FINE WINE
EDITIONS

# THE FINEST WINES OF
# RIOJA
## AND NORTHWEST SPAIN

## A Regional Guide to the Best Producers
## and Their Wines

JESÚS BARQUÍN | LUIS GUTIÉRREZ | VÍCTOR DE LA SERNA

Foreword by Hugh Johnson | Photography by Jon Wyand

UNIVERSITY OF CALIFORNIA PRESS
Berkeley | Los Angeles

University of California Press,
one of the most distinguished university presses in the United States,
enriches lives around the world by advancing scholarship
in the humanities, social sciences, and natural sciences.
Its activities are supported by the UC Press Foundation and by
philanthropic contributions from individuals and institutions.
For more information, visit www.ucpress.edu

First published in
North America by
University of California Press
Berkeley and Los Angeles, California

Fine Wine Editions

Publisher  Sara Morley

General Editor  Neil Beckett

Editor  David Williams

Subeditor  David Tombesi-Walton

Editorial Assistants  Anouck Mittaz,
Inés Rivera de Asís

Map Editor  Jeremy Wilkinson

Maps  Tom Coulson,
Encompass Graphics, Hove, UK

Indexer  Ann Marangos

Americanizer  Christine Heilman

Production  Nikki Ingram

Library of Congress Control Number : 2011922023

ISBN 978-0-520-26921-7 (paper : alk. paper)

Manufactured in China

10 9 8 7 6 5 4 3 2 1
17 16 15 14 13 12 11

| | | | | | |
|---|---|---|---|---|---|
| **ABV** | alcohol by volume | **g/l** | grams of residual sugar per liter of wine | ★ | A favorite wine or the finest in its range |
| **DO** | *denominación de origen* | | | | |
| **DOC** | *denominación de origen calificada* | **ha** | hectare (= 2.471 acres) | **[V]** | A wine that is a particularly good value in its class |
| | | **hl** | hectoliter (= 26.4 gallons) | | |

# Contents

# Foreword

## by Hugh Johnson

Fine wines detach themselves from the rest not by their pretensions but by their conversation—the conversation, that is, that they provoke and stimulate, even, I sometimes think, by joining in themselves.

Is this too surreal a thought? Don't you exchange ideas with a truly original, authentic, coherent wine? You are just putting the decanter down for the second time. You have admired its color, remarked on a note of new oak now in decline and a ripe black currant smell growing by the minute, when a tang of iodine interrupts you, the voice of the sea as clear as if you had just parked your car on the beach and opened the door. Picture the Gironde, the wine is saying. You know the slope with its pale stones and its long gray view. I am Latour. Keep me on your tongue and I will explain everything: my grapes, the sun I missed in August, and the baking September days up to harvest. Is my strength draining away? Then I am old, but all the more eloquent; you see my weak points, but my character is clearer than ever.

He who has ears to hear, let him hear. Most of the world's wines are like French cartoons, *sans paroles*. Fine wines are thoroughbreds with form and mettle, even on their off days or when they are outrun. If a seemingly disproportionate number of words and, naturally, money are lavished on them, it is because they set the pace. What do you aspire to without a model? And far from being futile, aspiration has given us, and continues to give us, more thoroughbreds, more conversation, and more seductive voices to beguile us.

Just 20 or 30 years ago, the wine world was a plain with isolated peaks. It had crevasses, not to mention abysses, too, but we did our best to avoid them. The collision of continents thrust up new mountain ranges, while erosion turned barren new rock into fertile soil. Do I need to mention the clambering explorers, the pioneers who planted at high altitudes with aspirations that seemed presumptuous at the time? If they started by making wine with little to

say, those who persevered found a new grammar and a new vocabulary, to add its voice to conversations that will soon, it seems, be worldwide.

Even among the most established there is continual change, as their language produces its own literature, and its literature new masterpieces. Far from being regions where everything has been discovered and every decision made, the classic regions of the wine world are where the finest tuning takes place—where it is financially rewarding to go to the greatest efforts and explore in the greatest depth every elusive nuance that soils and techniques can offer.

Rioja's career as an export wine is 150 years old. It began as an emergency replacement for a Bordeaux dried up by phylloxera, and that the emergency eventually produced one of Europe's most distinctive wines is a marvelous conjunction of history and geography. Keep a reasonably full-bodied example in a clean barrel in a cool cellar, and it becomes harmonious, bright, aromatic, and smooth: highly salable, but not a wine reflecting a single terroir. The Rioja tradition was for big bodegas buying in grapes to vinify in a house style.

This was fine in the restricted domestic market, but as the call for quality wine went global in the late 20th century, something more than a branded reserva label was needed. By the beginning of this century, the question was: "What is Rioja?" Is it the pale, sweet red long-aged in American oak, or the dark, intense rough-edged wine coming out of bodegas with modern ideas? Does it reflect a vineyard or just a cellar?

For Rioja, faced with serious competition from regions all over Spain, the question is critical. There is still no final answer, but an explosion of solutions has drawn the attention of the world to Spain's northwestern vineyards—not only to Rioja, but also to Navarra, Bierzo, Galicia, and the Basque Country. This book is perhaps the first to investigate and record this new wine world within a very old one.

# Preface

## by Jesús Barquín, Luis Gutiérrez, Víctor de la Serna

At the heart of northwest Spain lies Rioja. This famous region has long represented (with the even more historic Jerez) the peak of viticultural and winemaking achievement in Spain. But its overwhelming presence tends to obscure the important surrounding vineyards—those under the influence of the Atlantic. In this book, we look at all of them, considering the role wine has played over the ages in the culture of the region. We delve deep into subjects such as climate and soil, grape varieties, viticulture, and winemaking—from ancient to traditional and modern.

Viticulture was brought to northwest Spain by the Romans in the 1st century BC and quickly expanded. The last Christian strongholds after the Muslim conquest were in this region, and the reestablishment of vineyards throughout reconquered Spain started here. After a brief and prosperous era of exports to England from Ribeiro in the 16th century, the region reverted to the local trade in wine for some 300 years—a period marked by the most rudimentary viticultural and winemaking skills. The arrival of the French after phylloxera struck, and better transportation following the coming of railroads, launched the Rioja trade in the 1870s. The 20th century was an era of ups and downs—of upheaval, even!

"Diversity" is the byword when considering the climate, landscapes, soils, and subsoils of this part of Spain—a much-needed correction to the simplistic clichés about the country's wines. And diversity also applies to the region's grape varieties: Rioja is, for many, synonymous with Tempranillo, but several other grape varieties are also involved.

No less diverse are the fascinating winemaking cultures. We look at recent developments in the production of white Rioja and compare the relative strengths of varietals and blends. We examine the debate over the use of international varieties and local grapes in Navarra. And we tell the story of the triumph of Albariño and the rise of Mencía and Godello in Galicia and Bierzo, as well as discussing exotic local grape varieties like Hondarrabi Zuri.

The indisputable rise in quality that has been evident in northwest Spain in recent decades is largely due to greater efforts in the vineyards. From the 1990s, winemakers became much more directly involved with the sources of their fruit; they are now no longer mere masters of the blend. Moreover, the best producers are those who have managed to abandon (or who never indulged in) excessive chemical fertilization and the pursuit of exorbitant yields that accompanied the belated industrialization of much of the Spanish countryside in the 1960s and 1970s. In some areas, the steepness of the vineyards requires the exclusive use of traditional methods, which are very labor-intensive for both humans and animals.

In recent years, one of the most heated debates among wine enthusiasts has been the alleged disappearance of a classic or traditional style of Rioja, which has supposedly been displaced in preference for a "new taste" based on deep color, ripe fruit, and small new oak barrels. We discuss the extent to which this is really the case, as well as describing the different styles of winemaking that coexist in Rioja and other areas of northwest Spain.

It is in Rioja that the highest concentration of wineries and wines of merit is still found. Many of the region's greatest producers have roots in the 19th or early 20th century—a history that is very much alive in their glorious old wines. But there are also great producers whose story is just beginning, who promise much for the future.

In other regions, most producers do not have the noble heritage enjoyed by the oldest wineries in Rioja. So the producers from these regions have been selected solely on the quality of their more recent wines. In the introductory pages of each chapter, honorable mention is made of several very good producers who, for reasons of space, did not quite qualify for fuller profiles.

# From Myths to Modernism

There is a great deal of legend but very little by way of hard evidence about the origins of vineyards and wine in Spain—especially for its far northwest. This is a vast area that was colonized relatively late by the Romans, and where the Greeks and the Phoenicians—who are believed to have introduced grapevines to southwest Spain as early as the 11th century BC—never set foot.

Roman remains near Logroño confirm that viticulture was indeed practiced in what we now know as Rioja. But that unique Spanish feature—a centuries-long period of Muslim colonization, with the ensuing repudiation of wine and later Christian reconquest—intervened to destroy both viticulture and most of the evidence relating to its early development. So, in this instance, history starts in the Middle Ages, around the 10th and 11th centuries, when vineyard reconstruction began in the region and, later, in the rest of Spain. The Christian advance began in the northwest.

As Alain Huetz de Lemps pointed out in his seminal study *Vignobles et Vins du Nord-Ouest de l'Espagne* (1967), so many medieval charters mention vineyards that the planting of vines must have been a major preoccupation as the advancing Castilians rebuilt and repopulated the previously deserted valleys of the Ebro and Duero rivers, where war had been waged for centuries, as well as the many small valleys along the Miño basin in Galicia, an isolated region where Muslim presence had been minimal and intermittent.

Wine was considered a key component of the daily diet—an invaluable source of calories, not only for the privileged classes (noblemen, the clergy) but for the small growers themselves and for many workers. In 1205, Bishop Juan de Prejano established the food rations for all workers in the lands of the Albelda monastery in La Rioja, and they included wine for three meals a day: "So, bread, cheese, and wine were to be had at midday, bread and wine in the afternoon, and bread, meat, and wine in the evening."

Vines were planted wherever the climate and land would allow it, and by the late Middle Ages the area devoted to vineyard was probably the largest it has ever been in Spain. In Rioja, Gonzalo de Berceo (1197–1264), the first poet in the Spanish language, had already mentioned *un vaso de bon vino* ("a glass of good wine").

Where it was too cold and damp, cider replaced wine, as was the case along the northern coast. But wine was regarded much more highly, as attested by King Alfonso IX's decree of 1213, in which he pitied the poor canons in Galicia's Lugo cathedral who were forced to drink cider and made them a large gift of Ribadavia wine (from what we now know as the Ribeiro).

### The cost of protectionism

There was a little trade in wine from the very start of the Christian reconquest, but it was mostly limited to the privileged classes, since transport was difficult and expensive in a large and mountainous territory, quite apart from another very Spanish phenomenon: protectionism. The kings protected the wine regions by forcing their denizens to consume only local wine, at least until the year's harvest had been consumed.

Protectionism explains the survival of vineyards in very unfavorable habitats such as the humid mountains and valleys of Santander province (now Cantabria), west of the Basque Country. Huge amounts of tart Chacolí were produced there—simply because wines from elsewhere were banned. It was not until the early 19th century, when protectionism was finally abandoned, that richer white wines from La Nava del Rey (now Rueda), 100 miles (160km) south, near Valladolid, were freely allowed in. Within a couple of years, most of the Santander vineyards had disappeared.

**Left:** Rioja's landscape has dramatic reminders of the medieval past, but the origins of wine here are lost in the mists of time

Active trading in wine was almost absent, for these reasons, until the 19th century and the rise of Rioja—but for one notable exception. This was the national and international trade in the Ribeiro de Avia wines, which flourished in the 16th century. These wines, and particularly the prestigious whites, were shipped to the American colonies and cost almost as much as Sherry. They were also sold throughout northern Spain every time local production was not sufficient and outside replenishments allowed. But English, French, Venetian, Aragonese, and Flemish ships also loaded Ribeiro wine in Vigo.

The wines were particularly well known in England, and Huetz de Lemps believes this might be traced to an English incursion to Ribadavia in the 14th century. Jean Froissart (c. 1337–c. 1405)—whose *Chronicles*, written in the service of Philippa of Hainault, queen consort of England's Edward III, are a crucial source for the Hundred Years War—reported that the English soldiers found such powerful wines that, when they drank them, they could do nothing for two days. There are unconfirmed reports that small English ships were later able to navigate the Miño all the way to Ribadavia. What is confirmed is that the English wine merchants taught the locals new techniques, including the addition of sulfur to barrels.

King Philip II's ill-fated wars against England doomed the Ribeiro trade, and it died completely after Portugal's independence in the mid-17th century, when English merchants settled in Oporto and forgot all about Galician wines.

There were no bottled wines and no famous producers back then in northwest Spain, unlike in Jerez, where modern Spanish wine production originated. Wine with a name and a style—wine that was more than a not particularly pleasant part of the daily diet—would appear only in the mid-19th century, mostly in Rioja, but with a few bodegas also in Navarra, its eastern neighbor.

## The rise of Rioja

It was the spread of mildew and especially of phylloxera in France in the 1860s that gave Rioja, and in part Navarra, the opportunity to become leading wine regions in Europe during the 1870s and 1880s. French growers, seeing their sources of income dying because of the louse, went south in search of an alternative to their withering vineyards. They traveled to Rioja, and some Spanish entrepreneurs—most notably the two marquises, Riscal and Murrieta—traveled to Bordeaux (as Manuel Quintano had done almost a century earlier) to learn production methods that were soon adopted as the norm for the region.

The old-fashioned style before that, in Rioja and elsewhere in northwest Spain, was mainly a rustic version of carbonic maceration. Grape growers usually made wine for their own families. Because they lacked technology and probably space and money to buy barrels to age their wines, they tended to go for the easier old-fashioned way whereby whole bunches were fermented into wine in stone *lagares*, often foot-trodden. It was the *vino de cosechero* ("harvester wine"), which still exists today and is quite popular in Rioja Alavesa.

But the *méthode bordelaise* was soon adopted for the production of the best wines, both red and white, and embedded into the local tradition, soon becoming the *método riojano*: grapes were fermented in large oak *tinas* (vats) and aged in 225-liter oak barrels. This differed from the Bordeaux style in the long, often overly long, aging of wines in American oak. The wine was only bottled once it was sold.

Rioja's prestige grew so much—particularly in northern Spain, where these red wines became the staple in cities like Bilbao and San Sebastián—that for more than a century, this Riojan method was copied throughout the country. So, right up until the 1970s, most quality Spanish wines were merely Rioja wannabes.

**Above:** The Battle of Nájera (or Navarrete) in Rioja, April 3, 1367, fought between an Anglo-Gascon army (left) and a Franco-Castilian force as part of the Castilian Civil War; it was around this time, according to Froissart, that the English discovered the local wines

## Laying the foundations

The foundations for the oldest winery in Rioja were laid in 1825, when the first vines were planted on the Ygay estate and a winery started in 1852 by Luciano Francisco Ramón de Murrieta, later to be Marqués de Murrieta. In 1878, he acquired the Ygay estate and vineyards that ever since have been home to one of the great bodegas in Spain. He set the pace not only for classic red Rioja but also for white. The company remained in the family

until it was bought by another aristocrat, Vicente Cebrián Sagarriga, Conde de Creixell, in 1983.

In 1858, Camilo Hurtado de Amézaga, Marqués de Riscal, a diplomat and writer, founded the bodega that bears his title. He had been living in Bordeaux since 1836, so he decided to experiment with French varieties at his estate at Elciego and built his winery following the French model and techniques. He was the first in the country to use barriques. His wines soon started winning prizes, being favorites of King Alfonso XII. They became so popular that, in order to counteract fakes, the marquis had to invent the gold wire netting that makes it impossible to extract the cork without breaking the mesh. The netting itself soon grew fashionable and became a distinguishing feature of top Riojas.

Many wineries were started around this time. La Rioja Alta was founded by five wine growers from Rioja and the Basque Country in 1890; it is still in the hands of the same five families today. López de Heredia was founded in 1877 by Don Rafael López de Heredia y Landeta. Between 1913 and 1914, he planted the Tondonia vineyard, 250 acres (100ha) on the left bank of the River Ebro, which became one of the most famous vineyards and brands in Rioja. He also built a bodega in the popular location of Barrio de la Estación (the train-station neighborhood) in Haro, next door to La Rioja Alta and other well-known names such as Bodegas Bilbaínas and CVNE. These last two date from 1901 and 1879 respectively. The station and train from Haro played such a big part in the marketing and success of the wines that it made sense at the time to establish the business as close to it as possible. It became, effectively, the heart of Rioja's business.

Other relevant names from that era and still in existence today are Montecillo (1872), Berberana (1877), AGE (1881), Martínez Lacuesta and Lagunilla (1885), Bodegas Franco Españolas and Bodegas Riojanas (1890), Bodegas Palacio (1894), and Paternina (1896).

The Rioja appellation and its rules started taking shape early in the 20th century, but it was not until 1926 that the Consejo Regulador, the regulatory council, was put in place.

### Beyond Rioja

In Navarra, a few producers—most notably the Chivite family in Cintruénigo on the River Ebro—

**Above:** A barrique and its original inscription, still at López de Heredia, makes clear Rioja's late 19th-century debt to Bordeaux

were following the Rioja example. Active since 1647, they started a modern winery in the 1860s. Nearby, in Corella, Camilo Castilla built his bodega in 1856. Both firms remain active today, with Chivite playing a decisive role in the development of high-quality dry wines in the region and Castilla preserving an important part of Navarra's viticultural heritage, with its unique vineyard of Moscatel de Grano Menudo (Muscat Blanc à Petits Grains) from which others sourced the cuttings that would facilitate the spread of Muscat in Navarra in the 20th century.

But by and large, the history of northwest Spain's vineyards and wines in the late 19th century—and for much of the 20th century, too—

was centered on Rioja; one could say it was almost restricted to Rioja. Bulk wines prevailed elsewhere, and after phylloxera and the subsequent replanting of vineyards, much of the production was undertaken by cooperatives. These were actively promoted by the Catholic Church, and later by the Franco regime, as an attempt to ensure a reliable source of income for oft-impoverished peasants. Quality wine was not one of their objectives—indeed, the very notion of quality wine seemed totally foreign in most wine regions of Spain. Any small, quality wineries, such as Palacio de Fefiñanes in Galicia's Rías Baixas, which began bottling Albariño for the local aristocracy in 1904, were a distinct oddity.

### Post-phylloxera fortunes

Phylloxera finally hit Spain three decades after destroying France's vineyards, and by 1901 most of the vines in the country were dead. The French merchants had, by then, left Rioja and returned to Bordeaux and Languedoc-Roussillon.

It took a decade to replant the northwest's vineyards, but not much longer for Rioja to reestablish itself on the national scene as Spain's top region alongside Jerez. Interestingly, however, this prestige did not translate into Riojan domination of the mass markets of Madrid and southern Spain—at least not until the 1960s. Until then, the cheaper but gluggable wines of La Mancha were preferred there.

Spanish wine was on a roller coaster from the 1960s to the 1980s. Rioja expanded and, around 1970, made its first significant international push since phylloxera, with considerable growth on the British market. But by the end of the decade, overproduction and mediocrity undermined this progress. By the 1980s, Rioja's problems were obvious, and they gave an opportunity to other, previously unknown or forgotten areas of Spain to rise in terms of reputation and market success.

But the Riojanos recovered. The decline in prestige in the 1970s was due to the use of younger and more productive vines, as well as the less rigorous selection of grapes. More and more industrial techniques, and shorter macerations of barely mature fruit (to avoid high alcohol), produced poor-quality musts that lacked the aromatic potential or structure to withstand the oak regimes of the past. The result was thin, acidic, dried-out wines that reeked of coconut and vanilla and little else.

One of the causes of the problem was that bodegas didn't have vineyards of their own, relying on grape growers to supply them. This created conflicts of interest, because the growers, paid by weight, had very little interest in the quality of the grapes, concentrating instead on the quantity, while wineries hoped their suppliers would do exactly the opposite. In fact, some of these wineries were more like wine factories than anything else, and the bottles coming out of them during the 1980s, produced from vineyards with enormous yields, harmed Rioja's reputation.

Today, most wineries in Rioja and northwest Spain consider ownership of vineyards and full control of viticulture critical for their wines. Only a few—Martínez Lacuesta and Montecillo come to mind—still rely almost exclusively on external suppliers as the source of their grapes.

### *Alta expresión* and modernity

Even during the difficult decades, a few producers were experimenting with longer maceration and shorter maturation in wood, including French oak barrels. Relevant milestones were the creation of Marqués de Cáceres, with its fruit-forward wines crafted by France's Émile Peynaud in the early 1970s (a complete break with Riojan tradition), and Contino, which

**Over:** Most Riojan producers now see it as essential to control their vineyards; this picturesque example is near Lanciego

**Above:** Dinastía Vivanco and its sculpture symbolize Rioja's modernization, though the company also has Spain's best wine museum

pioneered the single-vineyard concept in the 1970s, when the norm was to blend wines from the different subregions to achieve consistency from year to year. Both Cáceres and Contino used French oak, and the wines were darker and fruitier than the average Rioja. In Navarra, Chivite launched its Gran Feudo brand in 1975, aiming for a similar style in less expensive wines.

There were other pioneers in Rioja. Bodegas Palacios developed its Cosme Palacio y Hermanos range with the help of French consultant Michel Rolland in the 1980s. But it was only in the 1990s that greater and more general change occurred in the region. Even if most of the

key players—Remírez de Ganuza, Roda, San Vicente, Torre Muga—were already in place by 1992, it was not until the release of the excellent 1994 vintage that the new movement came to prominence. The somewhat unfortunate term *alta expresión* ("high expression") was coined (were other wines "low expression"?) to designate the new style of wines, and everybody started talking about it. It even appeared on some labels.

It was good to move away from bad tradition, but trying to overextract from mediocre grapes was just as bad a recipe. The use of oak merely as a means of adding aromas to the wine served only to dissuade national and international customers from buying those Spanish wines. Put the wine into a heavy bottle, add a heavy price tag, and we would have the perfect path to disaster.

### The path to excess and back

While indifferent, industrial Rioja comprised the bulk of the production in the 1980s and 1990s, at the top end, a mentality of "the more, the better" caught on with some producers, and we started hearing about 400 percent and even 600 percent new oak. Overripeness, overextraction, and overoaking were the common excesses of the 1990s. Going from one extreme (thin, diluted, dried-out wines) to the other (black, overripe, jammy wines, flabby and heavy, with low acidity) is never good. But that's what happened.

Today, the pendulum is swinging back a little, and people discuss acidity, balance, and finesse, not only color, concentration, and power. Mid-market Rioja has also become cleaner and fleshier. In retrospect, 2001, another excellent vintage, could be seen as marking the beginning of a new era, where producers sought better balance and more elegance. The change, however, was not widespread, and it certainly never became a phenomenon like that of "high expression"; it was more of a silent revolution.

In fact, the best "modern" wines—not all, but the ones with acidity, balance, and concentration— are aging in the style of traditional Rioja. So the character and the terroir of Rioja are there, but they take time to show; the winemaking style makes the wines difficult to read when young. In any case, in the past, people didn't know what traditional wines were like when *they* were young, since they were never released at that stage. Now some commentators suspect that the wines from 1947, 1954, or 1964 must have been very similar in their youth to some of the modern-day Riojas.

Unfortunately, just as most people today drink their red Bordeaux or Vintage Port far too young,

so very few people lay down their Riojas and age them properly to drink when fully mature. The situation is exacerbated by the tradition whereby Riojas were aged by the wineries themselves and released only when they were ready. Keeping wines for years has never been common among Spanish consumers.

Today, excess and heavy-handedness are slowly receding in Rioja. An increasing number of producers look for balance and finesse in their wines, even though they are more concentrated than before. They consider the vineyards the key determinant of quality; they have respect for tradition once again but still make the most of modern techniques and technology. Most wines from the 1970s and 1980s were so thin and dried out that they could not be compared to the wines that came before. We hope that the two styles—pre-1970 and "high expression"—will converge, and that does indeed seem to be happening today. We also hope that this combination of the best of both worlds will allow wines from recent vintages to age like the glorious bottles from the 1940s, 1950s, and 1960s that can still give so much pleasure today.

### Navarra's missed opportunity

While this up-and-down period in Rioja opened up opportunities for other wine regions in Spain, none in the northwest was able to seize them. The most blatant case in point was Navarra, once heralded by British wine publications as the next Spanish wonder. It never happened, because most of Navarra's production was controlled by large cooperatives that relied on outside "experts" to restyle their lackluster bulk wines as competitive bottled wines for international markets. Like other Spanish wine regions in the 1980s, such as Penedès and Somontano, Navarra pandered to the international style, ripping out old Garnacha vines and planting large expanses of Tempranillo, Merlot, Cabernet Sauvignon, and Chardonnay.

A few producers, such as Chivite or Guelbenzu, stuck to their own style and avoided excessive homogenization. But most of Navarra's wine became formulaic Merlot or Chardonnay. After the initial interest, it became clear that Navarra was just another anonymous competitor for Australia, Chile, or South Africa on supermarket shelves—and it didn't compete well.

In the decade since 2000, a group of smaller Navarra producers has been agonizing over this decline and attempting a return to a more regional personality, with Garnacha and Tempranillo dominating the red blends; and Muscat and Viura, the whites. It will be a long, uphill battle, though.

## The cult of Mencía

A few red-wine regions in northwest Spain have fared better, but their size and total production are very small in comparison with Rioja and even with Navarra. Bierzo and Ribeira Sacra, with their hillside vineyards on slate soils and their interesting Mencía variety, took off in a big way after 2000. As so often happens, outsiders had to move in to shake the locals out of their complacency. In Bierzo, it was Álvaro Palacios, of Priorat renown, and his nephew Ricardo Pérez Palacios. In Ribeira Sacra, which produces some of Spain's freshest, most Atlantic-influenced reds, Bierzo's post-Palacios winemaker Raúl Pérez moved next door to produce the first glamorous wines there.

With a combined area under vine of 12,850 acres (5,200ha) and combined production around 4.75 million to 5.3 million gallons (18 million to 20 million liters), these two appellations are small in commercial terms, but they are among the growing number of regions in which individual producers, large and small, have acquired national or international reputations. Some of them have even attracted cult followings and entered geekdom in a way that none had managed to do until the end of the 20th century.

## Great white hopes

Much the same can be said of Galicia's reborn white-wine regions, practically forgotten since the decline of Ribeiro four centuries ago. As late as the 1980s, visitors to the region saw only bulk wines or wines anonymously bottled without labels by individual producers who made them in a haphazard fashion with primitive technology. Albariño was highly regarded as a grape variety, but its reputation seldom translated well into wine (except at Palacio de Fefiñanes). In the 1970s, retired engineer Santiago Ruiz began making very fragrant whites in the O Rosal subregion, and the acclaim these received, both nationally and internationally, turned the tide. Investment in viticulture, winemaking, and marketing followed—and with it, commercial success.

Unfortunately, overproduction and excessive reliance on technology have somewhat hampered real progress in Rías Baixas. Only a few producers—such as Gerardo Méndez, Pazo de Señorans, and Fillaboa—aspire to greatness, through lower yields and non-interventionist winemaking. The rest have been content to make technically correct but dull and unambitious supermarket wines.

With less commercial success so far, the other Galician regions have imitated Rías Baixas. Valdeorras, with its distinctive, ageworthy Godello wines (from a grape variety almost lost between phylloxera and the 1970s), and that old standby Ribeiro are the two regions that have made the most progress. Again, the proliferation of smaller growers and producers has been crucial for this renaissance, as it may soon be in much more obscure but potentially outstanding regions such as Asturias and Cantabria, as well as in the Basque areas producing much-improved Txakoli.

When climate change threatens and international customers turn away from heavy, alcohol-rich wines, these cool Atlantic regions may be the next great success story in northwest Spain.

# From Sierra to Sea

There is a general trend among wine lovers (amateurs and professionals) to think of the Spanish wine world as a uniform entity. As a consequence, there is a vague but widespread notion that the climate and geology of winemaking Spain are somehow homogeneous. It even makes a perverse sort of sense: if Spanish wines share a certain profile, then they must arise from similar growing conditions. In fact, it would be hard to find a more absurd cliché. Nothing could be further from the truth, in terms of geography, geology, or climate (not to mention grape varieties and viticulture, which we look at in later chapters).

Northwest Spain alone is characterized by a fascinating diversity of climates, landscapes, soils, and subsoils. In the regional chapters of this book, we shall find widely varying scenarios—from the quasi-desert conditions in southern Navarra (250mm [10in] of rain per year), to the abundant rainfall in western Galicia; from the flat valley vineyards in Rioja and Monterrei, to the steep hillsides in Bierzo and northern Navarra and the steep terraces in Ribeiro and Ribeira Sacra; from limestone in Rioja Alavesa, to schist in Bierzo, granite in Ribeiro, and sand in Rías Baixas.

Even within wet, Atlantic-influenced Galicia, areas like Monterrei and the Bibei subzone of Ribeira Sacra have a semi-continental climate. There are dramatic differences in temperatures between the seaside vineyards facing the Cantabrian Sea (Vino de la Tierra Costa de Cantabria and most Txakolis) and the inland valley vineyards (Vino de la Tierra de Cangas, Vino de la Tierra de Liébana). There are equally sharp contrasts between the Atlantic climate of much of Rioja Alta and the dry Mediterranean profile of Rioja Baja that extends into Navarra (with an average rainfall of 300mm [12in]).

In terms of soil composition, any apparent uniformity often masks remarkable variety. Most of the best soils in Ribeira Sacra are alluvial on a bed of slate and highly acidic. Most of those in Rías Baixas are of sand over granite, and most of those in upper Bierzo are slate. But there are exceptions to every rule, and it is not at all rare to find striking contrasts even within the same region. To take only one example, in the Navarra subzone of Tierra Estella, an area dominated by Mount Montejurra, we find alluvial sediment next to mountain limestone, a diversity that results in very different wines.

## Rioja's diversity

As for the region that takes up most space in this book, Rioja's diversity is characterized by the fact that it is spread across three autonomous communities: La Rioja (most of it), País Vasco, and Navarra. Even if this administrative division is discounted—and in an ideal world it would not be relevant to the profile of the wines—we are still dealing with a region that is roughly 60 miles (100km) long and up to 30 miles (50km) wide, crossed by the River Ebro from northeast of Haro to east of Alfaro. La Rioja is in turn divided into three subregions—Rioja Alta, Rioja Alavesa, and Rioja Baja—whose differences are determined by geography, geology, and climate. The climatic conditions are defined by the confluence of Atlantic and Mediterranean influences, with some areas closer to a true continental climate, as well as areas where the influences alternate. Average annual rainfall (which can vary widely corner to corner) is around 16in (400mm).

Soil differences allow distinctions between clay-limestone Rioja, ferruginous-clay Rioja, and alluvial Rioja—as established with characteristic precision by Manuel Ruiz Hernández in his monograph published in 1978.

Clay-limestone soils are typically infertile, yellowish in color, relatively low in iron, and with a limestone content of between 20 and 60 percent.

**Right:** The high hills of Rioja Alta and the sea off Rías Baixas
**Over:** The steep, old stone terraces typical of Ribeira Sacra

They abound in Rioja Alavesa, as well as around Haro, Villalba, and other towns of Rioja Alta. They produce wines whose high extract makes up for lower alcohol—a regional feature. For this reason, such soils predominate in the best Rioja terroirs.

Ferruginous-clay soils, comprising sandstone, clay, and marl, are low in limestone (5–15 percent) but high in clay and iron oxide. They are found in the higher regions, separating alluvial terraces and acting as boundaries between alluvial and clay-limestone soils.

Alluvial soils normally belong to the Rioja of the plains. They predominate in Rioja Baja and along the River Ebro and its subsidiaries. They often compensate for their poor limestone content with a high proportion of calcium carbonate in the subsoil, but they tend to be more fertile than other soils.

**Above:** Light, wind-blown soil in Rioja's San Vicente
**Right:** The very different stony soils in Rioja's Laserna

# The Triumph of the Indigenous

Spanish wine went through a kind of identity crisis during the 1980s and the start of the 1990s. Post-Franco, the country had finally joined the future; it had become modern and prosperous. But its wines suddenly seemed old-fashioned, and they were no longer appreciated locally. There was a tendency to underestimate local grapes, local traditions, local wines. French grapes were described in euphemistic terms as *variedades mejorantes* ("improving varieties"), as though indigenous grapes were not good enough and needed the help of more famous international grapes to produce wines that could be shown abroad. There was a big debate about Cabernet Sauvignon in Rioja. It was almost as though the Spanish were ashamed of their own grapes.

Then, in the 1990s, we witnessed the Garnacha "miracle" in Priorat, the recovery of Monastrell on the Mediterranean coast, Callet in Majorca, Mencía in Bierzo, Godello and Albariño in Galicia, Bobal in Valencia and Manchuela, Parraleta in Somontano, and Verdejo in Rueda. In Rioja, Graciano made a comeback, and other old grape varieties were completely rediscovered (like Maturana Blanca and Tinta, or Turruntés). This renaissance of the indigenous inevitably led some to ask if it was a mistake to plant Cabernet and Chardonnay. In retrospect, the answer is that, with some distinguished exceptions, it was. The thinking had been that since the world's most prestigious reds came from Bordeaux, Cabernet Sauvignon (or Merlot) had to be *the* red grape. It was the same with whites: on the basis of Burgundy, it had to be Chardonnay. We are not going to describe these varieties, though it's worth remembering that in Spain in the not-too-distant past, butter and smoke were believed ideal descriptors for Chardonnay, and green pepper for Cabernet Sauvignon, when in reality they indicated the excessive barrel fermentation and malolactic fermentation of the former and the lack of ripeness of the latter.

Catalonia (mainly Penedès), Navarra, and Somontano were the regions that bet the most on these French varieties. Today, these are the appellations suffering the deepest identity crises and the most serious marketing problems, which cannot be a coincidence. People are searching for a point of difference—for originality, personality, uniqueness. In this climate, the international is soon relegated to supermarket products that have to compete with a sea of similar wine from the New World, often at lower prices.

There are 750 acres (300ha) of Chardonnay in Navarra and up to 3,200 acres (1,300ha) of Cabernet Sauvignon. There are examples of interesting, well-made Chardonnays (Chivite's 125 Aniversario Chardonnay). There are good blends of Cabernet Sauvignon, Merlot, and Tempranillo, too (though these come at the expense of Garnacha being neglected and relegated to rosado). Syrah and Pinot Noir are permitted in Navarra alongside the local Garnacha, Graciano, Mazuelo, and Tempranillo. For whites, Sauvignon Blanc and Moscatel de Grano Menudo are also allowed, as are the three main grapes from Rioja: Viura, Malvasia, and Garnacha Blanca.

In Rioja, Cabernet Sauvignon can produce good results, and some vineyards planted with the variety are really old—in fact, the grape has a longer history in the region than Garnacha. Marqués de Riscal's Camilo Hurtado de Amézaga, in close collaboration with the local government, planted 9,000 vines of French varieties—Riesling de Johanisberg, Cabernet Sauvignon, Semillon Blanc, Furmint, Moissac, Pinot Gris, Pinot Blanc, Pinot Noir, and Pieponille—in 1862. Some of the best old Riojas are the cuvée Médoc bottlings, with a high proportion of Cabernet Sauvignon. After an experimental period in the 1990s, however, Cabernet was effectively outlawed. Today

**Right:** A bush vine, more resembling a small tree, of Godello, one of the many indigenous grape varieties returning to favor

it is tolerated—existing vineyards can be kept, and grapes used—but the variety cannot be mentioned anywhere. Riscal continued the tradition of a wine high in Cabernet with its Barón de Chirel, and other examples such as Campillo's Selección Especial are also made mainly with the same variety. Ironically, Chardonnay has finally been admitted as one of the region's white varieties.

## Varietals and blends

Varietal wines are a recent invention, and there is no tradition of them in Spain. In fact, grape varieties were already mixed in the vineyard—not only different varieties of the same color but red and white varieties together, with the aim of fresher and more aromatic musts. Using a proportion of white grapes in red wine is still practiced today, even though it's less common than previously. Indeed, it used to be said—and it is likely that this owes something to rural or urban myth—that the reason there were more white grapes in Rioja than reds was not only because there was a much higher demand for white wine than there is today, but because roughly 20 percent of the grapes in red wines were white.

Few grape varieties are complete enough on their own to make a complex and satisfying wine. Pinot Noir, Chardonnay, Nebbiolo, and Riesling come to mind, especially in northern climes. The farther south, the more necessary it is to blend different grapes to retain balance and complexity, since heat is a great leveler. There has been a recent trend for pure Tempranillo cuvées, usually in a modern and highly concentrated style, but the tradition has always been to blend in variable proportions of Garnacha, Mazuelo, Graciano, and Viura. Mencía, however, does stand well on its own. Albariño and Godello are usually bottled solo, too, and though they are not as long-lived as Riesling, they do keep and improve for a few years when well stored.

## Tempranillo

Tempranillo is Spain's flagship grape variety, the workhorse of Spanish viticulture. It is on the list of permitted grapes in more than 30 appellations and is the base for red Rioja, where its 125,000 acres (50,000ha) represent close to 80 percent of the total *viñedo riojano*—an astonishing rise from the 31 percent it occupied in the early 1980s.

### DOC Rioja 2008

| Grape | Area under vine |
| --- | --- |
| Tempranillo | 124,825 acres (50,515ha) |
| Garnacha | 15,204 acres (6,153ha) |
| Mazuelo | 3,978 acres (1,610ha) |
| Graciano | 2,454 acres (993ha) |
| Other reds | 151 acres (61ha) |
| Experimental reds | 420 acres (170ha) |
| Total reds | 147,032 acres (59,502ha) |
| | |
| Viura | 9,696 acres (3,924ha) |
| Malvasia | 141 acres (57ha) |
| Garnacha Blanca | 35 acres (14ha) |
| New whites | 49 acres (20ha) |
| Other whites | 168 acres (68ha) |
| Experimental whites | 12 acres (5ha) |
| Total whites | 10,102 acres (4,088ha) |
| | |
| Total reds and whites | 157,134 acres (63,590ha) |

The Spanish word *temprano* means "early," so the Tempranillo name hints at an early-ripening variety. Such varieties usually tend to originate in cooler areas and are adapted and forced to ripen early to avoid frost and other problems in these regions. In the case of Tempranillo, it is believed it may have originated somewhere in Rioja. It thrives in clay-limestone soils like those in the northwest of Rioja Alta and Rioja Alavesa. To get acidity and elegance, a cool climate is needed, but to get color and ripeness, heat is required, so a continental climate and some altitude is ideal. The wines are not particularly aromatic, acidic, or tannic, but they are very well balanced (as long as yields are controlled) and have a great affinity with oak, which is probably why they age relatively fast at first but then reach a plateau of maturity where they can stay for many decades. Today, the best examples from good vintages such as 1925, 1942, 1947, 1959, and 1964 are still alive and drinking well.

Legend has it that Tempranillo may be related to Pinot Noir, with cuttings allegedly having been brought to Spain by Cluniac monks and pilgrims walking the Camino de Santiago (St. James's Way). This story is lent credence by the fact that well-aged Rioja is somewhat reminiscent of red Burgundy, and the vegetative cycles of Pinot Noir and Tempranillo are also similar. Nonetheless, the grapes are genetically different, so such stories are really no more than legends.

Vines were traditionally pruned *en vaso* (*en gobelet* in French), but new plantings are usually on trellises, forming a double cordon. Synonyms used for Tempranillo include Tinta del País (in Ribera del Duero), Tinta de Toro (Toro), Cencibel (La Mancha), Ull de Llebre (meaning "Hare's Eye," in Catalonia), and Tinta Roriz or Aragones (Portugal).

## Garnacha

Research has shown that all grapes were initially red, and whites originated by mutation. This is the case for Garnacha Blanca, and all other Garnachas are also descended from the main Garnacha Tinta. Garnacha is certainly Spanish, probably from Aragón, but it is present in all regions of Spain, in France, Italy (in Sardinia, it's called Cannonau), Greece, Israel, Cyprus, Morocco, and Algeria. It's also widely planted in Australia, South Africa, the United States, Mexico, and Chile. The most recent figures indicate that, after widespread uprooting, it ranks only third among red varieties in Spain in terms of area (160,000 acres [65,000ha]),

behind Tempranillo and Bobal, but it is also third worldwide, behind Cabernet and Merlot.

As Huetz de Lemps reveals in his book, it was not until after phylloxera that Garnacha was planted in Rioja. At some point it was the most planted grape in the region, but it has been losing ground and currently accounts for 15,000 acres (6,000ha), or 11 percent of the total area under vine. It ripens well in Rioja Baja in stony and clay-rich soils but does not quite deliver in Alta and Alavesa.

Garnacha was once the main grape in Navarra, too, but as in Rioja, it has been consistently losing out to Tempranillo, as well as to French varieties. There are many different clones of Garnacha— from high- to low-yielding, from big to small berries, from pale to rich in color. Consequently, it produces a very wide range of styles—from fresh rosado in Navarra, to the reds of Château Rayas in Châteauneuf-du-Pape, to the concentrated Priorats of Álvaro Palacios such as Finca Dofí or L'Ermita. It can produce musts high in sugar and ripe wines characterized by red fruit (raspberries, strawberries, and cherry liqueur), as well as by Mediterranean herbs (lavender, rosemary, and thyme).

## Graciano

The word *gracia* is Spanish for "grace," so Graciano can be loosely translated as "graceful"— well, graceful for the winemaker at any rate. The viticulturist might have a different view on the matter, since Graciano is a nightmare for them, given its low yields. Indeed, some say the name must come instead from *gracias, no* ("no, thanks")!

The grape, found originally in Rioja and Navarra, and also now in Ribera del Guadiana, La Mancha, and Valencia, is the same as Tintilla de Rota in Andalusia, Morrastel in Languedoc, and Tinta Miúda in Portugal. It generally produces brightly colored wines, very aromatic

**Over:** Many of Rioja's grape varieties are indigenous, having adapted over the centuries to their often challenging conditions

and rich in acidity, which are ideal for enlivening Tempranillo. It almost disappeared during the 20th century but is now enjoying a comeback, approaching 2,500 acres (1,000ha). There are even some varietal wines, starting with a spectacular Contino Graciano from the 1994 vintage.

## Other red varieties

Mazuelo, also known as Mazuela, Cariñena, or Carignan, purportedly originated in Aragón's Cariñena, but it now accounts for just 6 percent of the vineyard surface there, while Garnacha dominates. But it has always been an important blending component in both Rioja (where its presence was recorded as far back as 1562) and Navarra, mainly for its color and acidity. On its own, it can be quite rustic, given its tendency to produce high yields (easily reaching 200hl/ha). It is quite light in aroma but deep in color and very rich in acidity and tannin. It is a variety that really benefits from the balance that old vines bring.

The newcomer among Rioja's red varieties is Maturano or Maturana Tinta. According to DNA tests, it is close to Espadeiro, but they are different varieties. It's still very early to give a definitive verdict on its quality, but if it delivers good color, aroma, and acidity, with moderate alcohol, it could be a very interesting complement to other grapes.

## Rioja's white varieties

There are some 10,900 acres (4,400ha) of white grapes in Rioja. That is not a small amount in absolute terms—it's 42 times the size of Condrieu in the Northern Rhône—but it still represents a mere 7 percent of the total 157,000 acres (63,500ha) under vine in Rioja. The main white grape, covering 10,600 acres (4,300ha), is Viura, which in Catalonia and parts of France is called Macabeo or Macabeu. (It is also one of the main varieties in the sparkling wine Cava.) Traditionally considered quite a neutral grape, it can create fresh, light

young wines that are straw-colored with green tints, relatively high in acidity, and have floral and herbaceous notes. It can also be barrel-aged or barrel-fermented following Burgundian methods, when the color deepens, the aromas combine fruit with creamy notes from the wood, and the texture becomes richer and rounder.

Until recently, the only other two white grapes permitted in Rioja were Malvasia Riojana, of which fewer than 150 acres (60ha) remain, and Garnacha Blanca (Grenache Blanc), representing no more than 40 acres (16ha) in total. Producers normally have a blend dominated by Viura, complemented by either or both of these others. Malvasia Riojana is found in Penedès as Subirat Parent, and in Extremadura as Alarije. Garnacha Blanca has to be handled carefully, in both vineyard and winery, to avoid the negative characteristics often associated with its wines: a dull, light-brown color and a certain heaviness on the palate due to low acidity.

Still, many people believed that you could not make good whites in Rioja with the existing varieties, even if others had already proved them wrong. They argued that unless new grapes were allowed, there was no future for white wine in the region. As the argument raged, the area devoted to whites continued to shrink—until, at last, it happened. In March 2008, new grapes were allowed under the DO, something that had not happened since 1925. A total of nine grapes were added to the list, and six of these were white. One could conclude from this decision that white Rioja was in need of change. The six newcomers include three traditional grapes that are being recovered (some were almost extinct): Maturana Blanca, Turruntés, and Tempranillo Blanco. The other three are rather better known: Chardonnay, Sauvignon Blanc, and Verdejo. Verdejo is not really an international grape, since it is mainly limited to its area of origin—Rueda, in the center of Spain.

The revolution was not quite as radical as

might first appear, however. The presence of Chardonnay, Sauvignon Blanc, and Verdejo has been limited, and may not surpass 49 percent of any blend. Moreover, the names cannot be mentioned on labels. They could help the average quality of high-volume wines, but in our opinion the really interesting improvements will come from the other three newly permitted varieties—at least in terms of wines with a marked personality.

The first of the "revived" grapes, Maturana Blanca, is also known as Ribadavia; confusingly, it is not related to the red grape of the same name. A low-yielding variety, it was quite important in the past but almost disappeared after phylloxera. It has been recovered by Viña Ijalba, an organic producer in Logroño. The project has taken more than 12 years to bear fruit, and the results seem promising. The wine has a bright golden color; a fine nose, with floral notes, ripe peach, and a hint of honey and wax; medium body; fresh acidity; supple texture; good length; and a remarkable finish. The same producer has also recovered and bottled separately an intriguing red Maturana Tinta.

Tempranillo Blanco was first identified in 1988 and is a genetic mutation from red Tempranillo; one of the canes of a red vine was suddenly full of albino grapes! Since then, a lot has been written about white Tempranillo—in fact, it has been more written about than tasted, since the process of propagating a new variety from a single cane is painfully slow. Apart from the color, Tempranillo and Tempranillo Blanco wines are quite similar: the nose of Tempranillo Blanco also has rich fruit but with an added dimension of white flowers and, when assembled with Viura and Malvasia, should give the resulting wines the density and weight that they now too often lack.

As for Turruntés (not to be confused with Torrontés from Galicia, nor that from Argentina), it seems to be what is known in Castilla y León

as Albillo Mayor, a variety low in alcohol but rich in acidity, which can bring some interest and differentiation to the whites from Rioja.

Before leaving Rioja and Navarra, we should explain that Cava is also produced in both regions, since the appellation is not limited to Catalonia, as is often supposed. It was initially opened to all those who wanted to produce wines in the Cava style. Faustino, Escudero, Olarra, Ondarre, and other wineries better known for their Riojas also make sparkling wines mainly from Viura, but Cava is the reason that we also find Parellada, Xarel-lo, Chardonnay, and even Pinot Noir there.

### Atlantic reds

Moving on from the two main appellations in the northwest, Rioja and Navarra, we find several other red varieties, mainly in Bierzo but also in Galicia and the Basque Country. The Mencía variety represents 65 percent of the area under vine in Bierzo (where it's complemented by Garnacha Tintorera, Merlot, Cabernet Sauvignon, and a little Tempranillo). Mencía is also authorized in all appellations in Galicia, Rías Baixas, Ribeiro, Ribeira Sacra, Valdeorras, and Monterrei, which makes it the king of reds in the northwest quarter. When cropped at limited yields, it produces juicy wines reminiscent of flowers and minerals, supple and fresh, somewhere between Burgundy and the Northern Rhône.

It seems that Mencía spread only after phylloxera at the end of the 19th century, and the limited genetic variation hints at a relatively recent variety. Though often linked to Cabernet Franc, this has been disproved by the experts, who have instead identified it as the same variety as that known as Jaen in Portugal's Dão region.

Garnacha Tintorera is present throughout the northwest, where it was the main culprit behind the acidic, harsh reds that gave the region a bad name. Internationally known as Alicante Bouschet, it's

one of the few Teinturier grapes, meaning that the pulp is colored, as well as the skin. The main characteristics of its wines are deep color and high acidity. A cross between Garnacha and Petit Bouschet (itself a cross of Teinturier du Cher and Aramon), it was developed by Dr. Henri Bouschet in 1866. Its high yields and resistance made it popular among grape growers; its color, acidity, and structure, among winemakers.

A multitude of red and white varieties pepper the Galician vineyards (many of them shared with Portugal). The names and spellings vary; there are different synonyms for the same grape; and the same name is often used for different grapes that are not related, which adds to the confusion. Most of these varieties are not well known, and little attention has been paid to them. But some of them certainly have potential. With proper viticulture, sensible yields, and care in both vineyard and winery, they could create wines with personality.

The potential of these varieties is being explored by the likes of Raúl Pérez, who started making wine in Bierzo with Mencía. Pérez is currently working all over the place as a consultant and in joint ventures, making highly personal Atlantic reds and several whites. Mencía was, until recently, considered capable of making nothing more distinguished than rosado. It owes much of its current prestige to Álvaro Palacios (of Priorat and Rioja fame) and his nephew Ricardo Pérez Palacios, with their wines Bierzo and Corullón and single-vineyard cuvées from their company Descendientes de José Palacios. Their first vintage was 1999.

Espadeiro, known in Asturias as Verdejo Negro, is one of the many low-profile reds in Portugal's Vinho Verde region, across the border from Galicia. There it is known as "the grape without color," because it produces very light-colored

**Left:** An ancient vine of Tempranillo, the flagship variety in Rioja but also permitted in some 30 other appellations

wines, and it is used mainly for rosados. Two good examples are those from Quinta de Gomariz (in Vinho Verde, not to be confused with Ribeiro's Coto de Gomariz) and Quinta de Carapeços. It's a vigorous, late-budding, late-ripening variety that is quite sensitive to oidium and needs plenty of heat to ripen properly. The musts are low in sugar and coloring matter, producing wines that are low in alcohol and very high in acidity. In Galicia's Rías Baixas, however, it has produced an impressive deep-colored red, Goliardo Espadeiro, with the help of that man Pérez.

Bastardo is common in Monterrei, where it is also known as María Ardoña. It is also fairly widespread in Portugal, in Valdeorras, and Ribeira Sacra (where it goes by the synonym Merenzao), and in the Jura (where it is called Trousseau). It produces aromatic reds, quite low in color, that have attracted the attention of many. (Look out for a Bastardo from Niepoort in the Douro.)

The list of unusual red grapes also includes Caíño Tinto, Loureira Tinta, Sousón, Brancellao, Mouratón, Ferrón, and Grao Negro. Undoubtedly some of these rarities will rise to stardom in the future, since the region has the potential for fresh and drinkable reds that are more and more favored by aficionados fed up with the low-acidity, heavy, and overoaked fruit-bombs produced anywhere and everywhere.

## Albariño and other whites from Galicia

Common sense tells us whites are produced in more northern, cooler regions; reds, in southern, hotter ones. This is why the Atlantic coast—from the Basque Country in the east, to Galicia in the west—and the northwest third of the country in general is where we find Spain's most exciting regions for whites (and Atlantic reds, for that matter).

Albariño is a white grape grown almost exclusively in the northwest of the Iberian Peninsula, mainly in the Galician region of Spain but also in Portugal. Legend links it to varieties from central Europe, Riesling in particular, that would have been brought to Spain in the Middle Ages, either by pilgrims walking St. James's Way or through the expansion of monasteries along the route. (The same logic also links Bierzo's red Mencía to Cabernet Franc.) But it all seems to be little more than legend. Recent DNA research by Spanish viticultural authority José Luis Hernáez Mañas shows that Albariño exhibits too much genetic complexity for it to have developed only since the Middle Ages. This evidence, and the fact that the variety is not found elsewhere along St. James's Way or in the monasteries, suggest a much older local origin. According to Hernáez Mañas, the mix of indigenous grapes with vine material brought in by the Romans, possibly with the help of birds transporting seeds, is the explanation—not only for Albariño but also for other varieties such as Godello or Treixadura, which would therefore have a common root.

In Galicia, Rías Baixas is the appellation where Albariño is king. When the DO was created in 1986, the intention was to call it simply Albariño, but the rules require a geographical reference for a DO and do not allow something as generic as the name of a grape variety. So, it was finally called Rías Baixas ("Lower Fjords") in reference to the numerous seafood-rich estuaries running through it. It's also present in the neighboring Ribeiro and Ribeira Sacra DOs—something Rías Baixas tried to prevent. The fight goes on, and the latest attempts at protecting the grape include banning the mention of it for non-DO wines. Maybe the appellation should have been for Albariño from Rías Baixas to start with.

Albariño drinks better in its second or third year, gaining complexity and depth in the bottle. In its youth, the nose is an explosion of flowers with some herbaceous and balsamic notes (freshly cut grass, laurel, fennel, mint, aniseed), a variety of fruits (apple and apricot), sometimes citrus (grapefruit, orange zest) or tropical (mango, papaya, lychee), and in the best examples a chalky minerality. After its first year, it loses some of the more primary aromas, the apple turning to peach but gaining in depth and volume, developing touches of quince and honey, increasing the balsamic notes (laurel, maybe rosemary or thyme) and amplifying the mineral echoes.

Godello is today the second most prestigious white grape after Albariño. It is found in Valdeorras, where the slate soils make for flinty, spicy, sometimes musky wines (Guitián and As Sortes are two names to investigate) and is also common in Bierzo, Rías Baixas, and Ribeira Sacra. It's called Gouveio in Portugal, and Verdello in Monterrei, a name also used in Portugal but not to be confused with Verdelho from Madeira.

There is a profusion of other white grapes. Loureira Blanca, or Loureiro, one of the main whites after Albariño, is quite widespread and appreciated on both sides of the border. It takes its name from its distinctive aroma: *loureiro* means "bay leaf" in both Gallego and Portuguese. Treixadura, or Trajadura, is one of the main ingredients for Ribeiro and is also available for the other appellations. Caíño Blanco, Torrontés, Palomino (the grape from Jerez), Doña Blanca, and Lado are other names that one encounters throughout the vineyards of Galicia. As with their red equivalents, some producers are already turning their attention to some of these grapes, and some interesting wines will surely result over time.

The three appellations for Txakoli—Bizkaiko Txakolina, Arabako Txakolina (a total of 170 acres [70ha] of vines), and Getariako Txakolina—correspond to the three provinces of the Basque Country—Vizcaya, Álava, and Guipúzcoa. They produce light and sometimes spritzy whites from the local grape Hondarrabi Zuri and a little red, most consumed locally, from Hondarrabi Beltza. Both grapes are believed to be local (even though the 20th-century French ampelographer Pierre Galet thought that the red might be linked to Cabernet Franc) and are not found in any other region. Other grapes vary from DO to DO, but we find small amounts of Petit Manseng, Petit Courbu, Gros Manseng, and Folle Blanche, and producers are also experimenting with Sauvignon Blanc, Chardonnay, and Riesling.

Finally, if we take a peek at Asturias, where cider reigns over wine (but Vino de la Tierra de Cangas exists), we still find some interesting and unusual varieties that could very well provide a few surprises in the future, such as Carrasquín, Verdejo Negro, and Albarín de Ibias.

## Grapes allowed in each DO

### Rioja
*Red*: Tempranillo, Garnacha, Mazuelo, Graciano, Maturana Tinta (Maturano), Monastel.
*White*: Viura, Malvasia Riojana (Subirat Parent), Garnacha Blanca, Chardonnay, Sauvignon Blanc, Verdejo, Maturana Blanca, Tempranillo Blanco, Turruntés.

### Navarra
*Red*: Cabernet Sauvignon, Garnacha (or Garnacha Tinta), Graciano, Mazuelo, Merlot, Tempranillo, Syrah, Pinot Noir.
*White*: Chardonnay, Garnacha Blanca, Malvasia, Moscatel de Grano Menudo (Muscat à Petits Grains), Viura, Sauvignon Blanc.

### Bierzo
*Red*: Mencía, Garnacha Tintorera (Alicante Bouschet), Merlot, Cabernet Sauvignon, Tempranillo.
*White*: Doña Blanca, Palomino, Malvasia, Godello.

### Monterrei
*Red*: Arauxa (Tempranillo), Mencía, Bastardo (María Ardoña).
*White*: Doña Blanca, Verdello (Godello), Treixadura, Caíño.

### Rías Baixas
*White*: Albariño, Loureira Blanca, Treixadura, Caíño Blanco, Torrontés, Godello.
*Red*: Caíño Tinto, Espadeiro, Loureira Tinta, Sousón, Mencía, Brancellao.

### Ribeira Sacra
*White*: Albariño, Loureira, Treixadura, Godello, Doña Blanca, Torrontés.
*Red*: Mencía, Brancellao, Merenzao, Garnacha Tintorera, Tempranillo, Sousón, Caíño Tinto, Mouratón.

### Ribeiro
*White*: Treixadura, Torrontés, Palomino, Godello, Loureira, Albariño, Macabeo, Lado.
*Red*: Caíño, Sousón, Ferrón, Mencía, Tempranillo, Brancellao, Garnacha Tintorera.

### Valdeorras
*White*: Godello, Doña Blanca, Palomino.
*Red*: Mencía, Merenzao, Grao Negro, Garnacha.

### Arabako Txakolina (Txakoli from Álava)
*White*: Hondarrabi Zuri, Petit Manseng, Petit Courbu, Gros Manseng.

### Bizkaiko Txakolina
*White*: Hondarrabi Zuri, Folle Blanche.
*Red*: Hondarrabi Beltza.

### Getariako Txakolina
*White*: Hondarrabi Zuri, Gros Manseng, Riesling.
*Red*: Hondarrabi Beltza.

# Back to the Future

Every region in Spain has a long and rich viticultural tradition, even those with less favorable climatic conditions. Such conditions are mostly in the humid northwest of the country, including the northern parts of Galicia, Asturias, and Cantabria, and the coastal part of the Basque Country. Put more succinctly, this is the wet, cloudy, and cool coastline of the Bay of Biscay, where, until the end of the 19th century, there were thousands of hectares of vineyards, most of which were destroyed by phylloxera and never replanted. Santander province (now the autonomous region of Cantabria) had 5,500 acres (2,225ha) under vine in 1857; by 1922, only 150 acres (61ha) remained. Recently, there has been a modest recovery in the region, with 320 acres (130ha) under vine in 2009 and nine wineries: a decade ago, there were none.

Even before the tragedy of the little louse that wiped out the vast majority of Europe's vineyards, a number of external events had shaped the development of northwest Spain's vineyards and contributed to their huge expanse—a typically Spanish phenomenon that led to this country having by far the largest area of land devoted to viticulture anywhere in the world. Most of that area was and is in the southern half of Spain, where drought conditions made it mandatory to plant very large vineyards to get a decent yield. But even northwest Spain has historically devoted a large amount of territory to the vine—there were some 358,000 acres (145,000ha) in its 11 provinces in 1889, immediately prior to phylloxera—and yields were much higher here than in the south.

Commerce, or rather the lack of it, explains many developments. In the context of the long Christian reconquest of Spain (not completed until 1492), wine was an important part of the diet, partly for political and religious reasons, and the bourgeoisie and merchants in each new Christian town soon surrounded it with vines. Anxious to preserve this asset, local authorities introduced protectionist measures, often supported by royal decree: no wine from outside the town could be sold there, at least until the year's local supply had been exhausted.

This protectionism was maintained by successive dynasties of Spanish rulers right up until the early 19th century. Even though the transport of wine over long distances was always difficult in this very mountainous part of Spain, there would have been much more inter-regional trade if those decrees had not been in effect. This would have benefited outlying areas such as Rueda, while the vineyards in poor viticultural areas—those producing thin, green, unpleasant wines on the damp Cantabrian coast—would have dwindled or disappeared altogether much earlier.

Only one area of the northwest ever knew a trade-led expansion of its vineyards before the 19th century—Galicia's Ribeiro de Ribadavia, which in the 16th century enjoyed a modest boom in exports to England. These were halted by King Philip II's aggressive policies, which culminated in the disaster of the Spanish Armada. British merchants looked instead to Portugal—a turning point for the international trade in wine.

The local trade of bulk wine and the dominant position of homemade wine (often solely for consumption by the winemaking family) were both crucial to the development of viticulture in the northwest. So was the ownership of vineyards. These normally belonged to kings, the nobility, or (particularly in Galicia) the Church. Peasants leased the land under more or less favorable conditions, and only very slowly did they acquire any kind of property rights. Under such conditions, viticultural practices were primitive and vineyards precarious. Finding enough high-quality vines to propagate by *provignage* (layering) was only one of the major problems.

**Left:** Plowing by horse, a practice that never died out, is one of the more visible signs of the return to traditional ways

## The French and the louse

It was against this inauspicious background that the advances of the 19th and 20th centuries took place. Before the twin scourges of oidium and phylloxera, one decisive development was the long-awaited abolition of protectionist laws— a royal decision that allowed red wines from Rioja and white wines from Old Castile (the area known today as Rueda) to supplant the mediocre coastal wines. At least as devastating for the latter was the oidium crisis, which hit Spain around 1855 (slightly later than France). Oidium, or powdery mildew, a destructive micro-fungus, was not a major problem in drought-stricken southern Spain or even in inland vineyards like those of Rioja Baja and Navarra, but it wiped out what remained of the vineyards on the Bay of Biscay.

Phylloxera, the all-devouring louse from the Americas, spread more slowly, and there was a quarter-century hiatus between the devastation of France's vineyards and that of Spain's, which occurred only at the turn of the 20th century. In the interim, northern Spanish viticulture experienced, for the first time in its history, a phenomenon that has recurred only sporadically since: prosperity.

The panic-stricken Bordeaux négociants needed a replacement for the lost production of red wines. They found a nearby source for good-quality, strong, well-colored reds such as the market demanded in Rioja and Navarra (as well as along the Duero farther south). They set up shop in Vitoria, Haro, and Logroño and encouraged the bevy of enterprising Spanish noblemen, led by the marquises of Riscal and Murrieta, who had already seized the opportunity to create wine estates patterned after those of the Médoc. They also created the first "industrial" wineries in northern Spain—the first in the country after those set up by the Sherry trade in the south a century earlier.

This period of upheaval gave rise to a number of viticultural developments whose influence can still be felt today. The oidium crisis sealed the fate of the most vulnerable grape varieties—including Gascón, which was reputed to make the best red Txakoli in Vizcaya. It disappeared completely and forever. Other coastal varieties were on the verge of extinction—particularly the best white grape, Hondarrabi Zuri—and were only reintroduced after effective anti-oidium treatments became commonplace. Inland, the more oidium-resistant Garnacha moved west from Aragón into Navarra and made its first forays into Rioja, where it would only become prevalent after the next major invasion—phylloxera.

## Foreign vines

Tempranillo, with some Mazuelo (Carignan) and Graciano, was still the prevalent red variety in Rioja, grown mostly on sloping vineyards, usually dry-farmed (though in 1889 there were some 5,000 acres [2,000ha] of irrigated vineyards), and head-pruned in a low *gobelet* very similar to the training system used in southeastern France and known locally as *vaso*. The arrival in 1862 of Jean Pineau—a Médoc *maître de chai*, engaged by the Álava authorities to aid the development of modern winemaking— accelerated the introduction of the first "foreign" vines, particularly after Pineau became the right-hand man of the Marquis of Riscal on his Torrea estate at Elciego.

From 54.5 acres (22ha), Torrea quickly grew to 190 acres (77ha), and some 20,000 of the new vines were Bordeaux varieties—not only the Cabernet Sauvignon that would be so instrumental in the greatest Riscal wines, but also other, less expected varieties such as Malbec and Semillon. But the innovations were received with a mixture of skepticism and scorn by the local growers, who insisted that indigenous varieties fared better. And they were right. The new plantings were more

**Above:** The small scale of much viticulture is exemplified by a grower on his donkey with only as much spray as he can carry

fragile—and their yields were only one-third those of the indigenous varieties. Ultimately, French varieties remained the exception in Rioja.

One of the main reasons for the relative lack of success of foreign varieties was the rapid realization by the French négociants that red wines made from the local grapes were certainly good enough for export. Another reason was that even Bordeaux-style properties, such as those of the Marquis of Riscal or the Marquis of Murrieta, were seldom able to cover their grape needs, and buying from local growers was a necessity. These growers never experimented with the Bordeaux vines and kept on delivering Tempranillo, Mazuelo, and the odd cartload of Graciano.

Pineau's work in the cellar was more influential than the choices he made in the vineyard. He imported the Bordeaux vinification methods such as the destemming and crushing of grapes, the use of small fermentation tanks, and the aging of reds in 225-liter barrels. These techniques were copied throughout Rioja. For the first time, bottled, ageworthy still red wines (and some whites) from Spain were offered on the market. This was a guarantee of stability for the region, even after the French vineyards were recovered, as the newly affluent middle class in the industrialized Basque Country, between San Sebastián and Bilbao, adopted these wines as their own.

### The apex of Navarra

Just before the phylloxera scourge, Rioja's vineyard area had grown to 128,000 acres (52,000ha), from 84,000 acres (34,000ha) in 1874. In nearby Navarra, the growth had been even swifter and more spectacular: from 74,000 acres (30,000ha) in 1877, to 119,000 acres (48,000ha) just 12 years later, of which 20,000 acres (8,000ha) were irrigated by the primitive inundation method, still used today in parts of Argentina. By the end of the 19th century, Navarra reached its highest-ever area under vine, at around 135,000 acres (54,500ha).

Navarra, like Rioja, profited from the woes of the French, though its coarser wines, from its warmer, Mediterranean-influenced terroir, never reached the high prices or reputation of those from Rioja. Bulk sales encouraged the planting of the vines in areas hitherto devoted to other crops, particularly along the banks of River Ebro—the Ribera—which had been covered with olive trees. Peasants began planting a row of vines between each row of trees. This was the area first colonized by the resilient Aragón variety Garnacha.

By the end of the 19th century, Rioja and Navarra had a combined area under vine of 300,000 acres (120,000ha) and an average crop of 2.2 million hectoliters—about 10 percent of Spain's total.

## Double whammy

In the far northwest, on the Bay of Biscay, hardly any coastal vineyards survived the double whammy of the end of protectionism and of oidium. In southern and inland Galicia, where viticulture had such a long and well-established tradition, recovery was slow at first, and the region's light, white wines did not benefit from large-scale exports to France. But by 1889, Orense province had recovered most of the area under vine it had 30 years earlier—some 44,000 acres (18,000ha). Just as in Rioja, the arrival of the railroad gave a boost to local production, which easily reached the large coastal cities of La Coruña and Vigo.

The situation was much less propitious in Pontevedra, Albariño's homeland. Due to the high humidity levels, vines were trained on pergolas; but even so, many still succumbed to oidium. Moreover, large-scale emigration to Argentina and Cuba meant that many vineyards were abandoned. This stagnation, which lasted until the 1980s, led to the import of wine, and even wine brandy, from Castile, Catalonia, and Andalusia.

By the turn of the 20th century, phylloxera had reached most of the northwest. The situation only got worse. The French market vanished, as did the Cuban, after the Spanish–American War of 1898—and Cuba had been Spain's best client for bulk wine.

The louse did not advance rapidly in Spain, so overall production did not drop precipitously. Accordingly, wine prices did not soar, but this in turn reduced the incentive to replant. On the contrary, the hike in cereal prices during World War I led many grape growers to switch to barley, wheat, or rye. So began a long period of crisis, prolonged by the Great Depression and the Spanish Civil War in the 1930s. In many regions, vineyards never recovered.

Phylloxera struck most of northwest Spain between 1890 and 1900 but came later to Rioja and Navarra. The belated destruction there was just as thorough as elsewhere, though. There were only 1,760 acres (713ha) left in Navarra in 1909. In Rioja, the crisis started in 1901, and despite some early replanting, the area under vine was halved by 1910.

## Quantity over quality

The dire economic and social situation of Spain in the first half of the 20th century—with whole-scale emigration and very little profit for growers—helps explain some of the egregious mistakes made in replanting, which delayed recovery further.

Despite the rustic winemaking practices and the almost total reliance on captive local markets, centuries of viticulture had made it possible to cultivate high-quality varieties in the region—from Albariño and Godello in Galicia, to Tempranillo in Rioja. Yet, in replanting after phylloxera, quality gave way to quantity as cooperative cellars and large négociants, from Navarra to Galicia, gave

**Right:** Though many of the best wines are from bush vines, those from well-tended trellised vines may be equally fine

farmers their only hope for a decent income. The dirt-cheap bulk wines they began making—and were still producing in the depressed Galicia region until 1990—could be made from any easy-to-cultivate, high-yielding variety, and indigenous varieties were pushed to the brink of extinction. By 1980, there were only some 400 Godello vines left in Valdeorras and around 500 acres (200ha) of Albariño in Rías Baixas.

Throughout Galicia, the hardy but neutral Palomino grape from Jerez (known locally as Jerez) and the dark-fleshed Garnacha Tintorera (Alicante Bouschet) replaced native varieties.

The search for vines that were less demanding in terms of human resources also largely explains the triumphant advance of Garnacha in Navarra and Rioja Baja when replanting started after 1910. In this case, the quality potential of the variety was much greater, but it was its hardiness that made it so successful (despite its susceptibility to *coulure* in the spring, which often leads to drastically reduced yields).

By the late 1960s, the area planted with Garnacha had overtaken that planted with Tempranillo in Rioja. It was only the renewed appetite for the native grape shown by such traditional producers (and buyers of huge amounts of grapes) as Marqués de Riscal and such new ones as Marqués de Cáceres that later reversed the trend yet again. So, by 2008, Tempranillo occupied an amazing 125,000 acres (50,000ha) in the Rioja appellation, and Garnacha just 15,000 acres (6,000ha), out of a total of 156,000 acres (63,000ha).

New investment and more receptive national and international markets made it possible to relaunch quality winemaking in Galicia, and this led to the recovery of native grapes—even the most arcane examples, such as Brancellao or Carabuñeira—and the welcome ripping up of

**Left:** Especially in small, steep hillside vineyards, local experience, expertise, and traditional tools are invaluable

most Palomino vineyards. But despite these developments, the unjustified bad press given to Garnacha cost it dear in Rioja and, even more so, in Navarra. Too many high-quality, old Garnacha vineyards were scuppered during the Tempranillo frenzy in Rioja, but the decisions made in Navarra were much more calamitous.

Like their counterparts in a number of other Spanish regions—most notably Somontano and Penedès—growers in Navarra grew tired of seeing the prices they could fetch rise barely above those of bulk wines. For that reason, they threw in their lot with French varieties (mostly Merlot, Cabernet Sauvignon, and Chardonnay), as well as with Tempranillo, in an attempt to rival New World wines on the one hand and Rioja wines on the other. The strategy backfired, and by the early 21st century a change of image toward stronger local personality was being attempted, with the accent on Garnacha and Tempranillo for reds and on Viura and Moscatel de Grano Menudo (Muscat Blanc à Petits Grains) for whites.

By then, the viticultural history of the northwest had taken yet another twist in Rioja, with the authorization to plant a bevy of minority regional grape varieties. Some of these varieties—particularly the red Maturana Tinta and the white Tempranillo Blanco—have attracted much interest among growers, which will probably result in other significant alterations to the vineyard map of the region.

The insistence by some quality-minded growers, such as Telmo Rodríguez at Remelluri, on returning to *gobelet* pruning and dismantling trellis systems—which have multiplied, because they make mechanical harvesting possible—is another example of the partial return to older, more local varieties and techniques as the region tries to build on its belated but genuine recovery of traditions after the long, hard years of the 20th century.

# Tradition and Modernity

In recent years, one of the most heated debates among wine enthusiasts—not only in Spain—has centered on the alleged disappearance of the classic or traditional style of Rioja. This style, characterized by long barrel aging in old American oak casks and secondary rather than primary fruit aromas and flavors, has supposedly fallen out of favor, to be replaced by a "new taste" based on deep color, ripe fruit, and small new oak barrels. But whether there is any such simple and stark dichotomy is very much open to question. Several different and overlapping styles coexist in Rioja. And while in other areas of northwest Spain the absence of a quality tradition akin to that of Rioja may mean that modern winemaking techniques are ubiquitous, in the vineyards the best producers are increasingly returning to the past.

### The old and the new

It's a truism that anything that does not remain active dies and rots. But whatever else one might say about the world of wine, it is nothing if not active. Innovation and new trends are very much the order of the day and have been for the past few decades. Ideas and philosophies abound, and the winemaker must decide where he stands on such diverse issues as biodynamics, the importance of terroir, canopy management, cold maceration, microoxygenation, reverse osmosis, barrel origin, new oak, the degree of toast, oak chips, and the level of sulfites employed. While we do not adhere dogmatically to any winemaking philosophy, we do think it enormously preferable to live in a winemaking climate that boils with innovation—and a wine-loving context that seethes with critical disagreement—than to be stuck with an incontestable canon set in stone.

In the case of Spain in general, and northwest Spain in particular, only a fool would claim that tradition is always superior to modernity. The Spain of quality winemaking (Jerez, Rioja, and Vega-Sicilia being virtually the only exceptions) is a recent invention, emerging from economic and social developments that have finally placed Spain on a par with other leading European countries.

Of course, some attempts at modernization have led to excesses of the worst kind. But very few people would argue that the Galician or Basque white wines of 30 years ago are superior to today's—and much the same could be said of Bierzo's reds of 20 years ago. We might also cite emerging areas such as Cantabria and Asturias, which have started to produce wines of real interest for the first time in centuries.

It is also true that the road to success is littered with the dead and injured. Tostado de Ribeiro is an example of one such casualty. A type of naturally sweet wine made from grapes dried indoors, Tostado de Ribeiro was very prestigious in its day. Now, however, it receives scant attention from producers in the Ribeiro DO because it is expensive to produce and could only ever be a niche wine. Only a few good examples remain, such as Vitivinícola de Ribeiro's Tostado de Costeira. At a lower level of quality and prestige, something similar could be said of Tostadillo de Liébana, a sweet wine produced at Potes in Cantabria that has all but disappeared in favor of red and white table wines made with local grapes and international (read global) winemaking techniques.

It is significant, however, that in almost all of these winemaking regions, the names that are building their reputations belong more often than not to a younger generation. In Rías Baixas, only Palacio de Fefiñanes boasts an honorable tradition in an appellation whose relatively recent ascent has been led by the likes of Gerardo Méndez and Marisol Bueno. In other Galician areas, too, one can still chat with the key figures behind the quality renaissance, be it as part of a vineyard or cellar

**Right:** Old oak vats are still used by traditional producers, but many of them were modern or revolutionary in their time

visit or at a commercial event or wine fair. Think of Senén Guitián, Emilio Rojo, Rafael Palacios, or Raúl Pérez. Together with another few dozen owners and enologists, they have built or are still building, the quality canon in their regions.

Navarra is, perhaps, a different case, since there a dubious era of innovation was marked by an excessive reliance on foreign varieties (oddly labeled in Spain as "improving varieties"). The result has not been as successful as some highly qualified observers predicted. Today, there seems to be a brighter future ahead for producers who strike a balance between terroir and traditional varieties and a quality-oriented viticultural regimen.

## Rioja's subtle nuances

It is in Rioja that differences of opinion about tradition and modernity are at their most pronounced but where we must also pay close attention to a broad range of subtle nuances, since the debate is not as black and white as is sometimes portrayed. For example, only somebody with an ax to grind or a highly questionable personal agenda would attempt to deny the talent of the fathers of such modernist wineries as Artadi, Contador, Finca Allende, Roda, or San Vicente. At the same time, a comprehensive list of Rioja's elite should, even today, be led by the names of people who shaped the history of Rioja decades, or even centuries, ago: Manuel Quintano, Luciano Murrieta, Guillermo Hurtado de Amézaga, Jean Pineau, Rafael López de Heredia, and others responsible for this region's winemaking milestones.

Indeed, there is a striking paradox here, in that those latter figures excelled precisely in their contribution to the modernization of Rioja wine—they are no less than the true fathers of modern Rioja. So why are their wines hailed as "classics" now? History shows that almost every classic

**Left:** Among meticulous modern techniques is rigorous fruit selection, carried out as grapes pass over a sorting table

was innovative, if not downright revolutionary, in its youth. And it is in understanding this paradox that we begin to understand what distinguishes Rioja from most of the rest of winemaking Spain. In Rioja there is now a tradition of quality winemaking that was once regarded as a novelty, as "modernist"—a movement that, in its day, had to struggle to succeed and only did so because of the efforts of a group of visionaries.

By contrast, in most other Spanish regions, prior to the recent quality explosion and with certain honorable exceptions, tradition meant dilution, mediocrity, rusticity, inordinately high alcohol for preservation purposes, and even, on occasion, the addition of unwarranted chemicals in the vineyard or in the winery—something not altogether dissimilar to the dire situation that the marquises wanted to fix one-and-a-half centuries ago in Rioja through the introduction of what was then regarded as "modern" viticulture and winemaking technology.

## Modernists and traditionalists in Rioja

In this context, it makes sense to ask whether today's "modern" styles and techniques represent genuine progress for Rioja vis-à-vis more classic (or rather century-old "modern") approaches. That the wine world is prone to partisanship and one-eyed debate is well known. For reasons that historians, psychologists, or sociologists would be better qualified than we are to explain, we humans have a tendency to rally to flags and to embrace tribal beliefs, even in situations where we cannot derive any real benefit—as the example of the soccer fan so vividly illustrates. A similar phenomenon takes place in the world of wine among wine lovers.

One line of thought is that the past two decades of "modernism" represent a kind of curse for Rioja. This highly conservative position is not one that we share—no matter how full our personal cellars may be with historic vintages of classical producers, or how often those bottles end up providing more pleasure than any others. Those who oppose change, it seems to us, generally have a bad case of selective memory: they only remember the best examples of decades ago, the best reservas and grandes reservas of CVNE, La Rioja Alta, Murrieta, Riojanas, Riscal, Tondonia, and the rest. They tend to forget the oceans of mediocrity that used to exist in even greater proportion than now.

The formula that made Rioja the second-greatest winemaking region in Spain in historical terms (Jerez came first) went wrong in the 1970s, with the uncontrolled growth of the area under vine and the even more excessive rise in yields—to the point of uprooting old vines in order to plant younger, higher-production clones that soon produced millions of bottles of what were at best mediocre wines. Of course there were always great historic houses to keep the standards high (Tondonia, first and foremost, but also La Rioja Alta for a time and, less consistently, CVNE), as well as new arrivals who struggled to balance tradition and innovation and cunningly made room for themselves at the top (Muga, Contino, Marqués de Cáceres and a few others).

The world of Rioja was for too long strangled by its own tradition, even beyond the limitations imposed by the region's regulations—which were later shown to be far from incompatible with innovation. There was a consensus on what an ambitious bodega needed to offer the market: first and foremost, a crianza, a reserva, and a gran reserva—all red. Sometimes there were two distinct lines under the reserva label: one in a *vino fino* style; the other, fleshier and more fruit-driven. Some producers retained a traditional young *cosechero*-style red. As for whites, the same oak-aging principle determined the classifications and offerings, with less emphasis on the older styles.

The last decade of the 20th century brought with it a group of producers who were prepared to confront this orthodoxy, to challenge the stylistic uniformity, and to produce highly individual wines in the process. This group included pioneers like the Martínez Bujanda brothers and their new ventures; special cuvées from long-established houses (Marqués de Riscal's Barón de Chirel, Muga's Torre Muga) or from newer producers (Bretón's Dominio de Conte); single-vineyard wines; Artadi's old-vines lineup; Viña Ijalba's groundbreaking Reserva with 50 percent Graciano; and the great reds produced outside the strictures of the crianza/reserva/gran reserva model (Palacio's Cosme Palacio Hermanos, the new Allende and Señorío de San Vicente).

What they achieved was no treason against Riojan authenticity. On the contrary, it represented a return to creativity and the pursuit of quality that constitute the true essence of Riojan tradition—the same tenets that inspired those influential figures at the end of the 18th century, during the second half of the 19th century, and in the early decades of the 20th century.

Shortly after the initial group of late 20th-century innovators came the likes of de Gregorio, Eguren, López de Lacalle, Madrazo, Mendoza, Muga, Remírez de Ganuza, Rodríguez, and Romeo. The key for all of them—as it was for their peers in almost every winemaking region in the world—was their courage. They were prepared to make difficult decisions about the control of grape supply and viticulture. They sought to transmit terroir with each and every decision. And their radical approach in vineyard and winery made them risk vintages.

In truth, all this should have come one or two decades earlier. But the winds of history blow in unpredictable ways, and every nation has its

**Right:** Among the many winemaking decisions that influence the style of the wine is the level of added sulfur dioxide

moment. This was Rioja's, and, well, better late than never. We are convinced that, no matter how great its past, Rioja's best is yet to come.

In a bright future based on exceptional terroir and winemaking techniques developed through generations, an important role will be played by the great houses that made and still make dream wines. The potential—while not yet fully realized—is tremendous, with the possibility of still greater complexity and richness. The best of the region's traditions are constantly being irrigated with the sap of the "moderns," the best of which will in turn become classics. After all, most of the artificial classifications that pretend to organize the world of wine are merely secondary when confronted with the one truly significant boundary: the one that divides great wine from ordinary grape juice.

Despite all this, we must admit that the dichotomy between traditional and modern in Rioja is anything but arbitrary, no matter how easy it may be to find wines that fall somewhere in between the two extremes. Moreover, it's important to stress that great wines are being made in both idioms. We'll discuss two widely available examples of the "old-fashioned" style: Viña Cubillo Crianza and Viña Arana Reserva. As for the moderns, we could cite Señorío de Cuzcurrita and Ostatu Reserva, or the more fruit-driven Pujanza and B de Basilio. Pouring a glass of any of these next to examples of classic Rioja can be a fascinating and illuminating exercise. And a most enjoyable one, too, provided that the wines are good examples (and in some of the wines we have mentioned above, the vintage makes all the difference) and that the taster bears no prejudice. The world of wine is too diverse and rich to bother trying to ruin it with boundaries and limits. Too many people are already too busy doing that.

## Traditional vs. modern

So, what exactly do we mean when we speak about traditional and modern Riojas? Which would be—for an uninitiated audience—the features that tell one from the other in this often imprecise territory?

As far as red wines are concerned, avant-garde wines are characterized by deep color, fresh-fruit aromas (severely overripe fruit in the worst cases), high extraction, and the use of new French oak with its vanilla and cedar aromas. The best examples will also be sourced from a low-yield vineyard, which could be due to old vines or to a viticulture that seeks concentration.

By contrast, classic Rioja reds are much less deep in color, with ruby and brick hues rather than the deep cherry color of modern versions. They tend to have been aged for a long time in older American oak, which gives the wines a characteristic bouquet (in good examples) of leather and dried flowers (including jasmine), and they often (but not necessarily) result from a blend of grapes sourced from different vineyards or even subzones within Rioja.

Nowadays, there are few representative examples of the 1970s standard of everyday Rioja wine, be it crianza, *cosechero*, or even carbonic maceration—and this is because only the best normally survives. Contemporary examples made in something approaching this style might be Tondonia's Viña Cubillo or La Rioja Alta's Viña Arana (a reserva)—but it's important to bear in mind that these are two of the best of their kind, then and now. When somebody says he misses the wines of the 1960s and 1970s, he is probably thinking of Imperiales, Continos or Arienzos—many of which are still alive and marvelously enjoyable today—but that would be a mistake. Let us open a Viña Cubillo and try to imagine it without its balance, with brutally rustic notes, with jarring leather aromas; let us subvert its subtle caramel notes into the characteristic stench of old barrels retoasted for sanitary purposes. That is what old mediocre Riojas were really like. In this

**Above:** The exceptionally ripe grapes used by some producers result in high alcohol levels, which need to be carefully monitored

context, the developments of the 1990s were a godsend for wine lovers, with the possibility of enjoying—without resorting to high prices or garage-scarce cuvées—clean and fruit-forward crianzas like those of Vallobera and Solábal, to mention just two solid producers.

## Types of Rioja: the regulations

To understand the framework of the debate between old and new winemaking, it may be helpful to explain the present regulations—which have remained essentially the same for the past few decades. The legal typology determines the specific aging seal that each wine can display on its label, which basically comprises the well-known trilogy of crianza, reserva, and gran reserva, plus the so-called generic back-label seal, which specifies only the vintage date. To these must be added the now out-of-fashion CVC (*conjunto de varias cosechas*, meaning "blend of different vintages"), which in the past had great commercial relevance.

In order to belong to the more prestigious categories (crianza, reserva, or gran reserva), the determining factor is the aging period, combining time spent in 225-liter oak barrels and a certain additional length spent in bottle afterward until the minimum requirement for whichever of the three categories is met.

**Crianza** A minimum of two years starting on October 1 of the vintage year, at least 12 months of which must be spent in oak barrels for reds and six months for whites and rosados.

**Reserva** *Reds*: A total aging period of three years, including at least one year in oak barrels.
*Whites/rosados*: A minimum total aging period of two years, six months of which must be under oak.

**Gran Reserva** *Reds*: At least two years in oak barrels, followed by at least three more years in bottle.
*Whites/rosados*: A minimum total length of four years, with a minimum period in oak of six months.

The generic seal is limited to the vintage indication and was designed originally for young unoaked wines, which should be made up of at least 85 percent of the vintage specified—since Rioja regulations permit (as do many of those elsewhere) the blending in of a small proportion of grapes from other vintages to "allow correction of certain parameters of musts or wines of any given vintage year." (Incidentally, this flexibility is also conceded to crianzas, reservas, and grandes reservas.) This generic label was the one chosen by avant-garde producers for their wines over the past few decades, since for them the Rioja regulations on aging were an unnecessary stricture.

To understand the relevance of those limitations from the point of view of marketing and winemaking prestige, it is essential to bear in mind the regulations of the Consejo Regulador but also the age-old local tradition whereby reservas and grandes reservas are by definition the most complex, rich, and harmonious wines of each bodega—an assumption based on the supposition that they are made from the best grapes and have the longest aging. This notion was challenged by a number of producers who applied vineyard management to its most rigorous extremes, distinguishing strictly between vineyards, vinifying separately, seeking concentration through exceptionally low yields, and using new French oak in pursuit of a specific structure for their wines. These producers were convinced of the excellence of their wines (something that would only later be confirmed or refuted, and of course there were countless disappointments), and therefore they believed that their labels should bear the most prestigious seal (gran reserva). However, at the same time, (a) they knew the wines would not be any better for spending extra time in barrel; (b) they wished to cater for a market segment that demanded fruit-forward wines of high extraction, powerful oak influence, and little or no bottle age (frankly, we do not regret the gradual loss of influence of this market segment); and above all, (c) they could not face the financial challenge of aging wines for up to five years.

Most of these new wines complied (and still do) with the requirements for crianza, but this designation detracts rather than adds prestige to wines that were marketed as unique. In all instances where it is not possible to enhance the label with the most prestigious seal, the solution is of course to radically ignore any age indication. In this way, the consumer's attention is refocused toward the brand name, in turn built around the producer's image—another breakthrough in the Spanish wine world, where the people in charge of viticulture and winemaking had always been obscured by the producers' brand image.

**Above:** Some Reservas and Grandes Reservas are identified as such (top), but others are labeled like more modest wines (bottom)

As a consequence of all the above, these award-winning, critically acclaimed exclusive and expensive wines were being labeled with the same generic seal (featuring only vintage indication) as the young and unambitious *cosechero* wines. It would be a mistake, however, to deduce that this rule had no exceptions, since there are also avant-garde producers who retain the reserva labels for their wines. This is not the case for gran reserva, though, which is practically restricted to classical profile wines.

The reserva indication does not, therefore, indicate that the wine has been produced according to a traditional Rioja style or even an intermediate style. It is a rich and complex world out there, and it cannot be reduced to an easy and fixed formula; it is necessary to learn about the different philosophies and styles of the different houses and even of each cuvée. We trust that the following pages, devoted to the most noteworthy producers, will provide readers with sufficient information to work their own way into the fascinating world of Rioja.

# Rioja

aro is the capital of Rioja Alta, and to many it is the wine capital of all Rioja. Tucked away in the appellation's northwesternmost extremity, it is the exact opposite of Alfaro, its counterpart in Rioja's far southeast, and the contrasts between the two cities define the parameters of climate and topography in Rioja. Consider the differences: Haro is Atlantic in climate; Alfaro is Mediterranean. Haro is at 1,450ft (440m) above sea level; Alfaro, 980ft (300m). The average temperature in Haro is 54.9°F (12.7°C); in Alfaro it's 46.8°F (13.8°C). Haro has an annual rainfall of 17.9in (455mm); Alfaro gets 14.5in (369mm).

It is the area around Haro that has traditionally been considered the best place for producing quality wines in Rioja, however. The reputation owes much to the composition of the soils—a complementary combination of argilo-calcerous and ferruginous clays that is ideal for growing Tempranillo. The chalky soils bring acidity and elegance, clay gives body and power, while ferruginous clays contain a number of different trace elements that deliver complexity. Broadly speaking, Haro is the place for Tempranillo blended with a little Graciano and Mazuelo to make serious but fresh wines, presented in Bordeaux bottles.

Wine has a long history here, but it was the arrival of French merchants in Spain just after 1850 that really made it take off. These négociants traveled to Rioja and Navarra, and many of them settled in Haro, searching for wine to supply thirsty France, wounded by oidium and phylloxera. They brought an unexpected prosperity to the town, as evidenced by the huge bullfighting ring that was built in 1886 and was inaugurated by the two most illustrious matadors at the time, Lagartijo and Frascuelo.

The prosperity brought more practical benefits, too. Haro became one of only two towns in Spain

**Right:** A statue in Haro of a man corking a bottle pays tribute to the role that wine has played in the town's prosperity

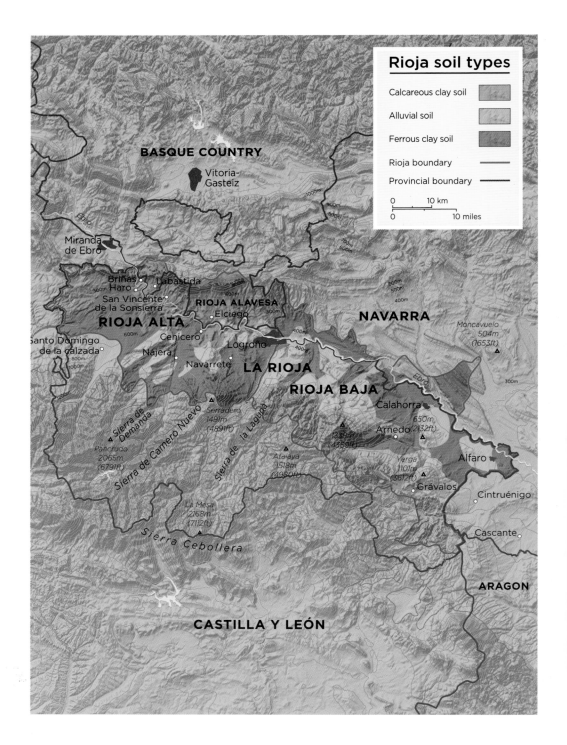

Rioja soil types

Calcareous clay soil

Alluvial soil

Ferrous clay soil

Rioja boundary

Provincial boundary

0       10 km

0              10 miles

BASQUE COUNTRY

Vitoria-
Gasteiz

1000m

900m

800m

Ebro

Miranda
de Ebro

700m
600m

Briñas
Haro    Labastida

San Vincente
de la Sonsierra

RIOJA ALAVESA

Elciego

600m
500m

600m
550m
400m

RIOJA ALTA

Cenicero

Logroño

NAVARRA

Moncavuelo
504m
(1653ft)

Santo Domingo
de la calzada

Nájera

Navarrete

400m

400m

LA RIOJA

300m

800m
1000m

1200m

Sierra de
Demanda

Sierra de Camero Nuevo

Serradero
1491m
(4891ft)

Sierra de la Laguna

RIOJA BAJA

Calahorra

650m
Arnedo (2132ft)

Ebro

Pancrudo
2065m
(6791ft)

1359m
(4389ft)

Alfaro

Atalaya
1518m
(4980ft)

Yerga
1101m
(3612ft)

Grávalos

Cintruénigo

La Mesa
2168m
(7112ft)

Sierra Cebollera

Cascante

ARAGON

CASTILLA Y LEÓN

5 6

to have electricity by 1890 (the other being Jerez). This had an enormous effect on the town's self-esteem and on the way it was, and to some degree still is, perceived by the rest of the country. There's even a saying from that era—*Ya estamos en Haro, ya se ven las luces* ("We must be in Haro, you can already see the lights")—that is still used today by young kids traveling toward Haro by car with their parents. At around the same time, in 1891, Haro's new-found status was acknowledged by Queen María Cristina, who granted city (*ciudad*) status to Haro, and the following year the Banco de España opened a branch there (a rarity anywhere other than provincial capitals). The Estación Enológica—the Enological Station, a major wine research center—also started operations in 1892.

These, then, were the golden years. And by the turn of the century, a popular phrase had been coined—*Haro, París, y... Londres*—a phrase you can still see printed on shopping bags today (though those bags tend to come from butchers rather than fashion boutiques). It may have come across as cheeky—impudent, even—to try to put Haro on the same level as the 19th-century world's two greatest cities. All the same, at the time, and especially for Haro's elite who were making a lot of money, it was not entirely facetious.

## Barrio de la Estación

The accumulation of historical names in Haro's renowned Barrio de la Estación, the district next to the train station, is unique. López de Heredia, CVNE, La Rioja Alta, and Muga are only a few of the wineries that established themselves in this quarter. In the wine world, perhaps only the Port-wine lodges at Vila Nova de Gaia across the Douro River from Porto offer a similar concentration of great names per square yard.

The explanation is quite straightforward: in a word, logistics. The train station was built just outside the city limits in 1880, using horticultural land in a place known as Cantarranas (which loosely translates as "frog's croak"), and was the hub for transporting the wines to Bilbao, where they were sold. Unquestionably, it was the railroad and, specifically, Haro's station that established Haro as the wine capital and the trading center of Rioja.

The concentration of wineries in the city left the surrounding villages dedicated to viticulture; places such as Casalarreina, Villalba de Rioja, or Rodezno have extensive vineyard areas but no big-name bodegas. In modern-day Rioja there are wineries in Sajazarra; and 7.5 miles (12km) southwest of Haro, at Cuzcurrita del Rio Tirón, lies the historical Castillo de Cuzcurrita, where an old winery has recently been revived.

Even if one had no interest in wine, the old wineries at the Barrio de la Estación would be worth visiting simply to marvel at the feats of engineering. Some, like López de Heredia or Roda, have impressive *calados* (literally "drilled," or "perforated") tunnels excavated through the rock to store barrels, running all the way to the edge of the River Ebro.

## Then and now

Most of the old stone wineries remain largely as they were when they were first built, but sadly, the same cannot be said about the town center. Here, beautiful stone *monasterios* exist cheek by jowl with ill-conceived urban developments from the 1970s that would be more appropriate for Benidorm. It's a legacy of a time when the antique was not appreciated and was considered merely old.

Another thing that strikes the visitor to Haro is its proximity to the Basque Country, which lies right across the river from Haro. The Basque influence has always been strong here—the CVNE labels said Haro-San Sebastián; those of La Rioja Alta, Haro-Bilbao—and it's amazing how Basque the atmosphere and population still are. There are *pintxos* bars not unlike those in San Sebastián, such as Mesón Atamauri in the Plaza Juan García Gato, ideal for a glass of aged white and some tapas.

Today, Haro's population exceeds 12,000, and most of those people are connected to the wine business in one way or another. It should come as no surprise, then, that the town's most popular event for visitors is also wine-related. *La batalla del vino* ("the battle of wine") takes place every year on the morning of June 29 and is very much what its name suggests: everybody throws red wine at each other until they are all drenched in purple. It all takes place some 4 miles (6km) from downtown in a place known as Los Riscos de Bilibio. It was originally a much more civilized event—a religious procession, dating from the 18th century or earlier, that steadily degenerated into its modern form until it acquired its new name in 1949. It is now an officially designated Fiesta de Interés Turístico Nacional (party of touristic interest), as declared by the Ministry of Tourism.

## Viticulture, horticulture

One curious and well-established Haro tradition, and one that plays an important role in defining the city's identity, alongside having so many people involved in viticulture and wine, is horticulture. The tradition dates back to Leopoldo González Arnáez, a wealthy landowner from near the city. Arnáez left some land to the city council in 1919 and instructed that it be lent to anyone in Haro who could meet his two conditions: that they would cultivate the land and that the produce they grew would not be sold. These communal vegetable gardens, some 200 of them, known as *venajos*, are divided into plots of between 5,400 sq ft (500 sq m) and 1,800 sq ft (1,000 sq m). Some are still available, but there's a waiting list open only to registered inhabitants of Haro.

For Jorge Muga of Bodegas Muga, the attraction of horticulture is obvious. "There's not a lot to do here during wintertime, so people are really into horticulture," Muga says. "Every day I pick the kids up after school, and we go and work at our plot. People like it, and there's even a competitive side, to produce better vegetables than your friends. We are also very much into eating naturally grown stuff." For those of us stuck in the city, it sounds fantastic, doesn't it?

## Ollauri, Briones, and San Vicente de la Sonsierra

One need not travel far from Haro to find places that are significant for wine in Rioja, whether those places are vineyards, wineries, or both. The three villages of Ollauri, Briones, and San Vicente de la Sonsierra are in the province of La Rioja, in the northwest, and therefore in Rioja Alta.

Ollauri—a tiny place with less than 170 acres (70ha) under vine, five wineries, and a grand total of 332 inhabitants—could almost be described as the outskirts of Haro. It belonged, until the 18th century, to Briones, together with Gimileo and Rodezno.

Other significant villages in the neighborhood are Rodezno, next to Ollauri, and Zarratón, important in viticulture, where nearby wineries either have vineyards or source grapes from growers. Briones and San Vicente are bigger and traditionally considered sources for some of the best grapes in Rioja, with a predominance of yellow soils rich in chalk around San Vicente and more reddish, iron-rich ones in Briones.

The inhabitants of Briones were the Berones, and the place is consistently mentioned in old books in discussions of the best vineyards. The historic, monumental village has a castle, noble stone houses, and an impressive church (Nuestra Señora de la Asunción), all of which reflect a rich past. Today it has an even greater area under vine than Haro—3,210 acres (1,300ha), compared to 2,470 acres (1,000ha)—but it is home to just seven wineries and 1,150 inhabitants.

The village has also become an important tourist destination, thanks to the wine museum at

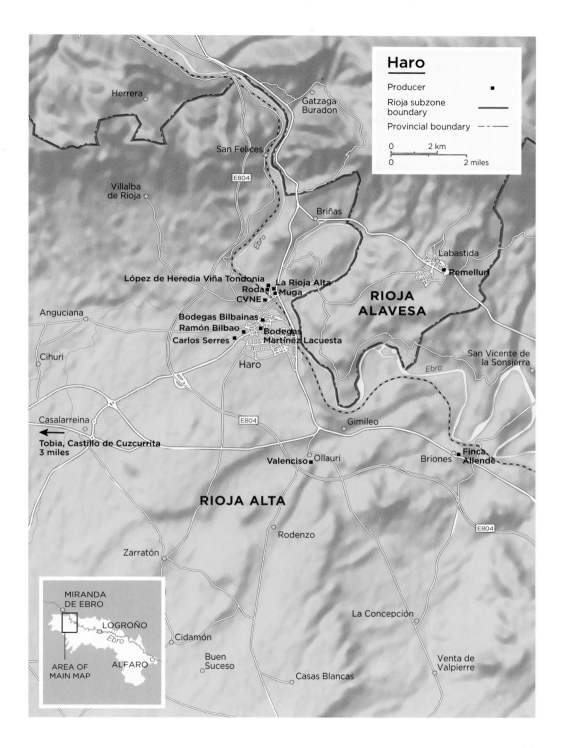

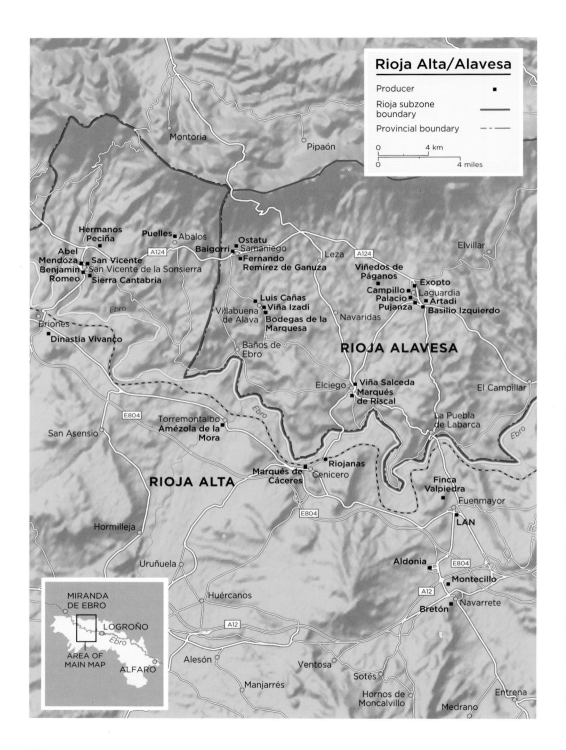

Rioja Alta/Alavesa

Producer ■
Rioja subzone
boundary ▬
Provincial boundary ▬ ▬ ▬

0           4 km
0                4 miles

Montoria
Pipaón

Hermanos
Peciña
Puelles  Abalos
Ostatu
Samaniego
Abel            Baigorri
Mendoza  San Vicente       Fernando
Benjamín  San Vicente de la Sonsierra  Remírez de Ganuza
Romeo  Sierra Cantabria
Leza
Elvillar

Viñedos de
Páganos
Exopto
Campillo  Laguardia
Palacio  Artadi
Pujanza  Basilio Izquierdo

Luis Cañas
Villabuena  Viña Izadi
de Alava  Bodegas de la
Marquesa
Navaridas

Ebro

Briones
Baños de
Ebro
RIOJA ALAVESA

Dinastia Vivanco

Viña Salceda
Elciego  Marqués
de Riscal
El Campillar

Torremontalbo
Amézola de la
Mora
La Puebla
de Labarca

San Asensio

Ebro

RIOJA ALTA
Marqués de  Riojanas
Cáceres  Cenicero

Finca
Valpiedra
Fuenmayor

Hormilleja
LAN

Uruñuela

Aldonia
Montecillo
Huércanos
Navarrete
Bretón

Alesón

MIRANDA
DE EBRO
Ventosa
LOGROÑO

Ebro
AREA OF
MAIN MAP
Manjarrés
ALFARO
Sotés
Hornos de
Moncalvillo
Entrena
Medrano

Bodegas Dinastía Vivanco. The Museo de la Cultura del Vino is not only the best private collection of objects and art related to wine but is probably one of the best wine museums in the world. It has pieces from Roman times, old utensils, a collection of 3,500 corkscrews, and objects of art and paintings related to wine from Sorolla, Picasso, and Jan van Scorel, to give only a few examples.

San Vicente de la Sonsierra, at the foot of the Sonsierra hills, is one of the most important villages in terms of wineries, with a total of 25. It also has some 4,200 acres (1,700ha) of vineyards, mostly red. In terms of population, it is also the biggest of the three, with 1,150 inhabitants. Though it is only 7 miles (11km) away from Haro, it is almost 330ft (100m) higher in altitude, at 1,730ft (528m) above sea level, which is reflected in the climate and the consequent delay in the ripening of the grapes.

San Vicente is an ancient place, with evidence of prehistoric inhabitants and a long, rich history, proof of which can be found in its churches, buildings, and monuments and in the ruins of the castle. Both in style and in geological composition, San Vicente has more in common with Rioja Alavesa: the soils are rich in chalk, the climate is cooler, and there is a noticeable Basque influence, starting with a steady tradition for *cosechero* wine, young and unoaked, made using carbonic maceration for consumption by family and friends. The latest news is that Vega-Sicilia, one of the most prestigious wineries in Spain, has bought 270 acres (110ha) of old vines around San Vicente in a joint venture with Benjamin de Rothschild. The venture made its first wine in 2009 from 132 tons (120,000kg) of grapes, and plans to reach an average production of around 300,000 bottles per year.

### San Asensio and Navarrete
There is a basic distinction to be made in this part of Rioja Alta—between San Asensio as a cluster of bodegas, and San Asensio as a terroir for vineyards. The latter is certainly less interesting, though it still serves a useful purpose—that of illustrating the soil variation in this part of Rioja. The N-232 road—which takes you from Briones in the west, with its distinctive clay-dominated soils, to Cenicero in the east, with some remarkable limestone terroirs—goes through San Asensio, situated between the two. Here the difference is striking, richer soils providing much greater fertility and lushness to the vegetation. It's pleasant to see but certainly not a great place to grow vines. Beets seem better adapted to this type of soil.

In fairness, as soon as you go south of San Asensio, on to higher and drier land, there are some remarkable old vineyards. But not many. What most of the many wineries around the village have, however, is land in surrounding areas, including Navarrete, where Bretón, Aldonia, Navajas, and Corral are established. Most San Asensio-based bodegas are relatively small and anonymous, except perhaps Perica.

### Labastida, Samaniego, Elciego, and Laguardia
The highest vineyards in the whole of Rioja are at Labastida, at the northern end of the Rioja Alavesa sub-appellation, at more than 2,300ft (700m). They are on the Remelluri estate, on the slopes of the imposing Sierra Cantabria mountain range, which effectively protects the region from Atlantic storms and keeps it relatively dry. Rioja Alavesa basically occupies the left (northern) bank of the River Ebro in the western part of the appellation, while Rioja Alta is on the right bank. From Labastida to Laguardia, the main town in Alavesa, however, the visitor will cross an Alta enclave—the Sonsierra area around San Vicente—and yet remain on the left bank. How come? Well, it's all political (or administrative if you prefer). Rioja Alavesa is in a different autonomous region—the Basque Country. (Basque nationalists would say it is in a different country.) Rioja Alta,

including Sonsierra, belongs, like Rioja Baja, to the autonomous region of La Rioja.

Administrative boundaries aside, there is no major difference in climate or terroir between Sonsierra and Alavesa. The climate in both is similar to that in the Alta sub-appellation, with annual rainfall around 22in (550mm). The areas directly protected by Sierra Cantabria are, however, slightly warmer, with a greater Mediterranean influence than there is on the right bank.

Alavesa wines are often somewhat different from those on the right bank, with bigger, more deeply colored reds and lower acidity. This is due to greater soil uniformity; as the white and yellow color of vineyards in winter attests, the limestone component dominates in most of Alavesa and Sonsierra, whereas there is much wider soil variation across the Ebro.

There are some 32,000 acres (13,000ha) of vineyards in Rioja Alavesa, which is the smallest of the three sub-appellations, and they have a common trait—this is the part of Rioja that comes closest to a Tempranillo monoculture. As much as 79 percent of the wine made here comes from the main regional variety. This is where the first Tempranillo varietals were made when such wines were a rarity in Rioja as a whole. There is in Alavesa a true cult of Tempranillo—"the soul of any real Rioja wine," as Juan Carlos López de Lacalle of Artadi likes to say. It is favored for its color and its ability to age well, despite its modest acidity levels. Also grown in the area are the white Viura, as well as the classic Garnacha, Mazuelo, and Graciano. But there isn't much of any of them.

You have to go back to politics to understand another Alavesa trait—the abundance of wineries, many of them built over the past few years. Much of this is due to the generous loan and subsidy scheme offered by the Basque government, which enjoys a greater degree of fiscal independence than most other autonomous regions, including La Rioja.

By subsidizing the construction of new bodegas, the Basque authorities have encouraged small-scale growers in Rioja Alavesa to become wine producers and (at least in theory) to get a better return for their efforts. It is not only small farmers who have benefited from this policy, though. Major Rioja Alta producers like CVNE or the Eguren family have moved across the border to Alavesa when expanding, building such new wineries as Viña Real or Viñedos de Páganos.

In addition to those profiled here, many of the lesser-known bodegas in the Labastida-Laguardia area are making quality wines. Some of the top names are Luberri-Monje Amestoy, Vallobera, Covila, Heredad de Ugarte, and Dominio de Berzal.

### Cenicero, Fuenmayor, Laserna, and Oyón

The part of Rioja centered on the small town of Cenicero (population 2,100) is often referred to rather dismissively as "Rioja Media," or "Middle Rioja," by its neighbors in Haro to the west, who claim that only their area is the real Rioja Alta. Bickering apart, there is a slight difference, because this is closer to Logroño and somewhat more open to the Mediterranean winds and their warmer, drier influence. But the Riojan authorities have long since decided that everything west of Logroño is Alta, and they make no further distinctions. Possibly they should, because this is too large an appellation—more than 150,000 acres (60,000ha) of vineyards over a 60-mile (100km) stretch—to convey a precise sense of terroir. But the freedom to use grapes from any part of the appellation in blends and to place them all under the same Rioja label has been central to the "négociant" ethos in the regional wine industry, and its leaders are not about to change that now.

The tradition of quality wine around Cenicero is as old as that in Haro. Montecillo was founded in 1874, Bodegas Riojanas in 1890. This tradition is more important in defining the general area

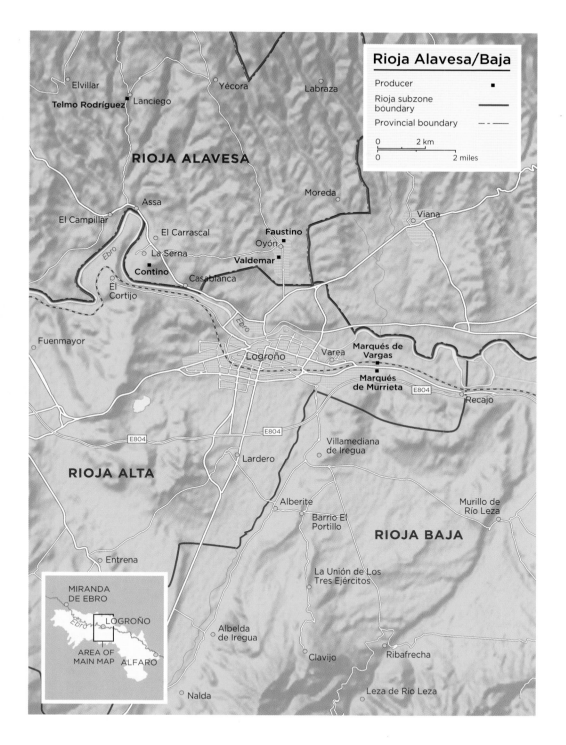

## Rioja Alavesa/Baja

| | |
|---|---|
| Producer | ■ |
| Rioja subzone boundary | — |
| Provincial boundary | – – – |

0  2 km
0  2 miles

Elvillar

**Telmo Rodríguez** ■ Lanciego

Yécora

Labraza

**RIOJA ALAVESA**

Moreda

Assa

Viana

El Campillar

El Carrascal

*Ebro*

La Serna

**Faustino** ■

Oyón

**Valdemar**

**Contino**

Casablanca

El Cortijo

Fuenmayor

*Ebro*

Logroño

Varea

**Marqués de Vargas** ■

**Marqués de Murrieta** ■

E804

Recajo

E804

E804

Villamediana de Iregua

**RIOJA ALTA**

Lardero

Alberite

Barrio El Portillo

Murillo de Río Leza

**RIOJA BAJA**

Entrena

La Unión de Los Tres Ejércitos

Albelda de Iregua

Clavijo

Ribafrecha

Nalda

Leza de Río Leza

MIRANDA DE EBRO

*Ebro*

LOGROÑO

AREA OF MAIN MAP

ALFARO

than specific terroir variation, since most bodegas in this central part of Rioja own vineyards or buy grapes in several adjoining areas—Rioja Alavesa, Haro, Ollauri, Logroño... If any aspect of terroir distinguishes the Cenicero area, it's the pervasive influence of the River Ebro and its tributary the Najerilla. Alluvial vineyards at relatively modest altitude are common, and the Ebro's many twists and turns have favored the creation of single-estate vineyards such as Contino or Finca Valpiedra since the 1970s.

Fuenmayor, Torremontalbo, and Navarrete are other main wine-producing towns in this central part of Rioja. But the concentration of important bodegas makes Cenicero a focal point, with the huge Marqués de Cáceres, Riojanas, and the Santa Daría cooperative, as well as Martínez Laorden, Berberana, Consejo de la Alta, Real Compañía de Vinos, and Sáenz de Santamaría. There is an even larger group of quality producers in the Fuenmayor area—not only Montecillo, LAN, and Finca Valpiedra, but Age, Altanza, Monteleiva, Marqués del Puerto, and Petralanda.

## Logroño

Logroño is the largest city in Rioja, as well as its capital—a historic frontier line and crossroads. This is not a land of privileged soils or special conditions for vine growing (though there are exceptions here as everywhere else, the most conspicuous being Finca Ygay). All the same, Logroño stands in the middle of a large winemaking region encompassing, among many others, the neighboring boroughs of Cenicero, Fuenmayor, Laguardia, Oyón, and Torremontalbo. This geographic position, together with its role as the region's economic center, helps explain why so many bodegas have chosen to put their headquarters in the city. It also explains why Logroño has become such an important link in Rioja's distribution chain, second only to Haro and its emblematic Barrio de la Estación.

But the times they are a-changing, and in today's wine world the emphasis has moved toward the vineyard, in terms of both production and, especially, communication. That is why so many producers are moving from this (growing) urban environment to locations that seem more appropriate to the rural nature of this business. Even so, many companies remain in Logroño, including a good few with long and distinguished histories, such as Marqués de Murrieta and Marqués de Vargas, as well as others like Franco Españolas, Viña Ijalba, and even Campo Viejo and Olarra.

## Albelda, Mendavia, Grávalos, and Alfaro

Until pioneers like José Palacios in Alfaro changed the course of things, this part of Rioja seemed destined to produce modest, alcoholic bulk wines or to provide well-colored grapes to bodegas in Rioja Alta and Rioja Alavesa, helping them overcome their own shortcomings in cool, wet vintages when ripeness was hard won.

Ripeness is not usually a problem in Albelda de Iregua, Alfaro, Aldeanueva de Ebro, and the other wine-producing villages in Rioja Baja. Instead of cool winds from the Atlantic, this sub-appellation is strongly influenced by the Mediterranean and is the driest and warmest in Rioja. This means that drought is a frequent hazard, partially alleviated now by drip irrigation. In summer, temperatures above $95°F$ ($35°C$) are not uncommon and rainfall is painfully scarce.

These harsh conditions have their advantages, though. Yields are low, wines are dense, and Garnacha does extremely well here. The Palacios family has shown that fine wines can be made in this once-despised region. Now other distinguished producers have followed suit: Bagordi, Barón de Ley, Biurko Gorri, Navarrsotillo, Ondarre, Ontañón, Alicia Rojas, Valsacro, and Viña Herminia. Rioja Baja is now a force to be reckoned with.

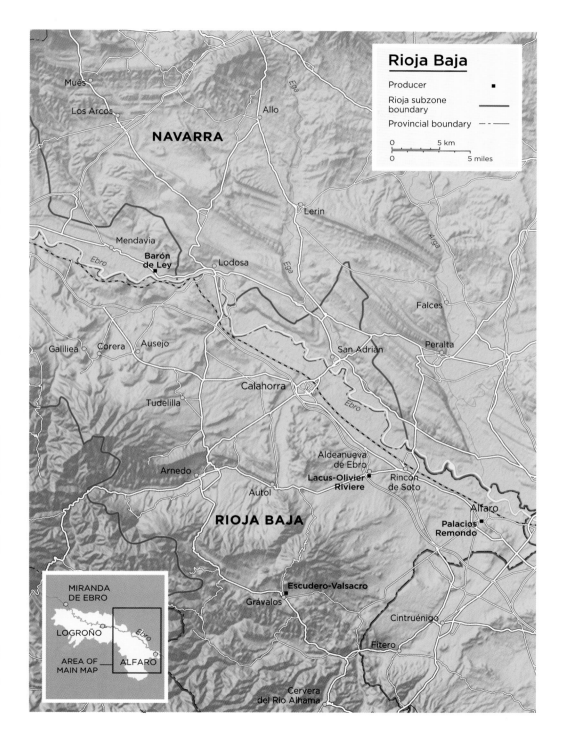

Producer ■

Rioja subzone boundary ——

Provincial boundary — · —

0       5 km

0       5 miles

Mués

Los Arcos

Allo

**NAVARRA**

*Ega*

Lerin

*Arga*

Mendavia

**Barón de Ley**

Lodosa

*Ebro*

*Ega*

Falces

Galilea

Corera

Ausejo

San Adrián

Peralta

Calahorra

*Ebro*

Tudelilla

Aldeanueva de Ebro

**Lacus-Olivier Riviere**

Rincón de Soto

Arnedo

Autol

Alfaro

**RIOJA BAJA**

**Palacios Remondo**

**Escudero-Valsacro**

Grávalos

Cintruénigo

Fitero

Cervera del Río Alhama

MIRANDA DE EBRO

LOGROÑO

*Ebro*

AREA OF MAIN MAP

ALFARO

# CVNE

The rather grandly named Compañía Vinícola del Norte de España (Northern Spanish Wine Company) is generally best known by its abbreviated form, CVNE. It was created in 1879 in Haro, the capital of the Rioja wine region, at the peak of the boom, when wineries sprouted up every other day to supply a France devastated by oidium and phylloxera. The founders were two brothers from Bilbao, Eusebio and Raimundo Real de Asúa, together with a friend from Rioja, Isidro Corcuera, and other minor stockholders. In fact, the company was called Corcuera, Real de Asúa y Compañía for a while. Today, the descendants of the founders are still managing the company from their base in Haro's Barrio de la Estación.

In the early days of its existence, the company acted solely as a négociant, but it soon started buying and planting vineyards and making wines (and brandies). As the years went by, the company gradually moved away from bulk wine (and brandy), and the CVNE name soon morphed into a brand, the more pronounceable CUNE. Master blenders were brought in from Reims in Champagne to make "sparkling Rioja," and the company started winning awards and medals at the universal exhibitions so popular at the time (Barcelona, London, Brussels, and Paris). It wasn't long before names that would become classics and pillars of the company—such as Monopole, Viña Real, and Imperial—were born, establishing CVNE as one of the great bodegas not only of Rioja but of the whole of Spain.

The company has always been forward-looking and modern and has always been prepared to buy the latest technology and experiment with new viticultural or winemaking methods. This pioneering mentality, which persists today, has served it well and is certainly one of the factors behind its continued success.

**Right:** CVNE's managing director Víctor Urrutia and his sister María Urrutia, in charge of sales and marketing

*The company has always been forward-looking and modern. This pioneering mentality, which persists today, has served it well, and is certainly one of the factors behind its continued success*

An early example of this innovative spirit was the construction of a new cellar as an extension to the winery between 1890 and 1909. Designed by the legendary Alexandre Gustave Eiffel, it was a startlingly original, innovative building in terms of both form and function. Conventional stone or brick columns were replaced with a metallic structure under the ceiling, which, as well as being spectacular, made working with barrels a lot more comfortable, with more space for moving, maneuvering, and racking. It has been used to age Imperial in oak barrels ever since it was built.

Imperial has been CVNE's flagship wine since the 1920s. It took its name from the imperial pint, since some bottles of that size were used to sell the wine. It is the archetype of Rioja Alta: a base of Tempranillo from Haro, Briñas, Briones, Villalba, Cenicero, Ollauri, and so on, balanced by some Mazuelo, Graciano, and even Viura to create a wine with good acidity, somewhat austere, and at around 13% alcohol, presented in a Bordeaux bottle. Traditionally it was two-thirds Rioja Alta and one-third Rioja Alavesa, while Viña Real was one-third Alta and two-thirds Alavesa. Nowadays, Imperial is made exclusively with grapes from Rioja Alta, and Viña Real with grapes from Rioja Alavesa.

In July 2004, King Juan Carlos I inaugurated the impressive Viña Real winery at Laguardia, the main building being a huge barrel room designed by French architect Philippe Mazières. Since then, Viña Real has been a separate company and winery, but we have decided to treat them together here, since Viña Real has played a key role in the history of CVNE. Contino is also part of the CVNE group, but it has always been independent, and its wines have therefore been profiled in a separate entry.

Viña Real was initially called Castillo San Mateo. (Other old brand names include Rioja Clarete, Cune Clarete, Rioja Toloño, and Lanceros.) A blend of Tempranillo, Garnacha, and Mazuelo, this is a powerful wine that ages for a greater time even than Imperial. The brand name was finally registered in 1940, and in the best vintages it was designated Reserva Especial.

Almost 130 years after the company was created, the same family is still running it, with Víctor Urrutia the managing director and his sister María Urrutia in charge of sales and marketing. The bulk of the production is today based on Viña Real Crianza; Cune Blanco, Rosado, Crianza, and Reserva; and Monopole. Corona Semi-Dulce is produced in very small quantities, Viña Real reservas and grandes reservas can be around 150,000 bottles, and Imperial, in the years when it is produced, ranges between 150,000 and 300,000 bottles.

The family owns 590 acres (240ha) of vineyards, mostly around Haro, but they also buy grapes from local growers. Given the quantity of wine the company produces, not to mention the extension of the vineyards, the variability of vintages, and the existence of some brands only in certain years, it is impossible to follow a fixed formula from vineyards to wines. But we can make some general points. The Cune brand, for example, is produced from grapes in Sajazarra. A large proportion of Viña Real comes from 260 acres (105ha) of vineyards in Laserna, planted between 1940 and 2001, that have been cultivated by CVNE for more than 30 years but do not belong to the company. CVNE's own vineyards in Laguardia also contribute to Viña Real. As for Imperial, the raw material is sourced from Villalba, Haro, Zarratón, Briones, and the oldest vines in Torremontalbo. Real de Asúa comes from grapes in Villalba, northwest of Haro.

Old vintages of Imperial and Viña Real are still available in shops and restaurants in Spain, and though prices vary a lot, you can find some bargains. The obvious question when you drink a superb

**Left:** CVNE's architecture, commissioned from Alexandre Gustave Eiffel, reflects its reputation for innovation

**Above:** Grapes for the Cune brand arrive at the winery from Sajazarra; a meticulously maintained traditional vertical press

Imperial 1968 or a Viña Real Reserva Especial 1962—to name just two magnificent examples—is, Would the wines from today age like this? To answer this question, we need some perspective. Old vintages from the 1920s through to the 1960s were bottled between 10 and 12 years after the harvest—something that is completely out of the question today, because of the financial cost and the space required. Until the 1970s, wood aging was never shorter than six years, and it was progressively reduced during the decades of the 1970s and 1980s. Nowadays, the wines age in barrel for about two years. And it is not simply the way the wines have been aged that is different. Many other things have changed in Rioja, too.

The answer to our question, therefore, can only be, "It depends." Not all old wines are good, and not all the wines from today will age faster. Today's wines, when they are made from high-quality grapes and when they are vinified and raised traditionally, will age like the old ones. When there

is a good vineyard, the wine will always emerge, regardless of how it was made. Some of the early new-wave Riojas from 1992–94 have a classic profile today. We believe that the Imperial Gran Reserva from 2004—bottled in October 2008 but still not released at the time of writing (2010)—will age magnificently, in a similar way to the old vintages.

Unfortunately, most people drink only the most recent vintages. Restaurant lists are full of immature wines—old Riojas have been ignored for a long time even in Spain—and we are in danger of forgetting what mature wine is. Happily, however, interest seems to be returning.

## FINEST WINES

### Monopole

Created in 1915, Monopole is the dean of white-wine brands in Spain. Though the first vintages were undoubtedly aged in barrel, the wine was originally intended to be fresher, fruitier, and paler in color than traditional whites. Today, the Viura grapes are given a soft pressing and cold clarification, and the must is then fermented in stainless-steel tanks at low temperatures to keep the primary aromas of fruit and flowers. All this counts against the wine's aging potential, but Monopole is intended to be consumed young.

## Imperial

Imperial is one of the icons of Rioja and one of the strongest and most prestigious brands in Spain. It is produced as Reserva and, in exceptional years, Gran Reserva, though the latter will most probably disappear in future, leaving only one Imperial. The wine was fermented in oak vats until the beginning of the 1940s, when the company changed to concrete, before coming back to oak *tinas* for the 2001 vintage. Current vintages age for at least 36 months in oak barrels, which is considerably less than used to be the case: until 1970, the wines spent at least six years in oak, and double that or more earlier in the century. Imperial is archetypal Haro: serious, austere, subtle, refined, fresh, and balanced. It ages magnificently and, along with Viña Real, remains our favorite of the CVNE wines, even though the company now has more expensive wines in its portfolio. We were lucky enough to taste (and drink) in 2010 a wide range of vintages of Grandes Reservas from 1928 to 2004. Our favorites among the old vintages were **1947★** (undoubtedly a world-class wine that could compete with the big names from Bordeaux of that year), **1959★**, and **1968**, while **1995** is remarkable among more recent wines.

## Real de Asúa

The Real de Asúa label was created with the 1994 vintage as a tribute to the founders of the company—it bears their surname—and it's made only in exceptional vintages from grapes from CVNE's vineyards in Rioja Alta. What makes it different from all the company's other wines is the aging process, which takes place in 100% new French oak. **2002** was not an easy harvest in the region, but as is often the case, the most exceptional wines are born in difficult years, and in the case of Real de Asúa this has been our favorite so far. A "Super-Imperial," if you like, with an international accent.

## Viña Real

Viña Real means Royal Vineyard, a name that comes from the vineyards located around the Camino Real ("Royal Way") in Elciego, the source for the initial vintages of the wine. Brands were quite volatile in the past, and trademarks were even more of a rarity in the early days of Rioja, so it's not clear which was the first vintage of Viña Real. It seems it was used during the 1920s and 1930s but not properly registered until 1940. Today, Viña Real is the name of a company, a winery, and a full range of wines, which includes three reds—Crianza (also called Plata, or "Silver"), Reserva (also called Oro, or "Gold"), and Gran Reserva—and a white, Blanco Fermentado en Barrica, a barrel-fermented pure Viura. The wine has always been dark and powerful, hearty and higher in alcohol than Imperial, somewhat hedonistic and bottled in a Burgundy bottle, symbolizing the wines of Rioja Alavesa. Originally the oak was American, but nowadays it's both American and French in the same proportion. Great bottles from **1954★**, **1962**, or **1964** can still be found and enjoyed. **Gran Reserva 2001** is our favorite of the current releases. The **Viña Real Reserva 1998** or the more recent **2005** have a good quality:price ratio, are easy to find, and can be enjoyed now.

## Pagos de Viña Real

This prestige cuvée was born with the excellent 2001 vintage and was the first to be vinified in the new Viña Real winery. It is 100% Tempranillo from *pagos* (vineyards) planted with old vines around the winery, with malolactic fermentation and aging in 100% new French oak, very much following the international taste and style, but somewhat against the traditions of the region.

## Corona

Corona, made from 90% Viura and 10% Malvasia, is only produced in years when the weather permits it, and as a semi-sweet wine, it's something of a rarity. Sweet wines are always an exception, but they are even less frequent in Rioja. The grapes should have developed some botrytis and are fermented and aged in new American oak barrels. It's usually consumed young, but the exceptional **1939★**, from the year when the Spanish Civil War ended, left in a corner for many years and discovered much later in the CVNE cellars, is an extraordinary wine.

**CVNE (including Viña Real)**
Area under vine: 850 acres (344ha)
Average production: 5 million bottles
Barrio de la Estación s/n, 26200 Haro, La Rioja
Tel: +34 941 304 800
Fax: +34 941 304 815
www.cvne.com

# Bodegas López de Heredia / Tondonia

**B**odegas López de Heredia is generally not known by its full name. It is better known as Tondonia or simply Heredia, which is what the local elders in Haro call it; recently the name López has become fashionable in the United States. But however you refer to it, the estate has become one of the flag-bearers for Rioja wines.

The company, based in its "cathedral" in the Barrio de la Estación, has never had a grand plan. The lofty reputation is a natural consequence of the bodega's own history, the character and quality of the wines, the determination not to deviate even an inch from traditional ways, and the two charming sisters, María José and Mercedes, who run the marketing and communication departments of the company in such a modern and efficient way. They are also responsible for

*The reason that Tondonia deserves a position of prominence on the Rioja podium is the sheer quality and seductiveness of its wines, across virtually the entire portfolio*

daily management and even production, though these tasks are shared with their brother, Julio César, and their father, Pedro, who, at well over 80 years old, is still at work every day of the year. This is a family business if ever there was one, where decisions on vine growing and winemaking have always been made by family members—from the founder, his son Rafael López de Heredia Aransáez, and his brother Julio César, to his grandson Pedro López de Heredia Ugalde and his great-grandchildren, the aforementioned Julio César, María José, and Mercedes. They are the backbone of this admirable, historic house, soon to celebrate its 150th birthday.

Let us return to our heroines, María José and Mercedes López de Heredia. These petite women

are sincere and obstinate in their convictions, yet at the same time extraordinarily kind and generous. (At a tasting with more than 200 people in Valencia in 2010, they could barely cope with the uncorking and pouring of dozens of bottles of such celebrated vintages as 1947, 1954, 1964, 1968, and 1970.) Mercedes and María José may well be two icons of Riojan tradition, but they are simultaneously two perfectly contemporary and informal hostesses. There is no paradox here, really; it is merely the expression of a rich complexity that contributes to the warm affection in which Tondonia is held by wine lovers all over the world. This is most likely because the role played by Tondonia in Rioja is similar to the little village in the celebrated Asterix stories by Goscinny, insofar as they are among the very few producers who will neither change the old-fashioned style of their flagship wines nor expand their lineup with modern reds or whites.

But the excellent reputation of the house of López de Heredia is definitely not built on the perfectly understandable affection toward its female co-owners or on the unquestionable attraction we tend to feel toward minority— some might say downright lost—causes. In fact, the reason that Tondonia deserves a position of prominence on the Rioja podium is the sheer quality and seductiveness of its wines, across virtually the entire portfolio. To use a formula coined a good 2,000 years ago and that does not look like losing its validity today (though its original meaning was indeed different), *in vino veritas*.

A walk with either of the sisters along the subterranean passages of the cellar full of dust-covered bottles is one of the most impressive experiences any fine-wine lover can enjoy. And sometimes one has the impression that the magnificence of these tunnels, the overwhelming

**Right:** María José López de Heredia, who, with her sister Mercedes, protects the proud reputation of the family firm

number of bottles they cradle, and their venerable sheen, together with the loving care of the family for their barrels, may cause the visitor to miss a fundamental truth to which the house gives more importance than might be apparent: wines are made, first and foremost, in the vineyard, and it is no affectation that all the great wines here are named after the vineyards from which they come. These were christened by the founder with resonant names: Viña Tondonia, Viña Bosconia, Viña Zaconia...

It would be an unforgivable omission not to mention here the fabulous figure of the founder, Rafael López de Heredia y Landeta. The great-grandfather of the current owners was one of those entrepreneurs of mighty personality whose ambition and initiative managed—despite the age-old Spanish mistrust of businessmen—to make the second half of the 19th century and the first third of the 20th slightly less disastrous than they would otherwise have been for Spain. It's a pity there weren't many more like him.

It was Don Rafael who bought the vineyards that—once unified and planted between 1913 and 1914—form the great estate known as Viña Tondonia, whose 250 acres (100ha) are one of the principal assets—symbolic and material—of the company. The other major vineyards were also bought and named by the founder in order to strengthen the corporate identity: Viña Bosconia (37 acres [15ha] in El Bosque), Viña Cubillo (60 acres [24ha] in Cubillas), and Viña Zaconia (60 acres, after Zaco, where it is located, and where today Viña Gravonia comes from). They are all around Haro, some of them very close to the cellar building, on the margin of the River Ebro, some 1,510ft (460m) above sea level. The varieties grown are the classic Rioja range: Tempranillo, Garnacha, Graciano, Mazuela, Viura, and Malvasia.

**Left:** The arresting architecture at López de Heredia is as original and impressive as the superb range of wines

Bodegas López de Heredia has a pretty radical approach to terroir, though at the same time there is a bit of a paradox here. For most people, terroir is inextricably linked to vintage variation. One might think that true terroir can only be expressed—even conceived—in the context of each different vintage, according to climate conditions during the season, especially during the final ripening cycle and harvest period. But at Heredia, the ultimate goal is to express the true character of each terroir consistently year after year: "one vineyard, one wine"

*The ultimate goal is to express the true character of each terroir consistently year after year: "one vineyard, one wine" is the philosophy*

was the philosophy propounded by Rafael López de Heredia, and it still pertains today. This naturally calls for more interventionist winemaking, since each year's wines are not allowed to express any vintage variation. Rather, Viña Tondonia Reserva is forced to behave like Viña Tondonia Reserva, Viña Cubillo must equally retain its identity, and so on. In fact, until 1981 none of these wines was labeled according to the vintage year but instead with reference to the number of years that had elapsed since; thus a Viña Bosconia 5° Año bottled in 1977 was really a Viña Bosconia Reserva 1972.

Regarding this practice, the López de Heredia sisters emphasize a distinction between two different lines within their portfolio. On the one hand, there is the line they call "commercial," the one spending little time on shelves and restaurant lists, which corresponds to wines labeled Crianza and Reserva. To these we might add Viña Tondonia Rosado, traditionally labeled Crianza, even though it is often released only ten or more years after the vintage (indeed, it has also appeared recently

**Above:** An ingenious way of making sure that the small hods of carefully harvested grapes are delivered as gently as possible

as Gran Reserva, for which it certainly qualifies). In the case of all these wines, what matters is not vintage variation but the character of every wine and every vineyard. That is why it makes little sense for them to emphasize vintages.

María José openly explains: "We correct vintage irregularities in a natural way, by blending in some wine from the same vineyard with a different color, acidity, or alcohol level. We use different vintages, within the legal limits, in order always to release wines of consistent quality and to maintain our house style." The sisters think that it would not be fair to single out any specific vintage above the others, because the guiding philosophy is to produce single-vineyard, brand-recognizable wines. "It is not the vintage but the label that matters: we produce Cubillo, Tondonia, Bosconia—never Tondonia 2000 or Tondonia 2001."

Even accepting that the story is basically as they have told it, it is still difficult to repress the suspicion that a mere 15 percent of wines from

other vintages will not be able to "correct" more extreme vintages, which inevitably leads to variation (maybe not brutal but certainly perceptible) from one year to another. From another point of view, as time passes, greater variation becomes inevitable; the wines evolve along different lines, which may not be discernible from one year to the next, but it becomes more evident over the longer term. Thus, we have the impression (subjective, of course) that the more recent releases of Tondonia Reserva are closer to their Bosconia Reserva siblings—at least as far as fruit and fleshiness are concerned—than they used to be 10–15 years ago, when the differences between both styles were more evident than now.

On the other hand, there are the grandes reservas (with the exception of the Rosado), which are all vintage wines by nature. They all retain—sometimes radically so, due to the winemakers' refusal to correct it—the character of the year they were born. These grandes reservas are always incorporated as such in the lists of historic wines of the house, so every tasting note remains untouched, save, of course, to account for the wines' evolution and bottle variation.

The historic grandes reservas of López de Heredia are truly wines to be contemplated with emotion and awe, to be enjoyed patiently in good company and, preferably, at a delicately assorted table—hence the understandable complaint of the López de Heredia sisters that many of their bottles are consumed by people who "merely want to be able to say that they have drunk them" and do not stop to appreciate what should be "an almost existential experience." Mercedes and María José are worried that the new possibilities afforded by new technologies may be contributing to this "dehumanization" of wine enjoyment—in particular of these drops of bottled history. That may be why they are not too keen on advertising the excellence of their historic wines. But how can one hold back the impulse of the world of communication? And how can we, of all people, silence the glories of their Bosconia 1954, Tondonia Blanco 1957, or Tondonia Tinto 1964, to mention only three wines that no self-respecting wine lover should miss? But please—with all due reverence.

## FINEST WINES

### Viña Tondonia Reserva v Viña Bosconia Reserva

While it is undeniable that the grandes reservas of historic vintages are truly exceptional wines (though we do not want to say that too loud, do we?), it would be a serious mistake to overlook the two great commercial wines of the house: Tondonia, in Bordeaux bottles, and Bosconia, in Burgundy bottles, following a tradition started by the founder, even though the Francophile differences are no longer quite as marked as they used to be (Viña Bosconia's predecessor was called Rioja Cepa Borgoña and included a small proportion of Pinot Noir). Today, a slightly higher proportion of Tempranillo and, above all, a deliberate wish to preserve a definite style give Viña Bosconia more body and color, riper fruit, and longer life than

Viña Tondonia, which in turn seeks a truer profile of Rioja "vino fino" that is perfectly ready and enjoyable upon release.

### Viña Tondonia Blanco Gran Reserva

The whites are probably the finest jewels in the López de Heredia lineup. And there is no doubt that the grandes reservas of Tondonia rank among the greatest Spanish whites. If we temporarily exclude those wines aged under *flor*, there are few candidates to challenge the supremacy of these noble Tondonias. Admittedly, they are not easily approachable, since the long aging in American oak barrels (nine years in the case of the sublime **Gran Reserva 1964★**) produces elegant oxidative notes that may disconcert novice drinkers. But this long aging process, preceded by another couple of years in oak vats and followed by a number of years in bottle, gives the wines an unmistakable profile, where a sharp and well-defined backbone is fleshed out by multiple layers of aromas and flavors that, in a mythical vintage such as 1964, reach astonishing levels. Other more recent vintages—some sharper, like the **1973**; others richer, like the **1976**—may one day reach a similarly perfect structure. But so far this 1964 is Tondonia's greatest white.

### Viña Tondonia Rosado Gran Reserva

The rosé is a majestic example of unique personality, as well as a cheerful table companion that combines harmoniously with a wide range of dishes. Considering its complexity, it does all of this at an unbeatable price. Mostly Garnacha with 30% Tempranillo and 10% Viura, it normally hits the market at age ten or older. Again, many people are put off by its oxidative profile, so distinctly removed from, say, 99% of other rosés. But in these days of globalizing and standardizing tendencies, everything that is singular and special must be celebrated with even greater emphasis. As far as we know, there is not another rosé like it in the whole world.

**Bodegas R López de Heredia Viña Tondonia**
Area under vine: 420 acres (170ha)
Average production: 500,000 bottles
Avenida de Vizcaya 3,
26200 Haro, La Rioja
Tel: +34 941 310 244
Fax: +34 941 310 788
www.lopezdeheredia.com

# Bodegas Muga

**W**henever the story of Bodegas Muga is told, the cast is almost always exclusively male. Well, perhaps a brief, cursory mention will be made of the founder, grandmother Aurora Caño, who passed away in 1991, or, rarer still, of her daughter Isabel Muga, who, at well over 70 years old, is today the first to show up at the winery every morning. Generally speaking, however, it is the Muga men who take the starring roles. And this rather chauvinistic interpretation of the bodega's history represents a major injustice.

There is no denying that Aurora's sons Manuel (also deceased) and Isacín (short for Isaac) deserve recognition for leading the major leaps forward that the winery took in the 1970s and then again in the 1980s and 1990s. And it is no less true that her grandsons (Manuel and Jorge, but also the younger

*It is astonishing to realize that Manuel and Isacín Muga managed to transform Prado Enea into a veritable icon of Riojan authenticity and tradition in a mere decade*

Isaac and Juan) are doing a great job this century, not only in terms of marketing but also, more importantly, in terms of the quality of the wines.

As important as these various male figures are and have been, though, Aurora Caño deserves a far more central position in the Muga narrative. It was Aurora, after all, who was the spring and the backbone, first by founding the company in 1932 with her husband Isaac Muga, shortly after their wedding (a partnership to which she contributed her solid winemaking knowledge), and later on by supporting the relocation to the cellar facilities in the Barrio de la Estación. In the words of Jorge Muga: "My grandma Aurora, a woman of great character, was always the cellar's alma mater. Besides that, she was a great taster. Until

her very last day, aged 85, she tasted, organized, and bossed about in her powerful voice."

But in Spain, as in many other countries, family names are transmitted via the male lineage, which in this case yields the paradox that today it is Muga and not Caño that is the house name. It is unlikely, though, that the family resents this, since Muga is an excellent brand name from the point of view of sonority, exclusivity, and linguistic compatibility. Moreover, the Muga family has been an active part of Haro viticulture since at least the 17th century.

The family had been growers until the experience of Aurora Caño and the entrepreneur spirit of Manuel and Isacín came together in the second half of the 1960s to start winemaking in vats followed by barrel aging. Wooden vats and oak barrels have, in fact, become a family signature that harks back to Aurora's memories of her youth among barrels at La Rioja Alta. Her father, Jorge Caño, was the cellar manager there, and she had to lend a hand after her mother's death in 1915. In her view, fine wine was born and matured in oak and oak alone; if other producers decided to move to concrete or stainless steel, well, that was very much their problem.

In 1964, as part of a process that took more than 12 years due to financial difficulties, Bodegas Muga took the leap from the small cellar on Haro's Calle Mayor to the imposing building in the Barrio de la Estación. The company also took the leap from producing young wines to making crianzas, reservas, and grandes reservas. And this was at a time when most others were abandoning oak.

Indeed, in those days, the trade of wooden barrels was not a particularly attractive business proposition. For a full decade between the 1960s and 1970s, Jesús Azcárate, from San Vicente de la Sonsierra, who was then the *cubero* (the cooper, the artisan who builds and repairs the oak

**Right:** Jorge Muga, who continues to develop both the more modern and the more traditional strands of his inheritance

**Above:** Large wooden vats, meticulously maintained by house cooper Jesús Azcárate, are very much part of the Muga signature

barrels and large wooden vats) and one of the few remaining masters of his trade, worked almost exclusively for Muga. Even then, the company was only able to keep him on thanks to the fortuitous sale of a vineyard for what was a small fortune at the time. Azcárate eventually joined the company, where he has now worked for 40 years. Along with his family, he is an integral part of the Muga story in his own right.

Muga's decision to venture into fine-wine production, trading a vineyard for cellars in the process, was the company's first radical move. The next came some 20 years later, and once again it centered on winemaking—specifically, Manuel and Isacín's pioneering decision to make a modern version of Rioja: Torre Muga. But this emphasis on winemaking should not overshadow the company's commitment to viticulture. The family's vineyard holdings are not large—1,000 acres (400ha)—and they could hardly grow any more except by venturing farther from Haro. All that notwithstanding, the vineyard remains a constant source of guidance and inspiration, and Jorge Muga says he is trying to leave large-scale viticulture in the hands of others so he can concentrate on smaller projects involving some of the most highly favored sites. Though always more terroir- than variety-driven, Jorge firmly believes that "minor" varieties can contribute complexity to Tempranillo blends.

Muga's gran reserva, Prado Enea, is sourced from grapes grown in Rioja's highest vineyards, among them Sajazarra. It is there, too, that their Cava Conde de Haro—produced only in selected vintages—obtains its freshness and lower alcohol. Other privileged vineyards include Baltracones and El Estepal, which yield the best Tempranillo (mainly), Mazuelo, Graciano, and Garnacha to produce the best Muga wines. But even these are complemented with myriad other parcels owned by small growers who have been associated with Muga for decades.

In fact, it would be hard to tell—even roughly—the area under vine controlled by the family. In part, that is because reaching a figure demands awkward calculations, adding together a huge number of plots, many of them extremely small. The calculation is further complicated by the fact that not all of the harvest goes into Muga wines (the balance is sold). What's more, the vineyards are dotted with dead vines and vines of subpar varieties—such as Moscatel and Calagraño, which is not even good as a table grape—that have survived from the days when the sole aim was to achieve maximum yields.

Equally, the total harvest figures are highly unpredictable, since they depend greatly on the quality of each vintage. The production of crianza, rosé, and barrel-fermented white represents about 800,000 bottles. From there on, total production figures may approach 2 million bottles in the best years, when all the house labels are produced.

## FINEST WINES

### Torre Muga
This pioneering modern Rioja, conceived in the late 1980s, is the greatest achievement of the brothers Manuel and Isacín Muga. Its first commercial vintage was 1991, though a 1989 was made and not released. The **2005**, from a vintage that was excellent in Rioja Alta, is the perfect expression of modern Rioja, characterized by what we have always loved in wines made in a style that was both powerful and extracted (a.k.a. modern). Understandably, the obvious toasty notes may put some off, but here is extraordinary balance, with flesh and fruit that do not merely compensate the oak but actually steal the show. Fresh acidity balances the first-class tannins. Modern, indeed, for today—but our bet is that this will be a future classic. Time will tell.

### Prado Enea Gran Reserva
There is a markedly intellectual character to the Prado Enea wines, which are made in a classical style. It's a character that is particularly apparent in the wines' youth, and it's also pronounced when they are tasted alongside wines made in a more modern style and released at about the same time. This is clearly true of the **Prado Enea 2001** versus the sensuous gush that is Torre Muga 2005. In Prado Enea we perceive floral notes, a hint of sesame on the nose that reaches the palate as mint and licorice, slightly tart, fruity acidity, and firm but elegant tannins. It is a wine that seduces as being deeply rooted in Riojan classicism and that—certainly in this vintage—promises a brilliant, decade-long future. Should we have the opportunity to open a perfect bottle at around 25 years old, we would do so with the highest hopes of finding a sublime wine. We are relatively familiar with the **Prado Enea 1982** (it is astonishing to realize that Manuel and Isacín managed to transform their brand into a veritable icon of Riojan authenticity and tradition in a mere decade), a wine that can be drunk with great pleasure, both sensorial and intellectual. The **Prado Enea 1978** was a rarer treat, but thanks to the generous hospitality of the Muga family, we have recently sampled a 25-year-old bottle. This is a beautifully elegant wine, evincing a strong sense of what might be described as decaying grandeur—the epitome of a well-matured *vino fino de Rioja*. A light robe, leaning toward the expected brick-orange, if barely presenting any sediment. The nose is marked by fine leather notes, dry autumn leaves, spices, and raw meat (a whiff of steak tartare), while the palate is still lively, with firm tannins and a harmonious finish.

**Bodegas Muga**
Area under vine: 500 acres (200ha)
Average production: 1.4 million bottles
Barrio de la Estación s/n, 26200 Haro, La Rioja
Tel: +34 941 311 825
Fax: +34 941 312 867
www.bodegasmuga.com

# La Rioja Alta

La Rioja Alta is one of the most traditional wineries remaining in Spain. It was founded by five wine growers from Rioja and the Basque Country in 1890. Today there are other stockholders, but control over the company is still in the hands of the original five families. The winery is situated in that most traditional of Rioja's locations, the Barrio de la Estación in Haro, next to other well-known names such as CVNE, López de Heredia, Muga, and Roda.

The company is one of the main guardians of traditional Rioja and is loyal to the classic profile of its wines. This does not mean it has avoided change or innovation (viticulture, vinification, and aging have all been updated through the years), but the basics remain the same, and their identity is scrupulously protected—a philosophy that sometimes means returning to old practices. They believe that American oak is best for their wines, for example, and they built their own barrels until the 1950s. In 1995, they returned to this tradition, and they now source, buy, and dry the wood, as well as making most of the barrels they use themselves. Though all their oak comes from the United States, they have a maturation cellar dedicated to experimentation, where one of the things they are constantly testing is wood of different origins.

The original fermentation room is still there, housing the original oak *tinas* that were used to ferment every vintage up to 1996, when the company built a new fermentation room in their winery at Labastida, only a couple of miles away from the headquarters in Haro. Here the oak vats have given way to stainless-steel tanks.

Rioja Alta is also, of course the name of a subregion within Rioja, considered by many to be the one with the greatest potential. To carry the name of a whole region—which can create some confusion among consumers—is a legacy of rights

**Right:** Guillermo de Aranzábal, chairman of La Rioja Alta and the current protector of its strong traditional reputation

*La Rioja Alta is one of the main guardians of traditional Rioja and is loyal to the classic profile of its wines. But this does not mean it has avoided change or innovation*

acquired long ago. The logo, used on their labels since it was registered in 1916, shows the River Oja framed by four trees, as well as the name La Rioja Alta in a distinctive and rather baroque italic font.

In the past, local wine laws meant it was not necessary to specify the vintage on the label, so the winery started selling its wines with 1890 on the label, referring to the year the winery was created. The name Gran Reserva 904 has similar origins; it was originally called 1904 after another significant date in the company's history, when it underwent a major expansion. Other wines took their names from vineyards named after the owning families: Viña Alberdi, Viña Arana, and Viña Ardanza.

In recent times, the company has expanded into other regions of Spain, with wineries in Rías Baixas (Lagar de Cervera), Ribera del Duero (Aster), and Rioja (Barón de Oña). But Rioja is still overwhelmingly the focus. Today the company owns 1,050 acres (425ha) of vineyards in the region, mostly in Haro, Briones, Labastida, Rodezno, and Cenicero, and this meets roughly half its needs. The most significant plots are the 222-acre (90ha) Finca La Cuesta (also called Viña Ardanza) in Cenicero,

planted with Tempranillo; and in Rodezno, Finca Las Cuevas (also called Viña Arana), initially 89 acres (36ha), now 188 acres (76ha), and Viña Alberdi, which is 54 acres (22ha). In 2006, a further 173 acres (70ha) in La Pedriza (Rioja Baja) were planted with Garnacha, which will contribute to the Viña Ardanza blend. Also of note are 62 acres (25ha) in Montecillo and 80 acres (32ha) in Cihuri. Yields are kept under 5,000kg/ha, and the average age of vines is 23 years old.

As a curiosity, the wire netting on Rioja Alta's top wines originally acted as a protective seal to prevent unscrupulous people from exchanging the contents of the bottle for another wine of inferior quality and then reselling it. Nowadays, it is used for aesthetic reasons, as well as to maintain a link with the past. The company was also a pioneer in keeping in direct touch with its customers by forming a special club (Club de Cosecheros), which allows customers to buy one cask of wine directly from the winery and to have access to its facilities for visits and dinners. In the past few years, the company has gone to great lengths to attract visitors by providing a restaurant and meeting services, as well as selling its wines in an ultra-modern shop inside the headquarters.

Rioja Alta has had its ups and downs over the years, and the quality of some wines during the early 1990s was not up to its historically high standards. But it seems to be back on track under the guidance of winemaker Julio Sáenz. Sadly, its stock of old vintages is small, but old bottles can still be found in shops and restaurants throughout Spain. The search is certainly worthwhile.

## FINEST WINES

### Viña Alberdi [V]

This is the entry-level wine—pure Tempranillo from Briones, Rodezno, and Labastida. It is sold as Crianza in Spain but Reserva elsewhere. It has been modernized since the very good **2001** vintage, sold as Selección Especial and dressed with a colorful label, displaying a fresher profile. It is aged for two years in American oak—the first year in new barrels, the second in barrels three years old.

## Viña Arana

Viña Arana is 95% Tempranillo that comes mainly from a 188-acre (76ha) vineyard in Rodezno, called Las Cuevas, with additional grapes from Las Monjas in Zarratón and Larrazuri in Labastida. The 5% of Mazuelo is also harvested in Rodezno. The wine is aged for three years in used American oak and is the archetype of the Bordeaux style produced in Haro and originally known as Rioja claret.

## Viña Ardanza

Ardanza is the surname of one of the founding families of the winery and a name often found in the management team through the years. It is also one of the strongest brands in Spain. Created in 1942, it was strong enough to survive some tough times. It was originally aged for 42 months—always in used American barrels—but this has been cut to 36 months. In the past, wines did not always carry a vintage date on the label, and this was also the case for Viña Ardanza. So, while old bottles do exist, it's difficult to know their age. The **2001** (released in 2009) is fantastic, taking its place alongside some of the finest vintages. It is being sold as **Reserva Especial**, only the third vintage ever to carry that designation (the other two being **1964** and **1973**). The downside with high-volume brands like this is that the different lots are necessarily heterogeneous. What makes Viña Ardanza different is the 20% Garnacha from Villalba. This is currently bought in from different growers, though in the future it will be sourced from the company's recently planted vineyard in the area, La Pedriza. The Tempranillo comes from the company's La Cuesta vineyard in Cenicero and Los Llanos and Montecillo vineyards in Fuenmayor. **Viña Ardanza blanco** was only produced for a few years, presented in 1988 (with the 1986 vintage) but abandoned early in the 1990s, when the company purchased a winery in Rías Baixas—Lagar de Fornelos—dedicated to whites made from Albariño under the brand Lagar de Cervera. At the same time, they gave up on all young wines, including the rosado **Vicuana**.

## Gran Reserva 904

Not only was 1904 one of the best vintages in Haro, it was also the year Alfredo Ardanza, one of the founders of La Rioja Alta, proposed the merger with his own winery, Bodega Ardanza. This was one of the milestones in the development of the company, and a special wine was named in honor of the event, Reserva 1904, later renamed Gran Reserva 904 to avoid confusion between name and vintage. The 904 is traditional in style, with good concentration and spicy fruit. It is 90% Tempranillo from growers in Briñas, Labastida, and Villalba, and 10% Graciano from the company's own vineyards in Rodezno and Fuenmayor. It is aged for four years in barrel and is possibly the longest-lived wine in the portfolio.

## Gran Reserva 890 ★

This is the top of the line—a wine that is produced only in exceptional vintages. It can age in wood for eight years (nowadays closer to six) and for another six years in bottle (this has also been gradually reduced over the years) before release. As one might expect from this formula, this is a wine of the most traditional style; spice from the barrels, vanilla, maraschino cherries, cedarwood, and smoke. The name alludes to 1890, the year the winery was founded, but the name was shortened to 890 to avoid confusion with the vintage year. It has never been a cheap wine. The vintage on the market in 2010 was the 1995. The scale of production is variable but averages around 40,000 bottles. Older vintages probably have a different composition, but nowadays the wine is 95% Tempranillo sourced from long-term suppliers in Briñas, Labastida, and Villalba; 3% Graciano from the company's own vineyards in Rodezno and Fuenmayor; and 2% Mazuelo from its vineyards in Rodezno. The color is translucent orange more than red, the coloring matter having precipitated out during the long periods in barrel and in bottle. The nose is mainly tertiary, with leather, forest floor, and mushrooms and a whiff of truffle and spice (clove), while the palate is polished, with suave tannins and good persistence. Great Gran Reserva 890 vintages include **1959**, **1970**, **1975**, **1981**, **1982**, **1985**, and **1994**. This is a textbook traditional Rioja.

**La Rioja Alta**
Area under vine: 1,050 acres (425ha)
Average production: 1.8 million bottles
Avenida de Vizcaya 8,
26200 Haro, La Rioja
Tel: +34 941 310 346
www.riojalta.com

# Bodegas Roda

**V**ery few producers fit more clearly than Roda in the group that the well-informed aficionado now refers to as "modern Rioja." The wines' organoleptic profile is unambiguous in that sense, at least during the first few years after bottling, and the cellar practices at Roda fall decidedly within the framework of Rioja winemaking innovation.

At the same time, however, few others can claim such complicity with tradition or such selective honoring of it. For example, right from its beginnings, Roda has respected and followed conventional terminology, releasing its Roda I and Roda II (the latter recently rebaptized simply as Roda) as Reserva wines. Equally, the company chose for its headquarters a neighborhood that is emblematic of Rioja classicism: the Barrio de la Estación in Haro. And finally, the subterranean wine cellars, ending in a balcony-like edge over the River Ebro, could not be more typical of historical Rioja practices.

This helps confirm what many of us instinctively believe: no matter how useful labels may be when it comes to simplification, few classifications are as worthwhile as the very intuitive and personal distinction between good wines and the rest. From this perspective, Roda wines belong largely in the first group. Indeed, it would not be going too far to suggest that some of its best wines—like the magnificent 1994 Roda I—have proved in their evolution a clear tendency to develop classic Rioja profiles. Some recent vintages, such as 2004 and 2005, point in a similar direction.

As is so often the case when one has the opportunity to taste and talk with a wine producer, a common topic of conversation with Agustín Santolaya—veritable factotum and visible head of Roda—is the rating of different vintages. It is surprising to discover his fondness for the difficult

**Right:** Agustín Santolaya, among whose principles is that Roda wines must be true expressions of their vintage

*Very few producers fit more clearly than Roda in the group now referred to as "modern Rioja." At the same time, however, few others can claim such complicity with tradition or such selective honoring of it*

**Above:** The name proudly displayed on the side of the winery comes from the first two letters of the owners' surnames

1997, especially for the 1997 Roda I (V). To be frank, it is a fondness we cannot share and one that we feel inclined to attribute more to the mental mechanics that make a father overprotective of his weakest child than to the wine's innate superiority. But it is nonetheless true that it is often the "parents" who know their wines best, so perhaps it would be worth keeping an eye on this wine, just in case time does indeed confirm Santolaya's hunch. It would not be the first time that has happened.

The owners of Roda are Barcelona-based Mario Rotllant and Carmen Daurella, whose surnames provided the winery moniker. Now divorced, they were married when they launched the winery in the late 1980s. They have always trusted the growing winemaking team led by Santolaya, which also includes Isidro Palacios, Carlos Díez, and Esperanza Tomás (in charge respectively of viticulture, enology, and research). Initially they flirted with the idea of following a château model: a single-estate wine produced in adjoining facilities. But they soon discarded this idea and

adopted a more flexible and modular approach— one might even call it "liquid," to borrow from Zygmunt Bauman's definition of postmodernity.

They were convinced that their peculiar location and weather north of Rioja would give very different results in different vintages, according to whether the predominant influence each year was Atlantic, continental, or even Mediterranean. Their mission, accomplished relatively speedily, was to control a respectable vineyard area planted with old-vine Tempranillo, Graciano, and Garnacha at different altitude levels (between 1,250ft [380m] and 2,130ft [650m]), and with different soil compositions (sand, chalk, limestone, and gravelly terraces). These old vines had been traditionally trained, with three irregular branches. For some reason, Roda is not interested in publicizing the identity of these vineyards, even when they are asked about it. In any case, control over the vines enables them to choose from a rich palette of fruit each year. The balance is sold as grapes to other producers.

The choice grapes then undergo a double selection process, first in the vineyard and later in the cellar. Fruit from each of the 17 plots is destemmed and fermented separately in 17 large wooden vats of 3,200–5,300 gallons (12,000–20,000 liters), which are replaced every ten years. Winemaking is divided into three steps: cold maceration, fermentation, and late maceration (up to about 20 days). Those 17 wines from the 17 vineyards are then transferred directly to 225-liter French oak barrels (50 percent new and 50 percent one year old), distributed around a dazzling state-of-the-art malolactic cellar where strict conditions of 68°F (20°C) and 75 percent humidity are maintained with the use of temperature-regulated floors. After December, once malo is completed, the heating is turned off and north-facing windows are opened, so that the wines are naturally stabilized at 43°F (6°C) by the winter cold.

A key moment in this process is naturally the decision, after sampling all the different barrels, of which wines will go into the cuvée Roda—sold until 2001 as Roda II, the best of which include Roda II 1995 (V), Roda II 2000 (V), and Roda 2005 (V)—and which into the more expensive Roda I. Here the criterion—not always evident in our tasting of the wines—is the dichotomy between red and black fruit, so the more youthful fresh-cherry profile goes to Roda, whereas the more profound and mineral, plummy/cocoa nose is destined for Roda I.

Bodegas Roda takes pride in its refusal to follow the (legal) practice of refreshing wines with up to 15 percent of wines from other vintages. We are to assume, then, that every drop in every bottle belongs to the vintage stated on the label. Santolaya defends this concept as a radical commitment to their no-compromise model, which aspires to bottle and bring to the consumer the liquid expression of the very precise nuances and spirit of the landscape, terroir, and climate of northern Rioja Alta, exactly the way they are every vintage.

## FINEST WINES

### Cirsion

Cirsion (written without an accent on the "o" but often pronounced as if it were written "Cirsión") is a concept wine, sourced from a most exacting selection of vines in the search for silkiness and early polymerization of grape tannins straight from the plant. Despite its high price, we have been fortunate enough to be able to follow fairly closely the development of the truly exceptional 2001★, starting before its commercial release. Already in November 2002 it expressed itself as a massive but elegant wine that (behind a still-closed nose) released an explosion of sensorial stimuli on the palate, with tannin that was sweet from the start yet loaded with personality—exactly the concept that its makers sought. Since then, this wine's evolution has been excellent, and by mid-2010 it was performing beautifully: powerful, still fruit-driven, serious, well structured, touched by subtle cedar notes, tobacco, and spice, with a delicious, endless finish.

### Roda I

Many Roda wines share, in almost every vintage, an exceptionally fine character, almost intellectual, marked by a sort of distant elegance. Sometimes one would appreciate—alongside their characteristically immaculate tannic structure—a little more fruit substance and a little more passion. In fact, it is not hard to imagine what Roda wines could be like if they consistently managed to match coolish intellectual perfection with worldly emotion: one need only reach for the 2004—or indeed the 1994★, a veritable classic—to show how great the best modern Rioja can be: an expressive nose, where perfectly integrated oak sustains clean mineral notes and black fruit of optimum ripeness, followed by a beautifully structured mid-palate, with bright acidity, powerful tannin, and intense fruit presence.

### Bodegas Roda

Area under vine: 370 acres (150ha)
Average production: 300,000 bottles
Avenida Vizcaya 5, Barrio de la Estación,
26200 Haro, La Rioja
Tel: +34 941 303 001
Fax: +34 941 312 703
www.roda.es

# Bodegas Bilbaínas

Among the Spanish wine lovers who reached adulthood—and with it the opportunity to pursue their passion—in the 1980s, the better informed and most fortunate were able to enjoy great wines made by Bodegas Bilbaínas 10–15 years earlier. By the 1980s, the company was nowhere near its best but, rather, had been lured (like many other producers in Rioja) onto the wrong path, leading to maltreatment of soils, excessively high yields, and the industrialization of wine production. What nobody can deny, however, is its long and noble history as one of the centennial producers in the Barrio de la Estación in Haro. In fact, at Bodegas Bilbaínas, 1901 is the official foundation date, the year when a firm of Bilbao businessmen bought Savignon Frères, a French company that had settled in Haro in 1859 to escape the successive scourges of oidium, mildew, and phylloxera in its native country.

*What nobody can deny is Bodegas Bilbaínas's long and noble history as one of the centennial producers in the Barrio de la Estación in Haro*

The turning point came in the early 1990s, when a powerful neighboring company tried to buy Bodegas Bilbaínas. That led the owners to hire the dynamic and prestigious winemaker José Hidalgo, whose helpful contribution meant a noticeable qualitative leap forward for the house's wines, best appreciated in the early releases of La Vicalanda, wines of modern profile whose first vintages are now—20 years later—in their prime.

But the financial investment required to renovate the vineyards as well as the winemaking facilities was enormous, and the company's sale became inevitable; in 1997, it was sold to the Codorníu group. For the first decade, all evidence of change came in the form of technological improvements. Then, in 2007, after the departure of José Hidalgo as head of production, a more intense search began for fruit character in the wines, accompanied by greater extraction and ripeness and more evident new oak. Time will tell whether these new wines will ever reach the level of excellence offered by classic vintages of Bodegas Bilbaínas in days past.

Bodegas Bilbaínas are supplied by over 1,000 acres (400ha) of vineyards, 600 acres (250ha) of which are its own, located in Haro on chalky

and sandy soils. The varieties planted are the typical Tempranillo, Garnacha, Graciano, and Mazuelo, and the white Viura and Malvasia.

Above: Bilbaínas's finest wines come from the Viña Pomal vineyard, between the rivers Ebro (above) and Tirón

## FINEST WINES

### Viña Pomal Reserva

This label is more than 100 years old, and the wine has always been made from grapes sourced from the Viña Pomal vineyard, between the rivers Ebro and Tirón. If we leave aside the exceptional old vintages—like the marvelous Bodegas Bilbaínas Vieja Reserva 1928 that we were fortunate enough to enjoy in the summer of 2010—Viña Pomal Reserva is probably the wine that today retains the most classical profile, despite the recent change from a traditional Rioja blend to varietal Tempranillo. By contrast, another traditional label, Viña Zaco, has recently been recast in a questionable international style. The Viña Pomal label also appears as Crianza and in two special versions: Selección Centenario Crianza and Reserva.

**Bodegas Bilbaínas**
Area under vine: 620 acres (250ha)
Average production: 2.8 million bottles
Calle Estación 3, 26200 Haro, La Rioja
Tel: +34 941 310 147
Fax: +34 941 310 706
www.bodegasbilbainas.com

# Bodegas Castillo de Cuzcurrita

From a winemaking point of view, the signature feature of this producer—and one that makes it unique in Rioja—is the vast walled vineyard (a *cerrado*, or *clos*) of more than 17 acres (7ha), planted in 1970, that in exceptional vintages produces the red Cerrado del Castillo. But this is not the only charm of this peculiar bodega. The facilities are located in Cuzcurrita del Río Tirón, in a medieval castle formed by a square wall around a central tower—all elegantly rendered in a contemporary style on the house labels.

It is perhaps that balance between ancient tradition and cutting-edge technology that best characterizes Bodegas Castillo de Cuzcurrita: labels featuring a minimalist representation of facilities more than 600 years old; calculation of foliar mass per bunch in traditionally trained vines; state-of-the-art cellar technology in a medieval castle...

The recent history of this bodega started in 1999, when new owners bought the castle and then the surrounding vineyards, starting an ambitious renovation project, with Ana Martín in charge of the winemaking. Her first vintage was 2000, still under precarious circumstances, remedied by the time the stellar 2001 arrived.

Castillo de Cuzcurrita produces Tempranillo wines only. One half of the 62 acres (25ha; with an average age of 35 years) under its control is its own, including the 18.5 acres (7.5ha) of El Cerrado, while the other half is under long-term contract. With the exception of the *clos*, the parcels are small, each less than 2.47 acres (1ha), and they are scattered all around Cuzcurrita on poor soils. Remarkable among them are the vineyards in El Monte, some of which were planted more than a century ago.

In contrast with the unequivocally modern style of this producer's wines, the viticulture aspires to the best Riojan tradition, using dry-farmed, densely planted, traditionally trained vines, and plenty of artisanal vineyard labor: regular pruning, green harvesting, bunch-thinning, and so on.

The winemaking philosophy is expressed in simple terms: "We respect tradition, but we want to show that true Rioja character can be conveyed in a modern style." In any case, wines cannot lie, and any experienced taster should be capable of identifying these as modern Spanish Tempranillo-based reds, almost certainly Rioja but not necessarily so. After all, the issue of typicity should not be a major concern, since we are dealing here with the westernmost section of Rioja, with a more continental climate and, therefore, with an area that is difficult to compare with the rest of the region.

## FINEST WINES

Production is limited to two labels. **Señorío de Cuzcurrita** is released every vintage in a larger number of bottles and **Cerrado del Castillo** only in exceptional vintages. There are no radical differences in concept behind them; the main difference is the source of the grapes, which in the case of Cerrado del Castillo is exclusively the walled vineyard next to the castle that gives its name to the wine. Quantitatively, though, there is a remarkable difference: in the latter, the intensity of extraction and the extra structure provided by new French oak are more obvious than in the former.

Cerrado del Castillo has been released in the 2001, 2004, and 2005 vintages, and the latter two are still somewhat tight and tannic. The great evolution of the **Cerrado del Castillo 2001**, which still needs to integrate its perfumed oak notes, but whose tannins have softened perceptibly, is enough, however, for us to imagine a promising future for these wines—which of course lack any track record, given the short history of the house.

**Bodegas Castillo de Cuzcurrita**
Area under vine: 62 acres (25ha)
Average production: 60,000 bottles
Calle San Sebastián 1,
Cuzcurrita de Rio Tirón, 26214 La Rioja
Tel: +34 941 328 022
Fax: +34 941 301 620
www.castillodecuzcurrita.com

**Left:** Juan Diez del Corral, managing director of Castillo de Cuzcurrita, who is helping realize its early promise

# Ramón Bilbao

In 1896, Ramón Bilbao Murga became a wine merchant in Haro, selling wines under his own name and that of Viña Turzaballa from premises in Calle de las Cuevas (*cueva* means cave). In 1924, he established the company Bodegas Ramón Bilbao in the very same place, on a street housing other names still around today, such as Bodegas Berceo and Carlos Serres, as well as relative newcomers like Florentino de Lecanda. The company was kept in the family until the death of its last member, Ramón Bilbao Pozo, in 1966.

In 1972 a new, bigger winery was built on the outskirts of Haro, on the road to Casalarreina, and the firm was transformed into a public limited company. It was in turn acquired in 1999 by the drinks group Diego Zamora, better know in Spain for its brand Licor 43. Responsibility for the day-to-day running of the winery is now in the hands of Rodolfo Bastida, at the same time managing director and winemaker, who appears to look after everything—from the style of the wines to the modernization of the facilities and the revamping of the company's brands and image.

Ramón Bilbao offers a full range of wines, from traditional to modern styles, showing a company that has adapted over time without losing its roots. All of the vineyards, 185 acres (75ha) in total, are located in Rioja Alta, Haro, Briones, Ábalos, San Vicente de la Sonsierra, Cihuri, Anguciana, and Cuzcurrita del Río Tirón. The company also has long-term agreements with grape growers, whose vineyards are controlled by the winery, totaling no fewer than 1,175 acres (475ha).

Unfortunately for lovers of traditional white Rioja, Ramón Bilbao has stopped the production of its white wines (as has happened at many other wineries as well), because the company now belongs to a group that also has Mar de Frades in Rías Baixas, known for its Albariño in a blue bottle, and a new venture in Ribera del Duero under the name Cruz de Alba.

## FINEST WINES

### Viña Turzaballa [V]
This is the most traditional label, kept for the gran reserva category and made only in exceptional—the winery's literature calls them "singular"—vintages, most recently 1994, 1996, 1999, and 2001. This brand has existed since 1924, but today it's almost unknown. Turzaballa is not a vineyard; this is pure Tempranillo from two vineyards in Haro—La Turca and La Zaballa, older than 75 years—and the name is a concatenation of both. It spends 40 months in American oak barrels and, later, the same time in bottle. It is intended for the long haul.

### Ramón Bilbao
The Ramon Bilbao label comprises the traditional red Crianza, Reserva, and Gran Reserva aged in American oak, as well as a Tempranillo Edición Limitada, a barrel selection aged in new French and American oak. For a while there was also a barrel-fermented white. The **1994 Reserva 75 Años** was released to celebrate the 75th birthday of the company and is a perfect example of balance between fruit and oak. The **Ramón Bilbao Tempranillo Edición Limitada** shows the telltale notes of cherries, spices, smoke and toasted wood, tobacco, and other balsamic notes, pitched somewhere between tradition and modernity.

### Mirto
This is a modern wine made from old Tempranillo from Haro, Ollauri, Gimileo, Cihuri, Villalba, and Cuzcurrita, fermented in small oak *tinas* and aged for 24 months in new French barriques. Dark, concentrated, and powerful, showing ripe fruit, mint, and licorice notes and toasty oak tones that require time in bottle to integrate. The **2001** and **2004** show very good balance and hint at a very good evolution in bottle. There are plans to build a new, modern winery exclusively dedicated to the production of Mirto.

---

**Ramón Bilbao**
Area under vine: 185 acres (75ha)
Average production: 2.5 million bottles
Avenida Santo Domingo 34, 26200 Haro, La Rioja
Tel: +34 941 310295
Fax: +34 941 310832
www.bodegasramonbilbao.es

# Bodegas Martínez Lacuesta

In 1895, at the age of only 21, lawyer, politician, and businessman Félix Martínez Lacuesta founded a house that was to become one of the most traditional in Rioja. It was one of the first registered brand names in the region (in 1909) and long enjoyed a reputation for high quality, sharing with other century-old houses in Haro and Logroño the favor of the connoisseur market. From the 1960s to the 1980s, the wines of Martínez Lacuesta had a privileged status in the best restaurants, even as house wines, in the days when this status conferred much-desired prestige.

Later, as the winds and the times changed in Rioja, as well as in Spanish gastronomy, the feeling was that Martínez Lacuesta was lagging behind, sticking to a model that emphasized corporate image and distribution channels over vineyards and winemaking. In that sense, the early 21st century seems to have been a turning point in the relaunch of a house that has nonetheless retained a notable presence in the market.

After many years in the very heart of Haro, in 2010 Bodegas Martínez Lacuesta moved to new facilities in the industrial belt of the city. It was a sensible logistical decision, based on the need for more space as well as the renovation of facilities and technology that had inevitably become obsolete. That was the second step forward; the first had already been taken with the purchase, starting in 1999–2000, of 150 acres (60ha) of vineyards. This was a radical and significant decision; since its birth in 1895, the house had always worked with bought-in grapes. Nowadays, these vineyards—together with some others that are rented—supply some 40 percent of the grape needs of Martínez Lacuesta, while the rest is bought from local growers around Haro, San Asensio, and Villalba, with whom there have been good trade relations for generations.

The spirit of renovation can also be found in the release of "special" wines of a more modern profile: Félix Martínez Lacuesta, Selección Añada, and Ventilla 71, which coexist alongside the traditional lineup best represented by the Gran Reserva and Campeador. There is also a highly reputed Vermouth Lacuesta, a product that has long been common in many Rioja bodegas and one that Martínez Lacuesta maintains at a particularly high quality level.

## FINEST WINES

### Martínez Lacuesta Gran Reserva

The Gran Reserva was for many years labeled as Reserva Especial, until the adoption of the more common terminology. We zealously keep in our private cellars some bottles of **Martínez Lacuesta Reserva Especial 1973, 1976★, 1981★,** and **1982**; every time we open one, it proves to be a real feast for the senses—all elegance and finesse in a perfumed bouquet, but also a fruit backbone and refreshing acidity that consistently shock those who never experienced the golden age of this producer. Recent vintages, especially **2001**, are particularly promising. It will be interesting to retry them in 15 or 20 years and to compare them retrospectively with their predecessors.

### Campeador Reserva

This is the other veteran label of Martínez Lacuesta, registered in 1917 and one of the pillars of the house's commercial expansion, both national and international. Throughout its long history, Campeador has been, and still is, the archetypal négociant Rioja Reserva—a blend of 50% high-quality Rioja Alta Tempranillo and 50% ripe and structured Rioja Baja Garnacha, specifically from the Alfaro area. This composition makes it exceptional in the Martínez Lacuesta lineup, though, because its reds are mostly Tempranillo-based, only sometimes touched by Garnacha and Mazuelo.

### Bodegas Martínez Lacuesta
Area under vine: 150 acres (60ha)
Average production: 1 million bottles
Paraje de Ubieta s/n, 26200 Haro, La Rioja
Tel: +34 941 310 050
Fax: +34 941 303 748
www.martinezlacuesta.com

# Carlos Serres

Charles Serres, originally from Orléans in the Loire, was a wine consultant in France. In 1855, he arrived in Rioja looking for wines to make up for the losses caused by phylloxera in his native country. He established himself in Haro, where he worked with Alphonse Vigier and Cipriano Roig trading wines. He brought with him the French way of making, selling, and promoting wines and a decidedly international outlook. In 1886, Vigier returned to France, and Serres and Roig started Bodegas Cipriano Roig, making and selling wine in the famous Calle de las Cuevas in Haro. In 1904, the firm was renamed Bodegas Roig y Serres, and when the second generation took over in 1932, the name was changed once more, to Bodegas Carlos Serres.

The winery continued making traditional-style Rioja and remained in the family, but it became a limited company in 1975 with the third generation of Serres. The company had already moved to a bigger bodega at the entrance of Haro in 1966, and this remains the headquarters, though it now looks ultra-modern both inside and out.

The company has 150 acres (60ha) of vines in Haro, all of them in Finca El Estanque ("The Pond"). The vines—Tempranillo, Graciano, Mazuelo, and Viura—are planted on argilo-calcareous soil and have an average age of 30 years. They are the source of fruit for the reservas, grandes reservas, and the limited-production Onomástica line. The rest of the grapes are always sourced within the vicinity of Haro from local grape growers.

Brands, labels, and wines have all changed a great deal over the years. A gran reserva blanco called Carlomagno, presented in a Rhine bottle, was discontinued many years ago, but it's still a very pleasurable drink if you are lucky enough to find a 1964 or 1968. A red Carlomagno was also made for a time. The Carlos Serres Reserva Especial from 1958 is still alive and kicking, showing that the word *especial* on the label really meant something

then (and also that 1958 was a superb vintage).

More recently, the name Serres has been used for an entry-level line of wines—red, rosado, and white—while the name Carlos Serres is used for the oak-aged wines—Crianza, Reserva, and Gran Reserva—and Onomástica for the *especial* wines.

The wines went through a dip in quality during the 1980s and 1990s, when the brand was relegated to supermarkets. But the company is very much back on track under the ownership of the Vivanco family, who acquired the bodega in 2002 and have renewed the image and the labels, which now have an old-style flavor that draws on the history of the company in the form of an old picture of the founder. This is a name to look out for once again, in both its modern guises and older vintages.

## FINEST WINES

### Carlos Serres

These are barrel-aged wines, made as Crianza, Reserva, and Gran Reserva. Tempranillo (with a touch of Graciano, and sometimes a little Mazuelo) is destemmed and fermented in stainless steel, then aged in a mixture of French and American barrels. The Reserva and Gran Reserva are sourced from the company's own vineyards in Haro. The **2004** vintage is recommended, and the range is on its way up, maintaining elements of the traditional but also incorporating more up-to-date techniques, so that more recent vintages also merit attention.

### Onomástica Reserva

These are the *especial* wines, red and white, from the oldest vines in the El Estanque vineyard. The red is a blend of Tempranillo, Graciano, and Mazuelo; the white is 100% Viura, fermented in stainless steel and aged for 24 months in new French and American oak barrels.

**Bodegas Carlos Serres**
Area under vine: 148 acres (60ha)
Average production: 1.5 million bottles
Avenida Santo Domingo 40, 26200 Haro, La Rioja
Tel: +34 941 310 294
Fax: +34 941 310 418
www.carlosserres.com

# Tobía

**B**odegas Tobía is so linked to Oscar Tobía that the two names are almost synonymous. Oscar Tobía was born into a grape-growing family in San Asensio. After completing his studies in agriculture and enology in 1994, he returned to the *cosechero* family winery and turned it into one of the modern *vino de autor* wineries exploding with the "New Rioja" renaissance.

In fact, though, the focus is as much on the terroir as on the author, since he aims to produce wines that express the former's characteristics. Allying tradition with innovation, old vines with R&D projects, he makes modern wines that come from a variety of areas in the three subregions of the DO. On top of the 42 acres (17ha) of vineyards that the company owns, it controls a further 148 acres (60ha), spread over 15 different villages.

*There is a wide portfolio of wines, produced in a modern, concentrated style—not shy in terms of oak, but well balanced overall. The wines are both powerful and elegant*

In May 2010, the company moved from San Asensio to its brand-new winery in Cuzcurrita del Río Tirón—43,000 sq ft (4,000 sq m), with a capacity to vinify 1,650 tons (1.5 million kg) of grapes—just in time for the 2010 harvest.

## FINEST WINES

There is a wide portfolio of wines, produced in a modern, concentrated style—not shy in terms of oak, but well balanced overall. The wines are powerful and elegant at the same time. There are four ranges: Viña Tobía (Blanco, Rosado, and Tinto); Tobía (Selección, Graciano, and Blanco Fermentado en Barrica); Oscar Tobía (Tinto and Blanco Reserva); and Alma de Tobía (Tinto, Rosado Fermentado en Barrica, and Blanco Fermentado en Barrica).

### Oscar Tobía Tempranillo Reserva

The company describes the Oscar Tobía range as representing "renewed tradition." The red is made from old-vine Tempranillo grown in Rioja Alta. The grapes are destemmed but not crushed and then undergo a cold, pre-fermentation maceration. Malolactic is carried out in barrel, followed by 21 months in French and Hungarian oak barrels, which are racked every four months. The unusual **2003** and the more classic **2001** are recommended. They show toasty oak and need some years in bottle for this to integrate with the ripe black fruit that tends to show through in time.

### Tobía Graciano

Graciano is more talked about than cultivated (or drunk), so there are not that many varietal bottlings. Tobía does one, and it's a good example, showing the concentration and acidity the variety can provide. We liked the **2007**, which shows a deep color, almost opaque, then the telltale structure, with lively acidity and freshness. Unfortunately, only 3,000 bottles were produced.

### Alma de Tobía Tinto de Autor

Alma de Tobía is the top range of wines, where innovation and longevity are crucial. The Tinto de Autor is a blend of Rioja Alta (40-year-old Tempranillo) and Rioja Baja (50-year-old Garnacha from Tudelilla), selected for the high altitude (1,400–1,900ft [440–570m]), the soil type (stony clay-limestone), and the low yields (3,100kg/ha). Malolactic takes place in new French oak barrels, followed by 20 months in these same barrels, after which the wine is bottled unfiltered. The result is a deep wine, with plenty of graphite and roses on the nose. It is medium-bodied, with good acidity and expression on the palate, where the floral note persists. We recommend the **2004**. Only a few thousand bottles are produced (7,200 in 2004).

**Bodegas Tobía**
Area under vine: 42 acres (17ha)
Average production: 275,000 bottles
Paraje Senda Rutia s/2
26214 Cuzcurrita del Río Tirón, La Rioja
Tel: +34 941 301 789
Fax: +34 941 328 045
www.bodegastobia.com

# Finca Allende

Miguel Angel de Gregorio grew up surrounded by vines, barrels, and wine. His family had moved from La Mancha to La Rioja when he was just six months old, so his father could take up a position managing the vineyards at Marqués de Murrieta. It was only a matter of time, therefore, before the young de Gregorio caught the wine bug. Sure enough, at the age of 25, once he had finished his university studies in agriculture in Madrid, and after a brief stint as teacher at the same university, he became technical director at Bodegas Bretón in Rioja.

Allende (its name derived from an old word for "further") was established as a company in 1995, a year that also saw the first vintage, produced while de Gregorio was still at Bretón. The wine was made using carbonic maceration and then aged in barrique, a formula somewhere between the ancestral method—carbonic maceration—and the new wave—new French oak—that attempted to find the best of both worlds. This balancing act has become Allende's signature: there's always a careful mixture of tradition and modernity, using both carbonic maceration and whole bunches, or destemmed grapes fermented in concrete, pumping over or punching the cap, malolactic in stainless steel or barrel, using American and French oak.

De Gregorio bought and restored the Palacio de Ibarra, at the entrance to the village of Briones, where since 2001 the offices and tasting rooms have been housed, with the modern winery built just behind it. The idea is to make village wines, designed to show off the character of de Gregorio's various small vineyard plots—138.5 acres (56ha) in total, all located around Briones. De Gregorio favors north, northwest, or northeast orientation, since he seeks to capture the Atlantic influence and counteract the extremes of the continental climate.

**Right:** Miguel Angel de Gregorio, who instinctively pursues his ideal of wines true to their terroir and indigenous varieties

*Somewhere between ancient and modern, Allende attempted to find the best of both worlds. This balancing act has become Allende's signature: there's always a careful mixture of tradition and modernity*

By 1997, de Gregorio had given up his job and was fully dedicated to his own project, which expanded with the introduction of Aurus, a wine that attempts to embody the aurean ideal of balance—hence its name—between Tempranillo and the indigenous Graciano. It was first produced in 1996 and remains top of the line, even though a single-vineyard bottling, Calvario, was later added.

In 1998, de Gregorio and his distributor in Catalonia, the renowned wine merchant Quim Vila, owner of Vila Viniteca in Barcelona, created a joint venture under the name Paisajes y Viñedos ("Landscapes and Vineyards"), to produce wines following the Burgundian idea of reflecting the characteristics of a given plot of land. They

*De Gregorio has always acted on his own impulses and shown a sometimes stubborn disregard for local wine laws—a tendency that has landed him in trouble on occasion*

buy the grapes, and therefore some of the wines are one-offs, while others are produced regularly. They started numbering the wines with Roman numerals (I through IX), adding just one other letter for the name of the village, since the rules in Rioja did not allow them to mention location, name, or vineyard. This law has now been changed, and vineyard names are now used as wine names— such as Cecias (85-year-old Garnacha from Aguilar), La Pasada (Tempranillo from Briones), and Valsalado. From the 2007 vintage, the numbers have disappeared. Vinification and aging are adapted to the vineyard and vintage, the aim always being to preserve the characteristics of each place in wines that are true to the land from which they spring.

De Gregorio has always acted on his own impulses and shown a sometimes stubborn

disregard for local wine laws—a tendency that has landed him in trouble on occasion. He continues to ignore the official designations of crianza, reserva, and gran reserva, and the wines carry a generic back label stating only the vintage. He has continued to focus on indigenous grapes, a Graciano cuvée and a single-vineyard white from old Viura being two recent examples. But then, this pioneering part of his personality runs in the family: his father was said to have found the first Tempranillo vine to produce white grapes (red grapes mutating to white is not, in fact, an uncommon occurrence), which has been the source of Tempranillo Blanco in the Rioja region ever since.

## FINEST WINES

### Allende [V]
Originally from 35-year-old Tempranillo vines grown in Briones, this wine was traditionally made using some carbonic maceration, since de Gregorio did not own a destemmer. It is aged in oak barriques, mostly French but with 10% made from Virginia oak. Dark and supple, it has been one of the flagship wines of the Riojan new wave since the mid-1990s. It offers a good quality:price ratio and is therefore one to look for on restaurant wine lists. De Gregorio believes **2009** is the best vintage ever, and we recommend **2005** and **2004** from the recent vintages and **1996** from the more mature ones. The latter is a remarkable wine, showing a very classic Rioja profile after a proper time in bottle.

### Allende Blanco [V]
This white is made with a proportion of Malvasia (20%, a little higher in the early vintages) and the rest Viura, aged in new French oak barrels for 12 months. The **1999** is delicious to drink and remarkably fresh a decade after bottling, while the **2007** hints at a similar future. The **2000** and **2003** vintages were warmer and the wines more mature but still with good freshness and intensity, a creamy, supple texture, well-integrated oak, and a flavor profile full of dried herbs, white fruit, and balsamic notes. A classic white, which needs time in bottle to reveal its true character.

### Allende Graciano

The **2004** Allende Graciano appeared ten years after the benchmark for Graciano-based wines, Contino's 1994 Graciano. The Allende wine is closed, mineral, austere, and serious—certainly not a drink for everyone. The color is intense, dark but not black, and bright. It already hints at a little leather and plenty of spice on the nose. In the mouth, it shows medium body and good acidity, but there's a sensation of balance and harmony that points to a long and stable evolution in bottle. This is a soil-driven wine rather than a fruit-driven one, with just 13% alcohol. A **2005** has also been released, and generally speaking de Gregorio finds it superior: "For me, it is a better vintage, but when you talk about Rioja as a whole, maybe 2004 is more homogeneous, because 2005 was more difficult in areas like Rioja Baja." He also considers that it's a vintage with "less alcohol and polyphenols but good acidity and easy fermentations." Allende is produced only in select vintages, including 2007.

### Aurus ★

This is a cuvée of very old Tempranillo and Graciano from nine north-facing plots in Briones, selected first in the vineyard and later at the sorting table, in search of the perfect balance. It is aged in new Tronçais oak barrels, with a very high proportion of them coming from the famous French coopers François Frères. This is a consistent wine, but **2001** is one of Rioja's best modern vintages, and the Aurus of this year goes one step further in balance and elegance, thanks to the fruit of old vines grown on a slope with a high clay content. Dark in color and very aromatic, in its youth it combines ripe berry fruit with floral notes (violet), even black olives, with some notes from the oak aging. Full-bodied, with lively acidity and plenty of fruit and tannin, it is nevertheless balanced and elegant and built for long life.

### Calvario

In 1945, a southwest-facing vineyard from Briones bearing the name Calvario ("Calvary") was planted with 90% Tempranillo, 8% Garnacha, and 2% Graciano. It belongs to the de Gregorio family, and Miguel Angel first vinified it separately in 1999, proceeding to age it in new French oak barriques for 14 months. The result is one of the few single-vineyard wines from Rioja. **2005** is a superb vintage for Calvario, and **1999**, the first one, still seems remarkably youthful, with a long life ahead of it.

### Mártires ★

This is the new kid on the block. A top-of-the-line, barrel-fermented white from a vineyard outside Briones called Mártires ("Martyrs"), planted in 1970 with pure Viura. **2008** is the first vintage and a very powerful wine. This is one to watch.

### Paisajes I

A pure red Garnacha—quite unusual in Rioja—from a 65-year-old vineyard called La Pedriza in Tudelilla (Rioja Baja). The soil is clay with gravel, covered with boulders not unlike those of Châteauneuf-du-Pape. **1998** was the first vintage, but our favorite is **1999**, full of red fruit, balanced acidity, and polished tannins.

### Paisajes V, Valsalado

This wine is sourced from a vineyard planted by Miguel Angel's father near Logroño and next to Ygay, with the four red grapes mixed in the field (40% Tempranillo, 40% Garnacha, 10% Mazuelo, and 10% Graciano). The 2.47-acre (1ha) vineyard, a southeast-oriented slope of clay and gravel, is called Valsalado and was planted around 1970 with 3,100 vines. The grapes are harvested and fermented together, resulting in a balanced and elegant wine. The first vintage was **1999**, but **2001**, one of the finest recent vintages throughout Rioja, is probably the reference for this bottling.

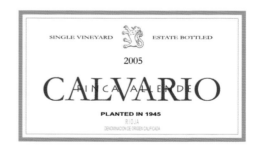

### Finca Allende

Area under vine: 138.5 acres (56ha)
Average production: 300,000 bottles for Allende and 12,000 for Paisajes
Plaza Ibarra 1, 26330 Briones, La Rioja
Tel: +34 941 322301
Fax: +34 941 322302
www.finca-allende.com

# Bodega Contador – Benjamín Romeo

Contador is the Spanish word for "counter," quite an unusual name for a wine or a winery. But then, almost everything to do with Benjamín Romeo is unusual. He was the winemaker at Artadi—of Viña El Pison and Pagos Viejos fame—from 1985 to 2000. In 1995, he started making wine from his family vineyards, getting ready to take over from his father, who was a typical *cosechero* in San Vicente de la Sonsierra.

Romeo then bought an old cellar on the hill above San Vicente, attached to the church whose bell tower is depicted on the Contador labels. Constructed in the traditional manner, it has a long tunnel excavated into the hill for storing barrels of maturing wine—and, historically, other produce that needed to be kept cool—and a wider entrance room, known as a *contador*, where the *pellejos* (goatskins) of wine were once counted in and out— hence the names Contador and Cueva del Contador for Romeo's first two wines.

Caves like these, which were built between the 12th and 16th centuries in San Vicente, were quite common elsewhere in Spain, mostly in regions such as Rioja (Labastida) and Atauta in Ribera del Duero. And as well as their principal role as stores for wine and food, they also served as meeting places for eating and drinking with friends.

Romeo, who is a firm believer in the idea that wine is made in the vineyard, finally left Artadi in 2000 to focus on his own business. In the meantime, he had restructured the family vineyards, locating and buying small plots in San Vicente and nearby villages (Labastida and Ábalos), all within 6 miles (10km), with mostly old vines (between 45 and 100 years old) on slopes between 1,300 and 2,000ft (400m–600m) above sea level. The vineyards, which have names such as La Raz, Las Olmazas, El Saúco, El Bullón, Azkueta, Mindiarte, San Juan, and Asnillas, are divided into 80 different plots,

**Left:** The idiosyncratic Benjamín Romeo, whose perfectionist viticulture and winemaking produce highly acclaimed wines

which Romeo believes adds to the complexity of the finished wines. In total, he owns 50 acres (20ha) and rents a further 25 acres (10ha). Most of these are planted with Tempranillo, head-pruned or *gobelet*-trained, and mostly massal selections of old genotypes, one of which is the now famous Tempranillo Peludo (meaning Hairy Tempranillo).

From the very beginning, the wines had an unusual profile, and they created quite a stir when they were first released, becoming widely known with the 2000 vintage. They're fresh, clean, and delineated, with silky tannins—very aromatic and with a texture and general character that reminded us of Chambolle-Musigny the first time we tasted them. The production of both wines is tiny.

The estate debuted with a single wine in the 1996 vintage. Romeo decided not to make anything in the difficult 1997 vintage and introduced his top wine, Contador, in 1999. Initially made only in select vintages, Contador was in fact made by Romeo's then wife, Marimar, for its first couple of vintages, while Romeo continued at Artadi. In 2001, Romeo's first year full time at Contador, he introduced a third wine, made from a single vineyard planted by Romeo's father, who also lends his name to the wine: La Viña de Andrés Romeo ("Andrés Romeo's Vineyard"). In style, it's warmer than either Contador or La Cueva.

It was only a matter of time before Romeo added a white, and when he did, he did so in style. Gallocanta (roughly translating as "Cock's Crow") is a blend of equal parts Viura, Malvasia Riojana, and Garnacha Blanca, barrel-fermented into a dense white, with the malolactic blocked to retain freshness.

All these wines have been unanimously acclaimed since the first vintages, but prices were high and quantities small. The 2004 Contador received a perfect score from *The Wine Advocate*, one of the first wines from Spain to receive 100 points. That sent the prices and demand through

the roof, but when the 2005 got the same score, the markets went berserk. Romeo's idea was to keep total production at a maximum of 25,000 bottles. However, by 2006 it was clear that the market was demanding a more affordable and available wine.

Romeo obliged with Predicador ("Preacher"), an entry-level wine made in considerably larger quantities and at a much more affordable price. The clean white label depicts the kind of hat that is worn by preachers in westerns but that reminds us more of the charlatans who used to peddle dubious potions as remedies. In reality, it's a tribute to Clint Eastwood and the film *Pale Rider*. With the 2007 vintage, Romeo added a white Predicador. Production stands at 120,000 bottles of the red and 10,000 of the white. Romeo has also just started bottling a new unoaked red called A Mi Manera ("My Way," probably more in homage to the Sex Pistols than to Sinatra), made with carbonic maceration carried out "his way," which will be released from the 2009 vintage.

The objective at this bodega has always been to produce great wines. To that end, Romeo does a green harvest, leaf-plucking, crop-thinning, and a manual harvest in small boxes; he's always looking for maturity (as opposed to overmaturity). In the winery, he uses manual destemming for some lots, fermentation in open oak vats (always below 77°F [25°C]), with as little sulfur dioxide as possible and gentle pumping-over. The wine is transferred to new, tight-grained, lightly toasted French oak barrels from a number of coopers, where the malolactic fermentation occurs. The wines are aged for some 18 months—depending on the wine and vintage—with racking always taking place on the waning moon, and they are bottled without fining or filtration.

Romeo vinified his first vintages in a small garage in San Vicente, before building a new winery in 2007. The reds are largely Tempranillo, and fully reflect his meticulous viticulture.

## FINEST WINES

### Gallocanta

Fresh and floral, this is a very powerful white, well oaked and unusual—in name, style, and indeed everything else. It has been released under slightly different names, but those names always refer to roosters. It is a blend of three different vineyards, one each of Viura, Garnacha Blanca, and Malvasia. Garnacha Blanca is the least common in the region, but it still plays a role in some blends, and it has recently become much more popular, largely thanks to this Gallocanta, where the bad characteristics often associated with the variety (dull, light-brown color, heavy and flat in the mouth due to low acidity) are completely absent.

### La Viña de Andrés Romeo

This is a single-vineyard wine whose name translates literally as "The Vineyard of Andrés Romeo"—a tribute to Benjamín Romeo's father, who, in the early 1980s, planted a 6-acre (2.5ha) vineyard in San Vicente de la Sonsierra with 7,500 Tempranillo vines, where each vine makes for one bottle of wine. The vineyard is located at a bend in the River Ebro, in an area called La Liende, opposite San Vicente de la Sonsierra. Here, we find more alluvial soils and a continental climate that make for a bigger, riper wine than Contador or La Cueva de Contador. Romeo is currently replacing dead vines with Graciano to add acidity, and he has added an adjacent plot (planted by a friend of his father's) to raise the total area to 9 acres (3.65ha).

### La Cueva del Contador

This was the first wine produced by the winery in 1996. It started as a second wine, a kind of mini-Contador. Its defining characteristic is the food-friendly high acidity, which is too much for some tastes but perfectly suited to ours. Production is around 7,000 bottles.

### Contador ★

First produced in 1999, Contador is made from a selection of the best Tempranillo vineyards, averaging 80 years of age. If you were looking for a single word to describe it, that word would have to be elegance. Fresh and pure and never showing the new oak in which it is aged, Contador is balanced and aromatic and a real pleasure to drink. Alas, it's also rather difficult to find, and it is expensive: production stands at just 4,000 bottles, and it

received 100 points from Robert Parker's *Wine Advocate* in the 2004 and 2005 vintages—a special wine, with a three-digit price. As is often the case, the very difficult **2002** vintage produced a very elegant wine—more restrained, with higher acidity—that is aging very well, and it is recommended. Another favorite of ours is the **2000**, but any vintage that can be tracked down and tasted is worth the effort, since this is certainly one of Rioja's greatest wines.

### Bodega Contador

Area under vine: 74 acres (30ha)
Average production: 150,000 bottles
Carretera Baños de Ebro km 1.8
41927 San Vicente de la Sonsierra, La Rioja
Tel: +34 941 334 228
Fax: +34 941 334 537
www.bodegacontador.com

# Abel Mendoza Monge

What are Abel and Maite Mendoza doing in San Vicente de la Sonsierra rather than, say, Nuits-St-Georges? The attitude, taste, and—quite obviously—winemaking philosophy of this endearing, down-to-earth couple are so Burgundian, so unlike almost everything else you are apt to find in Rioja, that the question is not an idle one. A glance at their vineyard holdings only confirms this impression: three dozen small plots in San Vicente, Labastida, and Ábalos—a spread of 10 miles (17km)—totaling under 40 acres (16ha), on myriad soil types, the great majority of vines head-pruned, with an average age of 40 years, an average yield of 30–35hl/ha, and an average altitude of 1,750ft (530m).

While Maite is an enologist with academic training, Abel is an experienced vine grower who has also become, through practice, a capable winemaker. The couple do most of the work on their estate on their own, and like the Burgundian vignerons they so admire, their obsession is, in Abel's concise description, "to understand the vine."

The Mendozas have been growers in the Sonsierra for generations, but it was Abel who first took the initiative of building a small winery, in 1988, and started making his own wine instead of selling the grapes. To finance his endeavor, he started out making young unoaked reds, with carbonic maceration of whole clusters, as so many Rioja families have done at home for many years. Under the Jarrarte brand, these wines showed a freshness uncommon among their competitors, and they still represent about half the total production, with local demand particularly strong.

For a full decade, nothing else was produced by the Mendozas while they improved the vineyards (90 percent Tempranillo), and Abel began recovering a small panoply of white varieties with massal selections from a few vines planted by his grandfather: four Garnacha Blanca vines, eight Malvasia Riojana, and seven Turruntés! The latter,

a native variety, was officially admitted in 2010 for Rioja DOC wines. There is also a 0.75-acre (0.3ha), 35-year-old patch of Viura. Whites remain Abel's hobby and a subject of endless research for him.

In 1998, the Mendozas began producing their first ambitious oak-aged wines: the Selección Personal, from an old vineyard in San Vicente, and the Blanco Fermentado en Barrica, a Malvasia/Viura blend that has consistently been considered ever since as one of the best whites made in Rioja.

Since that move, the Mendozas have concentrated on ageworthy wines that go from a basic Jarrarte crianza to the ambitious Grano a Grano, plus a varietal Graciano and a growing list of small-batch whites. "Small" is an adjective that applies to most of what is produced here, except for the two Jarrarte cuvées. The average production of Selección Personal is no more than 8,000 bottles.

The reds are fermented in small vats, some—those used for Grano a Grano—containing little more than a ton of grapes. Côte Rôtie–style, Abel likes to mix some white grapes with the red ones, a practice that has been shown to make color and aromas more stable. They are aged in French oak barrels from a bevy of different coopers—all part of a blending alchemy, including different soils at different altitudes, that Abel is convinced contributes greatly to a wine's personality.

Typical of that attitude was Abel's search for Graciano, of which he had none at first. But by searching out isolated Graciano vines in a couple of old mixed vineyards inherited from his grandparents, in 2003 he was able to ferment one barrel of it—a tiny production that rose slowly (500 bottles each of the two following years) as he grafted wood from those old vines on to old Tempranillo ones. Massal selection has always been his only way of planting new vineyards or transforming existing ones.

**Right:** Abel and Maite Mendoza, the passionate couple whose obsession with their vines is reflected in the art on their walls

Size remains one of the reasons why Abel Mendoza wines have not yet acquired more of a reputation, either in Spain or internationally. But the intentionally subdued, terroir-based character of these wines on release has also made that recognition more arduous. Significantly, the Mendoza wine that received the highest rating from Robert Parker was a basic Jarrarte crianza from the outstanding 2001 vintage, whereas the Selección Personal was consistently rated lower. But then this only adds to Abel Mendoza's Burgundian profile.

## FINEST WINES

### Abel Mendoza Selección Personal
This Tempranillo is from the 5-acre (2ha) El Sacramento vineyard, more than 40 years old. Fermented in concrete tanks and aged a year in French oak, about a third of it new, it is lively, personal, and terroir-infused, the opposite of a fruit bomb, and has always shown fine aging potential.

### Abel Mendoza Tempranillo Grano a Grano
A deep, powerful Tempranillo from two tiny plots in San Vicente, Gallocanta, and La Nava, yielding some 8,000 bottles annually. With malolactic in barrel and a year and a half in oak, this wine from grapes that are manually destemmed is made and aged ambitiously, aiming at a very long development in bottle, in the manner of the great Rioja classics.

### Abel Mendoza Malvasia Fermentado en Barrica ★
The misleadingly named Malvasia Riojana (actually the same variety as the modest Alarije from western Spain's Extremadura) has found a convincing champion in Abel, who coaxes an unexpected delicacy from it, with aromas of pears, wild flowers, and honey in a light, not especially powerful, but elegant wine.

> **Abel Mendoza Monge**
> Area under vine: 44.5 acres (18ha)
> Average production: 80,000 bottles
> Carretera Peñacerrada 7,
> 26338 San Vicente de la Sonsierra, La Rioja
> Tel: +34 941 308 010
> Fax: +34 941 308 010
> jarrarte@datalogic.es

# Señorio de San Vicente

San Vicente is sourced from La Canoca in San Vicente de la Sonsierra, a privileged vineyard of 44.5 acres (18ha) replanted in the 1980s with a selection of low-yielding vines from other parcels. La Canoca vineyard was given an unusually long rest period, during which a strict selection was made of lower-yielding vines among the many hectares owned by the Eguren family. It was Marcos Eguren who asked his father Guillermo—who was, at the time, responsible for vineyard management—to find and select the lowest-yielding vines as the first step in a severe selection process.

Their ultimate goal was to reduce yields drastically by choosing concentration over volume. Today, this approach is fairly widespread, but in those days it certainly was not; according to Marcos, "In this area, nobody wasted grapes until the mid-1990s." In fact, Guillermo Eguren went about his work compiling and selecting those vines in the belief that they were to be discarded. His surprise must have been great when Marcos, backed by his brother Miguel Ángel, told him that their intention was to plant the 18ha of La Canoca exclusively with them. These vines shared ampelographic characteristics that made them different from the rest: a peculiar shade in the foliage color, smaller berries in somewhat loose clusters, and a velvety bloom on the leaves—hence the name given to this subvariety, Tempranillo Peludo ("Hairy Tempranillo").

From 1985 until the moment they released (a good ten years later) the first commercial vintage of the wine emerging from this vineyard—San Vicente 1991—to great critical and sales success, Guillermo was forced to endure the scorn and derision of his neighbors. As Marcos says, the neighbors would ask, "What have you planted there, Guillermo, the worst plants?" Those were

**Right:** The cheerful Marcos Eguren, who remains modest despite the spectacular success of his family's wines

*With San Vicente 1994, the Eguren family pioneered the now-widespread
practice of releasing high-profile wines under the generic Rioja label.
Indeed, San Vicente is, of all its wines, still a favorite*

**Above:** The ancient hilltop fortress of San Vicente, which, ironically enough, has given its name to a pioneering modern Rioja

years of systematically poor yields that contrasted with the massive harvests and easy income made by other local growers, who were still focused on quantity.

According to Marcos, when the moment came to put a price on those first bottles of San Vicente 1991, he could not forget his father's patience in the face of the local growers' jokes in the taverns. The price—well above that of any other Rioja reserva then—had to compensate fully for his father's forbearance, as well as for the more

tangible expenses, purely to prove that all that effort had not been in vain. Even though the 1991 was followed by two poor vintages when no San Vicente would be produced, 1994 brought much needed vindication, and since then some San Vicente has always been produced, normally released three years after the vintage.

With San Vicente 1994, the family pioneered the now-widespread practice of releasing high-profile wines under the generic Rioja label. Jorge Ordóñez, its American importer, was confident he would be able to sell that 1994, whether or not it bore the reserva label that had graced the 1991 (and was used for the Spanish market), so the export lots were sent with the generic label only. It was an adventurous move but by no means foolhardy. They went on to test the Spanish market with a generically labeled 1995 vintage, and since the public seemed happy with it, they have persisted with it since 1996. This decision implied the loss of the commercial prestige of the reserva label (which was very influential then, and remains so today in some circles), but it also gave the family the freedom to decide on the length of the aging process and the date of commercial release.

*San Vicente is a wine of great concentration—100 percent Tempranillo from La Canoca vineyard, aged for 20 months in new oak barrels*

Consequently, San Vicente is a wine of great concentration—100 percent Tempranillo from La Canoca vineyard, aged for 20 months in new oak barrels. Originally, it was exclusively American oak, but after 1996, French oak was gradually introduced, starting at 20 percent and later moving to 40 percent, then 60, 80, and 90 percent, which means the latest vintages have seen a mere 10 percent American oak.

Indeed, San Vicente is, of all his wines, a favorite of Marcos's, mostly for sentimental reasons, since it was this wine that marked the family leap from traditional to modern wines right from the very first vintage in 1991. For as long as we've known him, Marcos has always been a cheerful guy, with a fondness for a laugh and a chat. It is not surprising, then, to see him exhibit a broad smile in recent years, his cheerful nature understandably enhanced by the impressive accolades obtained

by his wines and perhaps also by the sale of Numanthia-Termes to the LVMH group in 2008. This sale, presumably for a handsome sum, has put the family in a very comfortable financial position. All the same, it's hard to imagine Marcos being ready to accept even the most otherworldly offer for Señorio de San Vicente.

Not long ago, we asked Marcos, rather clumsily, for his favorite among his terroirs and wines. He answered both questions without hesitation, in two words: "San Vicente." And we must confess—if only because the reader is due some transparency on our part—that we, too, feel a special sympathy for San Vicente among the panoply of superb wines produced by the Eguren family. Our feeling for this wine owes something to the fact it was one of the first and most rigorous renovation projects in Rioja and one that we have tracked since its origins. But it also has something to do with its price, which, for all the praise, remains eminently affordable.

## FINEST WINES

### San Vicente
It would be hard to pick just one vintage of this wine, since Eguren has deftly crafted excellent wines from stellar years like **1994★**, **1995**, **1996**, **2001★**, **2004★**, and **2005**. But the level of other vintages is also remarkable, and in particular, the round and elegant San Vicente **2000** exhibits a beautiful and uncommon balance of aromatic complexity, acidity, and tannin. All the early vintages of San Vicente tend to show initially a perceptible presence of new oak but also powerful and balanced fruit notes that promise excellent integration, as well as fresh acidity to favor harmonious bottle aging.

### Señorio de San Vicente
Area under vine: 44.5 acres (18ha)
Average production: 55,000 bottles
Los Remedios 27,
26338 San Vicente de la Sonsierra, La Rioja
Tel: +34 945 600 590
Fax: +34 945 600 885
www.eguren.com

# Dinastía Vivanco

Vivanco is a very well-known surname in wine circles in Spain. Pedro Vivanco González started making wine in Alberite, a village south of Logroño, in 1915. His son Santiago later moved the business to Logroño, increased production, and expanded into the surrounding provinces. At the end of the 1960s, the third generation took over the running of the family firm, and Pedro Vivanco Paracuellos pushed the company even further, increasing both the area under vine and the sale of wine, all the while collecting all sorts of objects related to wine culture, his true passion. In the 1970s he made his fortune buying and selling wine; it is said that, at one point, one third of Rioja wine passed through his hands.

*Dinastía Vivanco has completely renewed its portfolio and built a new, state-of-the-art winery. The company has also opened the best wine museum in Spain*

In 1985, Vivanco Paracuellos bought land in Briones, one of the most prestigious towns in Rioja Alta, close to Haro, and in 1990 he created the company as we now know it, Bodegas Dinastía Vivanco. Today, the fourth generation—brothers Santiago and Rafael—is guiding the company alongside their father. They own a large area of vineyards—around 1,000 acres (400ha), mostly in Briones and Haro, from which they select fruit from the best 620 acres (250ha) for the Vivanco wines.

In the past, the name was associated with large volumes, but the company has completely renewed its portfolio and built a new, state-of-the-art winery, where the impressive barrel-aging room holds some 3,500 barriques. The company has also opened the best wine museum in Spain, displaying the family's private collection of pieces related to wine—from corkscrews, to paintings by well-known artists; from machinery, to Roman, Egyptian, and Greek artifacts. The museum was inaugurated in 2004 by King Juan Carlos I of Spain and became an instant success, as well as a major tourist attraction. Santiago, who is passionate about literature and archeology, is in charge of the museum and the Fundación Dinastía Vivanco, a nonprofit organization devoted to the research and promotion of wine culture. Its motto is, "Give back to wine what wine has given us."

Rafael Vivanco, who is now in charge of winemaking, trained in France and is very much aware of quality wines from all over the world. He has invigorated the wine portfolio with completely new wines, improving the balance between concentration and oak. Born in 1975, he still has years ahead to fine-tune his wines, so the future promises even better things.

## FINEST WINES

All the wines are presented in distinctive packaging: the recreation of an 18th-century bottle that now forms part of the family's museum collection. The entry-level Vivanco label is used for a white and a rosado. There are two ranges for barrel-aged wines. Even if the early vintages were sometimes marked by rather too much evident oak, the wines have improved tremendously since the middle of the first decade of this century, when Rafael finished his enological studies in Bordeaux and personally took over responsibility for the winemaking.

### Dinastía Vivanco
Two reds, Crianza and Reserva, are sold under this brand. The Crianza is pure Tempranillo and, like all the company's reds, it's cold-macerated (the winery has the facilities to chill grape temperatures down to 37.4°F [3°C]), fermented in French oak vats, then aged for 16 months in one-year-old oak barrels. The Reserva has 10% Graciano and comes from 35-year-old vineyards in Briones and Haro. Malolactic occurs in barrel, and barrel aging is extended to 24 months in 50% new oak. **2004** is one of the best vintages so far for both the Crianza and the Reserva.

**Above:** Rafael Vivanco, who, with his brother Santiago, has raised the quality and reputation of their family firm to a new high

### Colección Vivanco

These are the top-of-the-line wines, sourced from specific vineyards. Their finest wines, produced in very limited quantities, are three varietal wines— **Parcelas de Garnacha**, **Parcelas de Graciano★**, and **Parcelas de Mazuelo**—and a blend aptly called **4 Varietales**. In the promotional material, Vivanco explains all the different vineyards used for these wines, location, age, and characteristics. The **2007s** are consistently strong. The Garnacha and Graciano both come from Villamediana and Tudelilla and account for 2,500 and 5,700 bottles respectively. The 2,500 bottles of Mazuelo are from Agoncillo

and Alberite and were first produced in 2007. 4 Varietales is a single-vineyard wine, from Finca El Cantillo: 30 acres (12ha) surrounding the winery in Briones, made with all four red grapes (Tempranillo, Graciano, Garnacha, and Mazuelo), fermented and aged separately, then blended into 14,000 bottles.

**Dinastía Vivanco**
Area under vine: 1,000 acres (400ha)
Average production: 1 million bottles
Carretera Nacional 232,
26330 Briones, La Rioja
www.dinastiavivanco.com

# Bodegas Hermanos Peciña

Peciña is a minute village—with a population in 2009 of four, according to the Instituto Nacional de Estadística—belonging to the parish of San Vicente de la Sonsierra, in the northwest of Rioja Alta. The name derives from *piscina* (swimming pool), which comes not from any sports facilities in the neighborhood but from the 12th-century hermitage of Santa María de la Piscina, the best example of Romanesque architecture in La Rioja, which is located nearby.

Historically speaking, it was not unusual for people to take their surname from the village in which they lived or from which their families originated. This must have been the case—probably generations ago—for the Peciña family, owners of the Hermanos Peciña (Peciña Brothers) winery. Established in 1992 by Pedo Peciña Crespo and his three sons, the winery is quite a recent addition to the Rioja scene, and its wines are better known among lovers of traditional-style Rioja in the United States than in Spain.

The family has 125 acres (50ha) of vines, all in the environs of San Vicente de la Sonsierra, all within 6 miles (10km) of the winery, and all more than 15 years of age, some considerably older. The vineyards are located at altitudes ranging from 1,560 to 1,970ft (475–600m), all on clay-limestone soils. The plots are named Finca Iscorta, Salinillas, El Codo, La Liende, La Veguilla, La Peña, La Tejera, Llano Paulejas, and Valseca. The family likes to have a proportion of Graciano mixed in the field with Tempranillo, and all their wines have around 2 percent of Graciano.

In 1997, the company built a new winery and began making oak-aged wines. Since then, the family has been expanding and improving its facilities, always thinking about its customers, with a shop and the option of visits, tastings, and dinners. They even have guest rooms. They have enough capacity to vinify a million kilos—1,100 tons—of grapes and a stock of 3,500 barrels and 500,000 bottles.

Vinification is traditional; the grapes are destemmed and fermented with indigenous yeast in stainless steel, where the malolactic also occurs. To avoid the excessive taste of wood, the wines are aged in used barrels; and to avoid reduction, they are racked by gravity every six months. Time in wood is variable: two years for the Crianza, three for the Reserva, four for the Gran Reserva, but only nine months for the more modern wines. At the end of this process there is no need to filter or fine before bottling. The resulting wines have made Peciña a new classic.

## FINEST WINES

The style of the wines is generally very traditional, starting with a cold-macerated, fresh, and fruity white from Viura, then moving to the reds: a *joven*, a crianza, a reserva, and a gran reserva under the label Señorío de P Peciña, plus two special cuvées with a more modern flavor.

### Señorío de P Peciña

There are four different reds under the same label: the Joven is fruit-driven, but from the Crianza on, the wines show more tertiary notes, with plenty of leather and paprika and echoes of coconut from the American wood. There is limited production of the Gran Reserva, which is sourced from the oldest vineyards—as all grandes reservas should be, even though many are not—and kept for four years in American oak barrels and three years in bottle before release. The **2005 Crianza**, **2001 Reserva**, and **1998 Gran Reserva** are all recommended. Very classic wines.

### Peciña Vendimia Seleccionada Reserva

This is produced only in selected vintages, aged almost like a gran reserva (three years in barrel and two in bottle) but keeping a modern edge of more concentration and color. The 1997 is perfect for drinking now, with red fruit (maraschino cherries), balsamic notes, spicy and smoky, with a wood background. Medium-bodied, with good acidity, it keeps the fruit but shows signs of complexity in the shape of tobacco aromas. This is for those who like classic wines with a modern twist.

## Chobeo de Peciña

The top cuvée, quite different from the rest of the portfolio, is sourced from the oldest vines—more than 50 years old—which yield only 4,000kg/ha. The grapes pass over a selection table, and after alcoholic fermentation the wine is transferred to new American oak barrels for malolactic fermentation, where, after one racking, the wine will age for a period of nine months. This is a wine that is modern in style when compared with the rest of the portfolio.

**Above:** Santa María de la Piscina, from which the very exciting, relatively new firm of Bodegas Hermanos Peciña takes its name

**Bodegas Hermanos Peciña**
Area under vine: 125 acres (50ha)
Average production: 300,000 bottles
Carretera de Vitoria km 47,
26338 San Vicente de la Sonsierra, La Rioja
Tel: +34 941 334 366
Fax: +34 941 334 180
www.bodegashermanospecina.com

# Viñedos Sierra Cantabria

Guillermo Eguren belongs to a long line of Riojan growers. By the 1950s, he was already tending his own vines and making wine at San Vicente de la Sonsierra. Those were young carbonic-maceration reds, as demanded by the locals and Rioja's traditional markets. In recent years, Eguren's children Marcos and Miguel Ángel—the sixth winemaking generation in the family—together with his son-in-law Jesús Sáez, have given Sierra Cantabria a new impetus. Unlike some Riojan bodegas that are the product of a series of small leaps spanning a century, or others that have emerged recently from scratch, the Eguren family firm has followed its own path, starting with a solid base in the ever-growing

*Unlike some Riojan bodegas that are the product of a series of small leaps spanning a century, the Eguren family firm has followed its own path*

family vineyards (a treasure that Guillermo has carefully looked after and steadily increased) and culminating in the renovation efforts of the 1980s and 1990s by his two children, especially Marcos, on whom winemaking responsibilities now rest.

Of the many different ventures started and still owned by the Eguren family, Sierra Cantabria is the mother ship. It is certainly so in size but also in the number and variety of labels, both traditional (Murmurón—a carbonically macerated, young red—Crianza, Reserva, Gran Reserva), and avant-garde Rioja (Colección Privada, Amancio, Finca El Bosque, even Cuvée Especial, and Organza, a barrel-fermented white). It is nonetheless true that this coexistence is about to undergo a serious reorganization, and new facilities are being built to host the more ambitious modern-styled wines, sourced from the best vineyards—all of which

are grouped under Viñedos Sierra Cantabria. The designation Sierra Cantabria will remain for traditional wines still made in the original cellars in the heart of San Vicente de la Sonsierra.

The rationale for this decision has to do with Sierra Cantabria being the original brand name used by the Eguren family for their wines of the 1980s, which now cement the powerful and successful Eguren Group. Since then, the vineyards and cellars have been through many additions and transformations in the form of parallel ventures: Señorío de San Vicente and Viñedos de Páganos in Rioja; Numanthia-Termes (sold in 2008 to LVMH) and Teso La Monja in Toro; and Dominio de Eguren, produced as Vino de la Tierra de Castilla. While the group uses the Eguren name for its website, it is still somewhat striking that this—the signature name by which most aficionados identify the house and its wines—appears formally only on the humble wines of Dominio de Eguren (a label that seems to have a rather unexpected importance in the group's prosperity). The reason is actually very simple: the Eguren brand name belongs to a branch of the family that is not willing to sell it.

The winemaker, Marcos Eguren, is one of the stars of Rioja winemaking who matured in the 1980s and '90s, but his temperament is not at all that of a star. Calm and kind, he shows the combination of shyness and determination of one who does not wish to attract public attention but is at the same time convinced of the soundness of his work. He is a man whose feet are firmly planted in the Riojan soil. But he is also a man of some courage, someone who was prepared to implement innovations at a time when so-called modernity was a risky bet. This formula has been the key to the Eguren family's winemaking success.

Tempranillo is the main protagonist of these wines, with only minor concessions to Graciano and even fewer to Garnacha in the more traditional wines. Marcos explains: "In our Sierra Cantabria vineyards, only Graciano is occasionally—maybe once or twice every ten years—of sufficiently high quality to go into our Reserva or Gran Reserva; and even then it is only in a small proportion, because it is a very dominant sort of grape." In his opinion, Mazuelo and Garnacha do not work either in those cooler vineyards in the north of Rioja, which is why the monopoly of Tempranillo in his wines is not a random choice but rather is the result of natural selection in the local circumstances of climate and geology. On the other hand, he does think that some foreign varieties might succeed there—"I wish I could plant some Pinot Noir, if only to satisfy my curiosity," he says.

## FINEST WINES

### Sierra Cantabria Colección Privada
In the 1970s, Guillermo Eguren was already producing grandes reservas from carbonically macerated wines. Wines such as **Sierra Cantabria GR 1970** and **1973★** are virtually impossible to find today outside the family cellar, but they still give enormous pleasure to the lucky few who can sample them. Colección Privada is made following the same original concept, and the **2004** vintage is truly exceptional in our opinion—marked by an unlikely combination of jovial fruit, juicy acidity, and serious structure.

### Finca El Bosque
Together with **Amancio**, this is the flagship wine. It is sourced from a single Tempranillo vineyard near San Vicente de la Sonsierra planted in 1973. Originally it was conceived as a limited-release label for the subscribers of a wine club, but success soon led to continuity—save for the torrid 2003 vintage, in which none was made. For its timely combination of climate conditions and vineyard age, 2001 was the best year Marcos Eguren had seen, and for him it deserved special attention. Ten years after the vintage, the Finca El Bosque **2001** may seem restrained on opening, but it is a great wine that deserves long decanting to reveal spectacular aromatics, with excellent fruit and elegant spicy notes.

**Above:** A proud if weathered stone tablet identifies one of Sierra Cantabria's vineyards, with San Vicente at its center

### Viñedos Sierra Cantabria
Area under vine: 250 acres (100ha)
Average production: 800,000 bottles
Amorebieta 3,
26338 San Vicente de la Sonsierra, La Rioja
Tel: +34 945 600 590
Fax: +34 945 600 885
www.sierracantabria.com

# Compañia Bodeguera de Valenciso

It is seldom a good idea to play acronyms with producers' names in order to christen a business, because the results—convenient though they may seem—are more often than not unpleasant to the ear. But there are exceptions—like Valenciso, a winemaking company with a euphonic and resounding name deriving from the surnames of its founding partners, Luis Valentín and Carmen Enciso. Both partners had worked together for 25 years when, in 1998, they finally decided to embark on a joint venture of their own, leaving behind brilliant careers at Bodegas Palacio, in Laguardia, just months after its owner, Jean Gervais, sold it to a large Spanish business. Carmen and Luis speak marvels of Gervais. "He taught us a great deal of what we know, in every field," they say.

*"We seek wines with aromatic volume, wines that shine not out of weight but perfume. Many call this a 'feminine' wine. Whatever!"—Luis Valentín*

At the beginning it was just the two of them on their own, 100 oak barrels in a rented warehouse, and enough grapes (all bought) for the 24,000 bottles of the inaugural 1998 vintage. Of that Valenciso Reserva 1998 and the following '99, we were able to sample a few bottles labeled Crianza, which were exceptionally released a few months before the legal aging period required to deserve the reserva label. Understandably, a venture starting in 1998 may have lacked the financial resources to wait until 2002 before releasing its reserva and taking the revenue resulting from the first sale. But ever since the 2000 vintage the wine has always been bottled as Reserva.

Thanks to the reasonable success enjoyed by the house today, six people are working there full time, plus several others hired for specific seasonal work (pruning, harvesting, and so on). It is indeed a small company but also certainly one of those that contribute to the weaving of a sturdy business fabric in any country.

The most ambitious step in the meantime has been the building of their own cellar facilities in Ollauri. This was carried out one step at a time, avoiding excessive debt. In 2002, the grounds were purchased, and the works started one year later, not to be finished until 2008—though the facilities were ready for the 2007 vintage. The building has been designed for a production of 150,000 bottles per year, allowing for future growth.

Valenciso-controlled vines are almost 100 percent Tempranillo, averaging 27 years of age, some head-pruned and some on trellises with double cordon, all hand-harvested. The one exception is a small vineyard planted with white grapes (two-thirds Viura and one-third Garnacha Blanca). Valenciso grapes come from Briones, Ollauri, Rodezno, Haro, and Villalba (all of them in Rioja Alta), divided in 11 plots ruled by a strict work protocol that follows the French guidelines for *viticulture raisonnée*, with yield limits of 5,000kg/ha.

Valenciso Reserva is the only red produced yearly. The concept roughly corresponds with what the wine confirms in the glass. In the words of Luis Valentín: "We are not classicists; we prize fruit above oak, and we use French, not American, oak barrels. We are not radically modern, either: we are not after deeply colored or extracted wines. We seek wines with aromatic volume, wines that shine not out of weight but perfume. Many call this a 'feminine' wine. Whatever!"

The different plots are vinified separately, after destemming and no pressing. Extraction is by traditional pumping, without breaking or submerging the cap. Maceration periods depend on volume and vintage characteristics and range from under 20 days to well over 30. After wild malo, the wine goes into barrels—generally in May/June.

**Above:** The talented team of Luis Valentín and Carmen Enciso, successfully realizing their ideal of wines neither classic nor modern

The Valenciso team has broad experience in French oak aging, dating back to 1986, and it certainly shows in the fine structure of their wines. Every third is renewed yearly, so each barrel ages three vintages, for an average of 14 months. Again, the French influence shows in the subsequent transfer of wines to cement vats for blending and settling for about a year prior to bottling unfined.

## FINEST WINES

### Valenciso [V]

With quality and consistency in mind, vintage variation notwithstanding, the only vintage not released under the brand name Valenciso since 1998 has been 2003. From our perspective, the goal is being satisfactorily achieved, though we can wholeheartedly recommend the excellent **Valenciso Reserva 2004★**, a wine with a marked red-berry character, good typicity and length, pleasant balance between freshness and concentration, and an overall impression of depth. **Valenciso Blanco** is an austere, nicely focused wine of small production (roughly 1,000 bottles). Fermented and briefly aged in Caucasian oak barrels, it welcomes prolonged aeration during its first years of life.

**Compañía Bodeguera de Valenciso**
Area under vine: 42 acres (17ha)
Average production: 100,000 bottles
Carretera Ollauri a Nájera km 0.4,
26220 Ollauri, La Rioja
Tel: +34 941 304 724
Fax: +34 941 304 728
www.valenciso.com

# Bodegas Aldonia

Aldonia is a brand-new operation; its first commercial release was the 2004 vintage. It is the work of three friends—Ignacio Gómez Legorburu and brothers Iván and Mario Santos—who share both a common passion for wine and the luck to have inherited some family vineyards in Rioja. As early as 1994, they started working the vineyards. The first vinification was in 2000, but they sold the wine in bulk. Ignacio sold his share at the end of 2010, leaving the brothers working full-time for the bodega.

They have 37 acres (15ha) of vineyards in 12 different plots, mostly in El Villar de Arnedo, northwest of Calahorra in Rioja Baja, with close to 2.5 acres (1ha) in Navarrete (Rioja Alta). Their focus has been the vineyards: they want to get to know the soils and to work more on viticulture, because they believe grapes are the secret to fine wines. In their wines they want to express the balance already found in the vines. They work only with classic Rioja varieties—Tempranillo, Graciano, Mazuelo, and Garnacha—plus a little bit of an almost extinct white grape called Calagraño.

The project is still subject to some limitations: a brand-new winery in Navarrete is nearing completion, but in the meantime they are using rented facilities. Currently, the fruit is destemmed, then fermented at less than 90°F (32°C) for 10–12 days in stainless steel, where the malolactic also takes place. *Elevage* is in 300-liter used barrels (which are not permitted by the DO, so they are forced to use generic back labels), racked every six months. The wood is mostly French, but some American oak is also used.

Once their own winery is completed, they plan to experiment with concrete vats, whole clusters, and other techniques. They do not believe in varietal wines in the region, and their model is to produce one base wine—a village—plus some single-vineyard bottlings, crus following the Burgundian model. The friends are also marked out from many of their peers by their willingness to improve, to experiment, and to get to know the world's greatest wines—something that is not all that common among producers in Rioja.

So far, 75 percent of the production is exported, and since distribution in Spain is quite limited, they are also exploring direct sales—a side of the business that will also involve the sale of some of their favorite wines from Burgundy, imported by them, to their customers. A name to watch.

## FINEST WINES

### Aldonia [V]
The vineyards used for this wine are more than 30 years old, and they blend mostly Tempranillo with variable proportions of Mazuelo and Graciano. This is a drinkable wine, for those in search of something you can have with food—not heavy, not very extracted, not loaded with oak, but with enough acidity and balance to make you want to go back for a second sip. Red rather than black. This has a very good price:quality ratio. Some days we prefer the **2004**; others, the **2005**.

### Aldonia La Dama
This is a single-vineyard wine from a plot called La Dama ("The Lady"), a slope planted in 1968 at El Villar de Arnedo in Rioja Baja, with a field blend of Graciano, Mazuelo, and Tempranillo. It has deeper soils, with more clay and sand over a calcareous base, which has expressed a different personality from the surrounding vineyards. The black fruit, balance, elegance, freshness, and savoriness would make you think of a wine from the northern parts of the appellation. A bottle with the balance to age. It will be produced only in the very best years and will be limited to about 5,000 bottles. **2005** is our favorite vintage so far.

### Bodegas Aldonia
Area under vine: 37 acres (15ha)
Average production: 55,000 bottles
Gran Vía Juan Carlos I 43, 2E,
26002 Logroño, La Rioja
Tel: +34 670 62 84 98
Fax: +34 941 58 85 65
www.aldonia.es

# Bodegas Bretón

Things have changed so fast in Rioja over the past few decades that Bodegas Bretón is seen as a regional classic, as if it had been there forever. Yet it was only in 1983 that it was founded by Pedro Bretón and a group of local associates. Its early success has much to do with the work of two young men—winemaker Miguel Ángel de Gregorio and winery manager Rodolfo Bastida—who departed in the 1990s to pursue successful careers elsewhere, de Gregorio launching his own Finca Allende. It was also due to a respect for the classic style, which attracted conservative wine lovers in Spain.

The late 1990s were a period of flux and uncertainty for the winery, but since 2000 it has followed a path back to the elite level, now led by Bretón's daughter María Victoria, who took over after the founder's death. The arrival in 2007 of experienced winemaker José María Ryan from Viña Real strengthened this trend.

The original winemaking facility in the regional capital Logroño was finished just in time for the 1985 harvest. In 2003, the company moved to a handsome new winery on the St. James's Way near the small village of Navarrete, 7.5 miles (12km) away.

All grapes are obtained from estate and contract sources in the best areas of Rioja Alta. The estate includes a 104-acre (42ha) vineyard, Viña Loriñón, on the outskirts of Logroño along the south bank of the River Ebro, and the 54.5-acre (22ha) Dominio de Conte, which Steve Metzler of Classical Wines, Bretón's US importer, calls "a textbook vineyard" on a protected bend of the Ebro near Briones. The average vineyard age, more than 35 years, is "the highest of any major Rioja producer," according to the bodega. The grape varieties are mainly Tempranillo, with Mazuelo, Graciano, Garnacha, and Viura.

The estate vineyards provide about one third of the bodega's needs, the rest coming from several local growers.

The backbone of the production is the Loriñón line—from Crianza, to Gran Reserva. In the past few years, its Iuvene, a young unoaked wine, has gained a significant market share in the region, where those fruit-driven reds have traditionally had a strong following. Bretón was also a regional pioneer in the production of barrel-fermented dry whites, entirely from Viura grapes, and makes an ageworthy Loriñón Blanco Fermentado en Barrica.

But it was, of course, the elegant, timeless Dominio de Conte that won the winery its place as a significant producer along traditional lines, at a time when such wines were being discarded by many in favor of a more international style.

Actually, Bretón didn't fully escape the trend. In recent years it has been producing in small amounts a rich, quite modern, quite international wine, a Tempranillo from 80-year-old vines in Briones and aged in new French oak. This wine, Alba de Bretón, attracts attention in some circles but is not Bretón's most successful initiative.

## FINEST WINES

### Dominio de Conte
When it was introduced in the early 1990s—the vintage was 1989—this wine surprised Spanish aficionados because it didn't attempt to mimic the supercharged *alta expresión* style then prevalent. As Metzler says, "Benefiting from a perfect terroir for the ripening of the Tempranillo variety, Dominio de Conté serves as a reminder of the legendary Riojas produced in the late 19th and early 20th centuries, for its elegance and minerality and for its ageworthiness."

### Bodegas Bretón
Area under vine: 260 acres (105ha)
Average production: 1.4 million bottles
Carretera de Fuenmayor km 1.5,
26370 Navarrete, La Rioja
Tel: +34 941 440 840
Fax: +34 941 440 812
www.bodegasbreton.com

# Artadi

Juan Carlos López de Lacalle is a hugely successful winemaker who collects ratings between 98 and 100 points in the most influential American publications, yet he remains acutely conscious of the tasks that remain ahead and refuses to be swayed by local tales about Spain's wines having become the toast of the world. "I do believe that we make some great wines in Rioja, but also that Rioja and Spain in general remain the great unknowns on the international wine scene," he says. "We are far from being as well appreciated as some optimists say. We have a long way to go and also much to learn."

It certainly isn't the modest López de Lacalle's fault, for he has taken Artadi, once a fledgling cooperative cellar in Rioja Alavesa, to the top ranks of the world's wineries in just 25 years. The scion of a family of grape growers in Laguardia, he was one of the first enology graduates from Madrid's School of Viticulture in the mid-1970s, then studied agricultural engineering in Pamplona. That's a rather standard background in Spain's wine industry—one shared by many competent winemakers who turn out competently made, technological wines. What made López de Lacalle different was that he knew that the truth lay in the vineyards and that he traveled far and wide to the places where that tenet is truly practiced—from Burgundy, to the Rhine, to the better vineyards in the New World—to learn more about it.

As he recalls now, "Back then, there was a mere production-driven concept of quality, but no attention was paid to the soil, the climate, or the vintage. We were concerned about good color in the wine, about avoiding spoilage, but not about mouth feel or length. The great difference with my son's generation is that they know these things from the start, and they value what makes a wine's intrinsic quality."

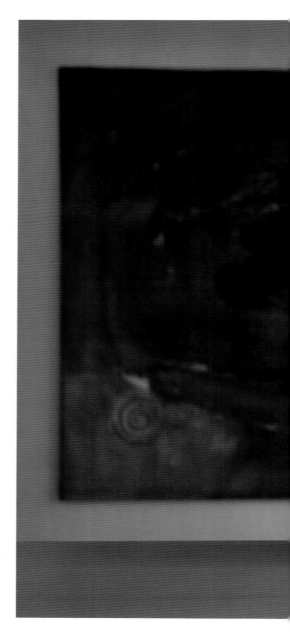

**Right:** Juan Carlos López de Lacalle, whose determination, skill, and vision have taken Artadi into the very top rank

*The modest Juan Carlos López de Lacalle has taken Artadi,*
*once a fledgling cooperative cellar in Rioja Alavesa,*
*into the top ranks of the world's wineries in just 25 years*

Back in the 1980s, these lofty concepts were hard to enforce for a young grower with little money, so López de Lacalle did what he could. He assembled a small group of colleagues and built a small cooperative cellar where they could bring their grapes and get a better return for their efforts than by merely selling them to private bodegas or to one of the larger co-ops. The name of the co-op, Cosecheros Alaveses, was soon superseded by its brand name: Artadi.

Like other fledgling producers of that era—Abel Mendoza comes to mind—the Artadi group made only the most inexpensive, basic wine for several years: the young, unoaked *cosechero* red traditionally made by whole-cluster carbonic maceration. This is the wine every family in Rioja drinks twice a day, the wine consumed in every bar in the region and in the Basque Country.

*López de Lacalle knew from the start that his forte was viticulture, in addition to providing the leadership to an enterprise set on returning to terroir-driven wines in Rioja*

Artadi's was better than the others because it was meticulously vinified and, more importantly, because it came from the sort of old vines, organically cultivated under López de Lacalle's supervision, whose grapes usually go into much more expensive cask-aged wines. Artadi Joven remains very good today, even though some customers grumble that it is no longer the same, because those top grapes now go into the more expensive wines made by the bodega, which is today a private company with López de Lacalle as the controlling shareholder. But that's a logical development, parallel to the development of the excellent barrel-aged and still prudently priced Viñas de Gain.

López de Lacalle knew from the start that his forte was viticulture, in addition to providing the leadership—some would say the ideological impulse—to an enterprise set on returning to terroir-driven wines in Rioja, instead of falling for the buzzwords of that era: technology and marketing. He chose from the start to have a top-notch enologist by his side, one with the skill to produce fine wines with a far less interventionist approach. As Artadi introduced its first barrel-aged wines—there are 1,300 casks in the cellar now, all of them made with French oak—that man was Benjamín Romeo, whose stellar work was soon widely recognized. Unsurprisingly, perhaps, there was not much love lost between López de Lacalle and Romeo when the latter decided to leave in 1999 and start his own successful bodega in nearby San Vicente de la Sonsierra.

But the loss was soon compensated with an exotic acquisition. López de Lacalle went all the way across Spain to the then-underappreciated region of Jumilla in the southeast to engage French enologist Jean-François Gadeau, who had arrived there years earlier with Altos del Pío, a French company intent on exploiting the old Monastrell vines that (under their French name, Mourvèdre) whetted their appetite for mass-produced, good-quality, inexpensive wine. Altos del Pío was ahead of its time and soon went bankrupt, but Gadeau stayed in Jumilla, working for Agapito Rico, one of the pioneers of the rebirth of the area. He didn't, however, hesitate at the chance to move to the already famous Artadi in Rioja. And with Rico and Gadeau, López de Lacalle created the El Sequé estate near Jumilla, now fully integrated into the Artadi group.

With Romeo, then Gadeau, in the cellar, the Artadi portfolio grew from the early 1990s, as did its vineyard holdings—from 173 to 217 acres (70–88ha)—which cover about 80 percent of its needs.

The all-Tempranillo cuvée Viñas de Gain (from the Basque word meaning "heights") has been the bread-and-butter wine for Artadi since that time, when the unoaked Joven was scaled back to its current annual production level of some 40,000 bottles—only one tenth that of Viñas de Gain. It was the other way around in 1987, when Viñas de Gain first timidly appeared.

The depth, the terroir feel, the complexity, and the sheer pleasure one finds in this cuvée are remarkable for a wine produced in such quantities and sold in the €15–20 range in Spain. Tom Cannavan, an experienced British taster, has described the 2004 Viñas de Gain in typically glowing terms: "Lovely, rich, deep, crimson black. Deep, sinewy, sensuous nose, with a plush red-fruit quality, giving a velvety impression with hints of herbs and wood smoke, its tight personality revealing hints of mocha and complexity. The palate has beautiful fruit, with that signature balance of concentration and richness and fresh fruit and acid character. Lovely, mouth-filling wine, with structure and presence, lovely fruit quality, and the potential to age."

The third wine in Artadi's basic range is a more recent addition, geared mainly to the international markets. Artadi Orobio, which retails below the price of Artadi Joven, is made from young Tempranillo vines. One half is briefly aged in French oak while the other half remains in tank before being blended. It comes under a screwcap—as the Joven also does now—and is an uncomplicated, fresh drink.

At the other end of the scale there has been a special blend made only in great vintages: Grandes Añadas, which now seems about to be phased out. But this remains the realm of López de Lacalle's obsession—old Tempranillo vineyards of great quality. A blend of three small ones is called Pagos Viejos, and Viña El Pison still reigns supreme.

But more is on the way. "One of the ways of discovering the truth of wine is distinguishing terroirs, since every single plot has its own personality," López de Lacalle said while showing barrel samples of three single-vineyard wines Artadi made for the first time in the outstanding 2009 vintage: El Carretil, La Poza, and Valdeparaíso. There will be ten barrels—3,000 bottles—of each of those old plots, which have formed the backbone of the Pagos Viejos cuvée since the early 1990s.

There is, of course, that fourth old vineyard whose grapes have always been harvested and bottled separately. Nominally, El Pison vineyard is no longer part of Artadi but of Viñedos Lacalle-Laorden—that is, the company bearing the last names of Juan Carlos and his wife, Pilar. In so doing, López de Lacalle is singling out the character of that fabled vineyard, inherited from his grandfather, as a *monopole* in Burgundian terms and as one of the true "grands crus" of Spain. That said, in practical terms Viña El Pison remains a part of the Artadi portfolio and is still the standard-bearer for the estate. The 2004 vintage was the first Artadi wine to win a 100-point rating in Robert Parker's *Wine Advocate*—a symbolic number with which Artadi had been flirting for a decade.

Another old favorite of López de Lacalle is white wine, with which he briefly tinkered in the 1990s before returning to it in 2006 with considerable success. There is little doubt that his forays into Burgundy played a role in his decision to start making whites again—which is remarkable in an estate that officially has no white varieties in its vineyards. Yet Artadi only needs to buy about 30 percent of the grapes it uses for its reborn Viura white. Old mixed vineyards in Rioja Alavesa have the advantage of yielding a few white grapes, which have now found a more interesting use than being added to the must used for the young, carbonic maceration reds.

## FINEST WINES

### Viña El Pison★

This small cuvée of some 8,000 bottles comes from a 7-acre (2.8ha) patch southeast of Laguardia, planted in 1945 with Tempranillo plus a little Graciano and Garnacha. It produces some of the most delicate and elegant expressions of the Tempranillo grape, and the wine often reaches amazing heights of complexity. A modern classic. The 2004 vintage is particularly successful.

### Pagos Viejos

A blend from the three best among the older plots owned by the estate, this is earthier than Viña El Pison but at least as complex and has shown outstanding ageworthiness over the past 20 years.

### Viñas de Gain Blanco Fermentado en Barrica★

Artadi has no dedicated vineyard for white varieties, but quite a few of its old plots are interspersed with ancient Viura vines. In the mid-1990s, they were harvested separately for a couple of years, and their must was fermented in oak barrels, giving a very fine white wine. The practice was discontinued, then resurrected in 2006. The wine is moved to stainless-steel tanks after fermentation and aged two years on its fine lees there. It resembles a fine Graves white, with a floral and mineral nose and some real depth, and it is definitely ageworthy.

Artadi
Area under vine: 217 acres (88ha)
Average production: 850,000 bottles
Carretera Logroño s/n, 01300 Laguardia, Álava
Tel: +34 945 600 119
Fax: +34 945 600 850
www.artadi.com

# Herederos del Marqués de Riscal

It's a fact of life that much of the world has rediscovered Marqués de Riscal because Frank Gehry designed a pink-and-silver mini-Guggenheim with a luxury hotel and restaurant inside that reigns over the entrance to the historic bodega. Yet Marqués de Riscal has more than the dazzling shiny building to show—it embodies Riojan history. Possibly its recent record has not been quite as brilliant as the Gehry creation, but there are signs of a renewed commitment to quality.

The company asserts that "as far back as 1858, it became the first winery in the Rioja to produce wines following the Bordeaux method"—a claim that remains controversial because the first Riscal wine was actually made in 1862, and Marqués de Murrieta also boasts of being the oldest producer.

It was indeed in 1858 that Camilo Hurtado de Amézaga, Marqués de Riscal was asked by the Álava province's local government to engage a *maître de chai* who could initiate the area's vine growers in the art of cultivating the vineyards and making wine as in the Médoc. (Described by his successors as "diplomat, journalist, freethinker," Camilo Hurtado owned vineyards and a winery on the Torrea estate in Elciego but had been living in Bordeaux since 1836 in a form of self-imposed exile that was frequent among Spanish liberals at that time.) The appointee was Jean Pineau, winemaker at Château Lanessan, who arrived in Rioja Alavesa with "9,000 completely guaranteed young vines" of Cabernet Sauvignon, Merlot, Malbec, and Pinot Noir, with the idea of launching an experimental vineyard.

Pineau's efforts with various Rioja vine growers bore fruit. They obtained wines of greater consistency and quality, with an unprecedented capacity to age because they were matured in Bordeaux barrels—in the end, the most decisive of the innovations brought by Pineau. But alas, barrel aging meant that wines couldn't be sold immediately, as the local growers were used to, so they all quit the project. His contract was not renewed, but the Marqués de Riscal jumped in, employed Pineau, and, in 1860, built new cellars designed by the architect Ricardo Bellsola, who had studied the leading *chais* in the Médoc.

That same year, Jean's son Charles Pineau made the first Bordeaux-style barrels in the cooperage installed by the Marqués, and the 96 acres (39ha) of vineyards at Torrea began furnishing grapes to the new winery. They included 25 acres (10ha) of the French varieties.

Riscal's long relationship with Cabernet Sauvignon would fuel controversy many years later as the Rioja appellation grudgingly gave the variety "experimental" status, provided its name did not appear on labels. It's been a different story in Ribera del Duero, which accepted Cabernet Sauvignon, Merlot, and Malbec because they have been part of the Vega-Sicilia estate since the 1860s.

Marqués de Riscal's greatest wines, in the first half of the 20th century, were its so-called Cuvée Médoc, which contained upwards of 60 percent Cabernet Sauvignon. One of them, the 1945, is considered by many as the greatest red wine ever produced in Spain.

Starting in 1986, Riscal renewed this tradition with its Barón de Chirel cuvée. It contains 15–20 percent Cabernet Sauvignon, which general manager and chief winemaker Francisco Hurtado de Amézaga calls "Cabernet Riojano." "It has been here so long that it is fully adapted and is no longer identical to those first vines," he says.

Indeed, according to French author Alain Huetz de Lemps in his 1967 book *Vignobles et Vins du Nord-Ouest de l'Espagne*, the fully accepted Garnacha variety has only been in Rioja, brought in from Aragón, since the vineyards were replanted after phylloxera struck around 1900. But Garnacha has been called "native" and Cabernet "foreign"—a capricious distinction in viticultural terms.

**Right:** General manager and chief winemaker Francisco Hurtado de Amézaga, intent on recapturing past glory

Cabernet Sauvignon did practically disappear from Marqués de Riscal blends after 1950, but vertical tastings at the winery—which has the most complete library of old wines anywhere in Spain—prove that, with or without it, the legendary grandes reservas have aged admirably. And their quality was recognized early on, winning gold medals throughout the century of the great exhibitions and a diploma in Bordeaux in 1895.

Barón de Chirel and Gran Reserva have kept up the level, but in recent years the basic Reserva has become a mass-production wine with more than 3 million bottles made every year. Always competently made, it's a good enough Rioja, but it has not helped the image of the winery. The new Finca Torrea wine, an interesting Tempranillo/Graciano blend, aims to restore it, as does the ambitious (and expensive) Gehry cuvée—one of

**Above:** The arresting, landmark architecture of Frank Gehry, which has helped many wine lovers rediscover Riscal's wines

the enticements, so the story goes, that convinced him to build part of a winery for the first time. But it may be a one-time-only wine—the 2001 150 Aniversario Reserva, made to commemorate the first 150 years of the winery—that comes closest to those great historic Riscal wines such as the 1936, 1945, or 1964. Pungent and lively as

the best Riscal wines have always been, it was named Spain's Red Wine of the Year 2009 by elmundovino.com, the respected wine website of national newspaper *El Mundo*.

Today, the winery owns a vast network of vineyards around Elciego, mainly Tempranillo, but also Graciano, Mazuelo, and Cabernet Sauvignon. But the 550 acres (220ha) are far from sufficient for what has become a very large winery, so in addition there are 2,435 acres (985ha) under contract with local growers.

There is still a rosé made in Rioja by Riscal, but no more whites. The decision 40 years ago to move production to the then-forgotten region of Rueda and to base it on the almost extinct Verdejo variety has paid handsome dividends and has indeed been crucial to the rebirth of Rueda. From that base, Riscal has expanded into red wines there, which it sells as Vino de la Tierra de Castilla y León. It campaigned strenuously, but ultimately in vain, to restrict the Rueda appellation to whites only.

## FINEST WINES

### Marqués de Riscal Gran Reserva
This wine is produced in minute quantities, if compared with the millions of bottles of Reserva, but it has all the subtle appeal of delicate, traditional Gran Reserva Rioja aged in old American oak.

### Barón de Chirel
Modern, concentrated, lavishly oaked (new French oak in this case), this does not automatically fall into the "international style" category, for the small proportion of Cabernet Sauvignon added to highly structured Tempranillo gives it some of the oomph and zing of those classic Cuvées Médoc.

### Herederos del Marqués de Riscal
Area under vine: 550 acres (220ha)
Average production: 4.5 million bottles
Calle Torrea 1, 01320 Elciego, Álava
Tel: +34 945 606 000
Fax: +34 945 606 023
www.marquesderiscal.com

# Bodegas y Viñedos Pujanza

Carlos San Pedro and his family bear one of the most genuinely wine-related names in the Rioja Alavesa area. So says history, both recent and remote. Remote, because there are 15th-century documents certifying the activities of the San Pedro family in the surroundings of Laguardia; recent, because the San Pedros follow several consecutive generations of growers and producers, starting with the great-grandfather Jenaro San Pedro, who planted Viña El Pison—now managed with great success for Artadi by his grandson Juan Carlos López de Lacalle.

Even present-day reality confirms this dedication: several members of the family run different winemaking companies in Laguardia, partly due to the splitting of the 200 acres (80ha) of vineyards that the family father Javier San Pedro used to grow in the now extinct Bodegas San Pedro (of course!). Among those companies we can count Bodegas Dios Ares (owned by Carlos San Pedro and his wife), Bodegas Las Orcas (owned by Carlos's sister Cristina), and Bodegas Vallobera (run by Carlos's brother Javier San Pedro). Vallobera was certainly a leading candidate for inclusion in this book, though in the end, space limitations have deprived us of this pleasure.

Finally, there is Bodegas y Viñedos Pujanza, the ambitious challenge adopted by Carlos when he was only 25 years old. With the humble spirit of one who is convinced he is on the right track (true modesty comes from those who know they are right but do not brag about it), he often states that his search for balance between the lightness and heaviness of Rioja's twin extremes may be a backward step for his family. We have a hunch that he is in fact sure that Pujanza is no such thing. He is grateful for compliments and good reviews, like anyone else, but like many people working in contact with nature, he tends to regard these things

**Right:** Carlos San Pedro, who has been succeeding admirably since founding Bodegas y Viñedos Pujanza at the age of 25

*With the humble spirit of one who is convinced he is on the right track (true modesty comes from those who know they are right but do not brag about it), Carlos San Pedro searches for balance between the lightness and heaviness of Rioja's twin extremes*

with a healthy dose of skepticism. What he enjoys best is selling his wines—"and so far, we are doing fine," he adds with a smile.

The vintage in which Carlos San Pedro and his team proved themselves was 2002. Not because they had, by then, settled into their own brand-new facilities but because of the extraordinary results they managed to obtain from such a difficult year. 2002 Pujanza was (and still is) elegant and polished, as well as expressive and fruit-driven: clean, with nicely integrated oak and mineral notes, the palate echoing the nose, with notes of raspberry and blackberry, good acidity, and remarkable persistence. Both previous and subsequent years have given riper vintages, when Pujanza wines have also been up to the challenge. (Especially noteworthy is the nicely balanced fruit of the 2007, though we think the oak notes will need time to integrate.) But few 2002 wines of the price (€11–12 at the time) hit such quality levels.

Pujanza and Pujanza Norte are the two top wines of the house. They have been joined by two novelties: on the one hand, the very exclusive Cisma—a red sourced from the old La Valcavada vineyard, with 1.7 acres (0.7ha) of low-yielding ungrafted Tempranillo vines (and some Viura); on the other, a varietal Viura white of mineral character, sourced from a different vineyard—Pujanza Añadas Frías, which will be made only in those colder vintages (as suggested by the wine's name), seeking to express not so much varietal nuances as those of the chalky terroir. So far, only the 2007 vintage (a September 2010 release) has met the specific demands for this wine to be produced.

The three vineyards mentioned are not the only ones owned by Bodegas y Viñedos Pujanza. It has patiently bought a grand total of almost 100 acres (40ha) of other vineyards in the area around Laguardia. Carlos San Pedro is particularly

**Left:** Some of the oak barriques in which Carlos San Pedro crafts expressive wines that avoid Rioja's two extremes

enthusiastic about a Tempranillo vineyard called San Román, only incorporated in 2009, which is among the highest in the region: 6.7 acres (2.7ha) at 2,360ft (720m) between Laguardia and Leza—in fact, the frontier between the two boroughs runs straight through the vineyard.

## FINEST WINES

### Pujanza
Pujanza is the higher-production wine—the one with which Carlos San Pedro introduced himself in 2001 with the 1998 vintage. It comes mostly from a vineyard called Valdepoleo or La Viña Grande, which consists roughly of 37 acres (15ha) of mostly Tempranillo planted on clay-limestone soils at about 2,070ft (630m) above sea level. Pujanza is normally a varietal Tempranillo, though in warmer years, like 1998 and 2003, it takes a little Graciano from a 3.7-acre (1.5ha) plot that is planted in the same Valdepoleo vineyard.

### Pujanza Norte ★
A mere one vintage after the inaugural release, in 1999 the only other wine produced here was made for the first time: Pujanza Norte (though Carlos tends to regard 2001 as the first vintage of Norte because it was the first vintage made at their own facilities). It comes from a vineyard on chalky-limestone soil called El Gancho or El Norte, with 6.7 acres (2.7ha), mostly Tempranillo, at 2,230ft (680m)—which comes close to the highest altitude of any quality vineyard in Rioja Alavesa. This is not a varietal wine, though Tempranillo is always predominant (and increasingly so, from the original 60%, up to 85% in 2004). It is remarkable that the Norte vineyard and the one producing Pujanza Cisma both include up to 5% of scattered Viura vines that—following traditional practices not exclusive to Rioja—are harvested and included in the production of both wines.

**Bodegas y Viñedos Pujanza**
Area under vine: 100 acres (40ha)
Average production: 140,000 bottles
Carretera de Elvillar s/n, 01300 Laguardia, Álava
Tel: +34 945 600 548
Fax: +34 945 600 522
www.bodegaspujanza.com

# Granja Nuestra Señora de Remelluri

Granja Nuestra Señora de Remelluri is located in what used to be the monastery of Toloño at Labastida, in the province of Álava, at the foot of the Sierra de Cantabria (the Cantabrian Mountains). It is an old property of the order of Jerónimo monks, who cultivated these lands with cereals and vines in the 14th century. It was purchased in 1967 by Basque businessman Jaime Rodríguez Salís, who rebuilt the vineyards and buildings, transforming the monastery into a winery and making it one of the most beautiful enclaves in all Rioja. Rodríguez's son, Telmo Rodríguez, one of the best-known and most influential winemakers in Spain, managed the company for nearly ten years before moving on to start his own Compañía de Vinos Telmo Rodríguez in 1994.

The place is rich in history, with a cemetery from the 10th century and an old stone *lagar* from the Middle Ages, where grapes were foot-trodden to make wine. Its grapes were also used by Manuel Quintano, dean of the cathedral of Burgos, to make the first Rioja wine following Bordeaux methods at the end of the 18th century. They now have a small museum where you can see pieces dating back as far as the Bronze Age—old engravings, objects, and a variety of archeological materials discovered on the property.

In more recent times, the Basque painter Vicente Ameztoy restored the 13th-century Santa Sabina Hermitage on the property, which contained the *Virgen de Nuestra Señora de Remelluri*. Ameztoy was one of the most important contemporary painters in Spain, and before his death in 2001 he was working on a series of five saints. One of them was San Vicente (St. Vincent), the grape growers' patron saint, wearing a kind of bib with a Remelluri label, and a scene of Paradise.

**Right:** Jaime Rodríguez with his son Telmo, who has returned to the historic property he now runs with his sister Amaia

*The initial vintages made Remelluri a benchmark for the modernization of Rioja, in that it was one of the few wineries to operate like a Bordeaux château, growing all the grapes used for its wines*

The initial vintages made Remelluri a benchmark for the modernization of Rioja, in that it was one of the few wineries to operate like a Bordeaux château, growing all the grapes used for its wines. It was also a pioneer in reducing the use of herbicides, mineral fertilizers, and synthetic products. Almond, peach, fig, and olive trees are planted to complement the vineyard in a wholly integrated agricultural system.

The 260 acres (105ha) of vineyards are planted with Tempranillo, Graciano, Garnacha, Garnacha Blanca, Moscatel, Malvasia, Chardonnay, Viognier, Sauvignon Blanc, Rousanne, and Marsanne. The dominant vine is Tempranillo, with an average age of 30 years, though there are terraces with

*The style, which initially followed Riojan tradition, was modernized. Remelluri was one of the first modern Riojas but is nowadays considered a classic estate*

pre-phylloxera vines, the oldest dating from 1876. Graciano appears to have been a traditional variety at Toloño, so it has also been included in the new plantings. The whites (among which there is no Viura) are planted at a higher altitude, around 2,300ft (700m), which makes them ripen considerably later, with some picked in October and even occasionally in November. The soil is poor, chalky, and very stony but with layers of clay that retain necessary moisture.

The methods applied in the cellar are closer to those of Burgundy than those of Bordeaux. Fermentation occurs in large oak *tinas* or *conos*, and the cap is punched down by foot rather than pumping the wine over, because the former technique is believed to give more polished tannins. The malolactic is also carried out in these large oak vats, and only a small proportion is carried out in barrique. The barrels are a mixture of old and new, depending on the wine, being newer for the more structured ones that need more oxygenation. The label has, however, an unmistakable Bordelais flavor.

The style, which initially followed Riojan tradition, was modernized during the years Telmo was at the helm. Remelluri was one of the first modern Riojas but, like Contino, is nowadays considered a classic estate.

The 2010 vintage marks the start of a new era for Remelluri. Like the prodigal son, Telmo has returned to the family property, which he now manages together with his sister Amaia. She did a *stage* at Domaine Leflaive in Burgundy, with the idea of converting the Remelluri vineyards, already cultivated organically, to biodynamics. They want to go one step further with the wines, too, strengthening traditions in the vineyards and the winery. The future looks exciting at Remelluri.

## FINEST WINES

### Remelluri Blanco ★
Telmo Rodríguez had an important part to play in the modernization of white Rioja. He had studied and traveled extensively and gained a good knowledge of wines and grapes from all over the world. He had the vision that a better white could be produced at the family winery of Remelluri at Labastida. That's how, in the 1990s and almost furtively, he started planting a number of experimental white varieties: Viognier, Roussanne, Marsanne, Grenache Blanc, Sauvignon Blanc, Chardonnay, Muscat, and Petit Courbu. The first few bottles went exclusively to the United States, since they produced no more than 2,500 bottles, they were using experimental grapes, and, because production was so small, they were forced to blend two vintages and made some lots of '94/'95, '96/'97, and '98/'99. But the wine attracted the attention of some sommeliers and fanatics of individual wines, and it even got some praise from Robert Parker. The white that Telmo created continues to appear in the family winery portfolio; it comes in a heavy Burgundy bottle—a clear declaration of principles—and is made in the

Burgundian style, barrel-fermented and aged in wood for 12 months or so. Some consider it the best wine in the portfolio. It is, without doubt, the most original offering. The wine ages well, so it's interesting to try any bottle you may come across, but from the most recent vintages, **2004** is a favorite of ours.

### Remelluri Reserva

The Reserva has always been the winery's flagship wine and one of the top examples of the whole appellation. The grapes are always harvested later than average, since the property lies in a colder place and is located at a higher altitude. The Tempranillo, Garnacha, and Graciano that make up the blend are harvested and vinified separately. **2005**, **2001**, and **1994** are personal favorites.

### Remelluri Gran Reserva★

Remelluri's Gran Reserva is only produced in selected vintages, and it's a category that has been consistently losing its share in the local Spanish market. As in the case of the Reserva, the different varieties are fermented separately in old oak *tinas* and then aged for some 26 months in barrels, approximately 85% of which are made of French oak, the rest being American. It is a classic Rioja, with fresh fruit and plenty of spicy balsamic notes, pipe tobacco, aniseed, and licorice hints. If you cannot find any older vintages, **1999** was the latest release at the time of writing (2010), and it shows the classic Rioja Alavesa profile.

### Remelluri Colección Jaime Rodríguez

A recent label, focusing on the terroir, using the oldest grapes from the property—a majority of Tempranillo, with just a dash of Garnacha, and aged in new French oak. This is a more concentrated, dense wine, marked by the oak, needing time in bottle to find harmony. Try the 2001 or the riper 2003, which is more accessible now.

**Right:** The gateway to the beautiful large estate of Remelluri, which has long been run on environmentally friendly principles

**Granja Nuestra Señora de Remelluri**
Area under vine: 260 acres (105ha)
Average production: 550,000 bottles
Carretera Rivas s/n, 01330 Labastida, Álava
Tel: +34 943 631 710
Fax: +34 943 630 874
www.remelluri.com

# Fernando Remírez de Ganuza

Fernando Remírez de Ganuza, who came from Navarra to settle in Rioja Alavesa, was in real estate for many years, and in that profession he came to know the vineyards in his region as very few people did. He bought them and resold them, he swapped them... and, being a wine enthusiast, he soon decided that he should keep some of the best for himself, create a serious estate, and build a winery.

He had started out in 1978 by specializing in land swaps involving tiny vineyards—the well-known Spanish *minifundios*—in order to assemble much larger, unified estates, several of which were bought by some of Rioja's best-known wineries. As he now recalls, "I'd say I have participated in about 2,000 acquisitions, sales, and swaps."

*Never afraid of being called a modernist, Fernando Remírez de Ganuza designed and largely built himself the equipment for a cellar that is different from all others*

So when he changed professions, he knew everything about the land. Then there was the winemaking part. And that's where he created a real surprise in the region, by revealing his brilliant technical inventiveness at the service of his idiosyncratic conceptions about cellar work. Never afraid of being called a modernist, he designed and largely built himself the equipment for a cellar that is different from all others. It was established in 1989.

Meshing perfectly with the rest of the beautiful, medieval village of Samaniego, the winery compound appears to be much older than it is, because it is faced with 200-year-old masonry stone blocks, with a perfect sheen. There is a little brook crossing the large central yard and a general air of bucolic peace. Only inside does one discover an amazing, state-of-the-art winemaking facility that resembles no other.

But before traditionalists start to cringe, the main fact should be stressed: Remírez's vineyard holdings—140 acres (57ha) around Samaniego and other villages in Rioja Alavesa—are amazingly good and provide sensational grapes. The average age—about 60 years, with some 100-year-old vines—is probably the oldest of any estate in Rioja. The varieties are 90 percent Tempranillo, 8 percent Graciano, and 2 percent Garnacha, all of the vines being head-pruned.

The minutiae of viticulture and harvesting (entirely by hand, in small baskets) are supervised to the *n*th degree by Remírez, and they include a system of *tries* (selective harvests) similar to that practiced at the grandest Sauternes châteaux. Ripeness levels are closely monitored, and each vine is visited several times, with only perfectly ripe bunches being picked each time.

Then it's on to Remírez's technical wizardry, which starts with a triple selection via three conveyor belts, with the first devoted to removing loose single grapes, the second to discarding damaged bunches, and the third to cutting the bunches in half horizontally. All of those processes are done by hand by skilled workers. The latter technique is a Remírez obsession, based on the conviction that the top part of the bunch (the "shoulders") is much riper than the bottom part (the "feet"). So the bottom goes for carbonic maceration, becoming the much-lauded Remírez young unoaked wine, while the top is fermented traditionally. The two wines are never blended back together. "There is a huge difference," Fernando insists. "There may be 1.5 percent more alcohol and 25 percent more anthocyanins—color—in the shoulder part."

Now the gadgetry comes into its own, as the half-bunches are pressed using an innovative

**Right:** Fernando Remírez de Ganuza and his daughter Cristina, the artwork hinting at his ingenuity in both vineyard and winery

Remírez de Gan

technique, designed by the wily Remírez, consisting of a flexible bag that is lowered into the tank of must and gradually filled with water, thus exerting a gentle but firm pressure on the grape pulp. The gentleness of the operation impedes the extraction of harshness or excessively herbaceous flavors. The idea stems from a time-honored local practice—*trasnocho* ("sleepless night")—in which traditional winemakers allowed the grape must to drip from sundown to sunrise.

Then it's on to the fermentation, done in peculiar, small, conical, stainless-steel tanks. And rather more conventionally, the wine then undergoes malolactic fermentation in new oak barrels. Overall, one-third new oak—both French and American—is used, because the barrel stock is renewed every three years.

What comes out of those barrels reflects Fernando's love for assertive, concentrated wines, where the superb quality of those grapes he so meticulously tends in the vineyard and treats in the cellar can shine. He doesn't favor sheer power for its own sake, however—contrary to what some critics say. Over the years, he has expanded his portfolio significantly, but that house style is prevalent throughout.

was a later addition, but it doesn't much resemble the red Erre Punto, since in this case it's an ambitious, rich, barrel-fermented wine.

Trasnocho was introduced as a more modern, more concentrated wine than Remírez de Ganuza, and Fincas de Ganuza as a less expensive wine from younger vines, but still with reserva-level aging.

With the 2001 vintage, Remírez de Ganuza presented its first Gran Reserva. It was the 2004 version of this wine, from another great vintage, that won Fernando his first 100-point rating in *The Wine Advocate*.

A selection of the ten best barrels in the cellar, giving some 3,000 bottles of the best wine in the house, was presented for the first time in 2008 under the name María Remírez de Ganuza—a poignant tribute to one of Fernando's daughters, killed by a car in front of the bodega when she was 14 years old. (His other daughter, Cristina, is now an enologist and his main assistant in the cellar.) A single-vineyard wine, La Coqueta, has been announced unofficially, but by late 2010 none had been released.

## FINEST WINES

### Remírez de Ganuza Gran Reserva ★
A combination of modern power and classic Rioja elegance, the **2004** made Jay Miller of *The Wine Advocate* gush with enthusiasm: "Purple/black in color, with a surreal bouquet of kinky spice, truffle, mineral, and black-fruit aromas; on the palate it is remarkably powerful yet elegant. Mouth-filling, complex, and staggeringly rich, it has the balance to evolve for 15–20 years and should easily have a 50-year lifespan." The projected longevity may be taken with a pinch of salt, but this is certainly one of the best new-generation Rioja wines.

**Fernando Remírez de Ganuza**
Area under vine: 140 acres (57ha)
Average production: 250,000 bottles
Calle de la Constitución 1, 01307 Samaniego, Álava
Tel: +34 945 609 022
Fax: +34 945 623 335
www.remirezdeganuza.com

The first wines produced at Remírez de Ganuza were, logically, the R. (or "Erre Punto," as it's called in Spanish), made with the bottom part of the grapes, and the Remírez de Ganuza Reserva, a wine that won many plaudits with its 1994 vintage—a peculiar one, because it was exported to the United States before the legal period of oak and bottle aging for a reserva had been completed, so in that market it was sold under a generic label. But it was all the same wine.

The white Erre Punto, made from the fruit of isolated white vines in some of the old mixed vineyards, and possibly from some bought-in Viura,

# Viña Izadi

Izadi is one of the main representatives of the *alta expresión* ("high expression") style—so much so that they even have a wine named Expresión. This is not, it has to be said, a label that we are particularly keen on. It seems to imply that everything else is somehow "low expression." But leaving aside that reservation, Izadi was nonetheless a pioneer of all that *alta expresión* is supposed to stand for: dark, tannic, highly concentrated, and generously wooded wines.

The venture was started in 1987 by Gonzalo Antón, businessman and restaurateur, manager of the Michelin-starred Zaldiaran Restaurant in Vitoria, and linked to the Alavés soccer club, where he was president for a few years. Always in search of the best wines for his restaurant, he thought it would be a good idea to produce them himself, supplying not only his wine list but also those of close friends in the Basque gastronomy world, like Juan Mari Arzak and Martín Berasategui.

In 1998, he surprised the wine world by tempting Mariano García—one of the best-known winemakers in Spain, responsible for winemaking at Vega-Sicilia from 1968 to 1998—out of his home region and into Rioja to advise on winemaking, mainly for the top cuvée Izadi Expresión. Since the restaurant is focused on modern haute cuisine, it was logical that the wines would also have a modern, quality-oriented profile. Antón's son, also Gonzalo but known as Lalo, is now in charge.

The bodega owns 370 acres (150ha) of vineyards around Villabuena and other nearby villages (Samaniego, Ábalos), divided into more than 100 plots, many of them located on small hillsides in the Sierra de Cantabria, in the heart of Rioja Alavesa.

The name of the company is actually Viña Villabuena, but it is generally known by its brand Viña Izadi. Thanks to its great commercial success, the bodega has expanded into a group of

wineries, known as Artevino, which also includes Finca Villacreces in Ribera del Duero, Orben in Laguardia, and Vetus in Toro. It has also diversified into enotourism, offering visits and tastings, as well as a restaurant—part of the Zaldiaran group, naturally—and a small hotel (11 rooms in a joint venture with the Hotel Conde Duque from Madrid).

## FINEST WINES

All the wines have a modern profile: concentrated, with ripe fruit and plenty of new oak. The Izadi line includes a barrel-fermented white, a red Crianza and a Reserva. They also have two special cuvées.

### Izadi Selección
Sourced from 22 acres (9ha) in Villabuena de Álava and Samaniego, comprising 80% Tempranillo and 20% Graciano. The grapes are hand-harvested into 15kg cases, put over a sorting table, and then fermented in stainless-steel vats. The wine is aged in new oak barrels, 75% of which are French and the rest American, for 20 months. Production for this wine is around 40,000 bottles. Would you be surprised if we recommended the **2001**?

### Izadi Expresión
This comes from a 15-acre (6ha) single vineyard in Villabuena de Álava: pure Tempranillo more than 70 years old, making for a very concentrated wine. As is the case with all Izadi wines, the grapes were hand-harvested in small boxes and selected on a sorting table. Alcoholic fermentation took place in stainless-steel vats, while the malolactic was carried out in new American oak barrels. The resulting wine was aged for 18 months in new French oak. Annual production is limited to fewer than 30,000 bottles. This is for lovers of heavyweight and highly concentrated wines. The **2001** was probably the peak vintage for this wine, but the **1998** was also very impressive.

> **Viña Izadi**
> Area under vine: 370 acres (150ha)
> Average production: 900,000 bottles
> Herrería Travesía II 5, 01307 Villabuena, Álava
> Tel: +34 945 609 086
> Fax: +34 945 609 261
> www.izadi.com

**Left:** Gonzalo "Lalo" Antón, the founder's son, who is now responsible for Izadi's acclaimed *alta expresión* wines

149

# Bodegas Ostatu

The Sáenz de Samaniego family has been in wine for many generations now. Like many other notable wine families in Álava, they can document wine activities dating back to the Middle Ages. As a token of this dedication, we can still see the impressive 18th-century manor around which the wine facilities are distributed today, as well as all the subterranean tunnels excavated in the rock walls of the Matarredo cellar, where for many years the family's wines were made.

*The Sáenz de Samaniego family are proud of their vineyards, which they very sensibly consider the greatest family treasure, as well as their way of life from time immemorial*

The present generation in charge of Ostatu includes Gonzalo, Ernesto, María Asun, and Íñigo Sáenz de Samaniego—four of the six children of Doroteo and Asunción, who are now retired after undertaking the house's transformation and definitive consolidation back in the 1960s. Following a trajectory shared with many other veteran Rioja growers from privileged locations, between the late 1970s and early 1980s Doroteo stopped selling young wines to the big houses and started to sell his own, first in flasks and later under his own brand name. This decision was partly triggered by the 1970s crisis, when several consecutive vintages remained unsold, thus pushing the family to take the plunge and start commercializing their own wines.

A new milestone was reached in 1996, with the first release of Ostatu Crianza, a wine that was immediately successful due to its beautifully clean and concentrated profile. It still offers very good quality at a reasonable price today (no longer a crianza, it is now labeled in generic terms as Ostatu Selección). In 2000, already under the management of the present generation, the modern approach was boosted with the release of an extreme wine in terms of concentration and use of oak: Gloria de Ostatu. Then, five years later, came the first bottling of Laderas del Portillo. The rest of the lineup (white, Reserva, Mazarredo Crianza), is all good, but nothing is quite up to the standard of the red on which the house has always sustained itself financially and the one that still constitutes an impressive 60 percent of the annual sales volume: the Ostatu Carbonic Maceration is where the family displays to great effect its decades-long experience in the elaboration of this *cosechero*-style red.

The Sáenz de Samaniego family are proud of their vineyards, which they very sensibly consider the greatest family treasure, as well as their way of life from time immemorial. Those 84 acres (34ha) of vineyards are located mostly around Samaniego, with some plots in Leza and Laguardia, and share some common features: ocher-colored earth, calcium-rich clay-limestone soils, and scattered hills and canyons. Their best vineyards are Revilla, El Portillo, Valpardillo, and Roancho, while the varieties planted are traditional: Tempranillo, Graciano, Mazuelo, Garnacha, Viura, and Malvasia.

## FINEST WINES

### Gloria de Ostatu

With Gloria de Ostatu, a wine produced under the aegis of Hubert de Boüard and Bernard Pujol, the house joined the modern style of concentrated, plump reds of solid structure and abundant use of new French oak. Gloria de Ostatu shares the basic pattern of most radically modern red Riojas: a varietal Tempranillo sourced from low-yielding old vines, uncompromising grape selection, cold maceration, repeated pumping and stirring, malo and subsequent aging for 18 months in new French oak barrels, and no cold stabilization, fining, or filtering. It is still too early to tell whether the wild power of its youth will polish and harmonize with bottle age. We certainly expect it to do so, especially in the best vintages, like **2001** and **2005**.

### Laderas del Portillo

Sourced from a single 2.7-acre (1.1ha) vineyard called Portillo, planted in the 1970s, Laderas del Portillo adds some exclusive production details—harvesting at more moderate concentration, a small proportion of Viura in the blend, a shorter aging period, use of 500-liter barrels—that result in a more fruit-forward and elegant wine, which shows itself in balance right from the start. This is a small-production operation of merely 3,000 bottles a year, made in collaboration with the team of Asturias négociant Ramón Coalla.

**Above:** Members of the Sáenz de Samaniego family, which has adapted by producing both modern and traditional wines

### Bodegas Ostatu

Area under vine: 84 acres (34ha)
Average production: 250,000 bottles
Carretera de Vitoria 1,
01307 Samaniego, Álava
Tel: +34 945 609 133
Fax: +34 945 623 338
www.ostatu.com

# Viñedos y Bodegas de la Marquesa

It would be hard to find a town anywhere in the world with a greater dependence on the wine industry than Villabuena de Álava. More than 40 wineries call the town home, and with a population that barely exceeds 300, that means there is a winery for every seven people. Alongside Izadi and Luis Cañas, de la Marquesa is one of the most notable names on the town's uniquely crowded wine scene.

There is a Spanish proverb—*quien tuvo, retuvo*—that suggests that anyone who stood out in the past is likely to shine again in the present. Whether consciously or otherwise, this idea has no doubt influenced our decision to select for this book a number of wineries that, while not necessarily at their best today, have consistently been responsible for some truly memorable

*A Spanish proverb suggests that anyone who stood out in the past is likely to shine again in the present. In the case of Viñedos y Bodegas de la Marquesa, it is apt*

bottles in the recent past. In the case of Viñedos y Bodegas de la Marquesa, however, the proverb is apt in a different sense, since this producer is currently touching the sort of heights that it has not reached since the years immediately following its foundation by Francisco Javier Solano, Marqués de la Solana. Back then, in the late 19th century, the ethos was, not surprisingly, Médocain (and post-phylloxeric), thanks to the influence of Monsieur Jean Pineau, considered by many to be one of the fathers of modern Rioja.

Under the trading names of Marqués de la Solana and then Bodegas de Crianza SMS, the house has remained in the hands of the marquis's descendants. In the 1990s, one of those descendants, Juan Pablo de Simón, the great-

grandson of the founder, with the help of his brothers—and, later, his sons Pablo and Jaime—made the decisions that led to the company's recent rise in quality. The company was also formally renamed, in honor of their ancestor María Teresa Solano, as Viñedos y Bodegas de la Marquesa, which was how it had been known unofficially in town for almost 100 years.

Valserrano (the company's other trading name) is medium-sized by Riojan standards, though it has been growing slowly but steadily over the past 15 years. The family uses only grapes harvested from its own vineyards—El Ribazo, Viña Montenuevo, Viña Monteviejo, and Las Carretas—which are scattered around Villabuena at an altitude of between 1,310 and 1,640ft (400–500m) above sea level.

## FINEST WINES

### Classic and modern
The range of wines produced by Valserrano straddles the two supposedly opposing styles of Rioja: classic and modern. In the former camp is a solid range of **Reserva [V]** and **Gran Reserva**, produced mainly from Tempranillo from their various vineyards plus around 10% Graciano. These wines are meant to be released ready for enjoyment, though a few additional years of cellaring will often add something to both wines. Representing Rioja's modern side is a single-vineyard wine, **Valserrano Finca Monteviejo**. This is 95% Tempranillo, firmly structured thanks to the obvious influence of new oak barrels; it is a wine that, in the best vintages, such as **2001**, **2004**, and especially **2005★**, will age splendidly once the concentrated fruit from the old (1948) vines in the Viña Monteviejo assimilates the wood tannins.

### Valserrano Graciano
Viñedos y Bodegas de la Marquesa deserves praise for its work in producing varietal wines from some of the "other" traditional red grapes in Rioja: Mazuelo, Garnacha [V] and, especially, Graciano, a wine that, in such vintages as **2001**, shows a delightful and improbable balance of freshness due to its marked acidity, firm structure, and depth,

**Above:** Juan Pablo de Simón, great-grandson of the founder, under whom the firm is surpassing its previous high points

with fine notes of tobacco. The first vintage of this wine was 1995, just one year after the first vintage (1994) of the varietal Gracianos released by pioneers Contino and Ijalba. Valserrano thus belongs to the group of producers that reasserted the quality of a grape that was, and still is, so often overlooked, even by those who should know better.

**Valserrano / Bodegas y Viñedos de la Marquesa**
Area under vine: 173 acres (70ha)
Average production: 450,000 bottles
Herrería 76,
01307 Villabuena, Álava
Tel: +34 945 609 085
Fax: +34 945 623 304
www.valserrano.com

# Bodegas Puelles

This estate has been in the grape-growing Puelles family since 1844, when it was purchased from the town council. But it was not until the current generation—Jesús (known in the family as Chucho) and Félix—that it dived into making, bottling, and selling its own wines, having established a modern winery on the property, an old water mill from the 17th century.

The family also made the transition toward wine tourism by opening a hotel right next to the winery. The Hospedería del Vino has six rooms and facilities such as a spa, a swimming pool, vinotherapy massages, and of course tastings and visits to the vineyards and cellars.

The family follows organic cultivation methods in the vineyard—some of its wines are certified as such—because they believe the wine is really made in the vineyard. The vineyards are all on the estate, in Ábalos, a winery-rich village in Rioja Alta (387 inhabitants and 15 wineries), at the foot of the Sierra de Toloño mountains, where soils are predominantly yellow clay-limestone, rich in chalk, which makes for elegant and supple wines. The vineyards are located at between 1,600 and 2,000 ft (490–610m) above sea level, under the shelter of the Sierra de Cantabria and its Atlantic influx.

The family believes in terroir and thinks great wines are a reflection of their origin. The methods followed in the winery are therefore very respectful of the grapes and oriented toward quality production. The destemming is very gentle, as is the fermentation in 20,000-liter stainless-steel tanks, which are naturally cooled by the mill stream running by. The family uses both American and French oak barrels in a similar proportion. This is a very consistent winery.

## FINEST WINES

Bodegas Puelles produces no fewer than eight different wines. Under the Puelles label there is a blanco, an unoaked tinto *joven*, a tinto that has aged for five months in barrel, as well as the standard crianza and reserva.

### Puelles Gran Reserva

The idea is that, in the Gran Reserva, the combination of fruit and oak results in elegance. They use 94% Tempranillo for this range, hand-harvested in October and fermented for 18–20 days. Malolactic fermentation is carried out in stainless steel, and the wine is then aged for 27 months in French and American barrels in equal parts, during which time it is racked a total of three times. The wine is clarified with egg whites and filtered before bottling. The **1996** shows an orange rim and plenty of ripe red fruit in the nose, as well as flowers, honey, balsamic notes, and some leather. Its elegant body and refreshing acidity make it very easy—and pleasurable—to drink.

### El Molino de Puelles

This is a single-vineyard wine, from El Molino ("The Mill"), a 11-acre (4.5ha) plot within the estate where the winery is located. It is certified organic. In this case, the wine is aged for 15 months in new oak, 70% of which is French, and is bottled unfiltered. It shows more black fruit than red on both nose and palate. The most highly recommended vintages are **2004** and **2002**.

### Zenus

This is the bodega's top wine, where the aim is balance and elegance, showing the characteristics of Ábalos. They source the best grapes from specific plots (San Prudencio and La Cañada) of 40-year-old vines. Malolactic is carried out in barrel and aging in 80% French oak for 18 months. Not surprisingly, the Zenus from **2001** remains our favorite, and as the oak is progressively integrating, the wine is becoming better and better.

**Right:** Jesús Puelles, who, with his brother Félix, has successfully managed the transition to bottling the family's own wines

**Bodegas Puelles**
Area under vine: 43 acres (17.5ha)
Average production: 250,000 bottles
Camino de los Molinos s/n,
26339 Ábalos, La Rioja
Tel: +34 941 334 415
Fax: +34 941 334 132
www.bodegaspuelles.com

# Bodegas Baigorri

Bodegas Baigorri announces itself with a glass cube emerging from within a sea of vines on a hilltop on the outskirts of the tiny medieval village of Samaniego. This eye-catching bodega was the brainchild of Jesús Baigorri and the architect Iñaki Aspiazu. Built in 1997 with a very strong focus on design, it is today considered a benchmark of modern winery architecture. It was acquired, ten years after its inauguration, by Pedro Martínez, a businessman from Murcia.

Just as the architecture is a mixture of tradition and innovation, so the winemaking employs cutting-edge technology with a nod to the past, as in the traditional oak *tinas* with ultra-modern conical stainless-steel vats. The winery is designed over six underground levels to facilitate working with gravity and to eliminate the need for pumps. Even when grapes, must, or wine need to be moved around, they are placed in small stainless-steel vessels known as OVI that are transported by a crane system.

All the grapes are passed over vibrating sorting tables that shake off any water or other unwanted matter that may come in from the vineyard, and they are subsequently selected by hand—sometimes even destemmed by hand one berry at a time to keep the grape intact and to make sure only the very best and perfect grains make it into the vats to create the top cuvées. The whole process is governed by a quest for the very highest quality, which means attention to the smallest detail, including strict grape selection.

As is the case at an increasing number of wineries, Baigorri is also focusing on wine tourism, offering visits, tastings, a shop, and even a restaurant, where modern food is served to pair with the wines. As you would expect, the Baigorri website is also a very accomplished, if rather minimalist, work of design and is also well worth a visit for those who cannot make it all the way to the winery.

## FINEST WINES

The winery has a full range of wines, including a rosado and an unoaked carbonic-maceration wine very much in the traditional Alavesa style, followed by the Crianza, Reserva, and a modern garage wine. The reds are dark and dense, rich in oak—the team here favors new barrels—in a modern profile, with black- rather than red-fruit aromas and echoes of licorice, chocolate, and smoke.

### Baigorri Fermentado en Barrica
A Viura fermented in new French oak barrels, aged on the lees and with frequent *bâtonnage*. In its youth, the wood comes to the fore, with a background of sesame seeds, dried herbs, and ripe stone fruit (nectarine, apricot, peach). It is made in a style to be drunk in the medium term.

### Baigorri Reserva
The grapes for this wine are chosen from the oldest Tempranillo vines. They are destemmed and hand-selected using vibrating sorting tables and are then fermented with a long maceration at a low temperature in stainless-steel vats with the cap submerged. Malolactic fermentation and aging take place in new French oak barrels for 18 months. We have been very impressed with the **2003** vintage. This wine and the Crianza are also available in 50cl bottles.

### Baigorri de Garaje ★
It was only a matter of time before a winery used the word "garage" in the name of a wine—a reference to Bordeaux's *vins de garage* of the mid-1990s. In Rioja, that winery was Baigorri, and this is a clear declaration of intent on its part. The wine is a paradigmatic example of the garagiste movement: dark, concentrated, and powerful from very ripe grapes, fermented in oak vats to extract all the aromatic and color components, then aged in new barrels to obtain an impressive result.

**Bodegas Baigorri**
Area under vine: 272 acres (110ha)
Average production: 600,000 bottles
Carretera Vitoria a Logroño km 53,
01307 Samaniego, Álava
Tel: +34 945 609 420
Fax: +34 945 609 407
www.bodegasbaigorri.com

# Bodegas Campillo

Julio Martínez had long dreamed of creating a top-quality winery along the lines of the French château model. His vision entailed the application of the finest architecture to the best available materials to build something modern, luxurious, and equipped with the very latest technology—somewhere that would be capable of making the very finest wines. Having established an empire with Bodegas Faustino, in 1990 Martínez was finally able to fulfill his dream.

The name he gave to this project was Campillo, which operates as an entirely separate venture within the Faustino empire. Located in Laguardia, it takes its name from one of the first vineyards owned by Faustino, a name that had also been used for one of the company's brands in the 1930s and 1940s. The project produces a full range of wines, with the emphasis always on quality. These are made in a traditional style, though there are concessions to modernity: the wines are produced using grapes from vineyards surrounding the winery building (including some single-vineyard bottlings), they are aged in French oak, and they sometimes include French grape varieties.

The palace-style winery might call to mind an abbey or maybe even the kitsch of Falcon Crest, but here things are done with taste, and the result is superb. The interior is as impressive as the exterior. For fermentation, they favor pneumatic presses and stainless steel; and the bottle- and barrel-aging rooms are spectacular, a combination of brick and wood, forming vaulted cellars full of perfectly aligned rows of barrels (some 7,000 in total) and up to 3 million bottles. Although production figures are not disclosed, the initial project envisaged up to 1.2 million bottles per year.

Campillo's vineyards are in Laguardia, where the Atlantic influence is stronger than the Mediterranean one, the soil is rich in chalk, and the grapes ripen to make structured wines that appeal to traditionalists and modernists alike.

## FINEST WINES

As is the norm in Rioja, the range covers a barrel-fermented white, a rosado, a red crianza (raised in American oak), a reserva (American and French oak), and a gran reserva (French oak), plus some other, "special" cuvées.

### Campillo Finca Cuesta Clara Raro Reserva

A single-vineyard wine from a vineyard (Cuesta Clara) planted with Tempranillo Peludo ("Hairy Tempranillo"), a rare (hence *raro*) clone of Tempranillo whose leaves are hairy on the underside. The vines are low-yielding, hand-harvested, selected at the winery, put through a long fermentation, and raised for 26 months in new Allier oak barrels. The result is a wine of intense color (but still with an orange edge), with both red and black fruit, underbrush, and some chocolate and spice. In the mouth, it is medium-bodied, with bright acidity, a supple texture, evident fruit, and a good finish.

### Campillo Gran Reserva

Red Campillo exists in the categories of crianza, reserva, and gran reserva. For the Gran Reserva, vintages 1978 (the first vintage), 1989 (made from centennial vines), and 1995 are still available, so for a reasonable price you can buy a mature wine for current drinking that has been kept in the winery in the correct conditions.

### Campillo Reserva Especial

This was also Gran Reserva. The **Gran Reserva Especial 1987** was an icon of modern Rioja and it featured a touch (up to 25%) of Cabernet Sauvignon. The wine was very good indeed, and if tasted today it would probably come across as quite classical in style. However, interest in this style of wine seems to have faded somewhat, and the Cabernet has disappeared from the blend, which is now just Tempranillo and Graciano.

> **Bodegas Campillo**
> Area under vine: 125 acres (50ha)
> Average production: not disclosed
> Carretera de Logroño s/n,
> 01300 Laguardia, Álava
> Tel: +34 945 600 826
> Fax: +34 945 600 837
> www.bodegascampillo.com

# Luis Cañas

Luis Cañas is both an old and new name in Rioja. The wine history of the family as grape growers goes back 200 years in Villabuena, one of the leading wine villages in Rioja Alavesa, and the firm dates from 1928. However, it was not until 1970 that it started bottling and selling its own wines.

In 1989, there was a generational change, with Juan Luis Cañas taking over from his father Luis and giving the wines an updated profile. In 1994, they built a new winery, and in the year in which "New Rioja" really started to boom, Luis Cañas was certainly one of the wineries that helped make this happen.

*In 1994, the year in which "New Rioja" really started to boom, Luis Cañas was certainly one of the wineries that helped to make this happen*

Luis Cañas has 222 acres (90ha) of owned vineyards and rents a further 500 acres (200ha). Every one of the 815 separate plots they work is treated individually in order to vinify each vineyard separately, depending on varieties, quality, and vine age. The company owns some 4,300 barrels, 70 percent of which are made of French oak, the rest being American.

The hard work has been reflected in the quality of the wines, which has increased tremendously, and they have obtained multiple international awards with some of their more new-wave, high-expression wines.

## FINEST WINES

The winery produces a big range of wines, from the traditional (Luis Cañas Gran Reserva), to the modern (Amarem), and on to the postmodern (Hiru 3 Racimos).

### Luis Cañas Gran Reserva

There is a full list of more classical-style wines (but still with a modern accent, favoring black fruit over red fruit and using some French as well as American oak barrels) under the Luis Cañas label, and the company bottles the whole spectrum—from a young unoaked blanco, to a gran reserva tinto. The Gran Reserva represents the top example within this label, and the fantastic **2001** vintage is highly recommended. The wine is made with 95% Tempranillo, with the balance provided by Graciano, Mazuelo, and Garnacha, fermented for seven days at a maximum temperature of 82°F (28°C). It is aged for 12 months in new French oak barrels and a further 12 months in second-year American oak barrels, then it rests for a further 36 months in bottle before being released.

### Amarem Graciano Reserva

The vineyards that produce the Graciano grapes used for this wine are close to 100 years old and are located in the village of Leza. This exceptional raw material is responsible for a dark-colored wine of great intensity on the nose, showing plenty of toasty tones intermixed with ripe black fruit, while on the palate there is lively acidity and good length on the finish. Try the **2004**, if possible on its 15th birthday.

### Hiru 3 Racimos

*Tres racimos* means "three bunches." In fact, the wine's name is quite tautologous, since *hiru*, too, is the Basque word for "three." The name comes from the extremely low yields obtained from the very oldest vines, which produce literally three bunches of grapes that are very small but full of flavor. It is a very, very concentrated and well-oaked wine, with a clearly modern accent. The wine is truly exceptional, and both the **2001** and **2004** vintages are highly recommended.

**Bodegas y Viñedos Luis Cañas**
Area under vine: 222 acres (90ha)
Average production: 1.6 million bottles
Carretera Samaniego 10,
01307 Villabuena, Álava
Tel: +34 945 623 373 / +34 945 623 386
Fax: +34 945 60 92 89
www.luiscanas.com

# Exopto

It doesn't take a long tradition or lots of start-up capital to begin making serious Rioja wines of depth and longevity—it takes passion and dedication, as a small group of friends who used to play rugby together have proven over just a few years with their modest but ambitious winery, Exopto. The name—Latin for "I hope fervently"—seems particularly well chosen for what started out as an apparently quixotic quest in 2003. After a few vintages and some very high scores from top international critics, hope is closer to fruition.

After seven years, Bordeaux-born, Bordeaux-trained enologist Tom Puyaubert, who still holds a day job as a sales manager in Spain for a large French cooperage, is now alone at the helm, since co-founders David Sampedro, a winemaker, and Javier Gómez Garrido, an agricultural engineer, have now gone on to different projects.

The initial idea was to reflect terroir and grapes more than anything else, rather than traditional winemaking techniques. The character of old vineyards in two separate parts of Rioja was sought out, and barrel aging was given a very Bordeaux-like importance and used accordingly.

Exopto owns no vineyards but has agreements with three growers in distinct parts of Rioja. While the small winery is in Alavesa, the Tempranillo and a little Graciano come from Ábalos in Rioja Alta, where it has 12 acres (5ha) across 16 parcels of *gobelet*-pruned, 25–90-year-old vines on clay-limestone. The Garnacha and most of the Graciano come from Monte Yerga in Alfaro, Rioja Baja, with 6 and 3.7 acres (2.5 and 1.5ha) respectively of 50-year-old Garnacha and 15-year-old Graciano on rocky soils, at an altitude of 1,600ft (500m), which imparts freshness to the fruit.

Tom, a proponent of blending, considers Tempranillo, Garnacha, and Graciano as the three most representative Rioja grapes. The grapes are picked manually in 33lb (15kg) boxes and vinified in small cement or oak vats, two materials liked because of the micro-exchanges of oxygen (a cause of better color stability and avoiding reduction problems) and also for the great thermal inertia they provide—an advantage over stainless steel. This helps keep the grapes cool for a cold soak, then to bring the temperature slowly up to 78.8°F (26°C). These vats also age Garnacha and Tempranillo for the blend of their youngest wine, BB de Exopto. Aging in barrel is meticulous. Two other wines, Horizonte and Exopto, go into barrel (90 percent French, the rest American) right after fermentation and are kept on their fine lees for six months.

## FINEST WINES

### Viña Turzaballa
Exopto makes three reds and one white, the latter from Viura, Garnacha Blanca, and Malvasia Riojana scattered among the old red-grape vineyards (originally to increase yields and to serve as early detectors of vine diseases). All are blends, the proportions of which vary according to the characteristics of the wine. Garnacha is used for fruit and sweetness, Tempranillo for structure, and Graciano for acidity and aromatic complexity.

The entry-level **BB de Exopto** is a blend of 50% Garnacha, 30% Tempranillo, and 20% Graciano, partially tank-aged to highlight fruit. Some 25,000 bottles are made.

**Horizonte de Exopto** is 80% Tempranillo, 10% Garnacha, and 10% Graciano. Production varies between 10,000 and 15,000 bottles.

**Exopto**, the top wine, is an atypical blend of 60% Graciano, 30% Tempranillo, and 10% Garnacha. Some 3,000 bottles are made in good vintages only.

**Bodegas Exopto**
Area under vine: 21.6 acres (9ha)
Average production: 40,000–45,000 bottles
Carretera de Elvillar, 26
01300 Laguardia, Álava
Tel: +34 650 213 993
Fax: +34 941 287 822
www.exoptowinecellar.blogspot.com

# Bodegas Basilio Izquierdo

For a while, this firm was called Bodegas Águila Real, which was not wholly consistent with the very personal nature of the project. Rather at odds with Basilio Izquierdo's decades-long discretion, his original two wines—red and white—are labeled B de Basilio, so he might have given his company his own name from the very beginning. At any rate, the bodega and the wines were—and are—inconceivable without the founder, owner, winemaker, and main cellar worker.

This is still a young project, with only a few vintages released onto the market at the time of writing (one of red, two of white). It is a very small operation whose wines had not even been tasted

*The wines are inconceivable without the founder, owner, and winemaker, displaying a rare combination of Riojan authenticity and finesse*

by the three authors of this book when they were first considering which producers to profile. When so many—some with long and successful track records—are inevitably missing, might it not seem somewhat risky to bet on Basilio Izquierdo?

Well, certainly not, having now tasted the wines, which display a rare combination of Riojan authenticity and finesse. But even before that, we were very confident, knowing Basilio as the cellar master for over 30 years at CVNE (including Viña Real and also, for many years, Contino). After his retirement in 2006, the master felt like making more wine, not playing bowls or golf. ("The search for top-quality grapes all over Rioja is much better gymnastics for someone like me," he says.) So, he started this brand-new project and is now fully committed to his winemaking passion. A bone-deep Riojan... born in La Mancha...

One of the peculiar features of this venture that somehow contributes to its even deeper rooting in traditional Riojan winemaking is that Basilio does not own any vines. He is convinced that the best Garnacha will always come from Rioja Baja, and so it is there, in Tudelilla, that he has found the 35-year-old vineyard from which to source his Garnacha—bunch by bunch, grape by grape. He takes pride in the sanitary perfection of his wines, where there is no room for a single raisiny, botrytized, or moldy grape. His pickers are well taught: "Do not worry about what is left behind in the vineyard; the owner may always harvest that and sell it or use it as he pleases."

## FINEST WINES

### Basilio Izquierdo
The flagship red wine (soon to be joined by a second label called Acodo) has a clear Garnacha character, ripe and perfumed, that evokes the traditional Riojan blend of grapes and vineyards. One-third Garnacha is complemented with two-thirds Tempranillo and a dollop of Graciano, all sourced from very old vines in Laguardia and Haro (in Rioja Alavesa and Rioja Alta respectively).

### B de Basilio
More Garnacha, white in this case, goes into this very scarce white wine (a mere 600 bottles). Three similarly styled vintages are available now (2007, 2008, and 2009), plus an experimental release in 2005 of only 200 bottles. A true rarity, it is made from Garnacha Blanca and a little Viura from a vineyard in Gallocanta, in San Vicente de la Sonsierra. It is barrel-fermented in new Burgundy barrels and aged there for six months; the secret to its unusually harmonious integration and finesse is the frequent *bâtonnage*, so the wine is always protected by its lees.

**Bodegas Basilio Izquierdo**
Area under vine: none
Average production: 7,000 bottles
Carretera Vitoria, Bodegas El Collado 9,
01300 Laguardia, Álava
Tel: +34 666 461 853
www.bodegasbasilioizquierdo.com

# Viñedos de Páganos

Taking its name from a borough in the Laguardia district of Rioja, Viñedos de Páganos is a relatively recent addition to the Eguren family's broad portfolio of wine projects.

The Eguren family feels most at home in Rioja, where they opened cellars at San Vicente de la Sonsierra (Sierra Cantabria, Viñedos de Sierra Cantabria, and Señorio de San Vicente) and, more recently, Viñedos de Páganos in Rioja Alavesa. The initiative crystallized in 1998 with the purchase of the vineyard and the construction of a cellar. The first commercial release was El Puntido 2001, and a wine has been made every year since then. The higher-profile La Nieta did not appear until 2004. Since then, both have enjoyed very good to excellent vintages.

One of the Egurens' guiding principles is that the winemaking and bottling should be carried out separately for each of their different ventures. Señorio de San Vicente, Sierra Cantabria, and Viñedos Sierra Cantabria are all made at their own dedicated facilities, and the same applies to Viñedos de Páganos. This strict independence—which incidentally is responsible for the different Eguren entries in this volume—is not at all compromised by the fact that, since 2005, Páganos has also doubled as the family company's headquarters. Indeed, Marcos Eguren emphasizes the exclusively logistical nature of this decision, since their other Rioja bodegas are still deeply rooted in San Vicente de la Sonsierra. They are certainly not contemplating any sort of centralization as far as winemaking is concerned: "At Páganos, we only produce El Puntido and La Nieta. And that is not going to change."

Following another of the Eguren's guiding principles, all the Páganos vineyards are planted with Tempranillo (including the apparently related Tempranillo Peludo and Tinta de Toro). One might have thought a new venture such as Páganos, where the core of old vines has been supplemented with freshly planted ones, would have been a good opportunity to take a punt on other accepted varieties such us Graciano, Mazuela, or Garnacha. But Marcos disagrees, arguing that the circumstances of weather and terroir are simply not favorable to anything other than Tempranillo. "The Páganos vineyards, like all our Rioja vineyards, are in a borderline region that is very cool, where varieties of a longer physiological cycle seldom give their best," he says.

## FINEST WINES

### El Puntido
This vineyard blend is the signature wine. It is remarkably consistent, but if we had to pick one vintage, it would be the **2004**: deep cherry, originally with a deep-purple rim of youth, now tamed a little; the nose hits you with fresh fruit and solid oak structure; spices, complex, clean, with a pleasant orange-peel note, some incense and a little sarsaparilla. The palate is well structured, with firm tannin, pleasant acidity, well-integrated alcohol, and a very serious fruit presence throughout, topped with an intense, long finish of licorice and mint.

### La Nieta★
La Nieta is named after a small plot of only 4.2 acres (1.7 ha) where the Eguren family applies the same principle of radically low yields and strict grape-by-grape selection that characterizes all their luxury cuvées. Working with extreme concentrations that are further structured by 18 months in new French oak, it is sometimes difficult to achieve balance—but there is no denying that the **2005** has it. It is a powerful but harmonious wine, marked by subtlety in the face of overwhelming complexity.

**Viñedos de Páganos**
Area under vine: 75 acres (30ha)
Average production: 60,000 bottles
Carretera de Navaridas s/n,
01309 Páganos, Laguardia, Álava
Tel: +34 945 600 590
Fax: +34 945 600 885
www.eguren.com

# Bodegas Palacio

This winery has a long and rich history. It was founded in 1894 by Cosme Palacio, moved its operations to Valladolid when phylloxera made its appearance in Rioja, and hired a winemaker that later went on to make Vega-Sicilia, which became one of the most prestigious wines in Spain and the seed for the growth of the whole Ribera del Duero region.

The Palacio family sold to a joint venture between Domecq and Seagram in 1972. Domecq soon left to create its own bodega, and Seagram continued on its own until 1987, when the winery was offered to its management and it was purchased by a group lead by Jean Gervais, who was Seagram Europe's former vice president. Gervais brought Michel Rolland in to revitalize the wine portfolio, and he created a revolutionary wine, for many the first modern Rioja: Cosme Palacio y Hermanos, a more concentrated wine in which the oak aging had been shortened and where the oak used was French rather than American.

*Michel Rolland was brought in to revitalize the wine portfolio, and he created a revolutionary wine, for many the first modern Rioja: Cosme Palacio y Hermanos*

The success of the wines led to a new change in ownership; in 1998, the winery was sold to the Entrecanales group (today Acciona), one of the biggest business groups in Spain, which already owned Viña Mayor in Ribera del Duero and Bodegas Barceló, known for its brand Peñascal.

They were pioneers in wine tourism, opening a hotel in the 19th-century winery building, where the 15 rooms each bear the name of a grape variety. As for the wines, like those of other entrepreneurs, what was once modern and revolutionary seems very classical nowadays.

## FINEST WINES

A wine called Milflores ("A Thousand Flowers"), has been the benchmark carbonic-maceration red in Rioja for years. The Castillo Rioja line—it should replace the El Pórtico line, which has disappeared from the portfolio—represents entry-level wines, while the red Glorioso, a brand created as long ago as 1928, is available in Crianza, Reserva, and Gran Reserva versions. All of the reds are Tempranillo, while the whites are Viura.

### Cosme Palacio y Hermanos Reserva Especial [V]
This was a revolutionary wine at the time it was created, because the wine was more concentrated than the norm and then aged in French oak, something that was then unheard of in the region. The label exists for both white and red. There is a number of wines under the Cosme Palacio label —two whites and three reds—but this is the one that is considered the first *vino de autor* from Rioja. It was created by Michel Rolland, who applied many Bordelais principles to the Rioja grapes, with very successful results. The **1994** was one of the best wines of this very famous vintage.

### Bodegas Palacio Especial
This is supposed to be the *alta expresión* wine from the winery, but the modern-looking bottle and austere label are, in fact, a very old design (we've seen examples as old as 1935) that was revived at the time of the "New Rioja" revolution. It is sourced from the oldest vines and aged in new French oak barrels for 24 months, then a further 12 months in bottle. The result is a well-oaked wine, black rather than red in color and fruit character, with the concentration, acidity, and balance to age with grace. If you can find it, the **1995** should be perfect for drinking now. If not, the **2004** is a good modern version that could be drunk from around seven years of age or kept for a few years.

**Bodegas Palacio**
Area under vine: 383 acres (155ha)
Average production: 1.5 million bottles
San Lázaro 1,
01300 Laguardia, Álava
Tel: +34 945 600 151
Fax: +34 945 600 297
www.bodegaspalacio.es

# Viña Salceda

From its discreet beginnings in 1969, obscured by local Elciego grandees such as Marqués de Riscal, Viña Salceda occupied a position best described as "middle class" in the Rioja hierarchy. It made correct reds at correct prices. Yet there was potential for more than that in its own vineyards, which surround the winery, and in those of its contract suppliers—156 small parcels, mostly old vines, in the same Rioja Alavesa area, and some across the River Ebro in Rioja Alta. That potential is what encouraged the Chivite family, of Navarra fame, to add Viña Salceda to its portfolio in 1998. Since then, progress has been steady.

The Elciego soils are excellent for quality viticulture—mostly silt loam on limestone-sandstone rock—as is the temperate climate, with sufficient rainfall in winter and spring. Add the contract growers' vineyards in villages like Cenicero, Laguardia, Ábalos, or San Vicente, and the result is a highly varied portfolio, with vine age a common trait, as is the fact that a great majority of these vineyards are head-pruned and dry-farmed.

As usual in the region, the great majority of these vineyards are planted with Tempranillo, with small amounts of Mazuelo and Graciano and some extremely old Garnacha Tinta vines.

All of the harvesting is done manually, with a careful selection process that starts right in the vineyard, following a detailed and precise harvesting schedule controlled by the winery.

Viña Salceda produces just four red cuvées, which run the gamut that so many Rioja bodegas know so well these days: one crianza, one reserva, one gran reserva, and the more expensive, more international Conde de la Salceda, made only in particularly good vintages.

The winemaking, however, is less run of the mill and gives a few clues to the seriousness of the Chivites' ambitions for their Rioja subsidiary. Well-controlled, slow fermentations with soft pumping-over of the must and skins are followed by some maceration of skins and wine on the fine lees and then by malolactic fermentation in barrel for the top cuvées—an indication of the premium placed on elegance by the bodega, and a very rare occurrence in Rioja.

Let's face it: for a few years, when the attention was totally focused on the infamously dubbed *alta expresión* wines, the efforts to upgrade Viña Salceda within the general framework of the Chivite style didn't make very big headlines. But as the exaggerations and mistakes made by some of the internationalists take their toll on the popularity of their wines and a new generation of more savvy consumers rediscovers the virtues of good traditional Rioja (there is quite a lot of bad traditional Rioja, too), Viña Salceda becomes more and more of a protagonist. It has the advantage of having done things right for a long time and having preferred elegance to power.

## FINEST WINES

### Viña Salceda Reserva

This wine combines the balance and lightness that group chairman Fernando Chivite favors in all of his wines with a more assertive fruit presence and more liveliness than in the classic Gran Reserva. It is aged 18 months in American oak and is fully in the traditional style.

### Conde de la Salceda

Produced exclusively from vineyards that are more than 80 years old, with head-pruned vines, this is a good example of modern Rioja without the excesses shown by some of its competitors, within the trappings of the style. Matured in 100% French oak barrels, it is 95% Tempranillo, with some Graciano for complexity and freshness, having excellent concentration and blueberry flavors.

### Viña Salceda

Area under vine: 111 acres (45ha)
Average production: 1 million bottles
Carretera de Cenicero km 3, 01340 Elciego, Álava
Tel: +34 945 606 125
www.vinasalceda.com

# Marqués de Cáceres

This is indeed a special case among Rioja producers: a house with a clear vocation for worldwide distribution of a huge volume of wine; a house whose conscious decision since it was founded more than 40 years ago was to renounce owning vineyards; a house that has deliberately followed its own path in the world of wine regardless of most trends and hypes; a house that cannot be considered traditional at all (just the opposite in a sense), nor small, nor romantic... But it is still a house that, despite it all, arouses sympathy from many knowledgeable wine lovers.

In the late 1960s, Enrique Forner returned from France to Cenicero, firmly resolved to renew his family's winemaking tradition—a goal that is mostly achieved with the important role played by his daughter Cristina at the head of this family company. In fact, Cristina Forner has been the visible face of Marqués de Cáceres for many years, strengthening the position of the company all over the world—a president in the most executive sense of the word, who has been deeply involved in the export management of the wines. Enrique Forner's main treasure was the experience he had acquired as négociant in Languedoc, as well as in the management of a couple of Bordeaux châteaux. As an essential support for his project, he brought with him the brains of Professor Émile Peynaud, with whom he had been collaborating in Bordeaux for quite some time. The resemblance to other great innovators—Quijano, Murrieta, Hurtado de Amézaga—is evident and reinforced by the use of the brand name Marqués de Cáceres, which inevitably invokes that past. And yet the perspective provided by Forner at the head of an investors' group was by no means retrospective but profoundly innovative.

Today, in the light of events over the past four decades in Rioja, his association with such an

**Right:** Cristina Forner, president of Marqués de Cáceres, who has fulfilled her father's vision for the company he founded

*This is a special case among Rioja producers: a house with a clear vocation for worldwide distribution of a huge volume of wine. But it is still a house that arouses sympathy from many knowledgeable wine lovers*

**Above:** The perfectly stacked ranks of barriques in the cavernous cellar of Marqués de Cáceres reflect the scale of its production

internationally prestigious enologist as Peynaud (and, from 1990, with Michel Rolland) comes as a clear precursor to the phenomenon of "flying winemakers," which has become so fashionable of late and is doubtless largely responsible for the homogenization of styles all over the world. There can be little question that the arrival of the first wines of Marqués de Cáceres on the shelves of wine shops was a genuine breath of fresh air, with their clear fruit aromas and plush tannins, in the midst of the rather faded landscape of Rioja wine at the beginning of the worldwide economic crisis of the mid-1970s. From this point of view, we tend to agree with those who consider that Marqués de Cáceres spearheaded the 1970s pioneering movement of modernization of Rioja wines, against the excesses and stale overoaking of many wines of those days, aged in often neglected, old American oak barrels.

Enrique Former and his partners, with the help of Peynaud, had of course the know-how, but also

enjoyed a small dose of serendipity in their first steps. The investors rented a little space inside the cavernous Cenicero co-op cellar and let Peynaud taste and blend among hundreds of barrels of Tempranillo wine made by the co-op and others. It was from the great 1970 vintage, and Peynaud concocted a sensational blend. Fruit-driven, fresh, with little overt oak, it was an entirely different expression of Tempranillo—and of Rioja—from anything anyone had ever tasted. They released the wine as a crianza in 1973, and it was an overnight sensation. Spain, then anxious for change in the waning years of the Franco dictatorship, fell for it completely. Marqués de Cáceres immediately became famous.

It adopted a typical Riojan model in deciding, from the very beginning, not to exploit vineyards directly. Never in the course of its history has Unión Vitivinícola (such is the formal name of the company) been the owner of the vineyards from which it sources an impressive 16,500 tons

(15 million kg) of grapes per year. Conditioned by the fragmented land-tenure system in the surroundings of Cenicero and the remaining areas of interest for the company, the model they have always used is long-term purchase contracts with growers, with technical support and quality control provided by Marqués de Cáceres, under the direction of winemaker Fernando Gómez Sáez.

In tune with the immense area under vine controlled by means of this system—almost 6,200 acres (2,500ha)—production figures are equally impressive and divided evenly between domestic and foreign markets. According to the company, its wines reach more than 100 countries. In terms of volume and market impact, we cannot overlook the importance of its Viura-based (and Malvasia-

*The outstanding 1994 vintage moved Marqués de Cáceres to release Gaudium ("Joy" in Latin) as another turn of the screw in a house style that was already openly modern*

touched) white wines: Marqués de Cáceres Blanco Joven, Antea Barrica, and Satinela Semidulce. There is also Marqués de Cáceres Rosado (80 percent Tempranillo, 20 percent Garnacha). These are all wines that—while not aspiring to impress the advanced taster—rarely disappoint and maintain a regular level, year in and year out. This is coherent with the company's marketing strategy, which hopes—and it would be hard to discuss its success—to seduce a wide range of consumers, not necessarily wine lovers, with sound wines and reasonable prices.

Red wines are dominated by Tempranillo, with an additional 15 percent between Graciano and Garnacha, and the Marqués de Cáceres range covers the full spectrum of classic types: crianza, reserva, and gran reserva. With even greater intervention of Tempranillo, there is an "extreme" range (in terms of ripeness and extraction) under two labels: Gaudium and its small brother MC. Both ranges include styles that could be called modern and ultra-modern, of which the finest examples offered by the house are respectively Marqués de Cáceres Gran Reserva and Gaudium.

## FINEST WINES

### Marqués de Cáceres Gran Reserva
Despite an outward image that might, for many observers, scream of Rioja tradition (the aristocratic name, a coat of arms, classic typography, and the gran reserva designation), this wine represents today the most faithful execution of the innovative style introduced by Marqués de Cáceres some 40 years ago. Consequently, it boasts a deep cherry color and notable extraction. In its first years there is a certain tension between the new oak notes and the ripe red fruit, with firm tannins that eventually polish with time, good balance between alcohol and acidity, and a memory of fine leather that in the best vintages—such as **1991** and **1994**—clearly invokes its Riojan origin.

### Gaudium
The outstanding 1994 vintage moved Marqués de Cáceres to release this Gaudium ("Joy" in Latin) as another turn of the screw in a house style that was already openly modern. Very deep in color, in its best vintages (**1994, 1996, 2001, 2004**) this wine is faultless within this canon: fine and elegant, with notes of Mediterranean herbs, red and black berries, spices, and well-integrated oak notes in the background. The palate is well structured, with good acidity and freshness, expressive, and with a reasonably round finish given the powerful style.

---

**Marqués de Cáceres**
Area under vine: 5,700 acres (2,300ha) on a long-term contract basis with local growers
Average production: 10 million bottles
Carretera Logroño s/n,
26350 Cenicero, La Rioja
Tel: +34 941 454 000
Fax: +34 941 454 400
www.marquesdecaceres.com

# Viñedos del Contino

One of the most pleasant spots in Rioja for a chat and tasting with friends on a warm spring or summer afternoon is an inviting shady grove behind the cellar facilities at Contino. Between the tree trunks, one can see the orderly and serene lineup of vines growing at Viñedos del Contino, sprinkled here and there with a few century-old trees: in the foreground, the famous olive tree; a little farther on, a couple of majestic holm oaks. In the background, we can make out the River Ebro, meandering around these almost 156 acres (63ha) divided into different plots, whose limits are not always evident to the casual onlooker.

*Every once in a while there are certain (sadly) very limited releases of wines under the personal seal of the house's brilliant winemaker Jesús de Madrazo*

On these sandy-limestone soils covered with pebbles are vineyards with rotund names: Olivo, of course, but also Juanrona, San Gregorio Encina, San Gregorio Grande, Don Vicente, Ribera Viconsa, and El Triángulo. No one will be surprised to hear that the vastly predominant variety is Tempranillo, complemented by 10 percent Graciano and slightly under 5 percent Mazuela, as well as a few acres planted with Viura and some Garnacha (both red and white)—or Garnacho, in the local nomenclature. Contino uses only a small part of the production in every vintage; the rest is sold to other producers.

On a corner of the Olivo vineyard, a little Cabernet Franc can be found, planted by José de Madrazo in the 1970s. The house co-founder was in love with French wines, and he also decided to bid seriously for the local possibilities of Gamay, thinking especially of its potential performance in carbonic maceration. Gamay was ultimately discarded, and a few years ago the vines were regrafted to Graciano, while the Cabernet Franc yields musts of excellent quality, year in, year out; these go into some experimental cuvées.

Every once in a while, there are certain (sadly) very limited releases of wines under the personal seal of the house's brilliant winemaker Jesús de Madrazo. These cuvées contribute to the great interest permanently generated around Contino among today's most passionate wine lovers. A perfect example would be Contino Blanco, a variable blend of Viura, Malmsey (the enologist's personal hunch), and Garnacha Blanca produced since 2006. The evolution of this very limited production is carefully tracked with a view to a future release once the company is fully convinced that the project has reached its maximum potential. These are not properly commercial releases, but they are available from the cellar door, at very good prices. The best is yet to come with the 2009 vintage, but in the meantime, 2006, 2007, and 2008 are different enough in style to be enjoyed for comparative purposes: 2006 is opulent and fat, and 2008 is extremely precise, 2007 being somewhere in between. They are still trying to find their style, but in the interim period, it is a truly fascinating process to witness.

Production started in the early 1970s following the Bordelais château model—a concept that Contino and Remelluri simultaneously pioneered in Rioja, where traditionally fruit from different vineyards would be blended, and winemaking facilities were located in the towns with the best connections, often a long way from the vineyards. In those early days, the key individuals were José de Madrazo and Ricardo Pérez Calvet. Less known is the decisive role played—purely for the sake of passion and personal friendship—by one of the fundamental figures of Rioja in the last third of the 20th century: Manuel Llano Gorostiza. It was

**Right:** Jesús de Madrazo, the brilliant but modest winemaker at Contino, who crafts a superb range of highly rated wines

Gorostiza who designed the San Gregorio logo, documented the historic origins of the Contino Don Pedro de Samaniego, and persuaded the owners to change the name of the firm, which was originally known as Sociedad Vinícola Laserna. For the first 20 years, the winemaker there was cellar master Basilio Izquierdo of CVNE.

Today, the production lies in the hands of the co-founders' children: on the one hand, we find Ricardo Pérez Villota, current manager of Contino and co-owner with his three brothers of 50 percent of the company (the other 50 percent belongs to CVNE); on the other, enologist Jesús de Madrazo, for a while assistant and disciple to Izquierdo until he took over in the late 1990s. De Madrazo is a Seville-born Bilbaíno whose ancestry is doubly related to Rioja winemaking, because his father's family also bears the name Real de Asúa, the same as the founders of CVNE. As if all this were not enough, Jesús also descends from the renowned branch of Madrazo painters of Cantabria, who in turn were related to the Fortuny family.

A simple anecdote, by now a decade old, illustrates the enologist's temperament. About a dozen wine lovers invited to the cellar had gathered and engaged in friendly conversation when Jesús de Madrazo arrived and quietly joined the party without anyone noticing. After a while he came up with a joke as naturally as one who had spent his whole life there (which is, by the way, almost true), and it was only then that the group noticed his presence and introductions were made and greetings exchanged. Shortly afterward began a series of comprehensive vertical tastings that would prove truly memorable. They took place precisely there, in the intimate grove behind the Contino cellars, facing the precious vineyards that were the source of the wines.

**Left:** The ancient olive tree amid the vines gives its name to one of Contino's greatest and longest-lived wines, Viña del Olivo

## FINEST WINES

### Contino Reserva

The house label, produced every vintage since 1974. Recent vintages such as **2001 [V]**, **2004 [V]**, and **2005 [V]** are certainly recommended, but these are wines that display their full potential only after 20–25 years. The already well-worn discussion about the merits of the **1982** vintage versus the **1981** could be solved, at least for us, by choosing the **1980**. Moreover, **1985** and **1986** are not far off those two celebrated vintages when it comes to the perfect expression of mature Rioja.

### Contino Graciano

Among Contino's modern-style wines, we generally prefer the idiosyncratic Graciano—a varietal bottling pioneered in 1994—versus the more expensive and exclusive Viña del Olivo. It is just a matter of personal taste, which in our case tends to favor fresh and well-structured acidity over higher concentration and raw power. **2000** is one of our favorite vintages, though barrel samples suggest that the **2009★** will be the best so far.

### Contino Viña del Olivo

Viña del Olivo is not a wine to show at its best on release. It has a lot of power, in both fruit and tannic structure, so needs time to integrate. At the release stage, it's often a matter of debate whether such a fusion will ever be accomplished—it's a matter, at any rate, that demands previous knowledge of the wine and its maker. If you were looking for evidence that this is one of the most reliable houses, all you have to do is reach for Contino Viña del Olivo **1996★**: a superlative wine, round and harmonious, the living proof that the best modern Riojas eventually turn classic in profile. On the nose there is a hint of olives, powerful and spicy, accented by creamy, coffee, and roasted notes. The palate is well structured and savory, with fresh acidity and an aftertaste that echoes the nose. The finish is simply fantastic: extremely long, full, and complex. A superb wine.

> **Viñedos del Contino**
> Area under vine: 155 acres (63ha)
> Average production: 300,000 bottles
> Finca San Rafael, 01321 Laserna, Álava
> Tel: +34 945 600 201
> Fax: +34 945 621 114
> www.contino.es

# Compañía de Vinos Telmo Rodríguez

We are all familiar with the term "flying winemaker." But Telmo Rodríguez, Spain's most celebrated itinerant vigneron, prefers the term "driving winemaker," which certainly gives more of a flavor of his lifestyle as he travels across Spain. Born into the family that owns Remelluri in Rioja, Rodríguez has lived wine since he was a baby. He studied in Bordeaux and worked for three years at Cos d'Estournel before setting off on a voyage that saw him meet and work with Clape in Cornas, Chave in Hermitage, the Perrins at Beaucastel, and Eloi Durbach at Trévallon in Provence. He then worked in the family winery for ten years, until he decided that he needed to make his own wine, to make it

*Born into the family that owns Remelluri in Rioja, Telmo Rodríguez has lived wine since he was a baby and is altogether rather successful at it*

exactly the way he wanted to. He works with other Spanish winemakers—the most important of whom is Pablo Egurkiza, disciple of Jean-Claude Berrouet de Pétrus and also educated in Bordeaux. Together they are rediscovering many appellations in Spain, as well as working in the classical regions, making wines north, south, east, and west and being altogether rather successful at it.

This is not a matter of one or two wines. Rodríguez makes ten, 15, 20, or more, in Toro, Ribera del Duero, Rueda, and Rioja, of course, but also Cebreros, Madrid, Cigales, Navarra, Valdeorras, and Alicante. He employs a young enologist in the various locations, rents space in a winery, and draws up agreements with viticulturists or wine producers, always in search of "wines with soul." Rodríguez's modus operandi is to enter a region by working with a local grower, to make a simple—

and inexpensive—wine. As he does this, he begins to understand the region, the character of the grapes, the soil, and the climate. Then he looks for exceptional vineyards to create a top bottling. This was the case in Toro, where he made Dehesa Gago and Gago before Pago La Jara, and in Rioja, where Lanzaga predates the top label Altos de Lanzaga.

The concept is quite Burgundian; simpler, négociant wines are made from sourced grapes and sold cheaper, whereas his own domaine wines (Matallana, Molino Real, and Pegaso can be added to those we've already mentioned), are limited in quantity and higher in price and quality, mostly single-vineyard wines from very old vines and extremely low yields.

The attention paid to the vineyards and the desire to work with the best grapes led Rodríguez to follow organic principles and, later, to start experimenting with biodynamics. This has called for a great deal of work in the vineyards, as he undertakes the slow conversion to these practices, and Rodríguez is currently in the process of certifying the vineyards with Demeter, the best-known certifying authority for biodynamics.

Relentlessly searching for forgotten areas and wines, he is interested in preserving traditions and preventing old regions and wine styles from disappearing under the pressure of commercial wines. He likes to talk to the older members of the community, asking how things were done in the past, how wines were made, how they tasted.

Rodríguez once heard Hugh Johnson OBE talk about a magical sweet wine from Málaga (a story we can all read in Johnson's autobiography *Wine: A Life Uncorked*), and he couldn't get it out of his head. He went to Málaga and talked to everyone. He walked the few remaining vineyards and selected the best spot. He inquired at Château d'Yquem about how to make sweet wine in barrel,

**Right:** Telmo Rodríguez, the self-styled "driving winemaker" who is among the most celebrated producers in Spain

**Above:** The wood and stainless steel at Telmo Rodríguez's new winery exemplifies his embracing of traditional and modern

and he experimented time and time again. Finally, the 1998 vintage turned out as he wanted, and the first Molino Real Mountain Wine was born. "Mountain wine" is what the British called this style of wine in the 18th century, and the example that had so enchanted Johnson had Molino del Rey written on the label.

Rodríguez is a true Riojano at heart, however, and the headquarters of his company is in Rioja. After many years spent traveling country roads and the world's airports like a rolling stone, he has finally settled. In January 2009 he moved to a brand-new winery at Lanciego, surrounded, as is his wont, by vines. Lanciego, in Álava, is at the foot of the Sierra de Cantabria mountains, where Rodríguez feels the blend between the Mediterranean and Atlantic influences is in better balance. He has vineyards with names such as Las Beatas, Guardaviñas—surrounded by olive trees—Viña Veriquete and Viña Venicio, usually old bush vines planted on a mixture of red and yellow soils. As many anticipated, in 2010 Rodríguez also went back to the family property of Remelluri, which he now runs together with his sister Amaia.

Though the biggest source for white wine has always been Rueda in Castilla y León, it was only a matter of time before Rodríguez did something in Galicia. In this case, the appellation that aroused his curiosity was not the obvious Rías Baixas but the obscure Valdeorras, where the white Godello grape and the red Mencía have the potential to produce wines of great personality.

Obviously, the vineyards are at the heart of the Rodríguez wines, but image is also something very important here, and Rodríguez works with famous artists, painters, photographers, and designers. The labels stand comparison with any in the world, as does the website, where you can see beautiful photographs of the many different regions in which he deploys his talents.

## FINEST WINES

Rioja represents only a small portion of the wines made by Telmo Rodríguez, and other areas are also very much worth exploring (Toro, Ribera del Duero, Rueda, Alicante, Málaga, and lesser-known Ávila or Cigales) but are not the subject of this book. To cover the northwest of Spain, we will also take a peek at his wines from Galicia. In general, the style of the wines is as close as possible to tradition, with as little intervention as possible but using modern techniques where it makes sense. The oak-aged wines are probably the most discussed by wine aficionados, since they show plenty of toasty oak on the nose in their youth, which gives them a modern profile. This smoky character is then absorbed after some years in bottle, and in fact these wines then age magnificently and into a very traditional style.

### Gaba do Xil [V]

A red from Mencía and a white from Godello, both from the Valdeorras appellation in Galicia, specifically from vineyards located in the tiny parish of Santa Cruz, belonging to Carballeda in the southeast of the province of Orense. The vines are found on steep slopes with rocky and acidic soils rich in granite. Both colors are fermented in stainless-steel tanks and bottled early without any aging in wood in order to retain their fruitiness. This is the region most recently added to the company's portfolio, so they are still in the phase of learning and understanding the region before attempting to make a top-end wine. But with the potential of the region and local grapes, it will certainly come.

### Lanzaga

The company also produces a wine called LZ, young juicy unoaked Tempranillo, whose name implies a little Lanzaga. Lanzaga is an oak-aged Rioja, mainly Tempranillo from 30 acres (12ha) of their own head-pruned vineyards worked biodynamically, plus another 20 acres (8ha) purchased from growers following *lutte raisonnée*. Located around Lanciego de Álava and bearing names such as Atalaya, Majadales, Arroyo la Losa, Pasocastillo, and Soto, the vineyards average 40 years of age and are situated at 1,640ft (500m) above sea level. The fruit is fermented in cement vats with wild yeasts and then aged for 14 months in 1,500-liter and 2,000-liter *foudres* and also 225-liter barriques. Some 25,000 bottles of this wine are produced yearly. We favor the **2006**, from an unusual vintage, but also recommend the **2001** and **1998**.

### Altos de Lanzaga★

This is the top Telmo Rodríguez wine from Rioja, from seven separate plots adding up to 10 acres (4ha) in total, cultivated according to biodynamic principles (in the process of being certified by Demeter), mainly Tempranillo with a little Garnacha and Graciano. The grapes are fermented with wild yeasts in small oak vats—they hold 6,600lb (3,000kg)—and are then aged for 18 months in 1,500-liter *foudres* and oak barriques. The wine was first produced in 1999, and production is limited to 4,500 bottles. The **2001** has a nice, dark pomegranate color and intense aromas with ripe black fruit and floral notes. Medium-bodied with good acidity, it is both supple and structured, and the lively tannins suggest a long life in bottle.

**Compañía de Vinos Telmo Rodríguez**
Average production: 100,000 bottles in Valdeorras and 110,000 in Rioja. Total production of the company is much higher.
El Monte s/n, 01308 Lanciego, Álava
Tel: +34 945 628 315
Fax: +34 945 628 314
www.telmorodriguez.com

# Finca Valpiedra / Viña Bujanda

When the large Martínez Bujanda group was unexpectedly split in June 2007, Carlos Martínez Bujanda and his sister Pilar kept all the non-Rioja holdings—essentially the huge Finca Antigua estate in La Mancha, the table-wine-producing company Cosecheros y Criadores, and the fledgling Rueda winery Cantos de Rueda. In Rioja, they basically had the unique Valpiedra vineyard and winery, lovingly built since the early 1970s by the family, which was the first member from the region of the Grandes Pagos de España ("Great Growths of Spain") association. But they also had to invent a range of less expensive wines to replace the profitable Conde de Valdemar and Valdemar lines, which were left in the hands of their brother Jesús in his new separate venture, and for that they have been using an appreciable collection of younger vineyards.

The family's obsession with creating its own core of vineyards, which has been a constant feature since it began making wine in 1889 but really took off in the 1980s, has turned into quite an asset for the brothers after the breakup.

Valpiedra is the cornerstone of the new group. Its 200 acres (80ha) produce not only their two single-vineyard wines—Finca Valpiedra and the new, more modest Cantos de Valpiedra—but a sizable amount of the grapes that go into the new Viña Bujanda portfolio, which also relies on an excellent holding of vineyards, all of them near Logroño, in both Rioja Alta (or Media, "middle," if you will—the status of the Logroño area has always been under discussion) and Rioja Alavesa.

In more harmonious times, almost four decades ago, the whole of Martínez Bujanda was united in its dream: Finca Valpiedra. At the time, single-estate wines were foreign to the Rioja concept of brand-name wines made from various

**Right:** Carlos and Pilar Martínez Bujanda, working to realize the full potential of the privileged Finca Valpiedra vineyard

*At an altitude slightly above 1,310ft (400m), well protected from Atlantic storms by the Sierra de Cantabria and with reasonable average rainfall, Finca Valpiedra has everything required to produce outstanding wines*

sources, including large amounts of grapes bought from small growers. But Valpiedra and another estate, Contino, which is 9 miles (15km) down river, changed all that. The winemaking facility at Contino, however, was built much earlier, and its wines became well known in the 1980s. Not so at Valpiedra, where the winery dates back only as far as 1999.

The land itself is spectacular, with the River Ebro and the riverbank trees harmoniously framing the picturesque vineyards, which cover three terraces, first planted in 1972, with new plots in 1992, 1994, 2000, and 2004. It's almost all Tempranillo, with a little Graciano and Cabernet Sauvignon and a tiny plot of white grapes. Then, on the third terrace, the great black hope: 10 acres (4ha) of the hugely promising Maturana Tinta, which were harvested for the first time in the 2010 vintage.

The soil is basically sandy loam and limestone, covered with *graves*, alluvial rolling stones. This is what gave the estate its name—Valpiedra ("Stone Valley"). The rocky surface retains the heat and also prevents vine dehydration by retarding the rapid evaporation of water during hot summer days. Another important feature is the high calcium content, combined with good levels of other nutrients (nitrogen, phosphorus, and potassium) and micronutrients such as copper and iron.

At an altitude slightly above 1,310ft (400m), well protected from Atlantic storms by the Sierra de Cantabria, and with reasonable average rainfall of about 20in (500mm), Finca Valpiedra has everything required to produce outstanding wines. It is only recently, however, that it has really begun to fulfill its potential.

The winery itself is equipped with 31 small (for Rioja, where everything seems big) 250hl individually temperature-controlled stainless-steel vats, which make it possible to vinify each plot separately. The grapes are harvested by hand,

transported in small crates, and go over a sorting table: the whole modern, quality winemaking environment. The new winemaker, Lauren Rosillo, who came from Finca Antigua with excellent credentials, began making good use of it in his first three harvests.

Further east, the panoply of vineyards now devoted to the new Viña Bujanda lines are on good-quality terroirs, both clay-limestone and red clay. But these parcels are much younger (the oldest having been planted in 1984) and of less homogeneous quality.

In the current economic climate, this large-production portfolio of moderately priced wines may well hold the key to the future financial success of the reborn Martínez Bujanda group. Until now, the lineup has been extremely simple: only three wines, all of them red, all of them 100 percent Tempranillo. One is a *joven*, fresh and unoaked; the second, called Madurado, is similar but spends three months in American oak; and the third is a classic crianza, which spends a year in small oak barrels (70 percent American, 30 percent French).

The wines have been well received. They are clean with good varietal expression, fruit-driven, and attractively priced. But of course they have to compete with better-established brand names, including one from the same family that got away: Valdemar. So, for that crucial part of the business there are still many unanswered questions.

For that reason, the importance of Finca Valpiedra as the prestige wine that will have to buttress the rest of the production increases significantly. The challenge over the next few years for Carlos and Pilar Martínez Bujanda will be to place and maintain Valpiedra at the very top of the Rioja hierarchy, alongside such wines as Viña El Pison, Contino, or Benjamín Romeo's cuvées. The estate has shown its potential. It now needs to fulfill it consistently.

**Above:** The smart, relatively new Valpiedra winery, where recent vintages of the flagship wine have been better balanced than ever

## FINEST WINES

Finca Valpiedra, from the fine vineyard surrounded by the River Ebro, is a Tempranillo-dominated blend that has better balance and more weight, in addition to its well-known smoothness, since the arrival of Lauren Rosillo, a young, motivated, and extremely talented winemaker.

### Finca Valpiedra's vineyards (with date of planting)
*First terrace*
La Casa: 37 acres (15ha) Tempranillo, 1972
La Vía: 40 acres (16ha) Tempranillo, 1972
El Monte: 35 acres (14ha) Tempranillo, 1972
Los Manzanos: 40 acres (16ha) Tempranillo, 1972
El Cabernet: 5 acres (2ha) Cabernet Sauvignon, 1980

*Second terrace*
La Calera: 30 acres (12ha) Tempranillo/Graciano, 1975
La Peña del Gato: 2 acres (0.8ha) Viura, 1980;
   Malvasia, 2008

*Third terrace*
Ribera del Ebro: 10 acres (4ha) Maturana, 2008

**Finca Valpiedra / Viña Bujanda**
Area under vine: 500 acres (200ha)
Average production: 1 million bottles
Término Montecillo s/n,
26360 Fuenmayor, La Rioja
Tel: +34 941 450 876
www.familiamartinezbujanda.com

# Amézola de la Mora

Despite the traditional style of its wines, this is a fairly young winery, a family business created in 1987. Their 173 acres (70ha) of vineyards, planted with Tempranillo, Mazuelo, and Graciano, surround the winery in the outskirts of the ghost village of Torremontalvo (population 17) in Rioja Alta, in the château style. The old stone buildings also feel like a real château.

The property, founded in the first half of the 19th century, had already been in the Amézola de la Mora family for three generations when phylloxera struck and winemaking was abandoned. Wine production was resumed when brothers Íñigo and Javier decided to restore the old cellars and to create the current winery—a task that was not completed until 1999 and that integrated the original buildings and facilities with new ones

*The original buildings are integrated with the new ones in exactly the same style, to blend both old and new, tradition and modernity— which is also the aim with their wines*

in exactly the same style, to blend both old and new, tradition and modernity—which is also the aim with their wines. Today, Íñigo's daughters Cristina and María take care of the business.

They own some caves excavated from the rock in 1816, which makes for a good tourist attraction, since these are some of the most beautiful caves in Rioja. It is logical that they offer visits and other wine-tourism activities, such as tastings, dinners, and visits to the area on horseback, as well as moving into art exhibitions, theater performances, and classical concerts. They offer on-demand visits in Spanish, English, or French.

As for the wines, they use only their own grapes, which are hand-harvested into 33lb (15kg) cases and then put over a sorting table for selection.

The clusters are destemmed and the grapes fermented in stainless steel. The wine is aged in oak barrels made of American and French wood, where they spend substantially more time than the minimum stipulated for the different categories of crianza, reserva, and gran reserva. The wines are fined and filtered before being bottled, then spend time in the cellars to settle and stabilize before release. They have also recently started producing olive oil under the Albomont brand.

## FINEST WINES

The broad range of wines includes a rosado (Flor de Amézola), a tinto crianza (Viña Amézola), and a tinto reserva (Señorío de Amézola).

### Solar de Amézola

This is the gran reserva red wine, made with 85% Tempranillo, 10% Mazuelo, and 5% Graciano, aged for 30 months in 25% new wood, 60% of which is American and the rest French. The **1999** is the perfect example of a traditional Rioja gran reserva, full of red fruits, tobacco, and leather aromas, while remaining polished and fresh on the palate.

### Íñigo Amézola ★

This top-of-the-line wine, which bears the name of one of the founders and comes from the best vineyard (San Quiles), is slightly more modern in style. It is pure Tempranillo, with malolactic fermentation carried out in barrel and aging for ten months in new barrels, half French and half American. It was very good in **2001** and **2005**. There is also now an Íñigo Amézola Blanco Fermentado en Barrica, which is 100% Viura.

**Right:** Cristina and María, now running the family estate where winemaking was resumed by their father Íñigo and uncle Javier

---

**Amézola de la Mora**
Area under vine: 173 acres (70ha)
Average production: 300,000 bottles
Paraje Viña Vieja s/n,
26359 Torremontalbo, La Rioja
Tel: +34 941 454 532
Fax: +34 941 454 537
www.bodegasamezola.es

# Bodegas Faustino

Faustino is one of Rioja's best-known producers. Indeed, the frosted Burgundy bottle with the label bearing a Rembrandt-style portrait (contrary to popular belief, the guys you see on the labels are not members of the Faustino clan) is pretty much synonymous with Rioja throughout the world, while Faustino I Gran Reserva is the world's bestselling gran reserva.

The foundations for this success story were laid by Eleuterio Martínez Arzok in 1861 when he bought the palace and vineyards of the Marqués del Puerto in Oyón, in the province of Álava in the Basque Country, but only 3 miles (5km) from Logroño. The main activity was to make wine and sell it in bulk—a good business that grew gradually, both in size and quality. Then, in 1930, Eleuterio's son, Faustino Martínez Pérez de Albéniz, took over and started bottling, an activity in which he was the pioneer in Rioja.

Brand names used in that period were taken from the names of the vineyards—names such as Campillo, Parrita, Famar, and Santana—an identification with the land that was later forgotten for many years, only to return 60 years later or so, when the company introduced some single-vineyard wines.

In 1957, the third generation, Julio Faustino Martínez, took up the reins, and he was responsible for launching Faustino as an international brand. Today, the brand is sold in as many as 47 countries.

The company's vineyards are in some of the best parts of Rioja—mainly in Logroño, Laguardia, Mendavia, and Oyón. Collectively, there are some 1,600 acres (650ha) of Tempranillo, Mazuelo, Graciano, and Viura, which makes Faustino the largest private vineyard owner in the whole of Rioja. The winery holds more than 50,000 oak barrels and a permanent stock of some 9 million bottles—without doubt, the largest bottle collection we've ever seen.

Bodegas Faustino, which remains a strictly family-owned business, has over time expanded to become Grupo Faustino. Other than Faustino itself, this includes Campillo and Marqués de Vitoria, also in Rioja; Valcarlos in Navarra; Condesa de Leganza in La Mancha; Bodegas Portia in Ribera del Duero; and Bodegas Victorianas, which offers varietal table wines from across Spain.

## FINEST WINES

The traditional style definitely used to be Faustino's flagship. But during the Riojan identity crisis at the end of the 20th century—a period that saw the rejection of traditional styles, largely pushed by market demand—it created a modern wine range with Faustino Crianza Selección de Familia and Faustino de Autor, plus some limited editions, such as Faustino 9 Mil (so named because the company only produced 9,000 liters of it) and Faustino Edición Especial, made 50 years after the first vinification of Julio Faustino Martínez. The traditional wines were produced in the three colors (red, white, and rosado), and they are all called Faustino, followed by a number (written in Roman)—I for the top wines, V for the middle range, VII for the entry level—and then the category (crianza, reserva, or gran reserva). The company also produces Cava, the sparkling wine that is most associated with Catalonia but is produced in different locations, including Rioja. The portfolio of sparkling wines includes Cava Brut Reserva, Cava Extra Seco, Cava Semi Seco, and Cava Rosado.

### Faustino V Blanco
Even though Faustino pioneered the new style of fresh, light, and crisp wines (together with Marqués de Cáceres), it now produces a whole range of white styles. The top three are sold under the Faustino V label: Crianza (brand new in the range, a sign that

**Above:** A sea of vines, like the many belonging to Bodegas Faustino, the largest private owner of vineyards in the whole of Rioja

traditional white Rioja is definitely making a comeback); Blanco Fermentado en Barrica; and a straight Viura that sees no oak, the first two in a Burgundy bottle and the last in a Rhine bottle. The fourth blanco is a fresh and unoaked Viura, labeled as Faustino VII.

### Faustino de Autor

This is the winery's modern wine, named after the trend of the so-called *vinos de autor*, an anti-terroir concept in which the most important thing is the signature of the winemaker. We're not really fans of the concept, but thankfully the Faustino de Autor doesn't take it too literally—it has a clear Rioja style. The **1995** is our favorite for this label.

### Faustino I Gran Reserva

The archetype of classical Gran Rioja, aged for a very long time and released a decade or more after the harvest, with a profile based on red fruit and balsamic notes. We welcome the fact that Faustino still offers what the company refers to as "mythical years" of this wine—**1964**, **1970**, **1981**, and **1994**—while the current release at the end of 2010 is still **1998**, and the previous release was **1996**, which is one of the best recent vintages. This is truly Faustino's top wine, and as such only very good vintages are produced.

**Bodegas Faustino**
Area under vine: 1,600 acres (650ha)
Average production: n/a
Carretera Logroño s/n,
01320 Oyón, Álava
Tel: +34 941 622 500
Fax: +34 941 122 106
www.bodegasfaustino.com

# Bodegas LAN

LAN is simply an acronym for the three provinces included in the Rioja DOC: Logroño (today called La Rioja), Álava, and Navarra. The winery was created around 1972; it's hard to be more precise, since various dates are used—the company, winery, and so on were created at different stages, and the 1974 vintage was the first to be vinified. Initially owned by a group of Basque investors, it was later sold to Rumasa, a big industrial group that ran into problems and was nationalized in 1983. The winery was owned by the government for six months until it was re-privatized and sold to businessman Marcos Eguizábal, who sold it on again after a couple of years to the original investors lead by Juan Celaya. It was finally acquired by the current owners in 2002.

*LAN's flagship vineyard is Viña Lanciano, along the River Ebro. It is planted with vines up to 60 years of age, the source of the higher-range wines like the Edición Limitada*

It's clearly been a bumpy ride. There have been ups and downs and changes in ownership, ranges, styles, and policies that make it a little difficult to get a clear idea of the company's wines and philosophy. For many years, the idea most people had about the wines was that they were rather simple, easy to drink, and produced in quantity. There was a dip in quality during the first half of the 1990s, followed by some crazy prices during the post-1994 Rioja boom. Lately, the wines seem to have improved and to have been made more consistently as the company gains ground.

The winery is located in Fuenmayor, in Rioja Alta. Their flagship vineyard is Viña Lanciano, a 178-acre (72ha) property along the River Ebro, northeast of Fuenmayor. It is planted with Tempranillo, Mazuelo, and Graciano up to 60 years

of age, the source of the higher-range wines Viña Lanciano, Culmen, and LAN Edición Limitada. The property has up to 24 different plots, each with distinctive features, all individually managed and hand-harvested. It also has some vineyards under contract from local growers and buys in grapes, since their own grapes barely cover their needs.

One of the distinctive features of the winery is the monumental aging cellar, which is often compared to a cathedral (though it looks more like an old train station to us). Constructed without columns, its 68,900-sq-ft (6,400-sq-m) floor space holds some 25,000 barrels that are stacked, handled, and racked using an elaborate crane system and the most advanced temperature-control technology.

Like most Rioja wineries, LAN has focused on red wines (and only oak-aged ones). But under its new owners (since 2002), investment group Mercapital, it has also acquired a winery in Rías Baixas as a source for white wines produced from Albariño—the historic Santiago Ruiz winery, one of the pioneers of Albariño in the O Rosal district.

## FINEST WINES

LAN Crianza, Reserva and Gran Reserva represent the largest volume, but the following three wines are made from grapes from the Lanciano vineyard, making them their finest estate wines.

### Viña Lanciano
This is the classic-style bottling within the estate wines from LAN, made with 80% Tempranillo and 20% Mazuelo and aged in a mixture of American and French oak barrels for 24 months. Vintages of Viña Lanciano such as **1996** can still be found at more or less the same price as the current vintage, so they are well worth looking for.

### LAN Edición Limitada
This is the most modern wine in the portfolio. The grapes are from El Rincón vineyard, and they are 85% Tempranillo, 10% Mazuelo, and 5% Graciano. The wine is aged for five months in new French oak barrels and another four months in new Russian oak barrels, before being bottled with neither fining nor filtration.

## Culmen

There was a shift toward more concentration and a slightly more modern profile with the creation of Culmen in the 1994 vintage. The wine was quite controversial because it was released with a huge marketing campaign and a similarly sized price tag that was hardly justified by the quality and the quantity of the wine. For subsequent vintages, the price level was reduced to a more realistic figure. This is a selection of the oldest vines, 85% Tempranillo and 15% Graciano, from the plot called El Rincón within the company's Viña Lanciano. It is fermented in small conical vats to maximize skin contact and color extraction, with the malolactic taking place in new French oak barrels, before aging 18 months in new wood and another 18 months in bottle. It is only produced in select vintages.

The Culmen Reserva from **2004** is the best wine we have yet tasted from the winery. It is dark in color, almost opaque, with an intense perfumed and fine nose with high quality toasty oak tones, a good structure in the mouth, correct acidity and density, and a remarkable finish.

### Bodegas LAN

Area under vine: 200 acres (80ha)
Average production: 4 million bottles
Paraje Buicio s/n,
26360 Fuenmayor, La Rioja
Tel: +34 941 450 950
Fax: +34 941 450 567
www.bodegaslan.com

# Valdemar

Few family businesses have split with quite as much publicity in Spain in the past decade as the erstwhile Martínez Bujanda group, whose best-known brand was Conde de Valdemar. Valdemar is now one of the two companies that emerged from the split, along roughly equal lines, of the group's holdings in the Rioja appellation. And here Jesús Martínez Bujanda—well known internationally as the former public face for the whole group—is on his own.

In a region where many large bodegas have not traditionally felt the need to own large areas of vineyard but have relied on bought-in grapes, the Martínez Bujandas have been known for building up their portfolio, particularly under Jesús's leadership over the past three decades. Now he finds himself managing almost 500 acres (200ha), most of which are in Rioja Baja, 22 miles (36km) from the winery, which is in Rioja Alavesa.

*Innovation has always been one of Jesús's strong suits—he made the first barrel-fermented white in Rioja from his outstanding Alto de Cantabria vineyard*

Innovation has always been one of Jesús's strong suits—he made the first barrel-fermented white in Rioja from his outstanding Alto de Cantabria vineyard, now owned by Valdemar, as well as the first Garnacha Reserva and the first Cabernet Sauvignon Reserva. The family also pioneered the production of rosé wines by the *saignée* method in Rioja. So, logically, more of the same was expected from him after the 2007 split.

Indeed, in addition to the continuation of the Valdemar and Conde de Valdemar lines, with that slightly high-toned, brisk style that some attribute to higher doses of Mazuelo in the red blends than other bodegas usually employ, the new company has led with its Inspiración Valdemar line—offbeat reds, including a varietal Graciano and several Cabernet Sauvignon-dominated blends.

In the 2005 vintage, Valdemar produced its first Inspiración Maturana Tinta varietal—a stunning introduction to this recently recovered (and officially admitted) native Rioja red grape. The stylistic kinship between Maturana Tinta, with its black-pepper and bell-pepper notes, and the Bordeaux Biturica family, which includes the two Cabernets and Merlot, is truly striking, and DNA fingerprinting may yet prove a genetic link. Then in 2009, the first 250 cases of barrel-fermented Tempranillo Blanco were made in the Oyón winery. This mutation is the most promising of the newly admitted white varieties in the region.

## FINEST WINES

### Conde de Valdemar Fermentado en Barrica
This is the 100% Viura, unusually fleshy and sunny, that pioneered barrel-fermented whites in the area as a whole.

### Inspiración Valdemar Maturana Tinta
First made in the outstanding **2005** vintage, this wine may shock Rioja traditionalists, but it is nevertheless a fine, pungent, deep red—and currently all on its own as a varietal wine.

### Conde de Valdemar Gran Reserva
This is a personal albeit traditional Rioja, with its marked acidity and freshness. Particularly fine in ripe vintages like **2001**.

**Right:** Jesús Martínez Bujanda, who is successfully maintaining his reputation for innovation with several striking new wines

Valdemar
Area under vine: 477 acres (193ha)
Average production: 100,000 bottles
Camino Viejo s/n,
01320 Oyón, Álava
Tel: +34 945 622 188
Fax: +34 945 622 111
www.valdemar.es

# Bodegas Montecillo

Montecillo is one of the historical names of Rioja. It was founded in 1874, during the Rioja boom of the 19th century, making it one of the oldest in the whole region. Montecillo can be translated as "Little Hill" or "Little Mount" and is the name of a small vineyard hill on the outskirts of Fuenmayor in Rioja Alta. It was developed by José Luis Navajas, grandson of Celestino Navajas Matute, who started a winery in 1874. His work was continued by his sons Alejandro and Gregorio under the name Bodega de Hijos de Celestino Navajas. In 1947, the name of the vineyard and the brand—very popular by then—was also adopted as the name for the company: Bodegas Montecillo.

In 1973 there was no one from the family to take over, since the proprietors didn't have any siblings, so the firm was sold to the Osborne family from Jerez and incorporated into their vast portfolio of wine and other drinks. They sold the estate with all the vineyards that then became Finca Valpiedra under the Martinez Bujanda family and focused on building an impressive winery with the objective of preserving quality and tradition through the use of the latest technology and winemaking. Today, they hold no vineyards, relying on producers in Rioja Alta to source their grapes—mostly, if not all, Tempranillo. They represent readily available, traditional Rioja—the wines can be found in supermarkets throughout the world—at competitive prices. They are therefore quite popular in export markets, which represent half their sales volume. The old bottles are well worth pursuing and savoring.

The new winery—first used in the 1975 vintage—is located at Fuenmayor, a popular village in Rioja Alta in wine terms, because it has no fewer than 3,700 acres (1,500ha) under vine and hosts as many as 28 different wineries. Here Montecillo ages the 30,000 barriques of wine it has in stock. Indeed, all the oak barriques

needed by the Osborne Group—for its wineries in Rioja, Malpica de Tajo, and Ribera del Duero—are hand-crafted at Bodegas Montecillo. There has been a gradual move toward French oak rather than American, but overall, Montecillo has remained faithful to the traditional style—not an easy task during the period when this was considered almost heresy.

## FINEST WINES

Montecillo has a broad range under the brands Montecillo, Viña Monty, and Viña Cumbrero, using the various available designations (crianza, reserva, and gran reserva), plus some special ones like **130 Aniversario** and **Selección Especial**. Somewhat confusingly, perhaps, it announced the introduction of Montecillo Verdemar Albariño from the Rías Baixas in Galicia—which has nothing whatsoever to do with Rioja—in 2009.

### Viña Monty
Viña Monty is nowadays present in the crianza and reserva categories (the Viña Monty Gran Reserva seems to have been discontinued), and the wines are still aged in American oak barrels. The good news for white Rioja fans is that, since the end of 2009, a Viña Monty Blanco Fermentado en Barrica has been introduced—further proof of the gradual, stealthy return of white Rioja.

### Montecillo
The whole Montecillo lineup is aged in French oak barrels, keeping an updated traditional style. The Gran Reserva is aged for 30 months in oak barrels, while the Reserva has 18 months, and the Crianza, 14. **Montecillo Gran Reserva Selección Especial 1991** and the **Gran Reserva 1994** rank among their finest wines and are textbook examples of traditional Rioja.

**Bodegas Montecillo**
Area under vine: none
Average production: 4.5 million bottles
Carretera Fuenmayor a Navarrete km 3,
26360 Fuenmayor, La Rioja
Tel: +34 941 440 125
Fax: +34 941 440 663
www.osborne.es

# Bodegas Riojanas

When Banco de Santander—then a mid-sized, strictly Spanish bank that was little known abroad—decided in the late 1960s to invest in the wine world, it asked Víctor de la Serna for advice. The Madrid-based journalist and wine writer was publisher of the *Informaciones* daily newspaper, another Banco de Santander venture, and he was, at the time, busy setting up the International Wine Academy, an august body of which he would soon be the second president. De la Serna did a thorough search of potential candidates among Rioja bodegas of good repute and eventually settled on two finalists. "Of the two, I strongly advised the bank to go for Bodegas Riojanas," he would later recall. "The reason was that it owned a magnificent vineyard portfolio, while the other bodega didn't own any vineyards." And Santander followed his advice.

That now seems like a logical decision, but 40 years ago it wasn't at all evident in Spain, and it was probably de la Serna's lifetime devotion to Burgundy that swayed him. At the time, Rioja was dominated by négociant-type firms that bought most or all of their grapes from contract growers, and the labor and expense involved in exploiting their own vineyards was considered by many a superfluous load. Only a few bodegas, like Riojanas or López de Heredia, were committed to sourcing their grapes from their own estates.

Some 40 years later, Santander has joined the world scene and completely moved out of holdings such as newspapers or wineries. But the Artacho and Frías families, the descendants of the founders, who for some time ran the company with their banking associates, stayed on. In 1997, they turned Bodegas Riojanas into a publicly traded company on the Madrid stock exchange. The company has now expanded into Toro and Rías Baixas.

The Riojanas vineyards are mostly around the town of Cenicero, in what some call "Middle Rioja"—between Haro and Logroño.

Riojanas was founded in 1890 and therefore rightly belongs to the club of historic, 19th-century bodegas headed by Marqués de Riscal and Marqués de Murrieta. The traditional style was maintained over the past two decades by chief winemaker Felipe Nalda Frías and general manager Felipe Frías, who retired in 2009 after 39 years at the bodega. He was succeeded by his son Santiago, a sign of continuity that is typical of the company. The current winemakers are Emilio Sojo Nalda and Marta Nalda—again the strong family connections.

Beneath that continuity, there have been ups and downs in the bodega's more recent history, with unconvincing attempts since the late 1990s to produce more modern, fruitier, oakier wines in the *alta expresión* mode, without producing any memorable results. Also, with the growth of production to more than 3 million bottles, a higher proportion of grapes comes from contract growers.

## FINEST WINES

### Monte Real Gran Reserva
A classic Rioja, this benefits from bottle age after a long stay in American oak. Its profile is powerful and well structured but with no harshness. Today it's a Tempranillo varietal from Cenicero vineyards.

### Viña Albina Gran Reserva
Sourced from limestone vineyards and submitted to the traditional winemaking procedures used for Rioja Fino, including less skin maceration, this is a more delicate wine than Monte Real but has shown great ageworthiness in such vintages as 1942. Today it is sourced from Uruñuela and Huércanos and contains some Mazuelo and Graciano.

---

**Bodegas Riojanas**
Area under vine: 300ha
Average production: 3.5 million bottles
Carretera de la Estación,
26350 Cenicero, La Rioja
Tel: +34 941 454 050
Fax: +34 941 454 529
www.bodegasriojanas.com

# Marqués de Murrieta

The weight of history is extraordinary at Bodegas Marqués de Murrieta, not only because of the century and a half that has passed since its official foundation (1852, the year of its first overseas shipping) and its continuous influence in the destiny of Rioja, but also for its presence—in the highest political circles—at the most decisive moments of the Spanish 1800s.

The key character was the founder, Luciano Murrieta, who doubtless belongs among the most select bunch of protagonists in the history of Rioja wine. Few other lives can illustrate so accurately the convoluted events of the 19th century in Spain as his 90-year-long one (1822–1911). His biography is closely linked to his mentor, the liberal leader General Baldomero Espartero, a stellar figure in the military and political history of Spain.

*The weight of history is extraordinary at Bodegas Marqués de Murrieta, because of its continuous influence in the destiny of Rioja*

Born into a wealthy Spanish-Bolivian family, Murrieta himself suffered the consequences of independence, and he was left behind by his parents in his native Peru when they fled the country after Bolívar's victory. At the age of two, he was sent to London, where his family had financial interests and where he would return in 1843, joining Espartero in his exile. The Wars of the Spanish Succession, and the influence of a branch of his family, kept him away from the world of business to embrace a military career—which he would pursue until 1860, always associated with Espartero, who hired him as his personal assistant and welcomed him into his family, almost like the son he never had. In 1848, Murrieta returned from his London exile (and long visits to Bordeaux),

determined to make his loyalty to the general compatible with the wine business. Murrieta was convinced of the winemaking potential of Rioja if Bordelais methods were applied in vineyard and cellar—just as Manuel Quintano had preached six decades before. At this moment, the role of the general was decisive again: having settled in Logroño after his marriage to a wealthy heiress, he loaned Murrieta his vineyards and cellar so he could put his ideas into practice. For a decade, the young Luciano still found time to dabble at winemaking while continuing his military career. While also looking after his aging mother, he pursued his winemaking experiments and laid the basis for the development of his business.

The key years were 1870–72, when Spain's King Amadeo I granted him the title of Marquis of Murrieta (and Espartero the title of Prince of Vergara), and he purchased the Finca Ygay, in the surroundings of Logroño, where he immediately started the building of the cellar facilities. As he relates in his memoirs, the title opened many a door for him, and the Ygay estate and cellar made his lifelong dream come true. After that came years of success and consolidation, helped by the crisis of French producers—devastated by mildew, oidium, and phylloxera—and also by the growing functionality of the Northern Railway, which stopped at Alfaro, Calahorra, Logroño, Cenicero, and Haro, conveniently crossing Rioja from east to west.

Murrieta had no children, so on his death the company passed to a collateral branch of the family, where it remained for several generations in the 20th century. After some years of relative decay, it was bought in 1983 by another noble family, of which the visible head since 1996 has been Vicente Dalmau Cebrián-Sagarriga, who has been deeply involved from a young age in the consolidation of the winery's

**Right:** Vicente Dalmau Cebrián-Sagarriga, of the owning family, and winemaker María Vargas, both at Ygay from a young age

quality and prestige. Bodegas Marqués de Murrieta has been much renovated and modernized, and crucial in that process has been the role played by winemaker María Vargas, appointed production manager, also at a very young age, in 2000.

The house uses only estate-grown grapes from Finca Ygay, which covers hundreds of acres, including the cellar and castle, baptized by Luciano as Château Ygay. Of this surface, 750 acres (300ha) of vineyards are in production, mainly of Tempranillo but also Mazuelo, Garnacha, Viura, and Graciano, with smaller amounts of Cabernet Sauvignon, Chardonnay, and Garnacha Blanca. The sites vary, though in general they share warm, alluvial, sedimentary soils with excellent draining capacity. As a result, the grapes tend to be rich in coloring matter and sugar, which accounts for the traditional Murrieta character: fat, highly pigmented, and slightly higher in alcohol.

The way Murrieta has adapted to the times has sometimes been controversial. As far as reds are concerned, there was the groundbreaking release of Dalmau—the archetypal modern Rioja, in which concentration, extraction, ripeness, and new oak are paramount. On the other hand, they have retained traditional labels like Castillo Ygay Gran Reserva Especial and Marqués de Murrieta Reserva. Both, but especially the latter, have experienced a serious transformation: fruit notes are more clearly perceptible now, and the tannic structure owes more to new French oak than to reused American oak barrels. The resulting wines are closer to international winemaking models and less clearly typical Riojas. At the same time, we must also note the higher cleanliness and precision found in recent vintages of Marqués de Murrieta Reserva, though it often reaches the market with tougher tannins than one would expect to find in a wine such as this.

**Left:** The evocative name of Ygay on the gatepost of the legendary estate purchased by Luciano Murrieta in the 1870s

## FINEST WINES

### Capellanía (and historic vintages of white wines)
Fans of now-lost El Dorado de Murrieta have reasons to lament its disappearance: it was a singular white wine in a markedly oxidative style, of high acidity, and touched by a characteristic note of fine carpentry. On a more positive note, its replacement, Capellanía (100% Viura, 18 months in oak) is superior in finesse and fruit freshness, though sometimes overwhelmed by oak, even if we would have loved El Dorado to remain on the market. In any case, Capellanía is a trustworthy candidate for a white *vin de garde*, especially when we consider its moderate price. Now that we mention old wines, in Spain it is still possible to find bottles from the first two-thirds of the 20th century of the magnificent Castilo Ygay Blanco★ in many different versions and vintages. As a rule, these bottles have shown excellent aging capacity and the ability to evolve gracefully, even under questionable cellaring conditions. No self-respecting wine lover should skip the opportunity to sample these jewels.

### Castillo Ygay Gran Reserva Especial
This wine has always aimed for Riojan classicism, if perhaps in the opulent and warm style characteristic of Murrieta: ruby with a brick rim, a nose of cherry liqueur and fine leather, medium body and fine acidity, with the odd volatile note at times and an overall impression of elegance. However, after the 2000 vintage, it has been somewhat revamped, with a bid for more fruit and a dollop of new oak at some point in its long aging—a risky decision, and the evolution in bottle will demand some attention. There is no Garnacha or Graciano in the blend—not even the small doses that were traditional—in order to give full voice to Tempranillo and Mazuelo, both from old vines sourced from the highest vineyards of Finca Ygay. María Vargas prizes Mazuelo as an ideal partner for Tempranillo, providing great aromatics and good acidity, especially in wines that undergo such prolonged aging.

**Marqués de Murrieta**
Area under vine: 750 acres (300ha)
Average production: 1.5 million bottles
Carretera Zaragoza km 5, 26006 Logroño, La Rioja
Tel: +34 941 271 370
Fax: +34 941 251 606
www.marquesdemurrieta.com

# Marqués de Vargas

The noble title of Marqués de Vargas is held by a Rioja family that has been closely related to the wine industry since 1840, when Felipe de Mata, the eighth Marqués de Vargas, planted the first vines in his Hacienda Pradolagar estate outside Logroño. Later, Hilario de la Mata was for many years the chairman and main shareholder of the historic Bodegas Franco-Españolas. His son, Pelayo de la Mata, the current Marqués de Vargas, realized his father's dream by building a winery on the hacienda.

Since then, the winery has been self-sustained, like a Bordeaux château, with Javier Pérez Ruiz de Vergara as winemaker. The current Marqués is the chairman of the powerful beverage distribution group Varma, which helped establish the new wines in the market.

*The vines are not irrigated, and organic viticultural practices are in place. "We treat our vineyards as though they were the most refined garden," enthuses de la Mata*

The 160 acres (65ha) planted with traditional red varieties Tempranillo, Mazuelo, Graciano, and Garnacha produce three cuvées, all of them in the reserva category. "We treat our vineyards as though they were the most refined garden," enthuses de la Mata.

The soil is a classic clay-limestone Rioja terroir, very poor in nutrients but giving fine-quality fruit. The vines are not irrigated, and organic viticultural practices are in place—so no pesticides or herbicides are used. Green harvesting is applied if needed to keep yields in balance—that is, between 28 and 35hl/ha.

The winery is technically sound, and it includes a large barrel room, since all the wines are aged in oak. Fine-grained American, French, and Russian barrels are used. As the winemaker points out, "We only want those barrels whose growth rings show the greatest quantity of spring wood, which is excellent for the aging of wines meant for a long life." Several toast levels are combined, with the aim of greater complexity.

The wines are neither fined nor filtered, and some of the better vintages have indeed shown excellent ageworthiness.

The winery raised some eyebrows when it was announced that its top wine would be aged exclusively in new Russian oak—a move apparently designed to give it a more original note and one that would set it apart from its competitors. But the intrinsic quality of Russian oak being what it is, this was a move that never fully convinced the critics. Nevertheless, the Russian oak barrels are still being used today.

## FINEST WINES

### Marqués de Vargas Reserva Privada

This wine is blended from a selection of grapes from the most favored plots within the estate, such as the El Cónsul, La Misela, and Terrazas vineyards. This is not a small cuvée, since the annual production hovers around 45,000 bottles and 1,500 magnums. It is aged 24 months in new Russian oak barrels. The deep color—a characteristic of Tempranillo grapes from these Middle Rioja terroirs—is a regular feature, as are the balsamic notes (leather and tobacco) from the oak. It is a big, somewhat monolithic wine when young but one that rewards bottle age.

**Right:** Pelayo de la Mata, Marqués de Vargas, who realized his father's dream of building a winery on the family estate

**Marqués de Vargas**
Area under vine: 160 acres (65ha)
Average production: 300,000 bottles
Carretera de Zaragoza km 6,
26006 Logroño, La Rioja
Tel: +34 941 261 401
Fax: +34 941 238 696
www.marquesdevargas.com

# Palacios Remondo

José Palacios, an Alfaro grower who had the foresight to build a modern (for the period) winery back in 1948, took one more step in the early 1980s as he decided to concentrate on quality, bottled wines only. This was unheard of in Rioja Baja, the warm, dry, Mediterranean-influenced eastern end of Rioja that has forever been pooh-poohed by snooty Alta and Alavesa types and seemed destined to produce modest bulk wines only. Thirty years on, things have changed, but for more than a decade Palacios and his offspring toiled alone.

One of those nine sons and daughters was to become a star a few years later, but he would have to move to an even more out-of-the-way place, Priorat, to reach that stardom with his amazing L'Ermita wine. Álvaro Palacios later formed a partnership with a nephew, Ricardo Pérez Palacios, in yet another forgotten region, Bierzo. In the meantime, two other brothers managed the family estate before striking out on their own: Antonio to Rioja Alta; Rafael to Valdeorras.

Finally, it was Álvaro who returned home to run Palacios Remondo after the death of his father in 2000. Few of his international fans know this, but Álvaro, while frequently commuting to Priorat, now lives in Alfaro, and he has taken head-on the challenge of bringing the family estate to the same heights he has reached in Priorat and Bierzo.

Altitude (around 1,800ft [550m]) and poor, healthy soils on the slopes of the Yerga mountain are the main assets of the Palacios vineyards. The soils are dominated by Quaternary Period sediments consisting of a clay-limestone subsoil covered with gravel and having excellent drainage. Most (272 acres [110ha]) of the family's vines are right there, in the La Montesa and Valmira vineyards.

"The most important thing about our wines is this vineyard," Palacios says when showing the Montesa vineyard, which is already old but, surprisingly, trellised, because that's the way his father wanted it when he planted it in the late 1960s. In that vineyard there is some Viura (20 acres [8ha]), the rest being the classic regional red grapes: Tempranillo, Mazuelo, and Garnacha. Álvaro regrafted the Graciano vines to Garnacha in 2007 because they did not do well on this soil.

After working with Garnacha since the late 1980s in Priorat, Álvaro has returned to Rioja Baja with a singular commitment to that often underappreciated variety. He will say with utter conviction, "Through its behavior, we can see that Garnacha is a very Spanish variety—perhaps even more than Tempranillo itself. It likes the sun, the heat, the stress from drought."

Once he gets started on the subject of vines and vineyards, Álvaro's eyes sparkle as he defends his theories on their origins. "All the great wines have monastic origins. When a microclimate, a good vineyard, and an abbey coincide, as happens in France, in Priorat, and along St. James's Way, which is right here, we find a great wine," says Álvaro, with something close to religious fervor. "The great wines appear where those small spaces are. They may not give more than a few thousand bottles, but they are great." You may tell him that there was never much of a monastic link to Bordeaux wines, or that there are great wines in the New World, too—but you won't change his mind about the subject.

After he returned home in 2000, succeeding his older brother Antonio, with whose ideas he didn't much agree, Álvaro set out, with the help of his brother Rafa and enologist Javier Gil, to reduce production to less than half what it was, concentrating on quality and making his La Montesa cuvée, with more than 50,000 cases a year, the basic product on which to build. It is very reasonably priced for the quality and is aimed at a wide public.

**Right:** Álvaro Palacios, who made his stellar reputation in Priorat but returned to run the family Rioja estate in 2000

With Garnacha predominantly featured, La Montesa has all the hallmarks of a pleasant, suave, traditional Rioja crianza, but it has been progressively acquiring minerality, as Álvaro has enhanced the expression of the terroir.

Before leaving for Valdeorras, Rafa established Plácet as one of the few praiseworthy whites in Rioja, overcoming the supposed aromatic shortcomings of the Viura variety, and it remains the lone white made here.

A small cuvée, Propiedad, is the most ambitious attempt yet on the Alfaro estate at a grand vin along the lines of a Finca Dofí or a Corullón, Palacios's top wines in Priorat and Bierzo, respectively. It's showing promising refinement.

Recently, an inexpensive but extremely attractive and drinkable cuvée, La Vendimia, was introduced. Aged for just five months in used oak barrels, it is a 50/50 blend of Garnacha and Tempranillo and is extremely easy to enjoy.

**Above:** The meticulously planted vines on the Remondo estate, whose free-draining soils are well suited to Garnacha

## FINEST WINES

### Plácet Valtomelloso ★
This is one of the most mineral Viura whites around, barrel fermented and aged 9–12 months in large oak *foudres*. It ages well and gains notable complexity.

### Propiedad
From some of the best, oldest vines on the estate, this Garnacha-led blend (40% Garnacha, 35% Tempranillo, 15% Mazuelo, and 10% Graciano) is the most aromatic and personal of the Palacios Remondo wines, with floral, spicy, and herbaceous overtones and some serious fruit on the palate.

Palacios Remondo
Area under vine: 370 acres (150ha)
Average production: 800,000 bottles
Avenida de Zaragoza 8, 26540 Alfaro, La Rioja
Tel: +34 941 180 207
www.vinosherenciaremondo.com

# Bodegas Lacus / Olivier Rivière

Every social organization benefits from a breath of fresh air every now and then, even the most solidly established ones. Indeed, it's often the organizations that have been around the longest that are most in need of renovation. There can be no question that Rioja, throughout its history, has been through this process many times, especially during the last decade of the 20th century, when not so much a wind but a hurricane of change blew through the region—a challenge to the status quo that still arouses serious controversy.

The first decade of the 21st century has been calmer, particularly regarding the assimilation of "modernity" and the regaining of balance between tradition and innovation; but already in recent years we have started to see pioneers with new ideas. By definition, these have little track record, so one would not want to bet one's house on them. But at least some of the ideas are interesting enough to make them worthy of attention, as is the case of Luis Arnedo (Bodegas Lacus) and the wines made by Olivier Rivière under his own name.

Olivier has played a fundamental role in Lacus as technical adviser since before the first vintage. In the words of Luis Arnedo, "Olivier is an essential figure at Bodegas Lacus, since his conception of vineyard management and winemaking perfectly complements the ideas I had originally when launching this project."

The key is certainly in the vineyard, both new and old (between eight and 40 years of age), located at heights ranging from 1,150 to 1,570ft (350–48), and including Tempranillo (45 percent), Graciano (32 percent), Garnacha (23 percent), plus a little old-vine Garnacha Blanca. Arnedo and Rivière think that Graciano has excellent potential in this area of hot summers with many sun hours and low rainfall. The same applies to Garnacha.

**Below:** Kindred spirits Luis Arnedo (left) and Olivier Rivière, who are among the most promising of Rioja's new generation

The goal is to obtain low yields and control the entire process, avoiding overripeness. In order to retain enough acidity, they play with slightly different blends every year and choose vineyards according to soils, orientation, altitude, and any other variable that may be of importance. Not all the production goes into the house wines; in fact, much is sold in bulk to other producers, especially in the early vintages, where the average production has been 15,000–20,000 bottles, even though the project has been conceived for an optimum yearly production of 80,000 bottles.

In the vineyard, as in the cellar, the basic idea is the minimum possible intervention, using exclusively indigenous yeasts and only 1 percent new barrels. The philosophy of Arnedo and Rivière is that oak should escort the wines, not mask them: "We want wines that are fresh, elegant, natural, with good fruit but also with a long life ahead." After sampling the 2008 and 2009, we can say that they are certainly achieving this goal, especially with the reds, both under Bodegas Lacus (the Inédito line: S, 3/3 and H12) and under Olivier Rivière's own name (Ganko and Rayos Uva).

**Above:** The sunlight on the ocher walls at Bodegas Lacus reflects the distinctly Mediterranean feel of this subregion

Olivier, after six years of experience as an enologist in Bordeaux and Burgundy, came to Rioja in 2004 to work with Telmo Rodríguez. Two years later, he decided to fly solo, buying grapes from different sub-areas and vinifying them in rented facilities (at Lacus since 2009). In this way, he has built a business releasing 50,000 bottles a year—90 percent of which goes to export markets.

Besides his participation in Bodegas Lacus, Olivier acts as consultant for Bodegas Emilio Valerio in Navarra and, since 2009, has grown his own vines in Arlanza. Everything suggests that Rivière will become a major figure in Spanish winemaking in the not-too-distant future. We should keep an eye on him.

**Bodegas Lacus**
Area under vine: 47 acres (19ha)
Average production: 20,000 bottles
Calle Cervantes 18,
26559 Aldeanueva de Ebro, La Rioja
Tel: +34 649 331 799
www.bodegaslacus.com

# Escudero / Valsacro

Escudero and Valsacro are the two sister wineries owned by the Escudero family in Rioja. (They also own Bodegas Logos in Navarra.) In the 1990s, the family was already producing a wide portfolio of wines—from sparkling wines under the Cava appellation, to the full traditional range of Rioja.

But they felt the need to open new paths and undertake innovative projects, including their own version of "modern" Rioja versus their own fairly traditional treatment of this theme. In pursuit of this goal, and in order to avoid legal complications involving the two appellations under which their wines fell (Cava and Rioja), they were advised to build a new winery and create a new company, so that they could detach production from trade.

That was the origin of Bodegas Valsacro, and once this project was consolidated, the production of sparkling wines became centralized at the original Bodegas Escudero in Grávalos, whereas the production of Riojas—both red and white, traditional and modern—has settled in the newer and larger facilities at Pradejón (a whopping 86,000 sq ft [8,000 sq m], versus a mere 21,500 sq ft [2,000 sq m] in Grávalos).

But few things in life are more inconsistent than the regulations that govern our lives and the bureaucrats in charge of interpreting them. And just a decade after making the division, the family was told to do exactly the opposite thing: merge again into a single company. In the near future, there will be just one commercial entity (which will most probably be called Bodegas Escudero, for historic and family reasons), while the winemaking will remain separate for practical reasons.

Benito Escudero is a key figure in the company as it is today. Generations of his ancestors devoted themselves to viticulture, until his grandfather, Juan Escudero, took the plunge and started producing wine under his own name in 1852. The next decisive leap was taken by Benito himself a century later. After studying enology in Haro and Penedés, he brought back the know-how of quality sparkling-wine production, which he immediately implemented in the family bodega. This was a genuine innovation, not just for his family but for the entire region. Originally, the means available were very rudimentary, and the family had to apply inventive solutions to daily tasks such as bottle rotation, *dosage*, disgorgement, and so on. Benito has been retired for a few years now, and his four sons are currently in charge of the four main areas of the bodega's activity: Amador (winemaking), Jesús (viticulture), Ángeles (financial management), and José María (marketing).

Escudero and Valsacro are mostly (80 percent) self-sufficient as far as their grape supplies are concerned. The family vineyards are located in Grávalos and Alfaro, the most remarkable of which is Cuesta La Reina, on Mount Yerga, at 2,300ft (700m) above sea level. They also have more than 75 acres (30ha; 60 percent Tempranillo, and 40 percent split equally between Garnacha, Mazuelo, and Graciano) at their Pradejón vineyard around the Valsacro facilities. The family also buys grapes from local Grávalos growers with whom they have had a long business relationship. This supply—mostly old-vine Garnacha and Tempranillo—amounts to around 20 percent of the yearly needs of both wineries.

As for the wines, the Cavas are actually fairly inconsistent, since the yields of vines devoted to Cava production are very sensitive to frost. And the Escudero family's vineyards are located at such high altitudes that they are particularly exposed to these dangers, with resulting oscillations in production that ranges between 100,000 and 200,000 bottles per year, averaging some 160,000. The production of Rioja is naturally far more stable, above 600,000 bottles, but with logical variations due to market dynamics.

## FINEST WINES

**Above:** Amador Escudero, winemaker for the family firm, which he runs together with three of his brothers

The portfolio is very wide and at a consistently interesting level. First, we have the historic contribution of Don Benito Escudero, which is deserving of a mention here in the field of sparkling wines—especially the top label, **Dioro Baco Cava Extra Brut Vendimia Seleccionada**, a blend of Chardonnay and Viura, with possibly more oak presence than it should have. Then, of course, there are the Riojas, where there is plenty to choose from. If you asked them for their own choice, they would probably single out their most recent examples of modern ageworthy Rioja: **Valsacro** and **Valsacro Dioro**. But in the 2005 vintage, they also released

two important novelties: **Arvum** and **Vidau**. Nor should we neglect the traditional reds sold as **Solar de Bécquer**: the Reserva and the Gran Reserva are both fine examples of traditional Rioja.

**Bodegas Escudero / Valsacro**
Area under vine: 445 acres (180ha)
Average production: 800,000 bottles
Carretera de Arnedo s/n, 26587 Grávalos, La Rioja
Tel: +34 941 39 80 08
Fax: +34 941 39 80 70
www.bodegasescudero.com / www.valsacro.com

# Barón de Ley

Mendavia is one of the few towns in the Navarra region on the left bank of the River Ebro that have been, from the start, part of the Rioja appellation, not of Navarra. There you will find an impressive, massive 16th-century monastery (which started out as a fortress) turned into the headquarters of a handsome wine-producing estate, Barón de Ley. The monastery and the noble title are about as far as the romanticism gets. This is a large corporation, quoted on the Madrid stock exchange, with subsidiaries in other appellations, such as Ribera del Duero.

That said, what sets Barón de Ley apart is the soundness of the project, its solidity, and the very good overall quality of its wines. The talent of chief winemaker Gonzalo Rodríguez has much to do with that. He has won acclaim both at Barón de Ley and at his own small winery in his hometown in Toledo province, Más Que Vinos.

The winery was launched in 1985 by a small group of Rioja-based investors who wanted to create a Médoc-style "château." They wound up making it much larger.

They first acquired the Imas estate in Mendavia, where 222 acres (90ha) of vines were planted. The soils were promising, and they had a history behind them to corroborate it. Already, back in the 16th century, Benedictine monks from the Monastery of Irache tended vines at Imas that were reputed to produce excellent wine.

Of that surface, some 25 acres (10ha) were planted to Cabernet Sauvignon, exploiting the Rioja appellation's tolerance toward that "experimental variety."

Since then, the estate has grown to its current size—790 acres (320ha) of vines—under the control of able viticulturist Fernando González. They are still insufficient for all of the winery's production, and as usual, they are supplemented by the grapes furnished by growers in and around Mendavia, under long-term contracts.

The bodega's technical literature stresses that "the alluvial character of the soil, stony on the surface and with clay in deeper layers, combines with a climate of marked Mediterranean influence, with high levels of sunshine and low rainfall, which proves ideal for obtaining wines full of extract and aromas."

Rodríguez believes that the drier climate of this area of the appellation, which is part of Rioja Baja, with its continental features, makes it "considerably easier" to achieve consistent quality from one harvest to another, by making it possible to reach the minimum alcoholic strength of around 13% while picking considerably earlier, around mid-September.

The winery makes a white wine entirely from bought-in Viura grapes from Rioja Alta, a rosé, a reserva, a gran reserva, and the top cuvée, Finca Monasterio, with its massive, somewhat pretentious, silver, embossed label.

The sheer size of the operation is obvious from its cavernous, temperature-controlled barrel room, which contains some 12,000 American oak barrels and 2,000 French oak barrels.

## FINEST WINES

### Finca Monasterio
A powerful, tasty blend of 80% Tempranillo and 20% Cabernet Sauvignon, this smooth, well-made wine will not win any medals for preserving tradition, but it is a serious, clean, well-structured wine that exemplifies how well this kind of blend can work if made with ripe, balanced grapes. The French oak gives it even more of an international profile.

**Barón de Ley**
Area under vine: 790 acres (320ha)
Average production: 2 million bottles
Carretera Mendavia a Lodosa km 5.5,
31897 Mendavia, Navarra
Tel: +34 948 69 43 03
Fax: +34 948 69 43 04
www.barondeley.com

# Navarra

Navarra's winemaking history stretches back to the Roman conquest of Spain. Its viticultural landscape is full of wonderful and varied terroirs—from the cool Valdizarbe, not far from the Pyrenees, to the Mediterranean Ebro Valley in the south. But it's also full of false starts and missed opportunities. Today, Navarra finds itself in flux, still seeking a path to success.

Being Rioja's neighbor was always part of the problem. With few exceptions—such as Chivite or Camilo Castilla—the Navarrese grape growers have been looking on enviously ever since the late 19th century, as bodegas multiplied in Rioja and succeeded with quality bottled wines. In Navarra, cooperatives proliferated from the 1920s—a movement that was meant to assure growers a decent price for their grapes. But all too often they lacked the drive, know-how, and markets to make anything but cheap bulk wine.

By the 1970s, a strategy to grow beyond mere subsistence was developing along two lines. First, modern production facilities were built, and more and more Tempranillo was planted to mimic Rioja. But soon, as the lack of suitable limestone in many parts of the region resulted in lower-quality Tempranillo, there was a simultaneous push for the official recognition of foreign grape varieties. And in 1973, with Franco still in power, the authorization of Cabernet Sauvignon, Merlot, and Chardonnay was one of the first significant liberalizing moves in a regulatory landscape that had hitherto been fiercely autarkical.

## International strategy

A new strategy slowly developed: to follow the tactics of Rioja in winemaking and marketing but to do so with more international wines. It was widely lauded at first. The British wine press, in the 1980s and '90s, led the chorus of plaudits for the

**Right:** The dramatic landscape of Valdizarbe, near the Pyrenees, represents one extreme of Navarra's varied terroirs

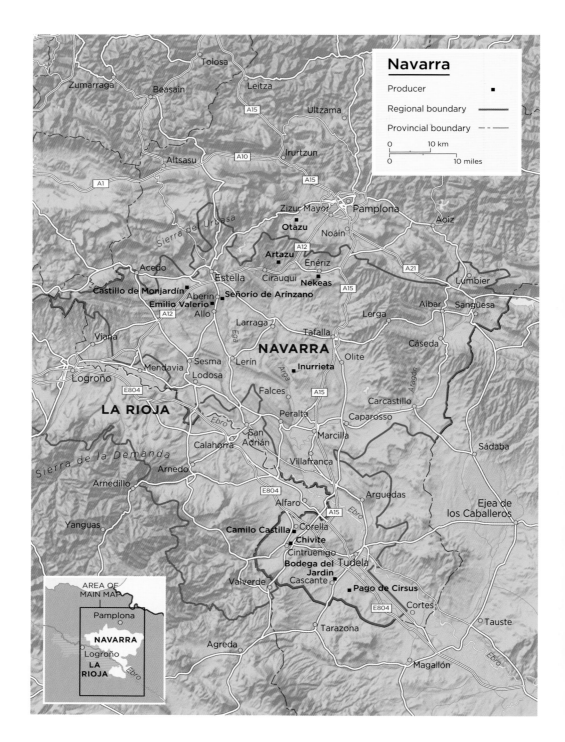

# Navarra

Producer ■

Regional boundary ———

Provincial boundary –––

0    10 km

0                10 miles

Tolosa

Zumarraga

Beasain

Leitza

Ultzama

A15

A10

Irurtzun

Altsasu

A1

A15

Zizur Mayor    Pamplona

Aoiz

Otazu

Noáin

Sierra del Urbasa

Artazu

Enériz

A21

Acedo

A12

Lumbier

Estella    Cirauqui    Nekeas

Castillo de Monjardín ■

Aberin

Señorío de Arínzano ■

A15

Aibar

Sangüesa

Emilio Valerio ■

Allo

Cáseda

A12

Larraga

Tafalla

Viana

NAVARRA

Olite

Lerga

Mendavia

Sesma

Lerín

Alagón

Logroño

Lodosa

Inurrieta ■

LA RIOJA

E804

Falces

Carcastillo

A15

Ebro

Peralta

Caparosso

Sierra de la Demanda

Calahorra

San Adrián

Marcilla

Sádaba

Arnedo

Villafranca

Arnedillo

E804

Arguedas

Ejea de los Caballeros

Yanguas

Alfaro

A15

Ebro

Camilo Castilla ■    Corella

Chivite ■    Cintruenigo

Cortes

Bodega del Jardín ■    Tudela

Pago de Cirsus ■

Valverde    Cascante

E804

Tauste

Tarazona

Agreda

Magallón

Ebro

AREA OF MAIN MAP

Pamplona

NAVARRA

Logroño

LA RIOJA

Ebro

new Navarra. This so-called modernization was generally considered positive, as gurus painted a picture of a world wine market with an unquenchable thirst for Cabernet and Chardonnay.

It didn't pan out for Navarra, though, as a new generation of overcropped, highly technological, international wines failed to convince international buyers that they were any better than Australian Chardonnays or Chilean Cabernets; while in Spain, the region's negative image as "poor man's Rioja" proved very difficult to dislodge.

Worse still, thousands of acres of the region's distinctive, native treasure—Garnacha—were ripped up in favor of imported varieties. All over northern Spain, Garnacha was decried as an inferior grape and its true potential ignored— even as the Grenache-led takeoff of Châteauneuf-du-Pape as a world-class wine region was taking place a short distance north of the border.

Enough Garnacha remained to make it possible to produce Spain's best but very cheap (and not very profitable) rosés. In the end, that lone local success story—and the worldwide switch to more local, more individual wines—led to a reconsideration of Navarra's situation after 2000. But by then, the region's wine industry had dug itself into a deep hole.

**Reconstruction**

The beginnings of reconstruction come amid the global economic recession, which is proving particularly painful in Spain. Equally inauspicious is the country's falling wine consumption. Quite a few of the new producers will not survive.

By now, most of the early converts to the international style have had to accept that all they achieve by putting "Chardonnay" or "Merlot" on a label is to compete head-on with New World varietal wines, which are often better and cheaper.

It isn't only the commercial imperative, though, that is prompting a return to roots and a search for a more Navarrese style. It's also the arrival of a younger generation of growers and winemakers who are convinced that European wines should compete in terms of terroir rather than variety. They are much more interested in Garnacha for red wines than their forebears were and are finally coming to terms with Moscatel de Grano Menudo as an indigenous white grape.

There are also other considerations with which Navarra must come to grips, however. The current market is increasingly polarized between "supermarket wines" (including most of those cheap rosés and international-style varietals) and "quality wines." The first of these markets should be important only to wineries producing many millions of bottles every year. Small and medium-sized bodegas need more added value.

In this market, the future belongs to those growers and winemakers—ever more numerous but still in the minority—who look critically on their own environment and decide what is best for them in terms of expressing their terroir and producing wines with personality. Personality will no doubt be even more important than sheer quality.

An increasing number of wine professionals in Navarra are therefore restoring and showcasing native varieties. They are finally learning the right lessons, in other words—even though they always have to fight against the ingrained national tendency to copy anything that seems to be successful anywhere. If Tempranillo was good for Rioja, then it should be good for everyone. Similarly for Cabernet Sauvignon and Merlot, both so successful in Bordeaux. So producers wind up planting Tempranillo, Cabernet, and Merlot, often in the wrong places, only to discover that it wasn't the right thing to do. The trouble is that, in viticulture and winemaking, you can't change things overnight. And for Navarra, it's a matter of correcting 30 years of mistakes.

# Chivite / Señorío de Arínzano

No Spanish family of wine growers can lay claim to an earlier start in the business than the Chivites of Cintruénigo in southern Navarra. A document signed by a public notary in 1647 recorded a request for a loan of 100 ducats by Juan Chivite Frías and listed as collateral "the cellar, with vats holding up to 150 *cántaros* [about 1,700 liters]" and "a vineyard on the road to Cascante, of 30 *peonadas* [about 30 acres (12ha)]." Obviously this was more than the usual vineyard and cellar capacity devoted to home consumption by families in the region, and so the Chivites settled on 1647 as the founding date for their commercial winery.

While common in Tuscany or the Rhine, the continued family ownership of a wine estate over three centuries is a unique case in Spain. The only comparable cases were in Jerez, but such families as the Osbornes and the Domecqs got their starts there a century later.

While the active local business of the Chivite family kept growing, particularly through the 18th and 19th centuries, it didn't take off internationally until 1860, when the wily Claudio Chivite saw the opportunity created by the onslaught of phylloxera in France. Almost single-handedly, he created an export business for wines from southern Navarra, using a route from Cintruénigo to Bayonne and on to Bordeaux.

The big Chivite winery was built in 1872, and it's still there today on Caballeros Street—a testament to a booming era. It was renovated in 1948 and received a full technical overhaul in 1988.

Félix Chivite, Claudio's son, ran the family business from 1877 until his death in 1928 and was succeeded by the youngest of his 13 sons and daughters, Julián. As it had after the French market was lost and Spain itself was hit by phylloxera, the company survived through tough times, which included the European fallout from

**Right:** Fernando Chivite, head of his family firm since 2009, champions elegance over extraction in his wines

the Great Depression, the Spanish Civil War, and World War II. Exports, always vital for Chivite, were hard hit by the disrupted economy and the high tariffs and trade barriers erected by governments. But the winery kept on selling abroad whenever and wherever possible and was one of the elite companies permitted to export in post–Civil War Spain.

Like his father's, Julián Chivite's reign was a very long one, lasting more than half a century, until his death in 1996. It encompassed the striking transformation both of Spain—from a backward agricultural society, to one of Europe's most modern states—and of Spain's wine industry. Some of the family-owned bodegas failed to adapt to the change and could not survive, particularly in Jerez, where the whole of the Sherry world was hit by a seemingly unending recession. But Julián Chivite's vision—like that of Miguel Torres Sr. in Catalonia—made it possible for the firm not only to survive but to thrive.

The company was making traditional, Rioja-inspired reds that were little known on the Spanish market outside Navarra when Julián Chivite launched, in 1975, a line of wines that was to be the springboard to nationwide and worldwide success. They were called Gran Feudo and were squeaky-clean, moderately priced wines made with the best technology available. Fruit-driven and with clear varietal characteristics, they were an instant hit and have since become the bodega's bestselling workhorse wines.

A decade later, the portfolio was completed with the introduction of Colección 125, a range of top-end wines (a red blend, a Chardonnay, and a sweet wine made with the native Moscatel de Grano Menudo grape) commemorating the 125th anniversary of Chivite as an exporting company. A few years later, some of the grapes used for this range would come from the Arínzano estate, 53 miles (85km) north of Cintruénigo, purchased in 1988.

The Chivites began replanting it shortly afterward. (The estate's historic vineyards had disappeared early in the 19th century.) There are now 316 acres (128ha) in production.

During the brief span of time since Julián Chivite's death, events have accelerated dramatically, with diversification and expansion on an unprecedented scale but also personal tragedy and family strife.

For some years after 1996, the company was run by Julián's four siblings—Julián, Carlos, Mercedes, and Fernando, who also became chief winemaker. Expansion into Rioja, with the acquisition of the well-known Viña Salceda winery in 1998, was followed by a foray into Ribera del Duero three years later, when 153 acres (62ha) in the privileged La Horra terroir were planted to Tempranillo, plus some Cabernet Sauvignon and Merlot. Finally, a move into Rueda was announced in 2009. (The brand used in both Ribera and Rueda is Baluarte.)

Meanwhile, tragedy had struck the family, as both Carlos and Mercedes succumbed to cancer within a few months of each other in 2005 and 2006. Later, in what has become a frequent scenario in family-controlled wineries in Spain over the past decade, Fernando and Julián Chivite parted ways. Fernando became chairman of the board in 2009 and assumed full control of the group, while in mid-2010 Julián announced he was starting a new winemaking venture, Unzu Propiedad, aiming to produce wines in several Spanish regions. He promptly introduced his first two products—a Navarra rosé and a Rueda white.

With some 1,110 acres (450ha) under vine in Cintruénigo and the surrounding villages of Aberín, Corella, and Marcilla, plus the Arínzano estate (not to mention interests in other regions), Fernando Chivite presides over the undisputed juggernaut of the Navarra wine scene. But he is following two very different strategies—one for the main winery, the other for the northern estate.

**Above:** Señorío de Arínzano, the first Navarra estate to be granted its own appellation and source of Chivite's top red wine

Arínzano became, in 2008, the first property in Navarra to be awarded its own single-estate appellation (Vino de Pago de Arínzano). It then released its first three vintages (initially only red wines): 2000, 2001, and 2002. The light, fresh style imparted by the cool climate of the Pyrenean foothills, tempered by the River Ega, is very much the ideal pursued by Fernando, who was one of the first among the new generation of enologists in Spain to eschew hyper-extraction and fruit-and-oak bombs. In the manicured, hillside organic vineyards (the estate is run in partnership with the World Wide Fund for Nature [WWF]), as well as in the spectacular winery designed by Pritzker prize-winner Rafael Moneo, the conditions fit Fernando's idea of great Navarra wine to a T.

Meanwhile, the Chivite brands from the Cintruénigo winery have undergone further diversification, with a new Varietal line (including a Tempranillo and an organic Merlot), and a top-of-the-line addition to the Gran Feudo lineup, Gran Feudo Edición (a Chardonnay, a rosé "on lees," a sweet Muscat, a Tempranillo, and a Viñas Viejas Reserva red blend from old Tempranillo and Garnacha vines).

## FINEST WINES

### Arínzano ★
The top red, from the northerly Arínzano vineyards, this is a delicate, subtle blend dominated by Tempranillo, with about one-third Merlot and some Cabernet Sauvignon—what some would call the quintessential modern Navarra blend but done in an unusually elegant style. The **2001** is particularly fine.

### Colección 125 Blanco ★
A lush, creamy, leesy barrel-fermented Chardonnay with enough acidity for balance, this is regularly rated among Spain's top whites.

### Colección 125 Vendimia Tardía
From botrytis-affected Moscatel de Grano Menudo (Muscat Blanc à Petits Grains) in the Candelero vineyard in Cintruénigo, this complex, delicate Muscat, vinified with Sauternes techniques, is one of Spain's very best sweet wines.

**Chivite / Señorío de Arínzano**
Area under vine: 1,435 acres (580ha)
Average production: 2.5 million bottles
Calle Ribera 34,
31592 Cintruénigo, Navarra
Tel:+34 948 811 000
www.bodegaschivite.com

# Pago de Cirsus de Iñaki Núñez

Iñaki Núñez is in Spain what Francis Ford Coppola is in America or Gérard Depardieu in France. No, he's not nearly as famous: the name of this Basque Country native won't ring a bell with many. But he's a movie-industry insider who has nevertheless made his mark on the wine scene. There are better-known personalities in wine, even in Spain (such as Antonio Banderas, who has invested in Ribera del Duero), but none has attained the same level of success, nor reached it so quickly, as this 57-year-old producer and distributor of movies. His first vintage in Navarra was as recent as 2002, and a mere seven years later he caused a bit of a stir by winning two of only 61 Grand Gold Medals awarded at the 2009 Concours Mondial de Bruxelles, that most international of wine contests.

*The sophistication and fleshy drinkability of Pago de Cirsus wines have attracted much attention. These are the most Mediterranean wines in all of northwest Spain*

Everything is rather grand about Núñez. His Pago de Cirsus is quite Hollywood in style—a 500-acre (200ha) property with a mock-medieval tower as its central feature. This is the main building of the modestly named Hotel Château Pago de Cirsus, one of the most luxurious establishments in the region.

The vineyards may have been envisioned by Núñez as little more than a romantic backdrop to his dream inn, but they have since become star performers in their own right. Despite their modest altitude (750ft [230m]) and the harsh continental climate of the central Ebro Valley where they are located, the poor, sandy-loam soils with plenty of limestone offer excellent potential for quality wines.

The next move by Núñez, a wine lover but not a winemaking specialist, was crucial to his success: he sought the advice of former Château Haut-Brion enologist Jean-Marc Sauboua, now an international consultant, and the Frenchman has been retained by Pago de Cirsus ever since. His role has been more active than that of the conventional flying winemaker, and he has been responsible for designing the whole wine range and overseeing vineyard development.

The sophistication and fleshy drinkability of Pago de Cirsus wines, which have attracted much attention since the young winery began releasing them, owe much to Sauboua. Some critics have objected to their "international style," but they are actually a faithful reflection of the Ribera del Ebro terroirs of southern Navarra, with power, warmth, and generosity in spades. These are no doubt the most Mediterranean wines in all of northwest Spain, which is logical considering their geographic location in a valley that is wide open to the influence of that sea. But they show none of the excessive heat or massive extraction that are sometimes the negative telltale signs of Spain's Mediterranean wines.

## FINEST WINES

**Pago de Cirsus Tempranillo Selección Especial ★**
Not surprisingly, Tempranillo (and Syrah) perform best in this warm, arid terroir. This Tempranillo has a powerful fragrance of toast, plums, and blueberries and is fruity, silky, and long.

**Right:** Iñaki Núñez, who first made his name in movies but now enjoys equal success through his wines

**Pago de Cirsus de Iñaki Núñez**
Area under vine: 334 acres (135ha)
Average production: 400,000 bottles
Carretera de Ribaforada km 5.3,
31523 Ablitas, Navarra
Tel: +34 948 386 210
www.pagodecirsus.com

# Bodega del Jardín

Bodega del Jardín is the most famous winery you've never heard of in northwest Spain. If we mentioned the name Guelbenzu, many fans of Navarra wines would recognize it. But the name is gone. These are hard times. And the eight Guelbenzu brothers and sisters are starting from scratch again. Well, not quite from scratch. The little bodega under the charming 19th-century villa—the bodega in the garden—is still there, as is the original family estate, with more than 50 acres (20ha) under vine around this village south of the River Ebro. That, and the proven know-how shown by the two siblings who directly ran the estate, Ricardo and Inés, is enough to guarantee that the tradition remains in Cascante. After tasting the first vintage of Bodega del Jardín, the 2007, there is no doubt that this phoenix-like producer deserves to be listed among the most interesting estates in Navarra.

What has been lost is the large modern winery in nearby Vierlas and its vineyards. A failed venture in Chile probably accelerated the partition of the estate and the loss of the name (Mondavi-fashion). So, a new Guelbenzu is now part of the Caja Navarra group of wineries, along with the likes of Señorío de Sarría and Palacio de Bornos.

With that load off their shoulders, the Guelbenzus went back to their roots. The Bodega del Jardín, reborn in late 2009, traces its history back to their ancestor, Martín M. Guelbenzu, who bottled the first quality wines in a region where coarse homemade Garnacha had hitherto been the only wine produced and sent them to the London World Exhibition in 1851.

Its success was fairly short-lived. But the winery was relaunched by the current generation of Guelbenzus and quickly gained an international reputation for its red wines. Now, under its new name, it is offering an interesting range of red wines—three of them to begin with.

**Left:** Inés and Ricardo Guelbenzu, the sister and brother who have taken their original family estate into Navarra's top flight

The vineyards, in 17 small plots, occupy parts of a 4-mile (6km) swath of land that runs between the Cascante county limit with Murchante, to the north, and Tarazona, in Aragón, to the south. Their altitudes run from 1,080 to 1,410ft (330m–430m).

The appellation used by Bodega del Jardín—Vinos de la Tierra Ribera del Queiles—straddles two of Spain's autonomous regions, Navarra and Aragón. The border between the two is just 2 miles (3km) or so from Cascante, and there is a natural unity in the terroir that led Ricardo Guelbenzu—not a great friend of the Navarra DO while he was still in it—to lobby the Agriculture Ministry until it was approved in 2003.

The underground winery has eight 200hl stainless-steel fermentation vats and holds some 500 barrels. The winemaking, inspired by Ricardo's back-to-the-land philosophy, is quite traditional and natural. No selected yeasts are used. Blends are preferred to varietals, in the belief that the former ensure greater complexity and personality.

The names of the new wines are less traditional and symbolize the rejuvenation of the estate. 1Pulso is a young wine made with Tempranillo and Garnacha; 2Pulso is a more structured Tempranillo/Merlot/Cabernet Sauvignon blend, with 12 months in oak; and 3Pulso is the grand vin.

## FINEST WINES

### 3Pulso ★
A wonderfully expressive, fleshy red with serious aging potential, this is an 80% Tempranillo/20% Garnacha blend from the estate's oldest vines, aged 24 months in French oak, half of it new. But it's no oak soup: the wine is concentrated and lively enough to carry the wood effortlessly.

### Bodega del Jardín
Area under vine: 58 acres (23.5ha) in Cascante
Average production: 120,000 bottles
San Juan 14, 31520 Cascante, Navarra
Tel:+34 948 850 055
Fax: +34 948 850 097

# Bodegas y Viñedos Nekeas

Bodegas y Viñedos Nekeas is a young estate, founded in 1992. It is a cooperative but very different from the massive co-ops launched in the early 20th century by the Catholic church to help poor grape growers improve their lot. In this case, it was just eight growers in the Nekeas Valley, in the cooler, northern part of Navarra, who combined their holdings to supply a new, state-of-the-art winery with native and international grape varieties.

Under the active leadership of Francisco San Martín, one of the founding growers who is now the company's president, Nekeas has specialized in good-quality wines at very competitive prices and has managed to gain more of a reputation on export markets, such as the United States, than in

*Concha Vecino's winemaking is precise, clean, and respectful of the fine quality of fruit she gets from the well-tended vineyards*

Spain itself. A crucial development was the arrival in 1993 of young winemaker Concha Vecino, who succeeded in developing a line of attractive, honest wines. She also helped steer Nekeas in a new direction, with more emphasis on native grapes in general and on Garnacha in particular. The success of the firm's first Garnacha varietal, El Chaparral, was a turning point.

The valley, in the Valdizarbe area of the Navarra appellation, is just 44 miles (70km) from the Atlantic Ocean, with cool temperatures (yearly average of 53.6˚F [12˚C]). Viticulture is made possible by the protective presence of the Perdón, Urbasa, and Andía mountain ranges, which shield it from the cold winds from the nearby Pyrenees and the humid flows from the Bay of Biscay. Slopes are often steep, and the altitude goes from 1,150 to 2,460ft (350–750m). The soils are poor, with pebble-strewn red and brown loams dominating.

Vecino's winemaking is precise, clean, and respectful of the fine quality of fruit she gets from the well-tended vineyards. Some of her creations, like the Viura/Chardonnay blend that's made a name in the United States, have inspired other winemakers in the region to follow similar paths.

The grape varieties are Tempranillo (173 acres [70ha]), Garnacha (111 acres [45ha], a third of which are old vines), Cabernet Sauvignon (100 acres [40ha]), Merlot (85 acres [35ha]), Chardonnay (80 acres [32ha]), Viura (37 acres [15ha]), and Syrah (12 acres [5ha]).

## FINEST WINES

### El Chaparral de Vega Sindoa
An oak-aged wine that well reflects the freshness and floral tones of cool-climate Garnacha, this is the winery's best-known product internationally. The **2007** was a fine example.

### Marain de Vega Sindoa
This pure Merlot, made only in selected vintages, shows a level of elegance rarely reached by the variety in Spain, where most terroirs are too warm for it. The **2001** was outstanding.

### Nekeas Chardonnay Cuvée Allier
Fermented and aged in fine-quality French oak, this Chardonnay from the estate's lowest-yielding vineyards eloquently shows why northern Navarra is one of the few Spanish areas that are cool enough for two very popular French varieties—Merlot and Chardonnay—to show any distinction. The **2007** and **2009** are fine examples.

**Right:** Concha Vecino, the winemaker who has helped ensure Nekeas's success, largely through native varietal wines

**Bodegas y Viñedos Nekeas**
Area under vine: 560 acres (225ha)
Average production: 800,000 bottles
Calle Las Huertas s/n,
31154 Añorbe, Navarra
Tel: +34 948 350 296
Fax: +34 948 350 300
www.nekeas.com

# Artazu

Artazu is named after the village where the small estate is situated. Not an easy feat under Spanish trademark law, which frowns on wineries carrying the name of their home town —but then again, we are in independent-minded Navarra, with its own regulations. This was, as Juan Carlos López de Lacalle recounts, "our first foray into an historical wine region such as Navarra," and the great magnet was old Garnacha vineyards.

López de Lacalle is the driven and highly talented owner and deus ex machina of Artadi, the bodega in Rioja Alavesa that he has brought from obscurity into the limelight as one of the best in Spain. He has a particular notion of Rioja: there, he likes only Tempranillo. But elsewhere he becomes hugely interested in other varieties that he deems well adapted to the terroir. A few years back, he found an able sidekick, the French-born enologist Jean-François Gadeau, whom he pried away from a job in Jumilla. Together they discovered Monastrell and now run El Sequé estate in southeast Spain. They are also making Garnacha wines from the coolest, most northerly of the subzones in Navarra, Valdizarbe

The geographic choice was interesting, because most Garnacha vines in the appellation are farther south, near the River Ebro. But López de Lacalle wanted as much freshness as possible from a variety that is known for its high sugar content and, therefore, the high alcohol in the wines made with it.

At Artazu, López de Lacalle and Gadeau assembled a 37-acre (15ha) estate comprising small plots of rare old vines (many of them 60 years old or more), plus 75 acres (30ha) that they rented, 32 acres (13ha) of them on steep hillsides. With the grapes, they make a rosé (using the classic Navarrese technique of *saignée*), a young red, and a more serious barrel-aged wine that, in its best vintages, can achieve world-class status.

On poor clay-limestone soils, and at altitudes ranging from 1,310 to 1,970ft (400–600m), these vineyards have small yields, despite the relatively high annual rainfall (24–28in [600–700mm]). The huge day/night temperature differential in summer is part of the explanation for the dark, intense color of these Navarra strains of Garnacha. The oldest of these plots, Santa Cruz, really stands out for its quality, which is what led López de Lacalle to devote it to producing an ageworthy, "serious" wine.

In the small, efficient winery there are 17 stainless-steel fermentation vats of various sizes, ranging from 30hl to 250hl. Only large, 500-liter French oak barrels are used—in very small numbers, since only Santa Cruz de Artazu spends any time (about a year) in them.

After the inaugural vintage (2000), variation between better and worse years was relatively marked, which led to some controversy in the United States. Since 2005, however, the Artazu wines have been much more consistent.

## FINEST WINES

### Santa Cruz de Artazu

A dense, concentrated, unexpectedly dark Garnacha made from vines nearing 100 years of age, with very low yields, around 2 tons per hectare, and showing the balance and harmony reached when a vineyard is perfectly adapted to its terroir. Simultaneously floral, peppery, and smooth, with super-soft tannins, a mouthful of this wine is sufficient to throw into disrepute all those "experts" who 30 years ago were dismissing Garnacha in the region as a second-rate grape with no future other than for dirt-cheap rosés.

**Bodegas y Viñedos Artazu**
Area under vine: 111 acres (45ha)
Average production: 200,000 bottles
Mayor s/n, 31109 Artazu, Navarra
Tel: +34 945 600 119
Fax: +34 945 600 850
www.artadi.com

# Camilo Castilla

Camilo Castilla in Corella, like Chivite in nearby Cintruénigo, is a true monument to Navarra's winemaking past—not one of the many Johnny-come-latelies in the region. Don Camilo Castilla Alzugaray founded the winery in 1856, and a century and a half later, it's still going strong—stronger than ever, perhaps. It's an interesting case: they make serviceable whites, rosés, and reds, but it's a small patch of old-vine Muscat and a staunchly traditional way of making old-style sweet wines that have won Camilo Castilla a unique place among the Spanish wine elite.

*It's a small patch of old-vine Muscat and a staunchly traditional way of making old-style sweet wines that have won Camilo Castilla a unique place among the Spanish wine elite*

For most of this long history, Camilo Castilla was exclusively devoted to the production of traditional, rancio-style Muscat wines, which gave it quite a reputation within the relatively small niche of consumers of such wines. Its strength was its large portfolio of vineyards around Corella, mostly planted with Moscatel de Grano Menudo—the Spanish branch of the small-berried Muscat family whose members go by a number of local names elsewhere (Muscat Blanc à Petits Grains, Muscat Canelli, Moscato Bianco, Muscat de Frontignan, Muscat de Lunel…). They produce more delicate wines than the large-berried Muscat of Alexandria, common elsewhere in Spain.

Moscatel de Grano Menudo was a great asset for Navarra's viticultural portfolio, but everyone forgot about it—except Camilo Castilla. Its vineyards would ultimately provide the plant material for the rebirth of the variety in the region in the 1990s, and they still account for one-third of the total Moscatel acreage in Navarra.

History changed in 1987, when Saragossa businessman Arturo Beltrán purchased the winery, with its large, rambling facilities in the center of the village, and decided to bring it into modern times by diversifying its production. He sent his 21-year-old daughter Ana, with her brand-new university degree in business administration in her pocket, to learn the trade, and two years later she became the general manager. Now, after two decades, she has developed a new range, under the Montecristo brand, of dry wines (including two reds, made with Tempranillo, Cabernet Sauvignon, and Mazuelo grapes purchased from local growers) and expanded the Muscat production to include dry whites and younger, more modern sweet wines.

But it's still those dozens of glass demijohns lined up on the roof of the winery that set this winery apart from all others, making it a reference point and a living museum that has protected valuable traditions through thick and thin over the years.

## FINEST WINES

### Capricho de Goya ★
Aged with the same techniques used by traditional producers in southern France—particularly in Maury and Banyuls—this is a stunning, treacle-sweet, but fresh, pungent, and complex Muscat wine of amazing concentration. From the 100-year-old Tambarría vineyard, it's aged for seven years—the first three in glass demijohns, outdoors, under the snow or scorching heat, and the last four in big old oak *foudres* in the 150-year-old cellar.

**Bodegas Camilo Castilla**
Area under vine: 136 acres (55ha)
Average production: 600,000 bottles
Santa Bárbara 40,
31591 Corella, Navarra
Tel: +34 948 780 006
Fax: +34 948 780 515
www.bodegascamilocastilla.com

# Bodega Inurrieta

Inurrieta is large, recent, and modern. In that sense, it resembles many—perhaps too many—Navarra wine estates. But over its one decade of operations, it has shown a sense of respect for the grapes and the terroir, as well as a knack for producing outstanding value. It has therefore placed itself at the head of this pack of newcomers and may yet develop into the sort of large-scale, terroir-conscious winery that Navarra needs.

In 1999, Juan Mari Antoñana—whose forebears were once vine growers in this tiny valley near the town of Olite, in the Ribera Alta sub-appellation—headed a corporate drive to relaunch winemaking in the area after many years of neglect. With winemaker Kepa Segastizabal, Antoñana has been the driving force behind Inurrieta's initial success.

*Over its one decade of operations, Inurrieta has shown a sense of respect for the grapes and the terroir, as well as a knack for producing outstanding value*

The valley is a beautiful place, with its vines, olive groves, and meadows amid gullies and rocky outcrops, not to mention a treasure trove of Roman ruins and medieval churches and castles. These remains bear witness to the birth of viticulture around the town of Falces, which dates back to the 1st century BC.

But all that's just the backdrop. The winery itself is all about sheer size and modern trappings. It is large (70,000 sq ft [6,500 sq m]), plainly functional, and able to hold 4 million liters of wine, part of that in 2,200 French and American oak barrels.

The vineyard portfolio is impressive in its area, with more than 500 acres (200ha), and in its diversity, since it included the top varieties admitted under the 1973 regulations of the Navarra appellation: the almost compulsory Tempranillo,

Cabernet Sauvignon, and Merlot, plus (fortunately) some Garnacha and Graciano, as well as Viura and Chardonnay. We soon discovered that there were other things, too, as some "experimental" plots were made official when Syrah, Pinot Noir, and Sauvignon Blanc were all legalized in a change to the regulations in 2007. The Inurrieta Sur red, a Mediterranean-styled wine that forms the backbone of the estate's portfolio (alongside Inurrieta Norte, which is a Merlot/Cabernet Sauvignon blend), had always been announced as a Garnacha/Tempranillo/Graciano blend. Overnight, in 2008, all mentions of Tempranillo disappeared and were replaced by Syrah. It's obvious that the wine's actual contents didn't change—only the nomenclature did. The same occurred with Inurrieta's top-selling white.

Commercially, the company is equally enterprising. It has, for example, established its Cask Club for clients who want to acquire a cask of limited-selection wine.

## FINEST WINES

### Laderas
An original Graciano from higher vineyards, aged for over a year in 100% American oak. Leafy, somewhat austere; there is some terroir here.

### Orchídea
A pleasant, fresh, citrussy, unoaked wine, with plenty of tropical-fruit aromas and flavors. This was announced in its first vintages as a Chardonnay/Viura blend, but in 2008, immediately after the DO's regulations were amended, it instantly became—lo and behold!—a pure Sauvignon Blanc.

**Bodega Inurrieta**
Area under vine: 568 acres (230ha)
Average production: 1.4 million bottles
Carretera Falces a Miranda de Arga km 30,
31370 Falces, Navarra
Tel: +34 948 737 309
Fax: +34 948 737 310
www.bodegainurrieta.com

# Castillo de Monjardín

Sonia Olano was Víctor del Villar's young wife in 1986 and quite the urbanite in San Sebastián when her husband took on the challenge of replanting vines on the family estate in Navarra. She joined him in bucolic Villamayor de Monjardín to learn everything about viticulture and winemaking. A quarter of a century later, she is Castillo de Monjardín's savvy general manager, and her husband has satisfied his passion for Chardonnay by establishing his wines as some of the best in Spain, including a rare Esencia that mirrors the best *liquoreux* made in France's Mâconnais by such producers as Jean Thévenet. But Monjardín has also developed a range of respected red wines, with distinguished Merlots.

The winery started in 1988 in the San Esteban Valley, in the Tierra de Estella subzone, near the northern limit of Navarra's vineyards. The trellised, cordon-pruned vineyards are on slopes surrounding the central building, on two different levels; between 1,800 and 2,000ft (550–600m), there is Chardonnay, while below 1,800ft there are Tempranillo, Merlot, and Cabernet Sauvignon. There is also an experimental Pinot Noir vineyard.

Pinot Noir was not included among the appellation's permitted varieties "because the Navarra climate is supposedly not right for this variety," Sonia says, with no little scorn in her voice. "No bureaucrat seems to have bothered to consider that in the high, northern vineyards, Pinot Noir can give excellent results."

The del Villar family's Burgundian dreams will have to wait. But a hopeful precedent is that of Syrah, banned at first but recently sanctioned and giving distinguished wines at Pago de Cirsus.

Monjardín's innovative attitude is also illustrated by its gravity-led winery—a large, 43,000-sq-ft (4,000-sq-m) facility that takes advantage of the slope to avoid pumping grapes, must, or finished wine. Nighttime harvesting of Chardonnay to take advantage of the cool temperatures was also practiced by the del Villars from the start—they were among the pioneers of the technique in Spain.

Other aspects of the modern approach taken by this estate are more controversial—from mechanical harvesting, to the lavish use of new oak for their top-end Chardonnay cuvées. They are common in Navarra and are obviously related to the once-lauded, now much more critically discussed approach to an international style in the region.

The Chardonnay grapes go directly into a closed pneumatic press, where they rotate for eight hours. The idea is for the grapes to be pressed naturally by their own weight, leaving unripe ones intact. This original process gives only 50 percent free-run juice. The white must is fermented in stainless-steel vats or in barrel. The red wines are produced traditionally, with the malolactic in stainless steel. They all spend time in barrel, including the fragrant Tintico, a Tempranillo aged for two months in 300-liter American oak casks.

## FINEST WINES

### Esencia ★
This botrytis Chardonnay is an explosive, truffle-scented, dense, sweet wine.

### Chardonnay Reserva
Fermented in new Allier oak, this is an ambitious, golden white, with good acidity and structure, beeswax aromas, and fruity but quite dry flavors.

### Deyo
A Merlot, aged eight months in new French oak, with clean, powerful fruit flavors (blackberries, dried apricots) and excellent smoothness.

**Castillo de Monjardín**
Area under vine: 334 acres (135ha)
Average production: 400,000 bottles
Viña Rellanada,
31242 Villamayor de Monjardín, Navarra
Tel: +34 948 537 412
Fax: +34 948 537 436
cristina@monjardin.es

# Laderas de Montejurra

Emilio Valerio is a prestigious lawyer, a prosecuting public attorney with a long career in environmental protection. His family has owned vineyards (and olive groves) on the southern hillsides of Montejurra since as early as 1342. In the 1990s, the agricultural crisis reached a point at which these old vineyards, low-yielding and trained as trees, became a financial burden. The alternative endorsed by the authorities and so-called experts of the time was the uprooting of those old vines and replanting with international ("improving") varieties on trellises—a real catastrophe that has often been repeated over the past couple of decades.

Valerio knew that this was not the right way—certainly not in terms of the balance between the land, its people, and the 700-year-old winemaking tradition of his family, and probably not in terms of financial returns, either. A first experimental harvest in 1995 won him over for the cause of authenticity: small production, low yields, and yes, comparatively higher production costs.

That was how he took the plunge and became more than just an attorney who defended the environment by means of the law. He adopted a hands-on defense by revamping the family's 35 acres (14ha) of old vineyards, buying another 15 acres (6ha) from growers who had no grape contracts, and applying vineyards and cellar-management techniques that are scrupulously respectful of the environment. Moreover, he has relied on biodynamics (rather questionably, if you ask our opinion, though of course everyone is free to proceed as they please in this respect).

The 50 acres (20ha) of vineyards are split into 40 small plots averaging 1.2 acres (0.5ha) in size. Some 35 acres are over 50 years of age, *gobelet*-trained, and mostly Garnacha (50 percent of the total area) and Tempranillo (20 percent). The rest are Cabernet Sauvignon, Graciano, Malvasia, and Merlot (which is being replaced now because they do not think it ideal for their vineyards). Of all the vineyards, only one is new: a small plot recently planted with Garnacha Blanca, massal selected and *gobelet*-trained. The soils, as the winery name indicates, are fairly infertile sandy and chalky mountain hillsides, unlike most other vineyards near Montejurra, which are mostly alluvial sedimentary.

## FINEST WINES

The image of Laderas de Montejurra in the first decade of the 21st century relied mainly on the reds—**Viñas de Amburza** (a blend of Cabernet Sauvignon, Graciano, and Garnacha) and **Viñas del Palomar en Argonga** (a Garnacha/Merlot/Graciano blend). Both wines were fermented in oak vats and then spent another 11 months in new and used French oak barrels. Since 2009, there has been a young, unoaked red **Emilio Valerio**, fruit-driven and Grenache-dominated, even though it is in fact a blend complemented by small proportions of other red varieties. From 2010, we should expect one or more old-vine Garnacha reds from the estate's vineyards: Arambeltza (80 years old, 1.2 acres [0.5ha]), San Martín de Leorin (60 years old, 1 acre [0.4ha]), Abbatia (75 years old, 1.2 acres), and Monte de Cicuruza (65 years old, 5 acres [2ha]). There will also be the white wines **La Merced** (Malvasia del Palomar) and **Abatía** (Viura). The finest wines have yet to hit the market, starting from the 2009 vintage, when two major changes occurred: French enologist Olivier Rivière joined the team; and their Dicastillo cellar, on the Palomar ridge, became fully operational. In our opinion, that bright future will be much more certain if Emilio and Olivier decide to prize the reasonable stabilization of the wines over extremely low sulfur dioxide levels.

**Laderas de Montejurra**
Area under vine: 50 acres (20ha)
Average production: 40,000 bottles
Paraje de Argonga,
Calle Ongintza 6,
31263 Dicastillo, Navarra
Tel: +34 678 908 389
www.laderasdemontejurra.com

# Bodega Otazu

Bodega Otazu (formerly Señorío de Otazu) is a spectacular estate near Pamplona that has been awarded its own appellation by the Navarra wine authorities—a rare honor in Spain. It combines an old tradition of winemaking, dating back to the 15th century, with a decidedly modern business model, pioneered by the company that recreated the winery in 1989, Gabarbide. The winery is run by manager Javier Bañales and winemaker Javier Colio.

It enjoys a magnificent setting in the Etxauri Valley, with the River Arga skirting the estate and the massive Sierra del Perdón in the background. After vineyards had practically disappeared due to phylloxera in the Merindad de Pamplona, Señorío de Otazu replanted some 227 acres (92ha) of a total area of 865 acres (350ha) with noble Spanish and international varieties. The vineyards surround the 16th-century palace, its 12th-century stone tower, a 13th-century church, and a 17th-century hermitage.

An old part of the winery was built in the French style and dates back to 1860. But the main, state-of-the-art facility, designed by renowned architect Jaime Gaztelu, was completed only in 1997.

This is an interesting area because it's very northerly and cool, with the Pyrenees lurking beyond the Sierra del Perdón. The Señorío de Otazu PR material claims it's the northernmost estate making red wine in Spain—which it is not (there are several others, in the Basque Country, Cantabria, and Asturias, that are farther north)—but the climate is certainly temperate. The soils are also conducive to quality wine production; sand and gravel dominate, with rocky surfaces and good permeability, while the clay subsoils retain enough moisture during the warm, dry summer months.

Technology dominates here—from viticulture to winemaking—and it's been both a plus and a minus, depending on one's viewpoint. No massal selection was used for planting the red varieties (Tempranillo, Merlot, and Cabernet Sauvignon) or the Chardonnay: 15 commercial red clones and three white ones were used. Clonal differentiation plays a large role in the winemaking, since certain clones are reserved for specific cask aging periods and, therefore, for different wines. There are 2,000 French oak barrels in the vaulted cellar designed by Gaztelu.

The results are decidedly international in style, very much along the lines chosen a quarter of a century ago by the Navarra appellation to make a name for itself: powerful, generously oaked reds; buttery, barrel-fermented Chardonnays (and also an unoaked, refreshing white), which were considered back then as the wines that could compete with New World ones in foreign markets. This perception has waned since then, as everybody realized that there was just too much Cabernet and too much Chardonnay in those markets, and European producers returned to native varieties or to blends with more local personality. Over the past few years, Otazu's wines, like some others in Navarra, have come closer to a more direct expression of the terroir, with fewer "international" trappings. But it's still a work in progress.

## FINEST WINES

### Señorío de Otazu Altar ★
A limited-production, refined, Bordeaux-style red (basically Cabernet Sauvignon, with 5% Merlot and 5% Tempranillo), a selection of the estate's best grapes, which is aged 18 months in new oak barrels. (There is also a similar but rarer super-cuvée, **Vitral**, of which only two or three barrels are produced each vintage.)

**Bodega Otazu**
Area under vine: 227 acres (92ha)
Average production: 550,000 bottles
Señorío de Otazu s/n
31174 Etxauri, Navarra
Tel: +34 948 329 200
Fax: +34 948 329 353
www.otazu.com

# Bierzo

Bierzo is a transitional region, and not only because the thousands of pilgrims who walk the St. James's Way go through its heart. It is also transitional in terms of climate, culture, traditions, agriculture, and, more pertinently for this book, grapes and wines. It is a coal-mining district in the western part of the province of León, surrounded by mountains, almost touching the provinces of Lugo and Orense, and the gateway to Galicia in the north from Castilla in the center.

The existence of vineyards in the region was documented in the writings of Roman author and philosopher Pliny the Elder and the Greek Strabo. The area predates the Romans, who brought the vines and viticulture, but the most significant period in its development was during the Middle Ages, thanks mainly to the Cistercian order of monks and the religious importance of wine.

For many years, the region was the most important source of red wines for neighboring Galicia and Asturias, where the bulk of wine production was white. But the attack of phylloxera and the development of transport, bringing with it wines from other regions, killed the captive market for Bierzo wines in northwest Spain. The region suffered. Dominated by the 1960s cooperative movement, it became a source of rosados and simple unoaked reds, and it remained that way for so long that some supposed that the region and its flagship grape, the red Mencía, were capable of nothing more. No one seemed able or willing to capitalize on Bierzo's very real and long identified potential for fine wines.

And so it was that a viticultural region rich in history and tradition was not granted its own *denominación de origen* until 1989. That the DO Bierzo was finally created at all was largely thanks to the work of entrepreneur José Luis Prada, whose winery Prada a Tope was created that same

**Right:** The mountain vineyards of Alto Bierzo, where the best wines often come from old, head-pruned vines on steep slopes

year, after he acquired the Palacio de Canedo and created a range of wines and other gastronomical treats, as well as a chain of restaurants serving and selling typical products from Bierzo.

Even then, it wasn't until Álvaro Palacios and his nephew Ricardo Pérez Palacios of the Palacios Remondo winery in Rioja committed to making great wines from Bierzo at the end of the 20th century that people really started to explore the potential of the area and of Mencía. Since then, Bierzo has exploded into life.

It has always been a beautiful area to visit. But it is perhaps best known in Spain for the gold mines of Las Médulas near the main town Ponferrada, which were the most important gold mines in the Roman Empire and are a UNESCO World Heritage site.

The area has a rich gastronomy; *cecina* (cured and smoked beef) and *botillo* (a pork intestine stuffed with different meats from the pig) are the flagship products, but peppers, apples, pears, chestnuts, and cherries are all equally good here.

## Soil, climate, grapes, and wines

In the 1,160 sq miles (3,000 sq km) within the DO covering 23 towns, there are some 9,900 acres (4,000ha) under vine. Vineyards are largely in the hands of small growers, with more than 4,000 proprietors, and the average holding is smaller than 2.5 acres (1ha). Winemaking is somewhat less fragmented, however. At the last count, there were just 55 wineries making and bottling wine.

The region is divided into two very different subregions: the mountain vineyards of Alto Bierzo (Upper Bierzo); and a flatter, wider section, known as Bajo Bierzo (Lower Bierzo). The climate, soil, and structure of the vineyards in the two subregions, and the resulting wines, are very different. The best wines often come from old vines on steep slopes.

The mesoclimate in Bierzo has many things in common with Galicia (humidity and rain), though in other respects it shares more with the hot and dry climate of Castilla. The average temperature is 53.6°F (12°C) but without going to extremes either in winter or summer, with 27.5in (700mm) of rain and 2,200 hours of sunshine. These are very good conditions for the development of viticulture.

The tiny vineyard plots in the mountains are on steep slopes, with soil rich in quartz and slate. The vineyards on the plains, planted in bigger plots, are on richer soil, with more clay and alluvial matter. The vineyards are planted mainly on humid, dark soil that is slightly acidic and low in carbonates and lime.

In terms of grapes, the main variety is Mencía, covering 65 percent of the total vineyard area, while Garnacha Tintorera (Alicante Bouschet) is losing ground. Tempranillo, Merlot, and Cabernet Sauvignon are permitted on an experimental basis, but some wineries bottle some wines without the DO label to take advantage of the good conditions for growing some of the French varieties. Similarly, the dominant whites are the local Doña Blanca and Godello, as well as Palomino, which was planted for quantity after phylloxera and, though it still represents 15 percent of total plantings, is now on the decline. Malvasia, Chardonnay, and Gewürztraminer are experimental and should represent less than 15 percent of a given wine.

Though white and rosado are produced, the overwhelming majority of wine from Bierzo is red (75 percent of the total volume). The crianza and reserva categories do exist here, but in practice they are mostly ignored. Production varies widely depending on the weather conditions of the year—from less than 10 million liters, to more than 20 million. Only 12 percent of the wine is exported.

Modern Bierzo is a young region, and most of the wineries included here did not even exist ten years ago. As for the style of the wines, the best description we have found comes from Álvaro Palacios, who says Bierzo sits "somewhere between the northern Rhône and Burgundy." Sounds tempting, doesn't it?

## Northwest Spain

Regional boundary ——————
Provincial boundary — — — —
International border ▬▬▬▬▬

0      50 km
0      50 miles

ATLANTIC
OCEAN

RÍAS ALTAS

Ortigueira

Viveiro

Ribadeo

Avilés

Ferrol

A Coruña

Betanzos

Villalba

Pravia

Tineo

Oviedo

Carballo

**ASTURIAS**

Cangas
del Narcea

Ordes

A9

A6

Lugo

Villablino

Corcubión

Santiago de
Compostela

**GALICIA**

Tambre

Baralla

Cordillera Cantábrica

Embalse de
Belesar

Muros

Ulla

Sarria

Noia

A Estrada

Lalin

Descendientes de
J. Palacios

**BIERZO**

Pazo de Señorans
Palacio de
Fefiñanes

A9

**RÍAS
BIAXAS**

Monforte
de Lemos

A53

Tapada-
Guitian

Ponferrada

Forjas del Salnés
Gerardo Mendez

**RIBEIRA SACRA**

Raul Perez

Pontevedra

Emilio
Rojo

**RIBEIRO**

AdegaAlgueira

Rafael Palacios

Astorga

Vigo

Viña
Mein

Ourense

Dominio
do Bibei

**VALDEORRAS**

Ponteareas

A52

Allariz

La Bañeza

Lusco

Viana
del Bollo

**CASTILLA Y LEÓN**

Fillaboa  La Val

Minho

**RÍAS BAIXAS**

**MONTERREI**

Verin

A52

Quinta
da Muradella

Embalse
Ricobayo

Chaves

Bragança

Guimaraes

Macedo de
Cavaleiros

Vila Real

**PORTUGAL**

AREA OF MAIN MAP

A Coruña

Barcelona

MADRID

# Descendientes de J Palacios

The idea of Bierzo had been in the head of Álvaro Palacios from the time he traveled Spain north to south and east to west selling oak barrels in the 1980s. He was looking for a forgotten area with high potential to create quality wines. In his internal debate, Priorat won over Bierzo. But ten years after the rebirth of Priorat in 1989, the Palacios name is also responsible for the revival of Bierzo. In this case, it's Álvaro together with his nephew Ricardo Pérez Palacios. Ricardo had been studying in Bordeaux and traveling throughout Spain. When he visited Bierzo, he was excited. He talked to Álvaro, and the idea that had been hibernating in his mind came back to life.

*Ten years after the rebirth of Priorat in 1989, the Palacios name is also responsible for the revival of Bierzo. Their first wines really surprised many people*

They looked for old vineyards high in the mountains rather than in the valley, where the berries were small, the juice concentrated and well colored. Until then, Mencía was considered a grape to make rosado and unoaked (often carbonic-maceration) reds but not much more. They found them in Corullón. They took their time, searched for the vineyards they liked, and painstakingly convinced many different proprietors to sell their few vines before revealing their plan. They also bought and restored a small stone winery in Villafranca del Bierzo. Today they own more than 85 acres (35ha) of vineyards, and another 37–50 acres (15–20ha) of other crops: chestnuts, cherries, apples, pears, figs, vegetables... They also run a farm, trying to get closer to the traditional agricultural structure of Bierzo.

The name of the company, Descendants of J Palacios, is a tribute to their father and grandfather respectively, José Palacios, the initiator of this great wine family with his Palacios Remondo winery in Rioja. The 1999 was their first vintage, vinified at Castro Ventosa, the winery from Raúl Pérez's family, who helped them get established in the region. It marked the beginning of modern Bierzo.

Corullón is the name of a tiny mountain village—the area they liked best for quality and the source of the grapes for all their wines. The vineyards here are very small plots of old-vine Mencía grown on steep slate slopes at variable altitudes, ranging from 1,310 to 2,950ft (400–900m), which have to be worked with a horse. They are often above the line of the clouds, which gives them very good light and enough temperature to ripen properly.

In fact, Bierzo and Priorat have much in common: old vines, local grape varieties of no great reputation, steep slopes, slate, and a bad or nonexistent image. Both also produce wines of strong personality: distinctive, elegant, and powerful, and marked by the minerality of the slate. Their first wines really surprised many people, gaining very high scores in the United States and showing the way for high-quality oak-aged Mencía, which some had thought impossible.

Their philosophy might be described as Burgundian, embracing the importance of place, the notion of terroir, respect for nature, and non-interventionist winemaking to create characterful, pure, and vibrant wines that give pleasure when drunk. It is a project run by the heart, not by the head. And when things are done with passion, when people believe in and enjoy what they are doing, it shows in the results.

They made 25,000 bottles of the 1999, under two labels, and began understanding the vineyards. Ricardo is very much into biodynamics—a true believer. He has translated Nicolas Joly's *Wine from*

**Right:** Ricardo Pérez Palacios, whose enthusiasm for Bierzo rekindled his uncle's interest and that of the region as a whole

*Earth to Sky* into Spanish and actively participates in the fight against genetically modified organisms. They started working the vineyards following those principles. Once they knew the character of the different plots, they saw the need to keep single-vineyard wines separate, so from 2001 they redefined their portfolio.

They use small wooden vats to ferment the grapes and have their barrels made to their specification by some of the world's top coopers. Their work in the winery, however, is not what they consider most important; and even when you ask them about it, they prefer to take you into the fields and show you the vineyards. It is there that these wines are made.

The 2001 vintage was very balanced in Bierzo— not one that made headlines immediately but, rather, one that gave elegant wines that are aging very well but took time to reveal themselves. In the same year, Álvaro and Ricardo launched their single-vineyard bottlings—Moncerbal, San Martín, and La Faraona. However, the quality of the Corullón blend did not suffer, as often happens when this diversification takes place; indeed, it actually improved, since the new wines were produced from vineyards that were not previously in their possession, and they allowed an even stricter selection for the Corullón.

What they wanted to make clear is that they did not take away the best grapes from Corullón to make other single bottlings; instead, they bought more vineyards. In other words, there was no cannibalization, as so often happens in such cases. A few more single-vineyard wines were to follow in subsequent vintages, and the nephew-and-uncle team has not looked back since.

In these ways, another historical wine region was brought back to life. Many other wineries, and even famous names from other regions, followed the Palacioses. But above all, it is them we need to thank for the renaissance here.

## FINEST WINES

They started with a couple of wines—one simply called Bierzo and the other Corullón, which is still produced—and then moved into several single-vineyard bottlings, as well as creating the very successful and affordable Pétalos del Bierzo, which represents the majority of their volume, with more than 300,000 bottles produced. Today, up to eight different wines are offered, all exclusively Mencía. Not all the single-vineyard wines are produced every year. All wines are produced in a very similar way and have a common profile, the differences as subtle as those between Chambolle-Musigny premiers crus Amoureuses, Charmes, and Cras. Most recently, they have focused on three of these single vineyards (in Spanish, they prefer to call them *parajes*, or "landscapes"): Moncerbal, Las Lamas, and La Faraona. Maybe one day these landscapes will be as well known, and their character as defined and studied, as those of the most elegant village of the Côte de Nuits mentioned above. All of the wines need plenty of air and benefit from decanting, because the production methods are highly reductive.

### Pétalos del Bierzo [V]
This is the entry-level wine, and it's a great success on restaurant wine lists. It offers one of the best quality:price ratios not only in Bierzo but in the whole of Spain. It is made of grapes from rented vineyards in Corullón and the surrounding villages, ranging from 40 to 90 years of age. The wine spends six to ten months (depending on the character of the vintage) in used barrels, resulting in a very perfumed wine redolent of flower petals— hence the name. On the palate, it is fresh, with plenty of fruit (strawberry, mulberry) and a spicy character, good acidity, and a salty edge that makes you want to drink more. Fortunately, it's produced in sufficient volume to quench your thirst!

### Corullón
Head-pruned Mencía, between 50 and 90 years old, planted at high density (6,000–7,000 vines per hectare), all on schist (slate), dry-farmed, and without any green-harvest. The vineyard is, and always has been, worked with mules. Yields are very low, at 20–30hl/ha. The wine is fermented in open wood vats with *pigeage* and aged 14 months in barrel. Around 18,000–20,000 bottles are produced. The dark color is followed on

the nose by plenty of balsamic notes intermixed with strawberry, red currant, blueberry, and floral scents. On the palate, there is a nice spine of lively acidity and focused flavors, making it delineated, pure, and long. Balance and elegance have always been the defining features, a style well represented in **2001★**. The **2005** is also among our favorites.

### Moncerbal ★

The Moncerbal vineyards are at an elevation of 1,970–2,460ft (600–750m) with centennial vines that barely yield 9hl/ha—extremely low considering there are 7,000 vines per hectare. This is an area with very little soil but a lot of rock, minerals, and even granite, giving very fine and elegant wines. It is a mountain where Mediterranean and Atlantic climates and forests coexist. They have vineyards on both sides of the mountain, the Atlantic and the Mediterranean, but the grapes used for the wine come from a plot called O Sufreiro ("The Oak Tree" in Galician) in the Mediterranean part, where the mother rock—always slate—is extremely old. As with all the other wines, it is bottled unfiltered, in this instance into no more than 2,500 bottles. The texture and nuances of this wine are distinctly Burgundian. We particularly liked the **2003**.

### Las Lamas

Las Lamas vineyard is only yards away from Moncerbal, but both the terroirs and the wines are very different. Here, there is more clay, and as in most of Bierzo, there's a lot of iron as well. This makes for rounder, more muscular wines. It's again very steep-sloping, south-facing, and planted with very old, head-pruned Mencía vines. Yields are extremely low, at 8hl/ha. Aging is for 13 months in new French oak, but none of these wines ever seems oaky. Only 1,200–1,800 bottles are produced.

### La Faraona ★

*La faraona* is the Spanish feminine form of "the pharaoh," a popular term in Alfaro in Rioja, where the Palacios family originates. When you buy bulk wine there, they give you all the wines to taste, but the best one is always kept till last. When they show it to you, they say, "And now, The Pharaoh!" It's therefore a brand name, not the vineyard name. At the same time, this is the only true single-vineyard wine, since it is sourced from a single plot, called El Ferro, comprising 0.75 acres (0.3ha) of 65-year-old vines in the highest part of the village of Corullón

**Above:** Some of the steep-sloped vineyards at Corullón, which are plowed, as they always have been, by mules

(at 2,805ft [855m]). The yields are minuscule, to the point of being uneconomical (it all depends on the price of the product, of course), and at 7hl/ha and 7,000 plants per hectare, this could compete for the lowest-yielding vineyard in the world. There are only two or three barrels each year. This is a great wine, with very powerful floral and fruit aromas. On the palate, it is quite light but sustained by acidity and an unusual tannin for Bierzo. It is a wine that transports you to the mountains of Corullón and makes you feel both Atlantic cold and Mediterranean warmth—a wine to which you can really apply the adjective "rare." The **2005** is highly recommended, but any vintage is worth trying.

**Descendientes de J Palacios**
Area under vine: 85 acres (35ha)
Average production: 350,000 bottles
Calvo Sotelo 6,
24500 Villafranca del Bierzo, León
Tel: +34 987 540 821
Fax: +34 987 540 851

# Bodegas y Viñedos Raúl Pérez

Raúl Pérez is currently one of the biggest names in Spanish wine. He is the most prolific and sought-after winemaker in the country, mostly in the northwest, partly because his wines have received very high praise and scores from Jay Miller in Robert Parker's *Wine Advocate*. Together with the low availability of the wines, this makes them very much in demand.

None of this was part of the plan of young Raúl Pérez Pereira, born in 1972 in Valtuille de Abajo. Indeed, despite there being a long tradition of wine in his family, by the time he reached his early 20s, he wasn't all that interested in wine—he didn't even drink it. He wanted to be a doctor. But somewhere along the line he caught the wine bug and never got over it. He started in the family winery, Castro Ventosa, in 1993, before the Bierzo revolution started, and was there until 2003. He was in fact another of the catalysts for the Bierzo revolution. It was at Castro Ventosa that he helped Ricardo Pérez Palacios make the first wines under the name Descendientes de J Palacios in 1999 and where he crafted fantastic wines like the Valtuille Cepas Centenarias 2001.

None of these achievements quite satisfied him, however. He needed to do different things, to express himself. We include him in Bierzo because he was born there and he makes some wines there, but he also makes wines in several other regions. He breaks the rules, he pushes the limits, he crosses the line and crosses boundaries—he is anything but conventional. He is, in our opinion, a genius, a wild, free spirit. He makes highly individual wines, including an incredible Albariño aged under the Atlantic, and a joint venture in Monterrei and Ribeira Sacra in Galicia. He even crosses the border into Portugal, where, with JL Mateo, he's making radical wines with names like A Trabe, Muradella, and Gorvía.

**Left:** Raúl Pérez, the highly idiosyncratic winemaker who, following rave reviews, is now the most sought-after in Spain

In Spain, though, Pérez makes wine in Bierzo, Ribeira Sacra, Méntrida, Cebreros, Asturias, Galicia, Madrid, and Valdevimbre. He makes wines like Pricum Prieto Picudo from Bodegas Margón in León; the biodynamic, old-vine Garnacha El Reventón from Cebreros (together with Daniel Jiménez Landi from Bodegas Jiménez Landi in Méntrida); the previously mentioned Quinta da Muradella; and Forjas del Salnés in Rías Baixas, where Pérez also makes the Leirana whites and Goliardo reds together with Rodrigo Méndez. In Madrid, Pérez advises the Bernabeleva winery; in Ribeira Sacra, he works with Guímaro (where he makes El Pecado) and with Algueira. No doubt there will be more in the years to come.

This is clearly not a regular operation with a fixed area of vineyards and an average number of bottles each year. Pérez works in many different places under a variety of arrangements (his own wines, joint ventures, consultancies), very often in very small vineyards (some owned, some rented, some belonging to others), making a few barrels of a wine that might not be made every year. It would be a marketing director's nightmare.

In 2010, some of the producers with whom Pérez works staged a tasting. They showed some 80 wines, but he says that there are more. In fact, one sometimes wonders if Pérez himself knows exactly how many wines he's involved with in some capacity or other—a situation complicated by the fact that some wines are not available commercially and are purely for drinking with friends. He appreciates the luxury of having seven or eight local grapes in Galicia, well adapted to the soil and climate conditions, which allows him to do something different. If you thought Mencía and Godello were exotic and obscure, wait and see the list of varieties Pérez uses: Caíño, Loureiro, Araúxa, Zamarrica, Albarín, and Merenzao (a.k.a. Bastardo, or Trousseau in Jura). He believes Ribeira Sacra is the region with most potential, but the problem there is the viticulture.

**Above:** One of Pérez's two "new" wineries, at Salas de los Barrios in Bierzo, where he makes his own range of Ultreia wines

Much of his work is based on intuition: he does not follow a formula—not even for the same wine from one year to the next. He wants to make wines with character, and most of the wines are produced in very limited quantities of around 1,000 bottles, the largest volume being 15,000 bottles. The diversity is mind-boggling. He is making some Loire-like reds, for example, that are sometimes a little fragile but have character to spare. He makes wines from tannic red varieties, as well as from less tannic, more aromatic ones. And he is very much committed to viticulture with no or little use of chemicals. Some wines are made with stems, fermented with indigenous yeasts in oak *foudres*, with variable use of new oak and low $SO_2$ (only at bottling).

His consulting business—and his full-time job as technical director at Bodegas Estefanía—gives him enviable financial independence. It means that when he doesn't like the vintage, he doesn't release the wine. None of his 2006 top wines made it into the market, for example.

The latest development is a bricks-and-mortar winery, which brings to an end the long period when Pérez was without a winery he could call his own. But he's not building just one winery—he's building

two! He bought an old winery, built in 1810, along with its vines in Salas de los Barrios, in Bierzo, and he restored the building. It's there he makes the Ultreia wines from Bierzo. He also bought a winery from the 1920s, with an amazing underground cave in Valdevimbre, where he's keeping the structure and building a brand-new winery inside; it was scheduled to be ready for the 2010 harvest. He will make two more wines at Valdevimbre, from Prieto Picudo, because he believes it's a variety that has a lot of potential and is only just beginning to be understood. The variety is tannic and needs gentle vinification, is high in acidity, and can be aged for a long time in wood.

When asked whether there are more wines in the pipeline, Pérez explains that he has just returned from South Africa, where he is working with Eben Sadie (Columella, Terroir al Limit) on a blend of Monastrell and Syrah that will be called Cabo Tormentas. He would like to do something in Chile or Argentina. He is also interested in the Rufete variety, which is found in Salamanca and the Douro. He has a Pinot Noir from Bierzo. And his Ultreia Douro, made with fellow maverick Dirk Niepoort, is already bottled. The man is simply unstoppable.

## FINEST WINES

This is an exceptionally difficult list to compile. Which of Raúl Pérez's wines are his finest? Which are his wines anyway? Names and labels come and go, and it's sometimes difficult to know if a given wine is his or belongs to a winery he works for. Some wines are sold with different labels in different markets, he makes small lots for or with friends, and when he tries to explain it all to you, your head starts spinning. There is a new Prieto Picudo sourced from 100-year-old vines and aged for 17 months in French oak, and this is one of the regions that he is going to grow in, with a permanent winery. Sacrata is a new label for Mencía from Ribeira Sacra; Vico, made in Bierzo for his American importer Patrick Mata, is sold as Ultreia in Spain. A white vinified as if it were a red, called La Claudina, a Godello from Valtuille de Abajo, comes to mind, because it received the highest score for a Spanish white ever in *The Wine Advocate*. At the time of writing, Pérez was making wines for his own company in Bierzo, León, Rías Baixas, Ribeira Sacra, and Monterrei, but this could very well have changed by the time you come to read this.

### Ultreia Saint-Jacques [V]
Ultreia was going to be the name of the project, and it comes from the old Latin greeting used among pilgrims on the St. James's Way, which can be loosely translated as "move ahead" or "continue." In fact, one of the wines is called Ultreia Saint-Jacques. This is pure Mencía from Bierzo, aged for 12 months in oval 1,500-liter oak casks with *bâtonnage*. It is very perfumed, with ripe red fruit and a mineral touch; concentrated and intense in the mouth but never heavy. Raspberry and graphite with a Burgundian accent. This is an entry-level, high-production wine, with 15,000 bottles that sell locally for less than €10. The only problem is finding it. Try the **2008** or **2009**.

### Ultreia de Valtuille ★
Once again, this is Mencía from Bierzo, from a vineyard planted in 1880 on sandy soils with a southern exposure. The **2008**, as seems to be the norm lately, is fermented in big oval-shaped casks. Elegant and powerful, the 15% ABV is perfectly integrated into the wine, though the wood needs a little more time to integrate. Production of the initial 2005 was a mere 1,900 bottles, and after it received a score of 98 points from *The Wine Advocate*, it is surely impossible to find.

### Sketch ★
The grapes for this single-vineyard Albariño from Rías Baixas are from 60–80-year-old vines, belonging to Forjas del Salnés, planted by the sea. It is made in the Burgundian way, in 750-liter barriques with *pigeage*. The bottles are aged under the sea for at least three months, now at 65ft (20m), because at 100ft (30m) the pressure caused problems with the corks. It is named after a restaurant in London of which Pérez is particularly fond. Great care is made to ensure the integration of the wood, but when very young, this wine is still a bit oaky, and it benefits from a year in bottle. He makes 900 bottles of this non-DO vino de mesa, or table wine. There's also another Albariño called Multi, aged in Austrian-style 1,500-liter oval-shaped oak casks.

### El Pecado ★
This is a red from Ribeira Sacra, made from 30–40-year-old Mencía vines grown on steep terraces of compact slate by the River Sil in a landscape that recalls the Douro Valley in Portugal. The wine ferments in open vats with *pigeage* and is then aged for a year in barrique. The winemaking takes place at Adegas Guímaro in the village of Sober, in the Amandi subzone of Ribeira Sacra. Some of the fruit is in whole bunches and foot-trodden, while the rest is destemmed, but no pumps or anything else aggressive are used for the fruit or wine. Pérez likes to make small quantities because it allows him to craft wines in an artisanal, hands-on way.

### A Trabe ★
This is a joint venture with Quinta da Muradella in Monterrei, but this wine seems to belong to Raúl Pérez. It is subtitled Viticultura de Montaña ("Mountain Viticulture"). A Trabe Red is a blend of indigenous varieties: 35% Bastardo (Merenzao in other parts of Galicia; Trousseau in Jura), 25% Mencía, 20% Zamarrica, 10% Verdello Tinta, 5% Serodia Tinta, and 5% Garnacha Tintorera. If you're interested in wine at all, you simply have to try it.

**Bodegas y Viñedos Raúl Pérez**
Plaza Alcalde Pérez López s/n,
24530 Valtuille de Abajo, León
Fax: +34 987 420 015
www.raulperezbodegas.es

# Luna Beberide

Luna Beberide is a family winery created in 1987. Its 200 acres (80ha) of vineyards have names such as El Francés and El Castrillón, on south-facing slopes in Villafranca, where the family lives, and in Cacabelos, where the winery is located. In the beginning they relied on French grapes such as Cabernet Sauvignon, Merlot, and Gewürztraminer, and they were quite successful. Unusually for Bierzo, they focus on white wines.

Luna Beberide has been the bridge between the old and new generations in Bierzo. At the end of the 1990s, the family approached Mariano García, who had just finished at Vega-Sicilia in Ribera del Duero after 30 years making their wines. They wanted his advice to improve their own wines. As a result, a friend who had studied in France with García's son Eduardo ended up as winemaker of Luna Beberide from 2001. He was Gregory Pérez, a Bordelais who had worked at Grand-Puy-Lacoste and Cos d'Estournel.

Alejandro Luna, together with Mariano García's sons Eduardo and Alberto and Gregory Pérez, also created a small project in Bierzo called Paixar. Gregory Pérez gave up Luna Beberide in 2007 to start his own winery, Mengoba, and also sold his participation in Paixar in 2010.

Today, the focus has shifted toward the local grape varieties, even though they have retained some of the French ones, and some of the wines made with them count among the best created from such grapes in Spain.

## FINEST WINES

The labels have changed a lot over time, and most of them are still not Bierzo DO, since they use ineligible French grapes (Gewürztraminer, Merlot, and Cabernet Sauvignon) and have to be sold as Vino de la Tierra de Castilla y León. They have recently started bottling a pure Godello white and a pure Mencía called Art, as well as a single-vineyard wine (also Mencía) called Finca La Cuesta and even a sweet wine made with Petit Manseng.

### Viña Aralia
A great commercial success, this 50/50 blend of Gewürztraminer and Chardonnay without the DO label is limited to 140,000 bottles. It works very well with Asian cuisine.

### Luna Beberide Gewurztraminer [V]
This is obviously a non-DO wine, but the Gewürztraminer works well here, and the wine is quite successful locally; indeed, it has a claim to being one of the best Gewurztraminers in Spain. It's made from 20-year-old vines yielding 25–30hl/ha, fermented in stainless steel and bottled young to keep it fresh. Drink it as young as possible.

### Tierras de Luna
This blend of Mencía, Merlot, and Cabernet Sauvignon is aged for 16 months in new oak and bottled unfiltered; it represents a more modern type of wine. The **2001** was showing well in 2005, which means that this wine needs time, since it's initially quite powerful with very present tannins.

### Luna Beberide ★
This is a red cuvée whose varietal composition has changed over time from the typical Cabernet Sauvignon (33%), Merlot (33%), Tempranillo (24%), and Mencía (10%) of the 1990s, lowering the proportion of French grapes (and the Tempranillo) and increasing the amount of Mencía to the current 40% Mencía, 30% Cabernet Sauvignon, and 30% Merlot. But it's still a *vino de la tierra* instead of a Bierzo DO wine. The 40-year-old Mencía is head-pruned, while the Cabernet and Merlot, planted in 1986, are on trellises. The wine is aged for 24 months in French and American oak, and even though technically it could be a reserva, this is not allowed for non-DO wines. We love the **1998** and **2000**, where the accent was clearly Bordelais.

**Right:** Alejandro Luna, who is strengthening the regional accent at his family winery through indigenous varieties

**Bodegas y Viñedos Luna Beberide**
Area under vine: 200 acres (80ha)
Average production: 400,000 bottles
Antigua Carretera Madrid a Coruña km 402,
Cacabelos, León
Tel: +34 987 549 002
Fax: +34 987 549 214
www.lunabeberide.es

# Bodega y Viñedos Mengoba

Gregory Pérez is the name behind Mengoba. Other than being friends with them, he has nothing to do with other famous Pérezes from Bierzo, such as Ricardo Pérez or Raúl Pérez. He's not even from the region; indeed, he's not even Spanish—he is a Frenchman from Bordeaux.

Pérez arrived in Bierzo in 2001 to work for Luna Beberide, where he stayed until 2007. Then he started his own project, which he named after the local grapes of Bierzo—"men" from Mencía, "go" from Godello, and since Doña Blanca didn't fit very nicely, and the grape is also known locally as Valenciana (meaning "from Valencia"), he decided to make a phonetic spelling mistake and came up with Mengoba. The name is quite unusual, but it reflects his interest in the local flavor, the native grapes, and the spirit of the project.

*Mengoba: the name is quite unusual, but it reflects Pérez's interest in the local flavor, the native grapes, and the spirit of the project*

Gregory had worked at Grand-Puy-Lacoste and at Château Cos d'Estournel between 1997 and 2000. He had studied in Bordeaux and met some Spanish friends who were also studying there. His great-grandfather was Spanish, which explains why he has a Spanish surname. At home, however, the family didn't speak Spanish, and even though they lived in Bordeaux, they were in no way linked to the wine business. But Gregory grew interested in wine, and went to study at Blanquefort. While there, he met Ricardo Pérez Palacios (from Palacios Remondo in Rioja and Descendientes de J Palacios in Bierzo), as well as Eduardo García, son of Mariano García, one of the most famous winemakers in Spain, who is the owner of Bodegas Mauro and also involved in many other wines in Ribera del Duero.

Mariano García was helping a winery in Bierzo—Luna Beberide—and they were looking for a winemaker. So when Gregory heard about it through Eduardo García, he packed his suitcase, arriving just before the 2001 harvest and without speaking a word of Spanish. Five years later, already completely integrated in the region, he took the next step and created his own project. He has a small winery in Sorribas, a small village close to Cacabelos, and vineyards in Espanillo, Valtuille, Villafranca del Bierzo, and Carracedo. Mencía and Godello are (now) better known, but Doña Blanca was almost lost, *gobelet*-trained and mixed with the Mencía in old vineyards.

Pérez is also involved in other projects. One is in León, where he is working with Prieto Picudo ("a tannic grape that we still need to come to know better," he says) sold under the brand name Preto. Another, Ibias, is based in Asturias, where Pérez works with grapes that are pretty much unknown and almost extinct. Pérez was also a partner in Paixar in Bierzo—together with Alejandro Luna from Luna Beberide and brothers Alberto and Eduardo García from Mauro in Valladolid—from its creation until 2010.

## FINEST WINES

The company started producing a red and a white under the Mengoba label and later bottled a varietal Estaladiña (a true rarity, since the grape is largely unknown); a sweet wine called Folie Douce, made from Petit Manseng, Godello, and Doña Blanca; and an entry-level red and white with the name Brezo ("Heather").

### Mengoba Mencía de Espanillo ★
This is Mencía with a small proportion of an obscure local grape, Estaladiña. Espanillo is a small village in the mountains of Bierzo, where the 80-year-old vineyards are planted on soils rich in slate. The wine is made in 400-liter integral vinification barrels, where alcoholic and malolactic fermentations are carried out, and the maturation is continued in the same barrel on its lees for a further 11 months.

This cool-climate red is fresh and mineral, with red-berry, balsamic, herb, and soil notes, fine tannins, and very well-integrated oak. It has only been produced since the 2007 vintage.

**Above:** Gregory Pérez, who has rediscovered his Spanish roots and is making exciting wines from indigenous varieties

### Mengoba Godello y Doña Blanca Sobre Lías

The white Mengoba is made from 50% Godello and 50% Doña Blanca. Pérez ferments the Doña Blanca in stainless steel and the Godello in 5,000-liter oak *foudres*, and the two are aged separately on their lees with weekly *bâtonnage* for eight months. The color is very pale, with floral and green-apple notes and echoes of Godello. The 2007 was the first vintage, with a total production of 15,000 bottles. A name to watch.

### Bodega y Viñedos Mengoba

Area under vine: 32 acres (13ha)
Average production: 82,000 bottles
Calle San Francisco E,
24416 Santo Tomás de las Ollas, León
Tel: +34 649 940 800
www.mengoba.com

# Bodegas y Viñedos Paixar

In 2001, Bierzo was the hottest region on the Spanish wine scene: the first wines from the born-again DO were hitting the shelves, and some were getting big points from the American wine press. It was an exciting area to be in. Luna Beberide was already established there, and the company sought the help of Mariano García, whom many rate as the best winemaker in Spain. He has a high public profile, having been winemaker at Vega-Sicilia, one of the most prestigious wineries in Spain, for 30 years, and now has a range of other projects such as Mauro, San Román, Astrales, and Aalto. García introduced his sons, Eduardo and Alberto, to Bierzo, as well as to Alejandro Luna, who is of a similar age to the young Garcías.

*The Paixar winery makes just one wine and in very small quantities. This could be a garage wine, but they don't even have a garage!*

Luna Beberide needed a full-time winemaker, and the Garcías proposed a friend of Eduardo, Gregory Pérez. The four young wine enthusiasts—Alejandro Luna, Eduardo and Alberto García, and Gregory Pérez—traveled the area together and discovered some very small patches of old Mencía vineyard around the tiny village of Dragonte (133 inhabitants), high in the mountains (2,950ft [900m] above sea level) in the municipality of Corullón. This was where Descendientes de J Palacios was sourcing grapes for the wines that were making the new Bierzo explode.

The quartet got really excited and decided to start a project together, making small quantities of high-quality wine from these vineyards. They heard the locals using the word *paixares* to refer to the highlands of Bierzo; they liked the word, adopting it for their project, Paixar. They made their first vintage, a grand total of 3,000 bottles, in 2001, at the Luna Beberide winery.

Today they control 12 acres (5ha) of vineyards, all old Mencía (50–80 years old), on steep slopes rich in slate, of which 7.5 acres (3ha) are generally used for the wine. This is why the production can be variable from year to year, sometimes reaching up to 8,000 bottles, with the average being around 5,000 bottles.

In 2010, the Luna family bought out Pérez's share of the business to allow Pérez to branch out on his own with his Mengoba project. Paixar is now, therefore, owned equally by the García and Luna families.

## FINEST WINES

### Paixar

The winery makes just one wine and in very small quantities. This could be a garage wine, but they don't even have a garage! Paixar is black both in color and—if that's possible—on the nose, with peat, coal, graphite, and black fruit. The wine is made in a non-interventionist way, trying to preserve the delicate character of Mencía. They put the grapes over a sorting table and then ferment them in stainless-steel tanks with pre-fermentation cold maceration, using only indigenous yeasts. The aging in French wood is determined according to the character of the vintage but averages 16 months, and the wine is bottled unfiltered. It is a dark and powerful wine, with a marked personality—Atlantic, earthy, intense, and structured, with enough balance and stuffing to age for a couple of decades. The **2004★** is a very austere, mineral vintage, much to our liking, and **2006** is another favorite of ours.

**Bodegas y Viñedos Paixar**
Area under vine: 1.2 acres (0.5ha)
Average production: 5,000 bottles
Calle Ribadeo 56,
24500 Villafranca del Bierzo, León
Tel: +34 98 549 220
Fax: +34 98 549 214

**Left:** Eduardo García, one of the founders of Paixar, which takes its name from the highland vineyards used for its wines

# Bodegas Estefanía-Tilenus

Bodegas Estefanía is a young company in the emerging appellation of Bierzo. Founded in 1999, it sells wines under the name Tilenus. It's a privately owned operation belonging to the Frías family from Burgos, a name linked to the dairy industry. They turned one of their milk-collection centers between the villages of Dehesas and Posadas del Bierzo, 4 miles (6km) away from Ponferrada, into one of the top wineries in the new Bierzo. They wanted to revive an old wine tradition in the family, since the grandfather used to make wine in Toro. The name of the company is a tribute to that generation: the grandmother of the owners was called Estefanía.

The base of the project was the acquisition of 100 acres (40ha) of old-vine Mencía, vineyards that ranged from 60 to 100 years old, the oldest vines planted in 1911. They have the latest technology for winemaking and a stock of more than 1,000 French oak barriques. The aim has always been to produce world-class wines, and no effort or money has been spared to achieve it. Raúl Pérez, who has become the most fashionable, prolific, and valued winemaking consultant in northwest Spain, has been in charge of making the wines.

The focus is on the vineyards, because they believe that the more care you take there, the less you need to do in the winery. The old vines yield no more than 2.6lb (1.2kg) of grapes per plant, which are hand-harvested. Fermentation takes place in stainless-steel vats; aging is in French wood. The bottled wine is aged in the winery and not released until considered ready—up to three years for some wines.

All of the wines are reds from Mencía. The range includes Joven (unoaked), Roble, Crianza, and two single-vineyard bottlings from extremely old vines. In 2004, they expanded to cover another indigenous grape, Prieto Picudo, with the brand name Clan, sold as Vino de la Tierra de Castilla y León. Of this there is a red crianza and a rosado.

## FINEST WINES

### Tilenus [V]
Joven, Roble, and Crianza exist for this label. This is the basic range, respectively unoaked, aged for 8–10 months in oak, and aged for 12–14 months in oak. The examples without oak show the pure fruit of Mencía, while the longer the oak aging, the more spicy notes and weight in the wines. The Crianzas from **2004** and **2000** are highly recommended.

### Tilenus Pagos de Posada ★
The vineyard Pagos de Posada is one of the oldest, located in Valtuille de Arriba, and the source for this wine. The grapes are harvested manually using small boxes at the beginning of September. Great care is put into every small detail, with the aim of producing fine wines. The destemmed grapes are fermented in stainless-steel tanks, always at temperatures under 82°F (28°C), for ten days. The wine remains in contact with the skins for a further 30 days. The aging occurs in new French barrels for a period of 13 months, and the wine is bottled unfiltered. The color is dark and very intense. It is marked by some toast notes such as coal, smoke, and roasted coffee in its youth, with cedarwood, lactic and spice notes (white pepper), flowers, and a core of red fruit (raspberry). On the palate, it has good structure, with lively acidity, but also plenty of fruit, supple tannins, and excellent harmony and length. The **2000** and **2001** should be ready and are very good examples of this wine. The **2004** will probably be one of the best.

### Tilenus Pieros
This comes from ancient vines—over 100 years old—grown at 2,300–2,630ft (700–800m) in Cacabelos. It is fermented in stainless steel and aged in new French oak for 18–22 months, then bottled unfined and unfiltered. It is marked by oak in youth and needs a few years in bottle. Only 3,000 bottles are made. It was first produced in 2001.

> **Bodegas Estefanía-Tilenus**
> Area under vine: 128 acres (52ha)
> Average production: 250,000 bottles
> Carretera Dehesas a Posada del Bierzo s/n,
> 24390 Dehesas, Ponferrada, León
> Tel: +34 987 420 015
> Fax: +34 987 420 015
> www.tilenus.com

# Dominio de Tares

Like most of the wineries in Bierzo included here, Dominio de Tares is a very young operation. When both critics and consumers got tired of heavy, alcoholic, overoaked, and overextracted wines, many turned to cooler regions able to produce fresh, elegant wines. Dominio de Tares was one of them, a company created by a group of investors interested in fine wine. At Tares, they combine tradition and the latest technology, with the aim of producing high-quality wines that reflect their origin, using only their local grapes, Mencía and Godello.

The vineyards are located in different parts of the appellation—not necessarily around the Bembibre area where the winery is located—because they believe that combining grapes from diverse soils and microclimates, in which Bierzo is quite rich, creates more complex wines. The winery can ferment up to 350,000 liters in 36 different stainless-steel tanks and thus keep the different vineyards separate. They also have 2,500 oak barrels, 30 percent new, where they age the wines from four to 24 months, depending on the wine, and then they are bottled unfiltered.

The harvest is carried out from the middle of September until the end of October, since each plot is harvested depending on the ripeness of the grapes. The bunches are transported in 33lb (15kg) boxes and put across a sorting table.

The first wine they put on the market was the Cepas Viejas ("Old Vines") from 2000. It was an instant success, because it was exactly what people were expecting from Bierzo at a good price. The portfolio has recently been broadened by some new labels and even a single-vineyard bottling.

## FINEST WINES

### Dominio de Tares Cepas Viejas [V]
*Cepas viejas* means "old vines," and this is a cuvée made from selected head-pruned Mencía vineyards over 60 years old, grown on clay-limestone soils with a high slate content. The hand-harvested grapes are put across a sorting table on their arrival at the winery to select only the perfect bunches. Alcoholic fermentation lasts for 15 days, and malolactic takes place in American oak barrels. The wine is later aged for nine months in a mixture of new and used barrels, of both French and American origin, and bottled unfiltered. This wine offers a very good quality:price ratio and has been quite successful. The initial **2000** vintage remains our favorite: it is very dark in color, almost opaque. There is good intensity of aroma, with dry straw, autumn leaves, and wild flowers covering a core of very mature red fruits. In the mouth, it is medium-bodied, with good acidity, balance, and length, both flavorful and powerful. The **2001** and **2004** are also recommended. Availability is high, since 160,000 bottles are produced. This is one of the best-known new-age Bierzo wines.

### Bembibre
In 2001, with the experience of the 2000 vintage, they selected seven different single vineyards that showed specific characteristics and their own personality. Each of these vineyards was cultivated according to the specific needs of its soil and climate. The blend from six of these vineyards was called Bembibre, the name of their village. Our recommendations are for the **2001**, **2002**, and **2004** vintages.

### Tares P3
The seventh vineyard identified and treated separately from 2001—planted with centennial vines on a steep slope that yield no more than 1lb (500g) of grapes per plant—was code-named P3 (*pago* 3). It showed a completely different personality, so they decided to bottle it separately, and this gave birth to the Tares P3 wine. Production is around 4,500 bottles. We'd love to see this bottling less marked by the influence of wood. The **2004★** remains our favorite vintage of this wine so far.

### Viñedos y Bodegas Dominio de Tares
Area under vine: 104 acres (42ha) owned, plus 25 acres (10ha) rented
Average production: 300,000 bottles
Los Barredos 4,
24318 San Román de Bembibre, León
Tel: +34 987 514 550
Fax: +34 987 514 570
www.dominiodetares.com

# Rías Baixas and the Rest of Galicia

The Rías Baixas DO is a composite of several subzones arranged alongside the southwest coast of Galicia, north of the River Miño—which acts as a natural frontier between Spain and Portugal—and around the *rías* of Vigo, Pontevedra, and Arousa. (A *ría* is the Spanish equivalent of the Norwegian fjord.)

The five subzones, from south to north, are O Rosal, Condado do Tea, Soutomaior, Val do Salnés, and Ribeira do Ulla. The most important by far is the Val do Salnés, which is where most of the historically prominent bodegas are located. It is also big enough to hold more than half of the appellation vineyards, responsible for over two-thirds of the total production. O Rosal and the Condado do Tea are intermediate in size and importance, while the more recent Soutomaior (1996) and Ribeira do Ulla (2000) account for only 4 percent of the vineyards and some 2 percent of the total production.

While reds are produced here (based on the local grapes Caíño Tinto, Espadeiro, Loureira Tinta, and Sousón), as well as whites from such varieties as Loureira Blanca, Treixadura, and Caíño Blanco, the region is dominated by the fresh and perfumed Albariño-based whites. A popular misconception is that these are wines to be drunk within one year of the vintage. But this only really applies to the lesser wines. A quality Albariño, bottled during the first spring after the harvest, with a balanced structure relying on fresh acidity and good mineral character, will be at its best after its second spring and will continue growing in bottle for some years.

A few additional comments may help contextualize the regional approach to wine culture. This is a region with a long tradition of popular winemaking that did not attain DO status until the mid-1980s. Since then, the region has been through something of a boom, largely thanks to its trademark Albariño—both in Spain and in some important export markets such as the United States.

But beyond the more obvious facts, there are certain aspects of the development of Rías Baixas that deserve attention. Perhaps the most striking thing about the region is the way its long winemaking tradition is rooted in popular practices that were technically poor—the region's winemakers had an unrefined, even reckless approach. Recent developments represent a huge leap forward in this regard. But this has come at a price: the region's new-found commercial success has been of such proportions that the 1987 figures of 500 growers, 14 bodegas, 600 acres (240ha), and 600,000 liters of total production have each grown by a factor of nine in a single decade. Today, there are 4,200 growers, 130 bodegas, 4,700 acres (1,900ha), and 5.5 million liters. In the past ten to 15 years, the pace of change has slowed a little in all but one rather worrying respect: total production is increasing at a higher rate than the area under vine—which means yields are steadily rising.

Thankfully, the dramatic expansion of the vineyards in the 1990s has a positive side, too. The young vines that once yielded wines devoid of true Albariño character are now reaching maturity and offer plenty of potential for quality winemaking. So the best may yet be to come.

### The contemporary Galician scene

Perhaps fueled by the greater availability of sufficiently old vines, a lot is happening on the Galician winemaking scene today. Having left behind the age of major financial investment by companies from other winemaking regions, a series of young growers from family estates are increasingly taking control. Committed to honesty and purity of expression, they are striving to produce small quantities of highly individual and original wines. Inevitably, the results do not always match up to the courage and enthusiasm

**Right:** The shores of the Atlantic, whose maritime influence gives a cooler, fresher character to the wines of Rías Baixas

of these young growers. But there is no doubt that they are a welcome breath of fresh air for the region.

To these young bucks we could add a number of established bodegas with a track record stretching back a couple of decades. Together, they form a short but promising list of producers who merit attention, even though we do not have the space to discuss them individually here: Manuel Villalustre's Adega dos Eidos and his Contra a Parede wines, Miguel Alfonso's Pedralonga, Zárate, Benito Santos, Tricó, Castro Martín, Torroxal, Santiago Ruiz, Pazo de Barrantes, Adegas Galegas, Terras Gauda, Viña Nora, Valmiñor. All these producers—the more commercially oriented, as well as the more radical—have, despite occasional ups and downs, proved that they have something of real interest to offer the fine-wine lover.

Rías Baixas has dominated the Galician wine scene for the past 20 years or so with its successful Albariños. But Galicia does not end there. Galicia has many natural advantages and the potential to produce both reds and whites of great personality, thanks to a wide variety of local grapes. This diversity is in part preserved by what might otherwise be regarded as structural problems—the scattered population and the small scale of land ownership, together with its challenging climate for viticulture. The most historic wine region is Ribeiro, better known in the past by the name of its largest town, Ribadavia. But there are also the ever more interesting interior regions of Ribeira Sacra, Valdeorras, and Monterrei.

Whites are made in all of these appellations, but many would argue that Galicia is even better suited to reds. These are Atlantic reds, of course, and the red-wine revolution led by Mencía in Ribeira Sacra (though still in its early days) has much in common with that of Bierzo. The work of Raúl Pérez, consulting for many small wineries trying

**Right:** Some of the vineyards in Valdeorras are in river valleys, as well as on hillsides, and the climate is more continental

to recover forgotten old grape varieties and making small batches of fresh reds full of character—and being commercially successful at it!—has become key to this movement.

The main artery of St. James's Way, known as the French route, cuts through the heart of Navarra, Rioja, and Bierzo into Galicia, then runs north of Valdeorras, Ribeira Sacra, and Rías Baixas to Santiago de Compostela, the end of the pilgrimage. Ampelography and, more importantly, DNA fingerprinting refute the legends whereby grape varieties were brought along the Camino from central Europe to Spain. But what is true is that, from the Middle Ages right up to the present day, wine has been one of the main sources of comfort and sustenance for pilgrims.

## Ribeiro

Even before Jerez, the land of Sherry, Ribeiro was Spain's first internationally renowned wine region. It attracted the attention of the Roman Empire, improved its wines under the Cistercian monks from Burgundy during the Middle Ages, then traded profitably with England in the 16th century. Then the British market disappeared after the fiasco of the Armada, which led to a considerable reduction in Anglo-Spanish exchanges. (This was the period in which British merchants turned their attention to the neighboring Douro region in Portugal.) But the terroir remained, the steep valleys where the Miño, Avia, Arnoia, and Barbantiño rivers meet in southern Galicia well protected by mountains from the Atlantic storms. So, Ribeiro kept producing wines that were well appreciated at least in Galicia itself.

All of the 19th-century scourges hit Ribeiro in succession—oidium, then mildew, then phylloxera. Its vineyards were totally destroyed. They were replanted in the worst possible way, with high-yield, nondescript Palomino replacing native grape varieties, and vineyards migrating from the hillsides to the fertile valley floors. It wasn't until the 1980s that, slowly at first, the native Treixadura, Torrontés, Lado, Albariño, and other white varieties regained the upper hand and the hillsides were reconquered. By 2010, high-quality whites—and, increasingly, reds—from Ribeiro were back on the market. But by then, other Galician regions had taken the lead in Spanish and international markets.

## Ribeira Sacra

The young appellation of Ribeira Sacra (created only in 1996), characterized by narrow valleys and spectacularly steep hillsides along the rivers Sil, Bibei, and Miño, is more fashionable than ever. At an increasing pace—almost by the day, it seems—more and more small growers are starting to make and market their own wines. This back-to-roots movement spans all of its five subzones, and we can only hope that it will not lead to the same mistakes that have cut short the promising future of other regions. Some of these emerging producers very much deserve the coverage they're receiving in the media and the growing prestige among wine lovers all over the world that goes with it: Algueira, Dominio do Bibei, Chao de Couso, Losada Fernández, Moure (whose owner José Manuel Moure is one of the region's great groundbreakers), Ponte da Boga, Regina Viarum, and Via Romana (another pioneer). One could also draw up a list of independent growers whose names are achieving recognition: Pedro M. Rodríguez (of Guímaro fame, working closely with Raúl Pérez), José Rodríguez (Regueiral), and Tomás Rodríguez (Barbado).

In these early years, small production goes hand in hand with an artisanal approach that is inevitably marked by irregularity—which is, at the same time, unquestionably one of the charms of these wines. They are, in general, difficult to obtain and not exactly cheap. But production is always going to be expensive when—together with investments in stainless steel to ensure cleanliness at the production stage—it requires intensive and skilled labor on the southeast-facing hillsides along the River Sil. As hard as these vineyards are to work, however, they create an unforgettable landscape that resembles some of the most prestigious riverbanks of the wine world.

Amandi, Chantada, Quiroga-Bibei, Ribeiras do Miño, and Ribeiras do Sil are the five subzones, marked more by climate differences than by soil variation—the soils are mainly alluvial, high in acidity, with a high proportion of slate. The dominant variety (with up to 90 percent of the total production) is Mencía. Some way behind, we find Garnacha Tintorera and Godello, smaller quantities of Albariño, Tempranillo, and Treixadura, and even smaller quantities of local varieties that may deserve attention in the long run: Brancellao, Caíño, Merenzao, Mouratón, Sousón, Doña Blanca, Loureira, and Torrontés.

## Valdeorras

Valdeorras is a small appellation in the northeast corner of the province of Orense (or Ourense in the local Gallego language, which is somewhere between Portuguese and Spanish), almost a continuation to the east of Ribeira Sacra. It has 3,340 acres (1,350ha) of vineyards spread over eight villages: Lauroco, Petín, O Bolo, A Rua, Barco de Valdeorras, Vilamartín, Rubiá, and Carballeda de Valdeorras. There are close to 2,000 grape growers but only 45 wineries, which between them produce some 3 million liters of wine, sold mostly (over 90 percent) in Spain. The average altitude of the vineyards is 1,640ft (500m) above sea level, but some are in valleys while others are on slopes, and the soils vary greatly, ranging from granite and sand, rich in stones, to shallower soils rich in slate.

The climate is continental, with some Atlantic influence, an average temperature of 51.8°F (11°C), and annual rainfall of 33–40in (850–1,000mm).

The DO was created in 1977 and covers whites based on Godello—often with Doña Blanca and Palomino—and a minority of reds made from Mencía, Merenzao, Brancellao, Sousón Tinta, Negreda, Grao Negro, Garnacha Tintorera, and even Tempranillo. Here, for almost two decades, the Guitián family has been producing from the native Godello grape some of the best and longest-lived whites in the country.

## Monterrei

Monterrei, southwest of Valdeorras and south of Ribeira Sacra, is in the province of Orense, on the banks of the River Támega and its tributaries, running into the border with Portugal. Though spread across four municipalities (Verín, Monterrei, Oimbra, and Castrelo do Val), it is much smaller than the other wine regions, with only 915 acres (370ha) under vine and 23 wineries producing around 1 million liters of wine. Valleys and slopes have different soils and produce different wines and are even divided into two separate subregions. Here, the export market represents 30 percent and rising, thanks to the international profile of wineries such as Quinta da Muradella.

The climate, which is again a combination of Atlantic and continental influences, is both drier and more extreme than the rest of Galicia, temperatures soaring to 95°F (35°C) in summer and sinking to 23°F (–5°C) in winter. Both whites and reds are produced here, with the whites being mainly Godello (also known locally as Verdello), complemented by Treixadura (known locally as Verdello Louro), Doña Blanca, and small quantities of Albariño, Blanca de Monterrei, Caíño Blanco, and Loureira. The main grape for reds is Mencía, the second being Arouxa, the local name for Tempranillo, with an interesting mix of other local grapes that often produce the wines with most character—Bastardo (or Merenzao), Caíño Tinto, and Sousón.

# Pazo de Señorans

bove all else, Pazo de Señorans is the product of one woman's courage. Soledad (Marisol) Bueno is a highly persuasive woman of ceaseless devotion, who one day set herself the goal of leading the cause of quality Albariño in the Galician region of Rías Baixas, both at her own bodega and as a formidable president of the local appellation. Very soon afterward—scarcely a year after the first vintage of Pazo Señorans Albariño was released—her team was joined by enologist Ana Quintela, who has been in charge of the house wines ever since, always in close cooperation with the head of the company.

As in most of the rest of Spain, the general level of winemaking in the area had, for centuries, been questionable at best, with notable local exceptions, of course. The project started by Marisol Bueno and several other 1980s pioneers was, therefore, far more than just a step forward: it was a radical reinvention of the Albariño grape.

Having said that, one should not ignore the long winemaking tradition in the region, which dates back several centuries. Evidence of this tradition can even be found on the premises of the historic Pazo de Señorans, in the shape of an old stone *lagar*. Today, this 14th-century building, which lends its name to the bodega's wines, is also the home of its winemaking facilities. Both the building and the 21 acres (8.5ha) of vineyards surrounding it are located in Meis, in the subzone called Val do Salnés.

The venture started in 1979 when Marisol and her husband Javier Mareque bought Pazo de Señorans, a 35-acre (14ha) property that included vineyards and some traditional winemaking facilities. For the first few years, they produced wine in a most rudimentary fashion and, like many of their neighbors, consumed part of

**Right:** Marisol Bueno and her daughter Vicky at the family property that led the revival of Albariño in Rías Baixas

*Pazo de Señorans is the product of one woman's courage. Soledad (Marisol) Bueno is a highly persuasive woman of ceaseless devotion, who set herself the goal of leading the cause of quality Albariño in Rías Baixas*

their production themselves, selling the rest to more established companies. By the late 1980s, in parallel with the creation of the Rías Baixas appellation, they grew in confidence and decided to take the plunge and bottle some Albariño produced in renovated facilities under their own brand name. Around 7,000 bottles were made of the first vintages, 1989 and 1990, and this volume would later grow steadily to reach 400,000 bottles of wine and more than 30,000 of *aguardiente de orujo* (a grape spirit, a sort of Marc d'Albariño) by the first decade of the 21st century.

Pazo de Señorans produces wines made from its own 20 acres (8ha) of estate vineyards, plus grapes bought from hundreds of other smaller vineyards whose total extension is

*Longer than anyone else, Ana and Soledad have defended something with which we entirely agree: that the best Albariños are not best consumed while they are still very young*

very hard to tell. These other vineyards are the perfect sociological illustration of the Galician *minifundio* ("tiny plot") land-tenure system, with more than 500 plots belonging to 180 families (averaging three per family). Although viticulturally speaking there is cooperation throughout the year, the weight of each family's tradition is powerful, and practices often differ from one family to the next—which adds extra diversity to the already different locations, altitudes, orientations, and so on. For years, the company considered expanding the estate, but prices in the Val do Salnés are steep. In any case, they seem to be comfortable with this state of affairs and cherish their relationship with growers for, among other things, the diversity that comes with the fragmentation.

The grape of choice is invariably Albariño, trained in *parra* (a sort of pergola, the traditional training method in the region, providing better control, though it is expensive) or on trellises. This is far from unusual in this subzone of Rías Baixas, where more than 90 percent of the vineyards are planted with Albariño.

Together with the unoaked whites—Pazo Señorans Albariño and Pazo Señorans Selección de Añada—the company released in 2009 the first vintage (2006) of Sol de Señorans. This is also an Albariño varietal, but after fermentation in stainless-steel tanks, it is aged for six months in Caucasian and French oak—500-liter barrels rather than 250-liter barrels, in order to soften the aromatic impact of new wood. This bodega has always acted as the spearhead in an otherwise slow-paced region, and its other new projects include experiments with large, several-thousand-liter oak vats for making Albariño whites with longer aging potential.

Though the bodega is not fond of malolactic fermentation, the extreme characteristics of a vintage may occasionally force them to use it to round out a wine that would otherwise be rather wild and spiky from high levels of malic acid: terroir rules here, and climate is part of it.

Longer than anyone else, Ana and Soledad have defended something with which we entirely agree: that, contrary to popular belief, the best Albariños are not best consumed while they are still very young (even before the summer following the vintage), in an attempt to preserve the primary fruit notes. The best Albariños have high acidity and low pH, and the structural qualities of the variety mean that the wines are at their best toward their fourth year of life—and sometimes even later. Pazo de Señorans has already proved this repeatedly, and these two women are quite prepared to carry on proving it even more convincingly than they have so far.

## FINEST WINES

### Pazo de Señorans Albariño [V]

A blend of the Albariño grapes of different origins bought by the house, the "basic" Pazo de Señorans label is, year in, year out, one of the most remarkable popular Albariños in Spain, as well as a most successful wine in export markets. It fully deserves such success, for these are fresh and aromatic wines that express a clean and well-defined minerality through a sharp structure. Part of a project aimed at quality rather than quantity, this formula has been so successful as to boost total production all the way to 400,000 bottles a year, thanks to steady growth from modest origins. Occasionally, this relatively large volume has resulted in slight variations among the different lots of the same vintage, but the general quality level remains very high. The best recent vintages are probably **2001**, **2004**, and **2008**.

### Pazo de Señorans Selección de Añada

This is the bodega's great contribution to the revitalization of the Albariño scene, at a time when the formula of fresh and aromatic wines was threatened with exhaustion—at least according to many in the media—after a number of years of remarkable success, especially in Spain. At the time of writing, more than ten vintages of this wine had been made by Marisol Bueno and her enologist Ana Quintela. The inaugural 1995 marked, almost by chance, the launch of a new style of Albariño—aged in stainless steel for three years—thus revitalizing this traditional winemaking technique. It is, moreover, a single-vineyard wine, sourced from a single plot from the highest part of the Pazo, but one whose sandy soil favors the ripening of the fruit. Golden with green hues, the nose is deep and complex with good intensity (flint stone, citrus, quince, olives, fennel...). The palate is ample, silky, even unctuous in texture but, at the same time, fresh, with very lively acidity. Released with a long life ahead, despite its time in tank, it has repeatedly proved the considerable cellaring potential of the best Albariños. It is one of the very few Spanish whites (other than traditional Andalusian wines, such as Fino Sherry and Manzanilla) that deserve to rank among the best in Europe. This is a consistently good wine, but among recent vintages we can perhaps single out for its quality the Pazo de Señorans Selección de Añada **2004★**.

**Above:** A bunch of mature Albariño grapes, whose potential for longer-lived wines has been proven by Pazo de Señorans

**Pazo de Señorans**
Area under vine: 100 acres (40ha)
Average production: 420,000 bottles
Vilanoviña,
36616 Meis, Pontevedra
Tel: +34 986 715 373
Fax: +34 986 715 569
www.pazodesenorans.com

# Palacio de Fefiñanes

Any generalization inevitably commits some sort of injustice, if only because there isn't time to stop and acknowledge every possible exception. This is very much the case where, in the pages of this book, we have stated that the history of quality Albariño started merely three decades ago. This is broadly true, save for a few honorable exceptions, the most conspicuous of which is Palacio de Fefiñanes.

In fact, well before Rías Baixas existed formally as an appellation and before Albariño became a trademark for elegant, fruity, high-quality white wine, Fefiñanes was pretty much the only label that gave prestige to the area. Forty years ago, Spain's elite wine and food connoisseurs (a much smaller circle then than now) would have been

*Before Rías Baixas existed and before Albariño became a trademark for elegant, fruity, high-quality white wine, Fefiñanes was pretty much the only label that gave prestige to the area*

more comfortable—and much more widely understood—ordering "a Fefiñanes" than "an Albariño," never mind "a Rías Baixas." If you're looking for proof about this, you might want to consult Juan Goytisolo's novel *Marks of Identity* (*Señas de Identidad*, 1966), in which Fefiñanes is ubiquitous and synonymous with good, fresh, white wine in a context where wine imports were simply out of the question.

The origins of any winemaking activity linked to the Palacio de Fefiñanes (or de Figueroa, as this impressively beautiful 17th-century building is also known) are hard to date precisely, but the bodega in its present incarnation was founded early in the 20th century, when Juana Armada and Miguel Gil, grandparents of Juan Gil de Araújo, undertook the rehabilitation of their palace.

Documents certify its existence in 1904, and the Albariño de Fefiñanes label appears to have been officially registered for bottling wines in 1928, together with the label designed by the Compostelan artist Mayer—which is roughly the same as the one used today. In the estate archives, there is a document from 1930 with the menu for the lunch celebrating the opening of the Hotel Compostela, in Santiago; the wines served then were Albariño de Fefiñanes and the red Marqués de Riscal.

Today's owner, Juan Gil de Araújo, likes to tell an anecdote that explains why so many people give credence to the idea that the Albariño grape may belong to the Riesling family. "My grandfather, a doctor who had studied in Germany," he says, "realized that the white wine produced from the Albariño *parras* growing on his lands was very similar in quality to the Rhine wines he remembered drinking during his study years in Germany. So he and my grandmother decided to produce Albariño whites commercially."

An important expansion took place in the 1950s, when the Marquis of Figueroa—son of the founder and father of the present owner—took control of the bodega. The next big change came in the 1990s, with the introduction of temperature-controlled stainless-steel tanks. Around the same time, a new management team arrived, too, and with it a new winemaker. After a period of uncertainty, Fefiñanes consolidated its privileged position in the context of the rise in quality of Albariño Rías Baixas.

Located on the coastal edge of the Val do Salnés, in the historic town of Cambados, Fefiñanes owes much of its growth to the atomized land-tenure system. While originally the estate's needs were satisfied by the *parrales* that surround the palace within the walled enclosure, nowadays

**Right:** Juan Gil de Araújo, grandson of the winery's founder, is improving its already high and legendary reputation

The 1583 Albariño de Fefiñanes undergoes alcoholic fermentation in French and American oak barrels, where it remains on its lees for about five months before going to a stainless-steel tank to settle. It is bottled early in the first summer after the vintage. The mild contact with oak produces a wine that resolves with unusual elegance the recurrent problem of excessive vanilla and spice so common in barrel-fermented Spanish whites.

Albariño de Fefiñanes III Año joins the trend of structured, unoaked Albariños. It is fermented in stainless-steel tanks, where it remains until it is bottled in its third year, including the first five months on its lees. Its powerful structure suggests that it needs two more years in bottle, especially in vintages that are as successful as the 2006★.

## FINEST WINES

### Albariño de Fefiñanes ★ [V]
This is the heir to the tradition of a century-old bodega. The house's two special wines—the 1583 and the III Año—certainly match up to expectations and rank among the appellation's top group every year, with excellent aging potential. But the special charisma of the Albariño de Fefiñanes, its history, and the fact that its quality has continued to rise over the past decade all combine to earn it a place among our "finest wines." Without rejecting new technology, its elaboration pays homage to the early production process: no maceration, slow fermentation, indigenous yeasts only, late bottling. The resulting wine, in the best years (which include most of the recent vintages, especially **2006**, **2008**, and **2009**), has golden hues, elegant citrus and flower notes, balanced acidity, and a persistent finish with a bitter note that confers distinction.

### Bodegas del Palacio de Fefiñanes
Area under vine: 50 acres (20ha)
Average production: 130,000 bottles
Plaza de Fefiñanes s/n,
36630 Cambados, Pontevedra
Tel: +34 986 542 204
Fax: +34 986 524 512
www.fefinanes.com

**Above:** The impressive facade of the Palacio de Fefiñanes (or de Figueroa), which dates back to the 17th century

90 percent of the estate's grapes—all Albariño—comes from tiny plots owned by as many as 60 different growers. The soils are sandy, of granitic origin, and are therefore acidic and quite shallow. Each grower contributes an average of 4,400lb (2,000kg) of grapes each year. Juan Gil de Araújo is genuinely enthusiastic about the relationship he enjoys with these growers. "The quality is exceptional, mostly from very old vines, averaging perhaps over 40 years of age, many of them grafted with the original palace vines," he says.

Three wines are now offered by Fefiñanes: the classic, basic label Albariño de Fefiñanes, plus two more recent additions.

# Bodegas Gerardo Méndez

Gerardo Méndez Lázaro, a grower from Meaño born in the mid-1950s, ranks high among those responsible for the qualitative leap made by Albariño whites in the 1980s. He takes his place alongside other famous names who, like him, are still the heads of their bodegas today.

At the very heart of Val do Salnés, Bodega Do Ferreiro is well known for controlling some of the oldest vineyards in Spain, with powerful pre-phylloxera vines of impressive appearance, whose twisted trunks climb toward the pergola structure that supports the leaves and bunches. Besides these ancient vines—some of them up to 200 years old—that provide grapes for Do Ferreiro's Cepas Vellas label, the winery sources grapes from younger vineyards, many of them necessarily not their own, planted mostly in the 1980s as part of the recovery of the Galician hillsides previously invaded by the eucalyptus trees that do so much harm to the local landscape.

The main vineyards and the winemaking facilities are located around the central building, the Casa Grande, in Lores, at the foot of Armenteira facing the Ría de Arousa. The present owner is known for his combination of strong faith in innovation and serious respect for the generations of growers who came before him. In Galician, *do ferreiro* means "the blacksmith's." As it happens, it was Gerardo's father, Francisco Méndez Laredo, known as "Pepe o ferreiro" ("Pepe the blacksmith"), who bought the estate and started to make wine, mostly for personal consumption, selling the rest to his neighbors. So, this wine eventually became *o albariño do ferreiro* ("the blacksmith's Albariño"). In the 1980s, Francisco (Pepe) was one of the prime movers behind the launch of the relatively young Rías Baixas appellation. When the moment came for the new generation to think of a brand name, Gerardo decided that there could be none better than the one by which it was already known.

Wine was an integral part of the daily life of most families in this rural area, characterized by a highly atomized *minifundio*. It was a natural element in the life and culture of this region, but it was made using rather pedestrian techniques. On the one hand, there was an abundance of very poor, sandy soils that were scarcely productive, except for the pergola-styled training that characterizes the landscape of the Galician coasts. On the other, wine was part of the regular diet of the region, so it was perfectly routine for many families (including that of Gerardo Méndez) to make their own wine. It was a wine sourced from the family vines and made without any sophistication in rustic containers, mostly for domestic consumption. Gerardo puts it more boldly, perhaps even exaggerating a little: "There is a world of difference between those domestic wines and today's careful elaborations; in fact, when I started, I had simply no idea."

Gerardo's enterprising personality moved him to bottle his wine, without labels, from very early on in his youth. He was already at it in 1973, which makes that year the first for his "bodega." But the winemaking impulse really arrived in the 1980s, and it's certainly no coincidence that the first vintage release of Albariño Do Ferreiro is 1986, the year the Rías Baixas appellation came into being.

The bodega uses state-of-the-art technology to obtain the purest expression from the grapes, combined with the most rigorous viticultural practices. Examples of the first abound, as in the obsessive cleanliness of the production process or the firm belief in cold macerations—a somewhat controversial practice in the area. The goal is to give the wines an unctuousness on the palate that contrasts with (and also complements in a way) their aromatic precision.

An example of the latter is the bodega's resolute faith in the *emparrado* system (pergola training) for the vines. Unlike other local producers, who think trelliscs offer a good alternative for the future (the traditional *parra* is highly demanding in terms of

**Above:** Gerardo Méndez Lázaro and his son Manuel, who believe that traditional pergola training is still best for their Albariño

skilled labor), at Do Ferreiro the creed is that there is no better solution for the local climate conditions, because *parras* isolate the bunches from the wet ground and, even more importantly, increase the amount of sunlight reaching the berries. Another important detail is the ceaseless devotion given to the vineyard, including individualized treatment of the stunning *cepas vellas* ("old vines"), each one of which is pruned differently every year, according to its specific needs and development.

Besides the "Blacksmith's" wines—Albariño Do Ferreiro and Do Ferreiro Cepas Vellas— Bodegas Gerardo Méndez makes two more wines. Tomada do Sapo is produced for a team of Spanish négociants (Valsegar de las Muelas). Also sourced from very old vines located at higher altitude (which emphasizes acidity), it is then aged on its lees for more than six months—which confers a more unctuous texture. Rebisaca is a departure from the varietal style, incorporating

with green hues while still young, it has superb, refreshing acidity, floral and fruit notes, and good volume and length on the palate—though these virtues are not always perceptible until a couple of months after bottling, when the wine has recovered from bottle shock. The bodega has decided to help the consumer by adopting a most commendable policy of stating the bottling date, since every vintage is bottled in several different lots during the year, starting in spring after the harvest. As with most quality Albariño whites, it is at its best after its second spring, and it continues improving for another few years.

### Do Ferreiro Cepas Vellas ★

Year in, year out, this wine consistently shows how intense the Albariño grape can be, emphasizing concentration, minerality, and complexity when compared to its younger sibling. Its distinctive feature is its origin in a single 2.5-acre (1ha) vineyard of extremely old Albariño vines, 10% of whose grapes are deliberately allowed to rot so as to intensify the wine's character. The existence of those vines was documented as far back as 1850, and word of mouth suggests they may be around 200 years old. Gerardo Méndez says that his grandmother's grandmother used to tell her that those vines were already old when she knew them. Regardless of these stories, always charming but hardly scientific, the undeniable proof is in the very existence and presence of such plants. Pictures of them are astonishing enough, but there is nothing quite like seeing the real thing. The harvest takes place in the second half of September, and after maceration and fermentation at low temperatures— which Gerardo applies to all his wines—the wine rests in tank until it is one year old and is then bottled by September. Like Albariño Do Ferreiro, Cepas Vellas only begins to show some time after bottling, ideally one or two years. Depending on the vintage, average production is between 7,000 and 12,000 bottles.

30 percent Treixadura and 5 percent Loureiro. After one year in stainless-steel, it is bottled for one of its major export markets, the United States.

## FINEST WINES

### Albariño Do Ferreiro [V]

Sourced from an assortment of vineyards, mostly planted in the 1980s and 1990s, this, the flagship wine in the portfolio, has gradually benefited from the older age of the vines. Albariño Do Ferreiro has always deservedly enjoyed a reputation as a pure and honest wine without artifice: pale yellow,

**Bodegas Gerardo Méndez**
Area under vine: 37 acres (15ha)
Average production: 120,000 bottles
Galiñanes 10 (Lores),
36969 Meaño, Pontevedra
Tel: +34 986 747 046
Fax: +34 986 748 915
www.bodegasgerardomendez.com

# Bodegas Fillaboa

This house was founded under the name Granja Fillaboa in 1986, almost at the same time that the Rías Baixas DO was formally created, making it a founding member. It is a beautiful and relatively large estate for the region (according to reliable sources, it may well be the largest in Pontevedra), located on the right bank of the River Miño in Salvaterra. For many years, the winery was family owned and managed, before being acquired in 2000 by the large Grupo Masaveu, which also owns other wineries in Rioja and Navarra.

Unlike the powerful *minifundio* land-tenure system that determines the size and vineyard holdings of most other important wineries in Rías Baixas, in the subzone Condado do Tea there is a much higher concentration of land. So a distinctive feature of Bodegas Fillaboa is that it is self-sufficient, supplying all of its grapes from its own vineyards: almost a *clos* of no less than 173 acres (70ha), mostly surrounded by an old stone wall that reaches 1 mile (1.6km) in length.

Apart from its two notable grape spirits, Fillaboa's production is confined to just two wines, both unoaked varietal Albariños: Fillaboa and Fillaboa Selección Finca Monte Alto. Fillaboa Albariño is produced on a much larger scale, using grapes from the Fillaboa plots Socalcos, Carasol, Terneros, Las Nieves, and Antigua. The winery, speaking through its public-relations staff (in big companies such as this, it's sometimes hard to get through to the people who actually make the wine), is proud of its commitment to sustainable viticulture. "This is the only sensible approach, since the vines are our dearest treasure," the PR person said. They are particularly concerned with the harmonious integration of the winery in its environment, which means the reduction of residues, integrated production, use of low-toxicity products in the vineyard and the winery, sexual-confusion strategies to reduce the proliferation of vine pests, and so on.

For a few years, Fillaboa made a French oak fermented Albariño, but the results were not as good as had been hoped, and the project was dropped. Following the same solidly established style as other wineries in the region, the company has staked its reputation on providing fruit where structure comes from the grapes themselves and from the wine's contact with its lees. This was a good decision, in our view. While barrel-fermented Albariños do occasionally result in interesting wines, the true greatness of this grape reveals itself through maximum purity and the minimum possible intervention during its making and aging.

## FINEST WINES

### Fillaboa Selección Finca Monte Alto ★

Of the 173 acres (70ha) in production, this comes from a small plot, planted in 1988, selected for its quality by the winery among the 11 parcels (all of them facing south) enclosed within the walls of this property. Production is even more limited for Monte Alto: around 2,000–4,000kg of grapes per hectare, which yield some 13,000 bottles. The best vintages of this wine, such as **2002** and **2005**, possibly also **2007**, undergo phases of fruit freshness and aromatic intensity: citrus, pear, aniseed, fresh herbs, and so on, but then age provides complexity, mineral emphasis, and overall balance. The ideal food-and-wine pairings change as the wine ages.

**Above:** José Masaveu, in charge at Fillaboa, which is in the privileged position of being entirely self-sufficient in grapes

While young, these wines find their best match in shellfish and simply cooked white fish, but after a few years in bottle they shine with richer fish dishes. The loss of aromatic exuberance is compensated by greater complexity and structure.

**Bodegas Fillaboa**
Area under vine: 173 acres (70ha)
Average production: 250,000 bottles
Lagar de Fillaboa,
36459 Salvaterra do Miño, Pontevedra
Tel: +34 986 658 132
Fax: +34 986 664 212
www.bodegasfillaboa.com

# Bodegas y Viñedos Forjas del Salnés

Behind the foundation of Forjas del Salnés stands one of the key figures of the recent history of Galician wine: Francisco Méndez Laredo, who passed away in 2001. He was the grandfather of the present owner, Rodrigo Méndez, who adored him and considers him his first teacher. A close second, and someone who also has a part to play in the story of this winery, is Raúl Pérez, the deservedly celebrated enologist from Bierzo.

Francisco was one of the key supporters of the appellation back in the 1980s, as well as starting two of the northwest's most interesting winemaking projects. First came one of the most widely respected cellars in Salnés, the vineyards and facilities of which he gave to his son Gerardo. Then, literally from scratch, Francisco started

*Behind the foundation of Forjas del Salnés stands one of the key figures of the recent history of Galician wine: Francisco Méndez Laredo*

another extremely promising venture: Forjas del Salnés. Indirectly, he has also lent his name to those wines, first through a tribute from his son—who borrowed his nickname "Pepe o ferreiro"—and then as homage from his grandson, who retained for the winemaking firm the same name Francisco gave his business of metal cages for mussel fishers: Forjas del Salnés.

Francisco's determination not to interfere in the business he had left to his son Gerardo probably influenced his decision to focus on red wines—which Rodrigo later adopted for himself. That is why the new vineyards planted by "Pepe o ferreiro" in the 1980s are all local red varieties: Caíño, Loureiro, and a smaller proportion of Espadeiro. So, when Rodrigo met Raúl Pérez in 2003 while selling him some Albariño grapes, he offered Pérez

a curious deal: "I won't charge you for the grapes if you help me make a red wine here." The first results of this promising collaboration were the 2005 reds Goliardo Caíño and Goliardo Loureiro. But of course, Rodrigo could not resist Pérez's insistent recommendation. "With your Albariño vineyards, it would be plain wrong not to produce a white wine, too." That inaugural 2005 vintage also, therefore, saw the first release of Leirana.

Those wonderful Albariño vines had reached Rodrigo and his uncle, Paco Méndez Lázaro, co-owner of the bodega, via his mother: the O Torno vineyard in Meaño had been planted one century earlier by Rodrigo's maternal great-grandfather. The vineyards of Forjas del Salnés are typical of the region: tiny plots of land never larger than 1ha (2.5 acres; the largest one, Xesteira, in Xil, is precisely that size); extremely variable vine age, ranging from pre-phylloxera *parras* in O Torno, to a few trellised rows of red Loureiro planted only recently in Xacobeira de Abaixo (Símes) and Xesteira de Abaixo (Xil), as well as 25-year-old vineyards like those in A Telleira (Dena). The bodega owns more than 7.5 acres (3ha), soon to be supplemented by recent plantations of their own. They also manage another couple of hectares for neighbors whose age or interests no longer lead them to the vineyards, among them a plot in Meaño with 1ha of Caíño Tinto and Albariño, where the vines are between 120 and 200 years old.

The growing portfolio of wines is wide enough, even if we ignore those made at the facilities by Raúl Pérez for himself (Sketch and Muti). The whites are always Albariño varietals. Leirana has the biggest production, but there are also Leirana Barrica (using grapes from O Torno), Leirana A Escusa, and Goliardo A Telleira. The latter is a sort of twin brother of Raúl Pérez's Sketch: the Albariño grapes of A Telleira vineyard barely fill two 750-liter barrels, so one is bottled as Sketch and the other one is Rodrigo's Goliardo A Telleira.

**Above:** Rodrigo Méndez with his grandmother, through whom Forjas del Salnés has some of its oldest, pre-phylloxera Albariño vines

## FINEST WINES

### Goliardo reds: Caíño★, Loureiro, Espadeiro★

The three varietal reds produced here (plus occasionally Bastión de la Luna, a blend of all three varieties) are made with destemmed grapes sourced from A Telleira. Cold maceration takes place before fermentation, and the cap is submerged three times per day. After pressing and some further contact with the cake, the wines go through malo and then age for 12 months in French oak barrels of diverse ages. The resulting wines are racy and authentic but also distinguished and elegant—likely the most refined expression that can be found today of the difficult Galician reds. If we add Galician weather conditions to the radical commitment of this bodega in matters of viticulture and winemaking, we are bound to find remarkable vintage variations.

This is even more perceptible when production is so small; we are talking here about 2,100–2,600 bottles, or just 133 magnums in the case of Goliardo Espadeiro 2008. In this context, there can be no room for barrel picking. The wines are simply true to each vintage as interpreted by the winemakers. And when the winemakers are Rodrigo Méndez and Raúl Pérez, this is most certainly a good thing.

**Bodegas y Viñedos Forjas del Salnés**
Area under vine: 30 acres (12ha)
Average production: 25,000 bottles
As Covas 5,
36968 Meaño, Pontevedra
Tel: +34 699 446 113
Fax: +34 986 742 131
rodri@inoxidablesdena.com

# Adega Pazos de Lusco

This winery was founded under the name Lusco do Miño by the experienced winemaker José Antonio López Domínguez, who teamed up with his US importers Stephen Metzler and Almudena de Llaguno. In 2007, the dynamic Bierzo winery Dominio de Tares became the major stockholder in the firm.

The winery is located in the subzone Condado do Tea, where the *minifundio* system is not as predominant as in Val do Salnés or O Rosal. This makes possible relatively large estates like the Pazo Piñeiro, locally known as Casa de Bugallal. The 16th-century manor—refurbished in the 19th century—is surrounded by Albariño *parrales*, and is now the operations center of Adega Pazos de Lusco. Early this century, an adjacent vineyard was added to the 12 acres (5ha) planted in 1970, so the total area of estate-owned vines tops 15 acres (6ha).

The remaining grapes used for Lusco wines are bought from small local growers in As Neves. These contracts, arranged by the firm's founder José Antonio López, were based on area rather than production, to discourage excessive yields. Equally, there is a ban on pesticides that is both coherent with the company's ecological principles and a guarantee of the microbiological activity indispensable for the life of indigenous yeasts. The use of these, together with strict temperature controls and the aging of the wines on lees, are the main winemaking criteria here.

From the technical point of view, a great advance for this bodega is the addition of Rafael Palacios—the talented winemaker of As Sortes in Valdeorras—as external consultant to the Dominio de Tares group. The first Adega Pazos de Lusco vintage in which Palacios had an input was 2009.

Time and experience have brought about an increasing belief in the longevity of the best Albariños, which are capable of doing much more than merely surviving after a few years in bottle but actually show their best in terms of character and structure. That has been the view here since the foundation of Lusco do Miño, and there is no doubt that the bodega's two main wines are now among that elite. The flagship cuvée—under the name Lusco since the 1996 vintage—was a leader of the quality revolution in Rías Baixas in the mid-1990s. And the bodega has also released the single-vineyard Pazo Piñeiro. Both wines age on their lees in stainless-steel tanks for as much as nine months prior to bottling.

Recently, a more modest third wine was launched for the US market: Zios. But that is not the style on which the winery wants to base its strategy. It wants to pursue the higher end of the market, especially with Lusco Albariño, which—at 55,000 bottles per year—is the heart of its production.

## FINEST WINES

### Pazo Piñeiro Albariño ★
This wine is named after the estate in Salvaterra do Miño whose 12 acres (5ha) of Albariño vines planted in 1970 constitute the main treasure of this house. The wine takes its singular character from the most exceptional vines of the Pazo Piñeiro. It's a style that is far removed from run-of-the-mill commercial Albariño bottlings, with their excessive youth and yields, their abuse of selected yeasts, and so on. In contrast, this wine is dry and mineral, fresh and fruity, structured and long. As with other serious Albariños, its virtues become more evident from its third year. Vintages **2005** and **2006** were outstanding, but 2007 and 2008 were not judged of sufficient quality. The **2009** seems extremely promising (as indeed is the **Lusco 2009**), even if this was not an absolutely top vintage in the subzone. Average production is 3,500–5,000 bottles.

**Adega Pazos de Lusco**
Area under vine: 35 acres (14ha)
Average production: 60,000 bottles
Lugar de Grixó – Aixén
36458 Salvaterra do Miño, Pontevedra
Tel: +34 987 514 550
Fax: +34 987 514 570
www.lusco.es

# Bodegas La Val

Founded in 1985, Bodegas La Val is another original member of the club of growers who promoted DO Rías Baixas from its very beginnings. For founder José Limeres, whose original motivation was to produce enough wine to supply his restaurants, finding a name for his business was easy: he simply borrowed it from the first vineyard he bought. To the 7.5 acres (3ha) of Albariño, Loureiro, and Treixadura that he found in the original La Val vineyard—in the subzone of O Rosal, near the mouth of the River Miño—he added two large Albariño vineyards at the heart of Condado do Tea in 1985: Arantei and Taboexa. Arantei also hosts the bodega's winemaking facilities, which makes it officially part of the Condado subzone.

Some years later, in 1998 and 2001, two more vineyards were bought: Xan Grande (8.5 acres [3.5ha] of Albariño and Caíño in O Rosal) and Pexegueiro (44 acres [18ha] of Albariño recently planted in Tuy). In all cases, regardless of the subzone, variety, or age of the vines, the plants are trained using the *emparrado* system. In 2010, the vineyard holdings were reorganized, including the sale of the greater part of the O Rosal vineyards, further concentrating the bodega's activities in the Condado subzone.

The fact that the vast majority of the vineyards owned by Bodegas La Val are planted with Albariño gives a clue as to how crucial a role it plays in its wines. The best labels are all Albariño varietals. That's certainly true of the main wine, La Val Albariño, where cold maceration and temperature control throughout the winemaking process give a fresh and fruit-driven white—a vehicle for the grape's pure expression. And it's no less the case in the more elaborate styles, whether the wine is aged in French oak (La Val Fermentado en Barrica), aged on its lees (La Val Crianza Sobre Lías), or has its origins in a single vineyard (Finca de Arantei).

La Val's range also includes grape spirits and Viña Ludy, a fruity, intense, and well-made Rías Baixas white from O Rosal, a blend of Albariño and Loureira with some Treixadura and Caíño. The varieties are vinified separately, then blended.

## FINEST WINES

### Finca de Arantei Albariño

Finca de Arantei is sourced exclusively from the vineyard of the same name, the largest vineyard owned by Bodegas La Val. Due to its inland location on the right bank of the River Miño, its orientation, and the soil composition (sand and pebbles), it is always one of the first plots to be harvested in Galicia each vintage. The La Val team selects this very special wine from the best lots, and in some cases the vintage enables them to obtain extraordinary results, as in 2002 (under the label Torres de Arantei) and 2006. In such years, Finca de Arantei Albariño has all the complexity, intensity, and finesse of the noblest Albariños, and it can also develop beautifully in bottle.

### La Val Crianza Sobre Lías ★

This is an impressive wine, very carefully made, and the few vintages released so far are fully convincing. In recent years, there has been debate as to whether sophistication in Albariño wines depends on working the lees in steel tanks or on fermentation and aging in oak. In our opinion, the former is the best way to express the true quality of Albariño, and La Val Crianza Sobre Lías is a powerful argument for our case. The three years that the wine spends on periodically refreshed lees favors the development of clean mineral notes worthy of the best German Rieslings, combined with an elegant but intense palate and a long, complex finish. A moderate aeration helps the wine express its character. 2003 and 2004 are excellent vintages of a wine that deserves careful attention.

---

**Bodegas La Val**
Area under vine: 143 acres (58ha)
Average production: 400,000 bottles
Barrio Muguiña s/n – Arantei
36458 Salvaterra do Miño, Pontevedra
Tel: +34 986 610 728
Fax: +34 986 611 635
www.bodegaslaval.com

# Viña Meín

Much of the best that Spanish Atlantic terroirs have to say has only been revealed over the past few decades, thanks to the happy combination of a return to the best local varieties—abandoned for years in the race for higher yields—and the use of modern technology that allows the expression of the essence of each region. A clear example of this phenomenon is DO Ribeiro in general, where increasing access to technology has enabled more and more small growers to produce their own wines (*colheiteiros*). Emerging immediately after the decay of the 1970s model of high production, Viña Meín is a pioneering house in this respect, too.

Leiro, located on the River Avia near Orense and the Miño, boasts a long winemaking tradition. This is derived from the Cistercian monastery of San Clodio, whose monks are originally responsible for the wine-dedicated atmosphere that pervades this valley covered with vineyards. In the context of the area's winemaking history, Viña Meín is a relatively young house, founded in the late 1980s as part of the push for quality winemaking in Spain. Despite its youth, it has become a benchmark for quality in the Ribeiro appellation and a model for more recent quality ventures such as the one led by film director José Luis Cuerda (whose wine, incidentally, is called Sanclodio). Javier Alén, head of Viña Meín, tells us that in 2010, for the first time since the foundation of the winery, they have had to buy grapes to satisfy the demand, after the 2009 harvest was 20 percent smaller than average. Those 11 tons (10,000kg) of bought grapes are sourced precisely from a vineyard recently purchased by Cuerda. For that very same reason, Viña Meín has bought a new 5-acre (2ha) vineyard in San Clodio and plans to replant it in 2011.

Together with Javier Alén, another important figure is Ricardo Vázquez, closely linked to the project since its origin in 1988. In those early days, he was responsible for replantation and vineyard management. Vázquez entered the cellar in 1993, when production started, and has remained there ever since as cellar master, having passed responsibility for the vineyards on to his son.

As a consequence of the failure of the high-production model, a number of vineyards planted mostly with Palomino were abandoned (and still remain, in some cases). It is 40 acres (16ha) of those plots that Javier Alén and his associates have been replanting over the past 20 years with indigenous varieties, scattered on southeast-facing hillsides in the boroughs of Gomariz and San Clodio in the Avia Valley (the appellation's name—Ribeiro—comes from its location on the Avia riverside, which is *ribeiro* in Galician). The dominant variety (around 75 percent) is the local Treixadura, with a ragbag of varieties completing the total: Godello (12 percent), Loureira (4 percent), Torrontés (3 percent), Albariño (3 percent), and a residual presence of Albilla and Lado, as well as local red varieties. This multivarietal character, with Treixadura in the lead role, chimes perfectly with local tradition, which bucked the monovarietal trend of other Galician appellations.

We find the first replanted vineyard in San Clodio, around the cellar building: 8.5 acres (3.5ha) of Treixadura (90 percent), Loureira, and Torrontés. The soil is mostly *sábrego*, a mixture of decomposed granite and clay, as in all their vineyards. As one leaves the estate, there are another 15 acres (6ha) evenly split between one's left (Cuñas) and right (Costas). In Gomariz, there are 7.5 acres (3ha): 2.5 acres (1ha) of Godello in Teja do Sal, and 5 acres (2ha) of Treixadura in Vilerma. In Osebe, 1ha of Godello and 1.2 acres (0.5ha) of red varieties. Small plots in Os Paus and Gallegos, also in San Clodio, complete the total surface of vineyards, which should soon amount to 44 acres (18ha) in production.

Besides the flagship wine, Viña Meín has produced, from the 2000 vintage onward, a

**Right:** Javier Alén, head of Viña Meín, which, despite its youth, has already become a benchmark for quality in the Ribeiro DO

barrel-fermented white, sometimes made in large oak vats and more recently in smaller 600-liter barrels. On release, it is often dominated by new oak, which is why it appeals to a market segment that prefers creamy and spicy oak notes over the sharp terroir character of the house wine: quite a marked contrast.

There is also a small-production red, made from local varieties Caíño Longo, Mencía, and Ferrón. Viña Meín Tinto Clásico is sourced from a single vineyard located in Osebe and displays typically high acidity and extraction, as well as deep color.

## FINEST WINES

The flagship wine has carried the winery name since its launch in 1995 (1994 was the first vintage). It accounts for more than 90% of the annual production and is the base on which the winery has built its reputation. It is also the wine that communicates the "magic" and authenticity of the house. This unoaked version aspires to the purest fruit expression held together by a tight structure. Bottled after six to eight months in stainless-steel tanks on its lees, it is a blend of all the varieties on the property, with Treixadura playing the leading role (70–85%, depending on the vintage). The best vintages of Viña Meín—for example, 2004★ or 2001★— combine aromatic intensity and freshness (bay leaf, white fruit, juicy acidity) in their youth with noble maturity after a few years of bottle age—the time needed for the aromas to develop. Since 2007, this wine has been bottled in two formats: for the local market, the label remains the one that made it popular in the 1990s, while for the rest of Spain and the export market, there is a more modern label and the description "Selección de Cosecha."

**Left:** The scenic Viña Meín winery, surrounded by vines, as is the rest of the Avia Valley, first planted by Cistercian monks

**Viña Meín**
Area under vine: 40 acres (16ha)
Average production: 100,000 bottles
Lugar de Meín s/n, 32420 Leiro, Ourense
Tel: +34 617 326 248
Fax: +34 988 488 732
www.vinamein.com

# Emilio Rojo

Emilio Rojo, like so many back-to-the-land vine growers in Spain, gave up a modern life and a modern career in a modern city. Unlike many of them, he looks and acts as if he had never left the vineyards surrounding the River Avia in southern Galicia. This small man cuts quite a dashing figure, which captured the fancy of Spanish and foreign journalists soon after his first highly distinctive wines were released.

The American wine writer Bruce Schoenfeld has described him very vividly: "The idiosyncratic Emilio Rojo works out of a glorified Quonset hut, deliberately turning his back on modernity. With his bristly moustache and black baseball cap, he is instantly recognizable in wine circles throughout Spain, appearing in magazine photos and attending symposiums. And yet, many Spanish consumers have never actually seen his wine."

Well, not many consumers anywhere have seen his wine. His production is tiny, as he is only willing to vinify the grapes from his small 3.7-acre (1.5ha) terraced vineyard, because "it faces east, not south or west, so the grapes mature more slowly and we harvest later, and it makes for a more delicate wine, which is what I want." In addition, his prices are the steepest in the Ribeiro region.

Rojo became, around 2000, the first instantly recognizable media figure from a then-forgotten, isolated wine region that is drastically different from most of the rest of Spain, where huge estates, mammoth cooperatives, and oversized négociant firms are common. In Galicia, minimalism reigns— indeed, the *minifundio*, the very small estate, is the rule in the region's farming sector.

André Tamers, a respected American importer of Spanish wines, took Rojo under his wing at the turn of the 21st century, and this helped the retiring grower gain the kind of media exposure in the United States that many European winemakers can only dream of. "I was lucky to meet André," he says. "He introduced me to the international markets."

This didn't change him one iota. He says he would like to "decrease, not increase" production in order to make better wines. And they still call him "the hermit of Ribeiro," a man who will sleep on a cot near his fermentation tanks at harvest time in order always to keep an eye on things.

It wasn't always like this. He did come from a very modest background, the scion of a family of grape growers and millers in the same village, Leiro, where he now lives again. But he was able, with scholarships, to go to university and graduate— not as an agricultural engineer or an enologist, but as a telecoms engineer.

He had a successful career with a large company when, in 1982, at the age of 30, he decided that the rat race was not for him. He spent a year in London and a couple more years in Leiro "doing nothing." Then, in 1987, when his father retired, he took over the modest family cellar, stopped making bulk wines, and turned his attention to bottled quality whites. That year he made his first 5,000 bottles.

The long sabbatical had changed his outlook on life completely. He felt an urge to restore the damaged terroirs and the varietal diversity of Ribeiro, as a few others were doing in the 1980s. Neutral Palomino and black-fleshed Garnacha Tintorera had been planted, often on overly fertile valley floors, after phylloxera struck.

Rojo took two steep, hillside vineyards that his wife had inherited, painstakingly rebuilt terraces with granite boulders, and replanted them with the long-ignored, low-yielding native varieties, led by the delicate Treixadura.

The site is called Ibedo ("Olive Grove") and is made up of 30 small terraces, mid-slope, at an altitude of 450ft (140m) on granitic soils. The eastern orientation dictates a late harvest date— usually in early October.

**Right:** Emilio Rojo, "the hermit of Ribeiro," whose perfectionist wines have attracted something of a cult following in the US

**Above:** Rojo's label, which proudly proclaims its indigenous variety, being affixed by his own hand to one of the 9,000 bottles

The winemaking is simple but demanding. The grapes are crushed and fermented at low temperature (68–72°F [20–22°C]) in stainless-steel tanks, with no help from cultured yeasts. Then the finished wine spends some time on its fine lees, again in stainless steel, before bottling.

Spanish consumers often have more difficulty appreciating Rojo's wines than do consumers in countries where ageworthy whites are more frequent. The reluctance by his fellow countrymen to wait for a couple of years to open a bottle of white—any bottle of white—is not conducive to such an appreciation. Often closed and seemingly inexpressive at release, these wines later show an austere, granitic minerality that doesn't entirely suppress the fine floral aromas and fruit flavors, in a complex combination that can only be described as refined and delicate. The vivid acidity makes it the kind of wine you want with fine Atlantic seafood.

Parts of the Spanish press, impervious to such refinement, have found other reasons to take notice of Rojo's accomplishments. "The wine retails for $150 in the United States," gushed a leading Madrid newspaper. Well, it isn't true, of course—

Rojo is no Coche-Dury yet. But they do sell for some $50–60, which is very unusual for any white wine from Spain in any market.

Whatever the price, it hasn't made Rojo a rich man. Selling fewer than 10,000 bottles a year will never buy him a villa on the Costa del Sol. He knows it; he knows his name is prestigious enough for him to consider making and selling a lot more wine; but he just shrugs. He only wants to make the best wine possible—and this is it.

## FINEST WINES

### Emilio Rojo ★

This is Emilio Rojo's only wine—a field blend dominated by Treixadura, which usually makes up 55–75% of the wine. There is often a good amount of Lado followed by varying proportions of Albariño, Loureiro, and Torrontés.

**Emilio Rojo**
Area under vine: 3.7 acres (1.5ha)
Average production: 9,000 bottles
Rey de Viana 5,
32420 Leiro, Ourense
Tel: +34 600 522 812
vinoemiliorojo@hotmail.com

# Coto de Gomariz

The Gomariz vineyards form what admirers have called "a golden shell," which is indeed what they look like in the autumn when seen from the top of the hills, looking down to the San Clodio monastery where the Cistercian monks introduced viticulture in the 11th century and made wines of great repute in the Middle Ages. Three estates share the site—Coto de Gomariz, Vilerma, and the very Monasterio de San Clodio now owned by film director José Luis Cuerda.

Of the three, the most ambitious and noteworthy is Coto de Gomariz, run by two young vine and wine fanatics, owner Ricardo Carreiro and enologist Xosé Lois Sebio. They are among the leaders in the recovery of red grape varieties in Galicia, they have produced some of the most expressive whites in Ribeiro, and they are now moving to fully biodynamic practices. "If you want to tell our vineyards from others, we're the ones with a lot of grass on the ground," says Sebio. "It gives us a lot of headaches and hurts some vines, but I refuse to use herbicides."

The oldest of those vines were planted in 1979. The total surface is now 66 acres (27ha), which is large for the region. Plant density goes from 5,000 to 7,000 vines/ha—high for terraced hillside vineyards. The idea is, as usual, to increase competition and lower the yield per vine, which stands at 2–3.5lb (1–1.5kg), depending on the variety—a guarantee of a better ripeness in this cool and damp climate. All the vines are trellised. The granite soils have some schist patches, and there is clay in the subsoil, helping retain water during droughts.

In 1978, Caco Carreiro—the current owner's father—started replanting the estate with native varieties, widely discarded since phylloxera. He began making wine from those vines in 1987. The current winery, combining traditional architecture with state-of-the-art cellar technology, was built in 2001. It also includes a distillery—an almost compulsory complement in Galicia.

The younger Carreiro and Sebio have expanded the portfolio to include tank- and barrel-aged whites and serious, oak-aged red wines, incorporating local grape varieties even before they were included in the lists of those that are officially admitted. An important one is Carabuñeira, native to the Ribeiro, much better known internationally by its Portuguese name: Touriga Nacional.

Much to the dismay of some authorities in the neighboring Rías Baixas appellation (who would like to prevent everyone else in the world from using the Albariño grape), one of the most distinguished Gomariz wines, Encostas de Xisto ("Schist Slopes") is 95 percent Albariño and 5 percent Treixadura, from a schistous outcrop that helps the famous grape, which needs more heat than it usually gets in Ribeiro. There is a Colleita Seleccionada—Treixadura-dominated, fermented in new, 500-liter oaks casks from Burgundy—an unoaked white, and a fresh, fragrant red made with Sousón, Brancellao, Caíño Longo, and Mencía and aged a year in used oak barrels. There are also intriguing, non-DO reds, including VX Cuvée Caco—a blend of Sousón, Caíño Longo, Caíño da Terra, Carabuñeira, and Mencía, fearlessly aged 20 months in new French and American oak.

## FINEST WINES

**Colleita Seleccionada ★**
This is as impressive as any barrel-fermented white in Spain, because, among other reasons, the oak is imperceptible, its only effect having been to further enhance the explosive, complex aromatic palate of this intense, balsamic, long wine.

**Coto de Gomariz**
Area under vine: 66 acres (27ha)
Average production: 60,000 bottles
Barro de Gomariz,
32429 Leiro, Ourense
Tel: +34 671 641 982
Fax: +34 988 488 174
www.cotodegomariz.com

# Dominio do Bibei

Located near the emblematic bridge built over the River Bibei by the Romans in the 1st century AD to connect the inland plains with the Atlantic, this producer has been key in the recent awakening of small producers in Ribeira Sacra since the release of its first wines in 2002. Not that Dominio do Bibei itself can be considered small or modest in any way, being quite different from others in the region.

It was founded by successful businessman (and native of Mendoia) Javier Domínguez to revitalize winemaking in the region, and the result of his initiative has been a powerful boosting of confidence in the potential of the almost-impossible vineyards along the rivers Sil and Bibei. Energy is the most obvious of the many qualities possessed by the management team at Dominio do Bibei: Suso Prieto, Laura Lorenzo, David Bustos, and Alin Lascu. Also crucial, especially in the early years, was the technical expertise of Sara Pérez and René Barbier Jr. in their first incursion beyond Priorat.

The estate's total extent is 304 acres (123ha) at an altitude of 650–2,300ft (200–700m)—a territory that seems impossible to control out of the sheer steepness and tortuousness of its landscape, following every twist and turn of the River Bibei. Though still subject to Atlantic influences, the climate of the Quiroga-Bibei subzone of Ribeira Sacra is far drier (28in [700mm]) of annual rainfall) and warmer than the Galician average, and even than other subzones of the same appellation. This explains the orientation of most vineyards toward the west. The soils are (with the inevitable variations from plot to plot), like most of those in Ribeira Sacra, granite-based slate, though there is a slightly higher clay component here.

More than 75 acres (30ha) are currently planted with a wide range of varieties, especially in the fairly chaotic 25 acres (10ha) of old vines. New plantings

**Right:** Winemaker Laura Lorenzo, who exemplifies the vitality that Dominio do Bibei has given to Ribeira Sacra as a whole

*The real spirit of Ribeira Sacra and of the terroir-driven approach of Dominio do Bibei is embodied by their two more fruit-driven and straightforward wines, Lapola (white) and Lalama (red)*

**Above:** Some of the many steep-sloping terraced vineyards in a landscape shared by other age-old pastoral pursuits

respect this historic mix but in a more orderly way, so that the different varieties can be harvested and vinified separately. The young vines are feeble and do not produce until they are several years old and their roots have had time to delve deep into the extremely poor soils. The main red variety is Mencía, supported by Garnacha Tintorera (all from old vines) and, on a more experimental basis, the local Brancellao, Caíño, Gran Negro (or Vella da Caxata), Mouratón, Merenzao, and Sousón. White wines come from the three Miño varieties: Godello, Treixadura, and Albariño, with fast-receding Doña Blanca (known as Merseguera in the Mediterranean area).

As well as the more straightforward Lapola (white) and Lalama (red), Dominio do Bibei releases two small-production single-vineyard wines every year. Lapena and Lacima are, respectively, a varietal Godello and Mencía, though Lapena 2009 may have some Albariño as well.

## FINEST WINES

### Lapola ★ [V] and Lalama ★ [V]

The real spirit of Ribeira Sacra and of the terroir-driven approach of Dominio do Bibei is embodied by their two more fruit-driven and straightforward wines, Lapola (white) and Lalama (red). They are blends of white grapes (Godello, Treixadura, Torrontés, and Doña Blanca) and red ones (Mencía, Brancellao, and Garnacha Tintorera), sourced from different vineyards. At Dominio do Bibei, there is a clear preference for large wooden vats, and even cement, for the fermentation process, where stainless steel plays almost no role at all. No new oak is used for the aging of the wines—in fact, newly purchased barrels are immediately filled with second-class wines before they are used for the house's top wines, including Lapola and Lalama.

> **Dominio do Bibei**
> Area under vine: 84 acres (34ha)
> Average production: 90,000 bottles
> Langullo s/n,
> 32781 Manzaneda, Ourense
> Tel: +34 610 400 484
> www.dominiodobibei.com

# Adega Algueira

This company was created in 1998 and is owned by Fernando González Riveiro. But he and his wife Ana Pérez have been in Ribeira Sacra for far longer, passionately tending their vineyards (now 27 acres [11ha]) for more than 30 years. In Doade (Sober), in the subzone of Amandi, they have 66,000 vines planted on *solcacos*, which is the local name (also used in the Douro in Portugal) for the small terraces that are the only way to plant and grow anything on such slopes. They have also six small monorails—each 500ft (150m) long—that make the transportation of grapes and tools possible.

The south-facing vineyards are located on the banks of the River Sil, on very steep schist slopes, in a landscape that looks very much like the Douro. They work exclusively with local grapes: the reds are Mencía, Alvarello, Merenzao, and Caíño; the whites are Godello, Loureiro, Albariño, and Treixadura. The winery is made of stone, in the style of the Romanesque monasteries, located in a very quiet site surrounded by oak and chestnut forests.

The wines to be aged in oak are always foot-trodden, because they feel this is the best way to extract without damaging the grapes (always the risk with a destemming machine). Fernando calls it the "de-mechanization" of the winery. They also try to use all the other traditional techniques and are experimenting with barrels made from the local oak. The ubiquitous Raúl Pérez is a consultant for the winery.

Their wines and spectacular vineyards—the descriptions often include words such as "vertigo" and "ravine"—have been praised by *The New York Times* and *Le Figaro*, so they are better known internationally than in Spain itself. The wines of Algueira are considered by many the finest and most elegant in Ribeira Sacra. O Castelo, their restaurant, is always ready to receive tourists and to give winery tours, which is something that is still quite unusual in the area.

## FINEST WINES

Under the generic name of **Algueira**, there is a core range of three wines, all sold in Burgundy-shaped bottles with simple white labels and letters in italics. First, there is an unoaked white blend, made from Godello, Albariño, and Treixadura. Next, a barrel-aged white, Blanco Barrica, which is actually the same blend as the previous wine but in this case aged for 12 months in French oak barrels on its lees, resulting in a more marked mineral character. Thirdly, there is a red varietal Mencía that has more in common with a fine Côte de Nuits than with the image most people have of Spanish reds.

### Algueira Merenzao
Merenzao is the name of the grape with which this wine is made—a grape that is also known in Ribeira Sacra as Carnaz or Godello Tinto. To add to the confusion, it is already known as Bastardo elsewhere in Galicia and Portugal, and it is none other than the Trousseau of Jura. It's a grape that gives little color, which may be one reason why it has been out of fashion. Fernando and Ana have been recovering it, as has José Luis Mateo from Quinta da Muradella in Monterrei. The **Algueira Merenzao 2008** is superb, with plenty of red fruit, spice, and slightly meaty notes.

### Algueira Pizarra ★
Whole clusters of Mencía are foot-trodden and fermented in oak vats, with a long maceration, and then spend 13 months in used French oak barrels. The grapes are selected from the best across their vineyards and give the wine a wild-berry and mineral profile that makes it fresh and calls for another sip (or another glass, or another bottle!). *Pizarra* means schist or slate, which is the main component of the soil and seems to show through in the wine. Some 22,000 bottles are produced each year. We recommend the **2005** and **2007** vintages of this wine.

**Adega Algueira**
Area under vine: 27 acres (11ha)
Average production: 70,000 bottles
Francos – Doade,
27424 Sober, Lugo
Tel: +34 629 208 917
Fax: +34 982 402 71
www.adegaalgueira.com

# Rafael Palacios

The Palacios family is, without doubt, one of the great wine families of Spain. Their home winery in Rioja, Palacios Remondo, was where they all grew up and learned to drink, love, and make wine. The second generation led the Priorat revolution at the end of the 1980s. At the turn of the 21st century they went to Bierzo, where they also played a big part in the revival there. Meanwhile, the home winery was not idle either; Rafael Palacios was the youngest son, and like all his brothers and sisters, he got involved in wine.

At the beginning of the 1990s he spent time in France, working for négociants and for châteaux like Pétrus and Moulin du Cadet while studying enology in Montagne-St-Emilion. It was there that he met Australian winemaker John Cassegrain, with whom he worked in his Hastings River winery in

*Rafa (as he's known to everyone) is passionate about poor hillside terroirs and is able to innovate in forgotten or poorly developed viticultural regions*

New South Wales. He also spent time in Coonawarra in South Australia, with stints in different wineries such as Wynns or Penfolds. During all these many experiences, he developed a real passion for white wine and learned how to make it well.

On his return to Rioja, he took on the technical management of the family winery. In 1997, he created the icon for modern white Rioja, a barrel-fermented Viura called Plácet. He soon realized that the only way to reach greater heights in whites was through improved viticulture. He continued working at Palacios Remondo until 2004, when he felt it was time to start his own personal project.

He had been exploring the white-wine potential of different regions and varieties in Spain, and he had been quite impressed with a Godello from Valdeorras. This was a variety that could provide the length and volume he was looking for. And he deemed Valdeorras—regarded by many as the region with the greatest potential for quality white wines in the country—equally suitable, having the highest vineyards in Galicia, as well as an Atlantic climate and acidic soils. That's why, in May 2004, he started buying small plots of old-vine Godello from veteran vignerons in the Bibei Valley subzone, bordering Ribeira Sacra.

Rafa (as he's known to everyone) is passionate about poor hillside terroirs and is able to innovate in forgotten or poorly developed viticultural regions. The most important objective was to work the vineyards in the traditional way, eliminating the need for herbicides and other treatments.

His vines are between six and 90 years old, in as many as 26 small and widely scattered parcels, with 48 acres (19.5ha) of Godello and 3 acres (1.2ha) of Treixadura. After years of renting, he has built his own winery.

Different lots are fermented in stainless-steel tanks, in big oak vats, or directly in barrel, depending on the harvest and the characteristics of the vineyard. For the aging of the wines, he favors oak *tinas* or even Austrian-style oval-shaped barrels instead of French barriques, because the contact surface is lower and the oak aroma is less marked, which he regards as essential for an aromatic variety such as Godello.

The end result is golden in color, with good aromatic intensity, fine toasty notes giving way to ripe fruit (green apple, pineapple), aniseed, and a powerful, flinty minerality. Medium-bodied in the mouth, with good acidity, it is fresh and unctuous at the same time, leading to a remarkable finish. It should develop even more complexity in bottle for at least five years. But this is only the beginning; the best is yet to come.

**Right:** Rafael Palacios, who left his family winery in Rioja to make exciting whites from indigenous varieties in Valdeorras

## FINEST WINES

Rafa currently makes two wines, but from the extraordinary 2009 vintage on, there will be a new single-vineyard wine when the weather conditions are favorable—a small batch limited to only 1,800 bottles that will be named after the vineyard, O Soro. Early tastings of this wine—which has been in preparation for some years—show tremendous minerality and an acid spine that suggests a long-lived wine of great personality. The idea is to release other single-vineyard wines, being careful not to take away anything from the other wines.

### Louro do Bolo [V]

Even though the first vintage of As Sortes was an instant success, the Spanish market demands entry-level whites, because we are not used to paying as much as for reds—a sign of what some call tinto-centrism. In 2006, Rafa created a new label, Louro do Bolo, with a mixture of his own and purchased grapes, fermented in stainless steel and aged in oak barrels on its lees for a few months. The idea is to preserve the fruit profile, and the result is a fresh wine, easy to drink, full of apple and pear with some minty, smoky, and spicy notes. The full name shown on the label is Louro do Bolo Godello Lías Finas Crianza Foudres Roble de Normandía, since the wine is aged in *foudres* made from Normandy oak. It is very good quality for the price.

### As Sortes ★

The predominance of small plots of land in the region is the result of inheritance drawn by lot (often out of a hat), called *sorte* in the Galician language. It was this important tradition that inspired the name As Sortes. The first vintage was as recent as 2004, but this wine shot straight to the top of the list of high-quality Spanish whites. It comes from high-altitude vineyards (at around 2,600ft [800m] above sea level), planted in granite soils, with vines ranging from 23 to 90 years of age. One of these vineyards, the oldest of all, is called Sorte 1920, because it was planted that year. **2007** was a very cool vintage, high in acidity, and as Rafa himself has said, "It is my Grüner Veltliner." **2009** is also highly recommended. This is one of the finest whites, not only in Valdeorras or Galicia, but in the whole of Spain: a truly mineral wine.

**Rafael Palacios**
Area under vine: 52 acres (20.7ha)
Average production: 88,000 bottles
Calle Avenida Somoza 81,
32350 A Rúa, Ourense
Tel: + 34 988 310 162
Fax: + 34 988 310 162
www.rafaelpalacios.com

# Bodega La Tapada

It was the Guitián family that, in the mid-1990s, elevated the white Godello grape to the highest category with their superb wines—for many among the best whites from Spain. This was achieved thanks to the singularity of their terroir and with the help of José Hidalgo and Ana Martín, one of the best-known winemaking teams in Spain. It was ten years before the region really took off, but it is now recognized as one of the areas with the greatest potential (already partially realized) for whites in the country. Martín and Hidalgo are still in charge of the technical direction of the winery.

*It was the Guitián family that, in the mid-1990s, elevated the white Godello grape to the highest category with their superb wines, for many among the best whites from Spain*

La Tapada estate, in the municipality of Rubiá de Valdeorras, where the 25 acres (10ha) of Godello grapes have been grown since 1985, is located at 1,800ft (550m) above sea level, and its soil is rich in slate, with gentle slopes (an inclination of 10–15 percent) on the south-facing vineyards. It has both Atlantic and continental influences and an annual rainfall of 33–40in (850–1,000mm). The average temperature is 53.6°F (12°C), with highs of 91.4°F (33°C) and lows of 23°F (−5°C), with 2,800 hours of sunshine a year. The vines, planted at a density of 3,100 plants per hectare, are driven on trellises and yield something between 8,000 and 12,000kg/ha, which is not exactly low. The wines transmit a strong sense of terroir.

This family winery was created by the Guitián brothers, led by Ramón, who was tragically killed in a car accident in 1996. Since then, Senén Guitián and his sister Carmen have taken the reins. They make wine only with their own grapes, so this is a true single-vineyard or single-estate wine. In our opinion, it deserves official recognition and its own DO, since its wines have a distinct personality that is quite different from others produced in the same appellation.

The first vintage was 1992. It was fermented with indigenous yeasts in stainless-steel tanks and without malolactic fermentation, which became the recipe from then on. Since 1994, they have also made a Fermentado en Barrica version, in which the smoky notes of the barrique are well integrated with the fruit. Since the 2002 vintage, they have also released a wine aged on its fine lees, called Sobre Lías. They were one of the first producers to convince Spanish consumers that whites can actually age and improve with a few years in the bottle.

## FINEST WINES

All the wines are 100% Godello. The Guitiáns produced a *blanc de noirs* for three vintages at the beginning of the 2000s—Guitián Merenzao—made with red Merenzao grapes, but they lost the source for the grapes and gave up. All wines are fermented using indigenous yeasts and are filtered and cold-stabilized. The bottles are dressed with a lovely Art Deco–style label, all with the same design, only the colors changing. All of the wines are highly recommended, but one has to wonder whether quality could be even higher if yields were a little lower and the wines were handled more gently.

### Guitián Godello ★ [V]
The grapes are fermented without the stems in stainless steel at a controlled temperature and aged in the same tanks for some six months before being bottled without malolactic fermentation. Godello is a very aromatic grape, and this unoaked version brings out all the potential of the fruit. A fine, complex, perfumed nose of marked personality: mustard, apricot, and elegant bay-leaf notes, fennel and citrus (grapefruit), and musky and mineral hints of flint and gunpowder. It is medium-bodied, well defined, elegant, and pure, lifted by a fine acidity, with intense, refreshing flavors and a very long finish. Some think it's better in the first five years

after the vintage, but it has been kept successfully much longer than that. It is a matter of taste which you prefer. It is ideal with seafood.

### Guitián Godello Fermentado en Barrica ★

In some vintages, a small proportion of the grapes (10%) are affected by botrytis, which could be responsible for the musky character that exists alongside the notes of grapefruit and gunpowder. The grapes are fermented in oak barrels, where the wine is aged for six months with daily *bâtonnage*. It is bottled without going through malolactic fermentation to keep the freshness, and it is aged in bottle a further six months before being released. It can age up to ten years. This is the black-and-golden label, a wine that opened many wine lovers' eyes in Spain to the potential of ageworthy whites from Godello grapes, though the unoaked version below ages just as well as this.

### Guitián Godello Sobre Lías ★

This wine follows in the footsteps of other Rías Baixas wines that are aged in stainless-steel tanks on their lees for some months to give them more character—an alternative to oak aging, which is considered by many as too aggressive for the more delicate and aromatic white grapes. The Guitián family keeps this Godello in stainless-steel tanks for some eight months, in contact with its fine lees, before bottling. On top of the signature peach, balsamic, and bay-leaf notes, the wine comes through as more yeasty than the barrel-fermented version, with toasty notes from the autolysis of the lees. The texture in the mouth has an added dimension, being both full and intense, while keeping its freshness. The label is very similar to the straight, unoaked Godello but with some orange thrown in. The **2008** and **2009** vintages are fantastic and should age for 5–10 years.

**Right:** Senén Guitián, who, with his sister Carmen, runs an estate worthy of its own DO, so distinctive are its wines

### Bodega La Tapada
Area under vine: 25 acres (10ha)
Average production: 130,000 bottles
Finca A Tapada
32310 Rubiá de Valdeorras, Ourense
Tel: +34 988 324 197
Fax: +34 988 324 197

# Quinta da Muradella

The fact that Quinta da Muradella is today considered the quality leader in Monterrei is due to the determination and hard work of José Luis Mateo, a true vigneron. The winery was created in 1991—the Monterrei appellation was created only in 1992—and now owns 35 acres (14ha) of vineyards across Pazos de Monterrei, Tamaguelos, and Vilardevós, on very different soils: slate, granite, iron, and quartz.

All these vineyards are replanted when needed, using a massal selection from the old vineyards, and are today certified as organic by CRAEGA (Consello Regulador de Agricultura Ecolóxica de Galicia). They are worked on biodynamic principles, but nothing is mentioned on the labels, because it is

*Mateo tries to follow traditional techniques without saying no to technological advances. The work with wood is very careful, so as not to mask the character of the wines*

done out of conviction, not as a marketing gimmick. There's also an impressive mix of grape varieties: Arauxa (the name given locally to Tempranillo), Bastardo, Brancellao, Caíño Longo, Caíño Redondo, Mencía, Sousón, and Zamarrica. But Mateo is also experimenting with Garnacha Tintorera, Prieto Picudo, Syrah, Tinto Serodio, Touriga Nacional, and Verdello Tinto. And that's only for the reds. For the whites, he works with Doña Blanca, Monstruosa de Monterrei, Treixadura, and Verdello, as well as experimenting with local and foreign varieties like Albariño, Bastardo Rubio, Torrontés, and even Sauvignon Blanc.

Since 2000, Raúl Pérez has been a consultant for the winery, and the arrangements—as is often the case with Pérez—are complex, because he gets paid in grapes or wine, and some wines are sold with the Rául Pérez label. A Trabe is a case in point, since it is actually sourced from vineyards in Quinta da Muradella.

There are four main vineyards. A Trabe is the oldest—indeed, it is one of the oldest in Galicia, planted shortly after phylloxera—with some vines over 100 years old. It has 3 acres (1.2ha) of head-pruned indigenous red and white varieties that belonged to Mateo's family and has been used for cuttings for new plantations. It's located at 2,850ft (870m) above sea level, the soil is decomposed slate, and the slopes are very steep (the incline up to 60 percent in some parts). This is a mountain vineyard, bordering Portugal and even crossing the border in some parts.

The Gorvia vineyard is also 3 acres but planted 15 years ago with material from A Trabe. Finca Notario is a very small plot close to Gorvia. The main Quinta da Muradella vineyard is bigger, at 28.5 acres (11.6ha), with recent plantings of different ages, five to 15 years old, and is used both for blends and for small lots of varietal wines.

On top of this, Mateo also manages 25 acres (10ha) of rented vineyards—a grand total of 60 acres (24ha) across 36 different plots. The winery has a maximum capacity of 75,000 bottles, but so far production has been smaller—some 4,000 bottles. Mateo tries to follow traditional techniques without spurning technological advances. The work with wood is very careful, so as not to mask the character of the wines; in general, French oak is used, and the wines spend 13 or 14 months there. He is experimenting more and more with bigger sizes.

## FINEST WINES

Muradella offers many different wines—13 to 17, depending on the year—often in very small quantities and different from one year to the next. Some are under the DO, and some are not, since they are experimenting both with old varieties and with international ones, trying to find the best expression of the different terroirs. Their entry line is called Alanda. These are wines for the table,

**Above:** José Luis Mateo, whose dedication and vision have established Quinta da Muradella as Monterrei's top winery

not for blind tasting, and are truly Atlantic wines of great personality. (Details of A Trabe can be found under Raúl Pérez.)

### Gorvia [V]
There is a red and a white, both from the eponymous vineyard. The red is Mencía (90%), complemented by Bastardo, while the white is mainly Doña Blanca aged in used 250- and 500-liter oak barrels.

### Muradella/Quinta da Muradella
Under the name Muradella or Quinta da Muradella are varietal wines from Bastardo,★ Doña Blanca, and Sousón, Albarello and Caíño Redondo (the Bastardo is our favorite so far). There is also a red blend from a selection of the oldest vines, and the white is vinified just like the red.

### Quinta da Muradella Finca Notario ★
This is a single-vineyard wine, from 0.75 acres (0.3ha) that belong to the notary of Verín, planted at the end of the 1940s at 1,380ft (420m) above sea level. It's 55% Mencía, 30% Bastardo, and 15% Garnacha Tintorera. The whole clusters of grapes are fermented in open barrels with two months of maceration and then aged for 14 months in French oak. The wine is of an intense cherry color, with ripe red fruit on the nose and very well-integrated wood. In the mouth, it has lively acidity and gives a profound mineral sensation—salty?—with a remarkable finish, leaving an overall impression of balance and harmony. A white wine is also made from the notary's grapes.

### Quinta da Muradella
Area under vine: 35 acres (14ha)
Average production: 45,000 bottles
Avenida Luis Espada 99,
32600 Verín, Ourense
Tel: +34 988 411 724
Fax: +34 988 411 724
www.muradella.com

# Basque Country / Cantabrian Coast

**B**asque Txakoli is the main protagonist of regional winemaking in the north of Spain facing the Cantabrian Sea, with Galicia to the west, Rioja to the south, and Navarra to the east. The total area is three-quarters of the size of Galicia, with which it shares common climate features marked by exposure to the Atlantic Ocean. It comprises three autonomous communities; from east to west, they are País Vasco (excepting the south of Álava, which is home to Rioja Alavesa), Cantabria, and Asturias. Of these, País Vasco, the Basque Country, is by far the most important, in terms of both tradition and the current production of Txakoli (or Chacolí in the Spanish spelling, though the pronunciation is the same). But Cantabria and Asturias also deserve recognition for their honest efforts toward quality winemaking.

### Euskadi, the land of Txakoli

Txakoli, in its different geographic origins, is a wine exclusive to the Basque Country, or Euskadi, as it is known in the vernacular language. (Visitors should be aware that this is a language with little or no resemblance to any other they may know, and many addresses and signs are written in Euskara alone, not in Spanish.) But let us not forget that part of winemaking Rioja spreads toward the south of Álava and is therefore part of the Basque territory. It would be unforgivable to ignore the fact that many top Rioja producers are located there.

*Txakoli* literally means "farm wine" or "home-made wine," which corresponds to the ancient Mediterranean tradition—widely practiced all over Spain—of growing vines on one's lands in order to make wine for family consumption, which may eventually include the neighborhood as well. In places like the Basque Country and Galicia, where land tenure is atomized and

**Right:** Basque vineyards are often very close to the edge of the Cantabrian Sea, which influences the style of the wines

**Above:** A temperature-controlled tank of the indigenous white grape variety Hondarrabi Zuri, the chief component of Txakoli

climate conditions are less favorable for the successful growth of vines, this tradition has survived for longer than in other regions where massive vineyard holdings, more regular harvests, and lower costs have favored the growth of the wine trade well beyond the local level.

There is, however, a degree of paradox here. For the remarkable rise of Txakoli over the past few decades rests squarely on the international success of Basque gastronomy, whose worldwide recognition is one of the pillars of the current reputation of Spanish cuisine. There may also have been a certain cultural inclination to favor Basque produce over anything foreign, which may have encouraged the consumption of Txakoli in the homes—and especially the restaurants—of the Basque Country. But to put too much emphasis on that aspect would be an oversimplification, since this is not an exclusively local phenomenon.

Anyone who keeps up with the latest news from the international wine scene will have noticed that Txakoli is attracting an increasing amount of attention from both consumers and wine writers. Export figures, especially for the

United States, seem to confirm this trend, which is easily explained as part of a movement that vindicates—as a reaction against excessive alcohol, body, and exuberance in many wines— whites that are low in alcohol, fresh, and structured by their notable acidity (all of which define Txakoli). But there can be no question that this phenomenon also has much to do with the existence of an ever-increasing number of serious producers, who have pursued quality above all. They have been helped by a series of sunny vintages in the early years of this century.

### The Txakoli appellations

Txakoli is produced in three appellations, each in a different Basque province: Bizkaia-Vizcaya, Gipuzkoa-Guipúzcoa, and Araba-Álava.

**DO Bizkaiko Txakolina** This is probably the most thriving of the three appellations—the one with the largest number of interesting producers and certainly the one with a more resolutely innovative attitude about the future of Txakoli, investigating new paths without renouncing tradition. One of the key factors has been a certain flexibility about the accepted varieties, which goes well beyond the indigenous two admitted in the neighboring appellation Txakoli de Guetaria. This is, besides, not a gratuitous decision; it is based on the tradition of the Biscay boroughs, where historically other varieties have been planted, especially Petit Courbu, known locally as Hondarrabi Zuri Zerratia. This extra complexity creates a far greater range of possibilities than the ancient, monotonous local offering of acidic and semi-effervescent Txakolis destined to be served in flat-bottomed glasses and drunk immediately (before the foam has disappeared).

**DO Getariako Txakolina** This was the first of the three appellations to be officially recognized as such, in 1989. While today it legally encompasses the entire Guipúzcoa province, this appellation is historically focused on two or three towns to the west of the province: Guetaria, Zaráuz, and Aya—but chiefly Guetaria, which concentrates around 80 percent of the production. The lovely town of Guetaria (Getaria in Euskara) was the birthplace of the man who proved once and for all that the Earth is round, Juan Sebastián Elcano, whose first round-the-world voyage began and ended in Sanlúcar de Barrameda, thus creating a symbolic link between these two maritime and winemaking towns of the north and south of Spain. To Guetaria's more obvious attractions—its picturesque port and rugged coastline—we must add the beauty of the vineyards on the hillsides around it. The varieties accepted by the DO are exclusively the indigenous white Hondarrabi Zuri and the red Hondarrabi Beltza—the former occupying 95 percent of the vineyards. As well as Bodega Txomin Etxaniz, whose owners played a key role in the foundation of the DO, there are several other interesting producers worth keeping an eye on—among them Ameztoi, Aizpurua, Talai-Berri, and Urki.

**DO Arabako Txakolina** The most recently created appellation for Txakoli (in 2001/02) is DO Txakoli de Álava, confined to the borough of Ayala (Aiara) to the north of the province, near Bilbao, facing the Cantabrian Sea. This is a region where vineyards (again mostly Hondarrabi Zuri and Hondarrabi Beltza) have been recovered thanks to the important support received by the Growers' Association from the public administration. This Asociación de Productores was founded in 1989, when only 12 acres (5ha) survived of the nearly 1,500 acres (600ha) counted in the second half of the 19th century. At present, there are more than 150 acres (60ha) and six producers, though in fact one of them (under the same name as the DO, Arabako Txakolina SL) accounts for 95 percent of the total production.

**Cantabria and Asturias**
In Cantabria, the region immediately to the west of Biscay, wine production is concentrated in two areas, protected by the *indicaciones geográficas* Vino de la Tierra Costa de Cantabria and Vino de la Tierra de Liébana—which, in practice, split the entire coastal territory of the province and the inland valleys facing the Atlantic.

There are now nine wineries in the region, with 317 acres (132ha) under vine. In both areas, however, there are now interesting producers, such as Picos de Cabariezo and Viña Lusía in Liébana. We must also single out two coastal wineries, which happen to be very close to each other, whose wines are consistently improving with every new vintage: Viña Lancina and Vidular (Ribera del Asón). Both are next to the border of the neighboring DO Bizkaiko Txakolina and share with it not only climatic conditions and grape varieties but also stylistic similarities with the best of those wines. This is not in the least surprising, since the local winemaking traditions of both regions have been developing in parallel, regardless of the political boundaries.

Despite the wide geographic extent of the Principado de Asturias (Asturias is about the size of Cantabria and the Basque Country together), winemaking there is limited to a small *indicación geográfica* in the southwest: Vino de la Tierra de Cangas. The impulse of local gastronomy and restaurants, as well as the support received from important names in the wine trade such as Ramón Coalla, have contributed to the recovery of a winemaking culture whose defining feature is Albarín Blanco (or Blanco Verdín), an ancient grape variety that exists hardly anywhere else (though it is also found exceptionally in some Galician whites). Corias is the most relevant bodega among the handful of producers in the areas of Cangas del Narcea and Degaña.

# Txomin Etxaniz

The seaside village of Guetaria is charming, one of those small places that are often overlooked by the reckless tourist but one that no serious traveler can afford to neglect. Among its attractions, it boasts a popular fishing port, very solid stone buildings, narrow streets, the silvery Cantabrian Sea foam splashing everywhere, to-die-for gastronomy (Kaia, Elkano), and, of course, the vineyards.

Those that surround Guetaria on the neighboring hillsides add a final irresistible appeal to the landscape of this village. And those vineyards are also the core around which Getariako Txakolina has expanded all over the province of Gúipuzcoa with stunning success over the past few years. The region has witnessed a similar growth concerning quality-oriented Txakoli producers, now numbering 20 or so. Among these, the pioneer (since 1930) and the benchmark is Txomin Etxaniz, a name that originally belonged to the grandfather of the current owners, the Txueka family.

*Txakoli Txomin Etxaniz still represents a satisfying achievement in terms of what Hondarrabi Zuri (plus a dollop of Hondarrabi Beltza) can yield on the Cantabrian coast*

If you wander the many steep paths up and down Mount Gárate, the likelihood of crossing this producer's vineyards—their own or those they rent—will be high. Those vineyards have resounding, unmistakably Basque names: first and foremost, Ametzmendi and Gurutze, where the winemaking facilities can also be found, since they outgrew their original location at the heart of the village, next to the Church of San Salvador. But there are also several others: Leoiaga, Tonpeta, Iturri...

Txomin Etxaniz produces three wines, of which the bodega's eponymous Txakoli is the unchallenged champion, for both its market dominance and its brand strength. The other two are a sparkling wine (Eugenia) and a late-harvest white wine (Uydi), which is mildly sweet and lacks the appetizing, typically sharp edges of the dry whites of the region.

## FINEST WINES

### Txakoli Txomin Etxaniz ★

There has been a noticeable increase in the production of Txakoli over the past few decades, which, in the case of Txomin Etxaniz, has been truly spectacular—with all the risks that this phenomenon brings with it in terms of young vines and the temptation to push yields beyond what is sensible. Even so, Txakoli Txomin Etxaniz still represents a satisfying achievement in terms of what the Hondarrabi Zuri grape (plus a dollop of Hondarrabi Beltza) can yield in the wet environment of the Cantabrian coast: short-lived primary fruit, lightness, marked acidity, a spritz on the palate... The keys to its production are the pressing of whole grapes, temperature-controlled fermentation to boost fruit aromas, and a few months on its lees and in contact with the carbonic gas generated during fermentation, prior to bottling. That is today's technological version of the traditional Txakoli style, and Txomin Etxaniz performs here like very few others. The majority of Guipuzcoan producers still choose this style, unlike their Biscay neighbors, who come from a crossbreed winemaking culture that is more open to new varieties and techniques that would have been deemed unthinkable in the old times of this popular Basque "farm wine."

**Right:** Iñaki Txueka (center) and other key figures at Txomin Etxaniz, amid traditional, high-trained Hondarrabi Zuri vines

**Txomin Etxaniz**
Area under vine: 150 acres (60ha)
Average production: 450,000 bottles
Calle Eitzaga Auzoa 13,
20808 Guetaria, Gipuzkoa
Tel: +34 943 140 702
Fax: +34 943 140 462
www.txominetxaniz.com

# Bodegas Itsasmendi

Under the expert guidance of one of the most influential professionals in Spanish winemaking, Ana Martín, and the technical direction of Garikoitz Ríos, Itsasmendi has unquestionably consolidated itself as one of the most solid projects in the Basque Country. A pioneering project in the Txakoli de Bizkaia/Bizkaiko Txakolina appellation, it has steadily matured, always learning lessons from the past. The approach here prizes integration with nature, as well as having serious respect for the environment and preservation of the terroir.

The origins of the project date back to 1989, when a group of Biscay growers, aware of their tradition and the potential of the region, decided to start a new venture committed to quality winemaking. The facilities in Muskiz opened with a great fanfare in 1995, and the 25,000-bottle capacity would soon prove insufficient. In 2002, the cellar was moved to the emblematic town of Guernica, where, in an ideal vintage like 2008, the company can confidently handle up to 275 tons (250,000kg) of grapes—including those from its own 75 acres (30ha) of vineyards.

The vineyards are located in different areas of Biscay, half of them within the Urdaibai Biosphere Reservoir. The varieties planted are mostly the indigenous Hondarrabi Zuri and Hondarrabi Zuri Zerratie, complemented by 5 acres (2ha) of Riesling. Yields are restricted to a maximum of 7,500–8,500kg/ha. (The appellation admits up to 13,000kg/ha.) This intervention is crucial for the quality of Itsasmendi wines, especially given the relatively young age of the vines; in normal conditions, they should yield increasingly good wines as they age.

The wine with the largest production in the portfolio is the young Txakoli Itsasmendi, a vintage wine like that produced by every Basque grower. To this we must add Itsasmendi No.7, which we describe below, and Itsasmendi Urezti, a late-harvest white with some 80g of residual sugar per liter, overripened on the vine and harvested as late as November.

## FINEST WINES

### Itsasmendi No.7 ★

For the average Spanish wine consumer, any unoaked white wine is automatically deemed a wine meant to be consumed very young, perhaps only months after bottling. This prejudice is even more extreme in the case of Txakolis, and producers seem to be conscious of it, to the point that very few of them keep any stock from previous years. This No.7 (which is simply named after the stainless-steel tank where it matures) is Itsasmendi's serious attempt at an unoaked white, with aging potential, to evolve elegantly and smoothly in bottle, with no major loss after the inevitable drop in primary-fruit notes. The blend is based largely on indigenous varieties, and the distinctive feature of Itsasmendi No.7 is a selection of the better-structured lots plus 20% of Riesling. From a winemaking point of view, the difference is the aging of the wine in tank on its lees for several months prior to bottling. The resulting wine has a body and volume unlike any typical Txakoli. The producers predict a gain in complexity during the first three to four years of bottle age, which we have indeed verified for both typical vintages and unusually warm ones like **2006**. The **2008** vintage looks particularly promising. It is worth adding a number of bottles to one's personal cellar as they are released each year and storing them carefully to find, years later, a serious, expressive, and complex white that most certainly belongs in that often imprecise category, "fine wine."

**Bodega Itsasmendi**
Area under vine: 75 acres (30ha)
Average production: 180,000 bottles
Barrio Arane 3,
48300 Guernica, Vizcaya
Tel: +34 946 270 316
Fax: +34 946 251 032
www.bodegasitsasmendi.com

**Left:** Respected winemaker Ana Martín, who has helped establish Itsasmendi as one of the region's best producers

# Egia Enea

Alfredo Egia Cruz, founder and very visible head of Egia Enea Txakolina, is one of the best representatives of that group of small Txakoli producers who started to bottle under their own labels in the late 1980s and early 1990s. Now there is an abundance of quality producers, and ordering a random bottle of Txakoli in a Basque restaurant need not mean finding an acidic skeletal wine marked by annoying sulfur notes or a coarse carbonic presence. The odds are that the wine will at least be interesting and often a pleasant surprise.

This movement is particularly strong in the Biscay area of the Txakoli region, where the area under vine has multiplied by six (and production volumes by nine) over the past 15 years, and where more than a dozen growers have emerged, making a resolute statement in the cause of rigorous viticulture and winemaking.

In many cases, complexity is provided by the presence of other varieties—especially Hondarrabi Zuri Zerratia (Petit Courbu), which enjoys a relevance in the Bizkaiko Txakolina appellation that is missing elsewhere in Txakoli.

Alfredo Egia is a profound believer in an idea that has become something of a cliché in recent years but ois nonetheless true: that a wine is made in the vineyard. Egia says the concept behind Egia Enea Txakolina, which existed in his mind for many years before it came into being, was to express the terroir in such a way that it would produce a white where the typical freshness and liveliness of Txakoli could be complemented by good structure, leaving an impression of complexity and volume on the palate.

That was why he started by choosing the soils for his vineyards so carefully. For years he studied the best south-facing hillsides in the Biscay area of Encartaciones. It was only in 2001 that he bought a plot that met his criteria, in Balmaseda. This plot had been a vineyard for centuries until 1915, in the same area where Txakoli Balmasedano was sourced—a wine whose reputation lasted until phylloxera marked the decline of Cantabrian winemaking tradition. To the original 7.5 acres (3ha) planted in 2001, he added another 5 acres (2ha) in 2007, intended to provide for the growing production of his one and only wine.

There is a special mesoclimate here because of the vineyard's location. Its southern orientation and steep hillsides (with a gradient of 25 percent) combine to keep the vineyards free from the abundant mists that cause so many sanitary problems in the region. These are poor soils that limit yields to around 7,000kg/ha—well under the norm among Txakoli producers.

Alfredo is fond of Hondarrabi Zuri Zerratia, which makes up 80 percent of the final blend, the remaining 20 percent being Hondarrabi Zuri. He says, "HZZ is very sensitive to mildew, but with proper vineyard management it produces Txakolis of superior aromatic range, with white-pepper notes and better body and structure on the palate. With our smaller percentage of HZ, it is minerality we are after." He believes it's vitally important that any vineyard work is carried out to the letter, and he is constantly monitoring the vineyard's performance to ensure that the timing of every action and every treatment is exactly right. He is very emphatic about the benefits of a severe green-harvest in order to delay picking and thus help the complete ripening of the berries.

As a result, Egia Enea is a serious wine: precise, with sharp but not excessive acidity, a well-handled vegetal element of grass that gives it personality, and an elegant finish with a pleasant bitter note.

**Egia Enea**
Area under vine: 12 acres (5ha)
Average production: 17,000 bottles
Artebizkarra 18, 3° izda,
48860 Zalla, Bizkaia
Tel: +34 661 922 101
www.egiaenea.com

# Picos de Cabariezo

The Liébana Valley in Cantabria is a very peculiar place, a north–south gash in the Picos de Europa mountains that are part of the long coastal range separating Spain's northern coast from the Castilian plateau. Liébana is wide open to the south and perfectly protected from the Atlantic gales by the mountains. As a result, it's a drier, warmer Mediterranean microcosm in the middle of Atlantic Spain. There are orange and lemon trees, cork oaks good enough to furnish stoppers for Vega-Sicilia, and vineyards, too, in general near the village of Bedoya.

Scattered across small plots, mostly on steep hillsides, are old, gnarled, head-pruned vines to which no one paid much attention until recently. There is an old distilling tradition in the valley, but the commercial distilleries of *orujo* brandy, Spain's version of grappa, weren't even using those grapes—they brought them in from Zamora, south of the mountains. Apparently, the vines were only used for homemade, often illicit, booze.

So no one had ever seen a wine from Liébana, much less a properly made and bottled one, when five enthusiastic friends set up a small winery and distillery near Potes, the main town in the valley, back in 2000. They had noticed that there were more vines around than were at first apparent— some 150 acres (60ha) ten years later. Most of these were Mencía vines, often 80–100 years old, clinging precariously to schistous or limestone slopes. That promised some interesting quality if anyone ever set their mind to it.

The first wines were made in 2006 by the new company, formally called Compañía Lebaniega de Vinos y Licores—which sounds grand, but it's actually very small, tucked beneath a mountainside hotel, with a few fermenting vats, a small barrel cellar, and 12 beautiful copper *alquitaras* (stills).

Next door is the experimental vineyard planted in 2000, with the help of the regional government, to study the adaptation of Spanish and foreign grape varieties. But for winemaking purposes, the winery counts mainly on the 30–40 tons of old-vine Mencía grapes it purchases from small growers in the valley. There are also some Palomino vines, but these are used only for the *orujo*.

The experimental vineyard yields a mixed bag of white grapes, which are all used for a late-harvest white. In addition, Picos de Cabariezo makes a soft, unoaked red (a blend of 40 percent Mencía with Garnacha and Tempranillo) and a serious but pleasurable Mencía varietal called Roble.

The wines were first developed from a distance by their own flying winemaker Pere Escudé, a pioneer of the Costers del Segre DO and later the chief winemaker of the large Cellers Unió co-op in the Montsant DO.

Picos de Cabariezo is no longer alone on the Liébana highlands—having being joined there fairly recently by Lusía—and they share the Vinos de la Tierra de Liébana appellation. There are, in addition, half a dozen Cantabrian wineries near the coast, specializing in white wines. A whole generation of Spaniards who had learned that no wine at all was made either in Cantabria or in Asturias is having to relearn the nation's viticultural map.

## FINEST WINES

### Picos de Cabariezo Roble
Aged in French and American oak barrels for at least four months, this old-vine Mencía is balanced, fresh, and luscious, with abundant fruit but also a mineral backbone that gives it some elegance. This is an honest, terroir-driven wine, with no artificial gimmicks getting in the way.

**Picos de Cabariezo (Compañía Lebaniega de Vinos y Licores)**
Area under vine: 27 acres (11ha)
Average production: 50,000 bottles
39571 Cabezón de Liébana, Cantabria
Tel: +34 942 735 176
www.vinosylicorespicos.es

# Year by Year 1990–2010 and Select Older Vintages

In this chapter, we aim to give an overview of recent Rioja vintages and also to look back at some significant older ones, to shed some light on the region's finest wines. Moderate quantity usually goes hand in hand with quality, but there are years when high production coincided with high quality—that is to say, there is a correlation between quantity and quality, but it is not always direct. At the same time, it is not always the famous vintages that age better. Official scores of vintages are often, with the benefit of hindsight, put in their proper perspective. It's not unusual for wines from less touted vintages—maybe less ripe and higher in acidity—to age for longer. For example, Muga's 1969 Prado Enea is today fresher and livelier than the much more famous 1970 Prado Enea.

All the wines we feature here in the old vintages have been drunk between 2005 and 2010, meaning that old red—and white!—Rioja is extremely ageworthy. Of course, after 30 years there are no good vintages as such, just good bottles; but it's surprising how few old bottles have to be poured down the drain. Tempranillo reaches maturity quite fast but then remains on a mature plateau for a very, very long time. Some wines are over the hill and have taken on a disgusting compost and rotten-carrot character. But most are still very drinkable, while a few have just faded quietly away. And we are talking here about bottles stored in Spain—not all of them, by any means, at perfect temperatures.

## 1925

The official vintage ratings start with 1925, the year the Consejo Regulador was set up. Well-kept bottles of Castillo de Ygay and Marqués de Riscal are drinking beautifully 85 years later. Of course,

*Left:* Some of Rioja's greatest old bodegas—like Marqués de Riscal—still have relatively good stocks of mature vintages

those wines were made in a very different way; for example, the Ygay was aged for more than 30 years in wood (one has to wonder what was used to top up the barrels), and it was bottled only in April 1964, before being launched on to the market in 1973. That's why it's still relatively easy to find.

## 1928

Officially designated *muy buena* ("very good"), this vintage was not without its difficulties, such as northeast winds and frost during harvest. It's not, in fact, one of the more famous years, and there are not many well-known wines from the vintage. However, Bodegas Bilbaínas Vieja Reserva ("Old Reserve") is truly world-class.

## 1934

An excellent vintage that achieved both quantity and quality, with balanced wines. The Castillo de Ygay Tinto, which, amazingly, was not put on the market until 1961, is one of the best wines from the vintage and one of the best Riojas in history.

## 1942

A classic vintage that produced powerful, deep-colored wines that have aged gracefully. Castillo de Ygay Tinto, Viña Tondonia Tinto, and Viña Albina from Bodegas Riojanas are still in top form today.

## 1945

Though 1945 was not really a great vintage, it somehow produced one of the best Riojas ever—the Marqués de Riscal Cuvée Médoc, a wine with a high proportion of Cabernet Sauvignon that has remained dark and powerful throughout its life.

## 1946

The 1946 is an unheralded vintage—officially declared "normal," or the fourth-highest official

category, something almost never used nowadays—
but it's worth mentioning if only for the magical
Castillo de Ygay Gran Reserva Especial white, a
wine with incredible acidity and intensity. Truly a
world-class wine, this was released as late as 1973.

## 1947

A superb vintage, dry and warm, across Europe,
and Rioja was no exception. Somehow, 1948 was
officially declared to be "excellent," while 1947 was
only "very good." In retrospect, however, the
declarations should be reversed, and CVNE's
Imperial can easily compete with the greatest wines
from the vintage in Bordeaux. Imperial and Viña
Tondonia, both in gran reserva format, represent
the peak of the vintage.

## 1954

This vintage qualified merely as "good," because
there were frosts in April and a cool summer. But
time has proved CVNE's Viña Real Reserva
Especial and López de Heredia's Viña Bosconia
two of the best Riojas ever.

## 1958

An excellent vintage, as per the official rating,
with some unusual parameters: a short vegetative
cycle and only 16in (410mm) of rain (one quarter of
which fell during summer, which was beneficial).
All the same, many top wines were not produced
this year, while some unheralded ones, like Carlos
Serres Reserva Especial, have lasted to the present
day in pretty good shape.

## 1959

A vintage initially considered lower in quality than
1958, thanks to its 20in (506mm) of rain (quite
spread out during the vegetative period, but low at
budding time and quite high in September), spring
frosts, and a cold July, which resulted in a vegetative
cycle of 200 days. Many people think it is one of the

most classical vintages and certainly better than
1958. CVNE's wines stand out, especially Imperial.

## 1964

This was greeted as "the vintage of the century."
There are so many great wines from 1964 still
available and eminently drinkable that it's difficult
to single out the best of them. However, anything
from López de Heredia—Viña Tondonia Tinto,
but especially the Blanco and Viña Bosconia—is
superb. Since the 1960s, records have been kept
showing the volume of wine granted DO status,
so we know that 1964 produced 135 million liters,
when the average for the decade was only
100 million. This is a vintage of both quality and
quantity—something not that unusual. All even-
numbered vintages from the 1960s would deserve
to be on this list, but somehow 1964 and 1970 are
even better than 1962, 1966, and 1968.

## 1970

Marqués de Cáceres is one of the most famous
wines from this magical vintage—the first year for
a revolutionary and modern wine, breaking with
tradition by keeping the fruit and using French oak.
Technically a crianza, it was the first wine from a
new producer that, at the time, had no fermentation
vats, no barrel cellar—in fact, no winery at all as
such. But the wine was so skillfully blended by
Emile Peynaud that it became an instant classic,
establishing the brand, the winery, and modern-
day Rioja. The year produced a sizable 113 million
liters, which somehow seemed to last forever. The
vegetative cycle lasted 195 days, since sprouting was
quite late after a cold, wet winter, but there were no
spring frosts, and there was a warm but wet summer
(some hail in June) followed by a mild autumn.

## 1973

This vintage has recently been rediscovered. Viña
Tondonia Gran Reserva Blanco and the whole

lineup from La Rioja Alta (890 and 904, Ardanza) and Muga's Prado Enea are superb. Somehow, the official qualification was only "good," the third-best category.

## 1981

Total production was on the increase throughout the 1970s and 1980s, and 1981 saw a large crop that yielded 135 million liters of wine of excellent quality, even though the official rating was only "very good." It was overshadowed by 1982, which is one of the most famous vintages ever.

## 1982

An excellent year, with a reputation on a par with the same vintage in Bordeaux. The year yielded 125 million liters of wine after a vegetative cycle of 210 days, a mild winter with 4.5in (115mm) of rain, warm weather at budding, very high temperatures at the beginning of June, moderate rain in July and August (0.7in [18mm]), and then 1.5in (40mm) in September. Most houses produced very good wines, making it a remarkably consistent vintage.

## 1987

After some difficult vintages in the early to mid-1980s (including a catastrophic 1984), the region was in need of a very good vintage, but one did not come until 1987. It was a typical continental year, with a cold winter and a warm and dry summer. (The year saw only 11.2in [286mm] of rain, when the usual quantity is around 17.7in (450mm].)

## 1990

People often think that vintages across Europe are similar to those in Bordeaux. However, this is not the case in Rioja, as can very clearly be seen in 1990—which was only an average vintage here, not a world-renowned one, as it was in Bordeaux. It was a warm and dry year that produced 161 million liters.

## 1991

This vintage produced some wines of great tannic structure, with the ability to age well. Production was down to 145 million liters, and the vintage earned the "very good" rating.

## 1992

A very rainy year, with 26.5in (673mm) of water. The vintage was equally marked by torrential rains during the harvest, which started on October 12. That date stands as a dividing line: the grapes harvested before were excellent, while those harvested after were not up to standard and resulted in light-colored and unstable wines. A total of 150 million liters of uneven wines were produced. It was the first vintage for wines such as Torre Muga, Roda, and Remírez de Ganuza.

## 1993

This was a difficult vintage for Rioja and the other regions of central Spain. The year yielded 174 million liters of wine, to be drunk earlier rather than later.

## 1994

The year that "New Rioja" exploded. It was rated, correctly, as "excellent," but the official vintage scores became quite meaningless in the 1990s (few years ever seemed to have negative scores), and most people lost track and interest. A good vintage was also very much needed in the region, after a series of average and difficult years. It was a warm and dry summer, and ripening was fast. Artadi Pagos Viejos, Marqués de Vargas, Remírez de Ganuza, and Roda were the names that made headlines at the time. Torre Muga, a modern-style wine aged in French oak, is one of the best wines of the vintage, and the profile today is that of classic Rioja, demonstrating that when the grapes are good, the character of the region, the terroir, will always show through in time, no matter how the wine is made or aged. The Gran Reserva from Viña Tondonia, released in 2010, is built to age for decades. A total of 169 million liters were produced—around 20 percent lower than the average at the time. But with the increase in wineries, the area under vine, and the press impact of the new wines, annual production volumes soared from this point on.

## 1995

This was a truly great vintage—it merited the same "excellent" rating as 1994—but it suffered commercially because it came in the wake of the very widely praised previous year. It produced very good, powerful wines but with good acidity; the wines are more austere than those of 1994. The warmth of early September was balanced by cooler days, with rain just at the right time and a dry, mild October. Very healthy grapes were harvested quite late—the second and third weeks of October in some cases. It was probably the last of the classic CVNE Imperial Gran Reserva vintages, and Viña El Pison got 99 points from Robert Parker, which put Artadi, Rioja, and Spain in general in the spotlight.

## 1996

This vintage suffered the opposite fate of 1995, in that it was rated too highly given what we now know of the wines. On paper, the conditions were perfect—a cool, dry summer, a warm September with some rain, then a cool, dry October—the total production reaching 224 million liters. Torre Muga and Roda I (today called Roda), Aurus, and the regular Allende were all very good, as was Contino's Viña del Olivo, the first year of this single-vineyard bottling, a tendency that was to gain ground gradually in Rioja.

## 1997

This vintage got bad press from the beginning, and it's true that the weather conditions were difficult, with rains in June bringing mildew and oidium. Production went up to 254 million liters of uneven quality. However, despite the initial bad image, many wines—Aurus and Finca Valpiedra, in particular—are aging superbly.

## 1998

After the bad press for 1997 and the difficulties in selling the wines, Rioja was waiting for any opportunity to declare a good vintage. That's how 1998 came to be touted as a good year (officially "very good"), whereas it was probably one of the worst of the past 15 years. Many wines are already past their best. Quantity was steadily on the rise—274 million liters this year.

## 1999

This was a cold vintage, and the wines did not really achieve good balance; there was plenty of acidity but probably not enough concentration. It was an early-budding year, but frost destroyed all the buds, and a secondary budding did not happen until mid-May, so flowering was one month later than normal. Naturally, yields were down from previous years, to a total of 216 million liters. Grape prices went through the roof, breaking all records. This is a vintage for early consumption—with some exceptions, like Finca Allende's superb Calvario.

## 2000

Until August, the outlook was for a great and very large vintage, but rains in September and throughout October made the ripening of grapes difficult, resulting in an unusual and uneven year, with the longest vegetative cycle ever. A still-unbroken record of 311 million liters produced variable quality; for the best producers—those working with limited yields and old vines—2000 is a very good and at the same time an easy-drinking vintage, only overshadowed by 2001. The wines from Benjamín Romeo, Contador, and La Cueva del Contador made a huge impact this year, joining Artadi, Allende, Roda, Muga, and the Eguren family at the peak of modern-day Rioja.

## 2001

This is, in every respect, a truly great vintage, with textbook conditions, perfectly healthy grapes, and all the rest. It also got all the press, scores, and hype it deserved. It's an even vintage, built for long aging, with plenty of everything (color, alcohol, acidity, and tannin). We'd love to taste Aro from Muga, Aurus or Abel Mendoza Selección Personal, Barón de Chirel, Contino Graciano, and the like in 20 years. On the other hand, 2001 also represents the return of great traditional wines, with some fantastic grandes reservas—a category that was apparently dying. Superb examples are Viña Ardanza (in what was only the third vintage to be labeled Reserva Especial), Viña Real Gran Reserva, and Monte Real Gran Reserva. Yields were relatively moderate, with a total production of 242 million liters.

## 2002

A warm but rainy September brought botrytis into the vineyards of Rioja. Cool northern winds at the end of September prevented a real disaster, but it was nevertheless a very difficult vintage that produced wines for early consumption. Yields were considerably reduced, sinking to a total of 197 million liters. The vintage was officially rated "good."

## 2003

The year of the heat wave. As it was throughout Europe, 2003 was an unusual vintage in Rioja. Budding occurred early, and the year was very warm and dry, with an extremely hot summer that blocked phenolic ripening, led to high sugar, and made acidity drop dangerously, resulting in wines that were often overripe and heavy. Grapes should have been harvested much earlier, but some habits die hard—one of them being the date of the harvest. However, Rioja still managed to produce 298 million liters of wine.

## 2004

Officially declared "excellent," this vintage initially enjoyed a very good reputation, because it followed 2002 and 2003, though many now prefer 2005, which has more acidity. Having said that, 2004 represents one of the best vintages—if not the best ever—for Artadi's Viña El Pison. It was a warm year, with only October being cooler and wetter. Total production was 270 million liters. The top wines of the vintage include Aurus, Contador, Contino Viña del Olivo, El Puntido, and Roda I.

## 2005

A truly great year. A warm spring still provided the necessary rain in April and May, and it was followed by a moderately warm summer but with cool nights that helped preserve the acidity—in other words, textbook conditions. Mostly perfect bunches were harvested in mid-October, and the grapes had perfect parameters in terms of anthocyanins, coloring matter, sugar, and acidity. It is a year with great aging potential, comparable to 2001; and though it might still be a bit early for such a comparison, some rank it alongside 1995, predicting a similar evolution for the wines. For us, it is also a better vintage than 2004, especially because it has better acidity, which gives the wines extra freshness. As for the top performers, there are no great surprises, with all the usual suspects appearing among the best wines of the vintage: Aro, Calvario, Cirsion, Contador, Viña El Pison... If you want something different, try Pujanza Cisma or Pujanza Norte. Total production was 274 million liters of consistently good quality. A balanced year.

## 2006

A very warm year, with an average temperature higher than any other year of the past decade. Some producers, like Muga, consider it very good, much better than 2007, though judging by the wines we have tasted, in most cases the vintage was too warm, resulting in fat wines low in acidity. We much prefer the fresher 2007s. The weather conditions produced a difference in sugar and phenolic ripeness, which is probably why the year seems to be quite heterogeneous, with good vineyard work separating the good from the bad. Total production was in line with the previous year, at 278 million liters.

## 2007

A cold vintage, with good acidity and lots of tannin, that broke the cycle of warm vintages the area had experienced since 2000 and made wines for the long haul. There was a delay in maturity, September was quite warm, and harvest started very slowly around September 21, finishing on October 12. The result was Tempranillo with very low yields and good acidity, usually under 14% ABV. The wines are fresh, and the oak influence seems to be receding in more and more wineries. Total production remained stable at 274 million liters. María José López de Heredia thinks 2007 could be "another 1947, which, according to my father, is the best vintage ever for our bodega. Discussing with others, it seems as though it has not been the same everywhere—for example, around Briones they were hit twice by hail, and mildew was strong. We did not have hail in Haro, and mildew only reduced yields. We picked exceptional grapes, both red and white, and the evolution of the wines is extremely promising. It could be another historic vintage." Grandes reservas and some other top wines have not yet been released, but the crianza level showed very promising wines. Artadi's El Pison was back on track after a relatively weak 2006, and Contino surprised us with a fantastic white.

## 2008

If 2007 was the year when the warm cycle was broken, 2008 was again a cool—but in this case more uneven—vintage, with more acidity. There was frequent rain during the vegetative cycle and at the end of October, which slowed down the harvesting and increased the need to sort the grapes. All in all, it was a difficult year. Finca Allende released a new white, Mártires, from old-vine Viura. The top red wines have not yet been released, so for those we will need to wait and see. The region yielded 272 million liters of wine.

## 2009

A return to the hot vintages of earlier in the decade, 2009 was complicated by severe hail during the growing season. This resulted in an uneven vintage, with some producers really enthusiastic about the quality of their wines, while others are not so optimistic. Over the past five years, the region has produced roughly the same amount of wine—278 million liters in 2009—despite the increase in vineyards, which means lower yields per hectare, in line with the DO rules getting stricter.

## 2010

Grapes are still being harvested as we write these lines, so it's far too early to talk about the quality of the wines. But as was the case in 2008 and 2009, 2010 is again looking like an irregular year. It was a very warm summer, with little temperature difference between day and night. The oft-repeated comment is "uneven," since grapes achieved high sugar ripeness quite quickly but were much slower reaching phenolic ripeness. The wines will not have much structure, but they will probably be high in alcohol, to drink young. Now that the first decade has drawn to a close, the "vintages of the century" so far seem to be 2001, 2005, and 2007.

**Right:** To the victor, the spoils. María José López de Heredia holds the key to her family's treasure trove of old vintages

# Top Restaurants in Northwest Spain

In present-day foodie circles, northwest Spain is pretty much synonymous with "gastronomic paradise." It's a reputation that has developed in a remarkably short space of time. Just a generation ago, in the mid-1970s, the *Michelin Green Guide* was advising foreign tourists to be wary of Spain's dastardly habit of using olive oil in its cuisine. Now, San Sebastián has the greatest concentration of three-star restaurants of any city its size in the world. The vital input of a bunch of young Basque chefs in the waning years of the Franco dictatorship has spread over this whole humid slice of Atlantic-influenced Spain, simultaneously highlighting cutting-edge techniques, great local ingredients, and even those old-fashioned traditions that were pooh-poohed only a few years back.

The movement began four decades ago with Juan Mari Arzak and Pedro Subijana's seminal group The New Basque Cuisine. Their influence soon spread across Spain—first in the neighboring areas, then reaching all the way to Galicia. Once the Galicians discovered it, they embraced it with a vengeance, and they are now dazzling everyone.

Today, the density of outstanding restaurants from Navarra to Galicia is matched in very few regions anywhere in the world. Given this wealth of talent, a list as short and as subjective as this one will inevitably omit some very fine restaurants. All the same, the names featured on the next few pages provide some of the finest current eating (and drinking) in Spain.

Ratings system:

| ★★★ | Good to excellent |
| ★★★★ | Exceptional |
| ★★★★★ | Outstanding |
| R | Regional specialties |

**Left:** The proud proprietor of Rekondo in San Sebastián, with one of the many superb wines in its extraordinary collection

## Rioja

### Casa Toni ★★★R

Jesús Sáez wittily updates Riojan classics—witness his cream of potatoes *a la riojana* with a piquillo pepper foam and crunchy chorizo wafers.

Calle Zumalacárregui 27
San Vicente de la Sonsierra
Tel: +34 941 334 001
www.casatoni.es

### El Portal de Echaurren ★★★★★R

In his family's traditional inn, Francis Paniego has steadily developed a personal, technically modern, but sensible style, rising to the top tier of Spanish chefs. He uses low-temperature techniques particularly well, leading to surprising dishes such as his crunchy, nutlike asparagus that has been cooked at 150°F (65°C) for six hours.

Calle Padre José García 19
Ezcaray
Tel: +34 941 354 047
www.echaurren.com

### Las Duelas ★★★

In the spectacular cloister of an ancient convent, Juan Nales cooks ambitious modern dishes with some regional touches. *Duelas* means "wooden staves"—a vinous reference that seems entirely appropriate for a restaurant in Haro. A typical dish is the desalted codfish steak with a golden onion and soy sauce.

San Agustín 2
Haro
Tel: +34 941 304 463
www.hotellosagustinos.com

## La Vieja Bodega ★★★R

This beautiful cellar is certainly old, as its name indicates—dating back as far as the 17th century. But Raúl Muñiz's cooking is anything but ancient, as exemplified by his monkfish with leek couscous and leek essence.

Avenida de La Rioja 17
Casalarreina
Tel: +34 941 324 254
www.viejabodega.com

## Terete ★★★R

Sharing old refectory tables in a convivial, informal atmosphere, the customers of this old-style inn revel in timeless regional classics led by the great roast baby lamb, preceded by the traditional vegetable *menestra*. Rioja wines, of course.

Calle Lucrecia Arana 17
Haro
Tel: +34 941 310 023
www.terete.es

### Navarra

## El Molino de Urdániz ★★★★

David Yárnoz, ably assisted by his family, is a beacon of molecular inventiveness right outside Pamplona, attracting attention with such creations as roasted foie gras with carrot root, juice, and roasted leaves in brine, or suckling pig bathed in an Iberian garlic reduction.

Carretera Francia por Zubiri (Na-135) km 16.5
Urdániz
Tel: +34 948 304 109
www.elmolinourdaniz.com

## Enekorri ★★★

This 25-year-old restaurant has been strikingly redecorated in a modern style, and its cuisine has also been updated. With Fernando Flores in the kitchen, Enekorri offers such dishes as langoustines and spinach with a pine-nut "praliné" and toasted butter.

Calle Tudela 14
Pamplona
Tel: +34 948 230 798
www.enekorri.com

## Maher ★★★★R

Ribera del Ebro, famed for its vegetables, expresses its culinary potential best in Enrique Martínez's welcoming hotel-restaurant, where you'll find such things as a comforting dish of codfish with olive oil, glazed bell peppers, a "pil pil" sauce made with aromatic herbs, and tender vegetable sprouts that exemplify Martínez's refined approach.

Ribera 19
Cintruénigo
Tel: +34 948 811 150
www.hotelmaher.com

## Rodero ★★★★R

This is Koldo Rodero's long-established refuge from either boring conservatism or unbridled molecular deviations. When he cooks a large *txuri ta beltz* ("white and black") cannelloni made with blood sausage, cauliflower, and red kidney beans, he is simultaneously innovating and staying close to his Navarra roots.

Calle Emilio Arrieta 3
Pamplona
Tel: +34 948 228 035
www.restauranterodero.com

## Túbal ★★★R

Atxen Jiménez is a great hostess. Her restauránt is a bastion of traditional Navarra dishes, as well as a showcase for Ribera vegetables, always combined with meat or fish in the Spanish style—for instance, cardoons with clams, or sautéed artichokes with cep mushrooms and foie gras.

Plaza de Navarra 4
Tafalla
Tel: +34 948 700 852
www.restaurantetubal.com

## The Basque Country

## Akelarre ★★★★

Bucolically isolated on green meadows overlooking the sea, Pedro Subijana's restaurant retains its creative spirit and houses an impressive cellar. His recent, whimsical dishes include some toasty Ibérico pork *panceta* with jellied raw vegetables, and shrimp with string beans, or scalded hake with goose barnacles, olive oil pearls, and arugula. Thirty-five years ago, in a much more subdued Spanish culinary scene, Subijana was a revolutionary with his famed sea bass with green peppercorns. The truly remarkable thing about him is that he has never stopped being creative.

Paseo Padre Orcolaga 56
San Sebastián
Tel: +34 943 311 209
www.akelarre.net

## Arzak ★★★★★

Juan Mari Arzak, with his wife Maite at his side in the dining room, and now their daughter Elena as the much-lauded co-chef, is recognized as the pioneer of fine dining in Spain. Like his old friend Pedro Subijana, he keeps up the good work with an increasingly avant-garde cuisine instead of resting on his laurels. Customers who have not visited Arzak in years will be surprised at its constant evolution. The egg and white truffle flower with goose-fat-and-date chorizo is a far cry from the scorpionfish pâté of years past.

Avenida Alcalde José Elosegui 273
San Sebastián
Tel: +34 943 278 465
www.arzak.es

## Elkano ★★★★R

A temple of Basque-style grilled fish and meat, where hake, sea bream, turbot, and beef steaks reach perfection. Customers come from as far as away as Japan and Canada to enjoy some amazing large fish straight from the boat and prepared in the most simple, even primitive fashion—but one that reaches an art form here.

Herrerieta 2
Getaria, Guipúzcoa
Tel: +34 943 140 024
www.restauranteelkano.com

## Etxebarri ★★★★R

Víctor Arguinzóniz is the Ferran Adrià of the grill, a revolutionary chef who enchants by applying his imagination to the choicest fish and meat and even paella and ice cream. His custom-made special grills sing. Arguinzóniz uses mostly holm oak and grapevine cuttings but also orange and olive branches.

Plaza San Juan 1
Atxondo, Vizcaya
Tel: +34 946 583 042
www.asadoretxebarri.com

## Jolastoky ★★★R

Sabin Arana (in the kitchen) and his sister Itxaso (in the dining room) are keeping this monument to bourgeois Basque cuisine, opened in 1921, alive and kicking. The stewed woodcock with turnips is a time-honored classic, as are the clams with rice, fresh vegetables and a parsley sauce.

Avenida de los Chopos 24
Getxo, Vizcaya
Tel: +34 944 912 031
www.jolastoky.com

## Kaia-Kaipe ★★★R

This is the alternative to Elkano in Getaria. The best grilling techniques are applied to fine fish, with a more varied cuisine in the Kaialde Room.

Calle General Arnao 4
Getaria, Guipúzcoa
Tel: +34 943 140 500
www.kaia-kaipe.com

## Marqués de Riscal ★★★

With Francis Paniego of Ezcaray as consulting chef, this striking restaurant in the Frank Gehry–designed building of the historic Riscal winery complex offers a delicate, modern take on Rioja classics.

Calle Torrea 1
Elciego, Álava
Tel: +34 945 180 888
www.luxurycollection.com/marquesderiscal

## Martín Berasategui ★★★★★

Amid the bevy of starred restaurants around San Sebastián, this is possibly the most finely balanced between classic inspiration and cutting-edge creativity. Berasategui's sense of finesse and balance is such that he pulls off amazingly complex dishes while making it look easy. But there's great complexity in, say, a cold basil essence with a lime sorbet, juniper *granité*, and touches of raw almond.

Loidi Kalea 4
Lasarte-Oria, Guipúzcoa
Tel: +34 943 366 471
www.martinberasategui.com

## Mugaritz ★★★★★

This is not an easy place to find, but it is well worth the effort. Andoni Luis Aduriz, a fanatic of wild herbs, is perhaps the most experimental, Adrià-like of the Basque chefs. Currently, only two full tasting menus are served, and they may include such whimsical dishes as a simple roast of deboned coastal small fry with St. George's mushroom fibers and a bunch of garlic flowers in a savory broth.

Aldura Aldea 20
Errenteria, Guipúzcoa
Tel: +34 943 518 343
www.mugaritz.com

## Rekondo ★★★R

This is the place for tasty Basque fare such as hake in green sauce and particularly for top wines at decent prices from one of the world's great cellars.

Paseo de Igueldo 57
San Sebastián, Guipúzcoa
Tel: +34 943 212 907
www.rekondo.com

## Zuberoa ★★★★R

Some modernists say Hilario Arbelaitz is too much

of a traditionalist. As a chef working in a wonderful 16th-century farmhouse, it wouldn't really be so surprising if he were. However, he is about more than the past: his forte is to update classic Basque dishes using modern techniques and first-rate, fresh ingredients. From the lobster stew to the baby squid with onions, this is as close to perfection as it gets.

Plaza Bekosoro 1
Oiartzun, Guipúzcoa
Tel: +34 943 491 228
www.zuberoa.com

## Cantabria

### Bar del Puerto ★★★

Creativity and modernity are certainly not the buzzwords here, but this is the place for some of Spain's best seafood. The size of the langoustines is amazing in itself, and their taste is, too. The horse-mackerel croquettes are also delicious.

Hernán Cortés 63
Santander
Tel: +34 942 213 001
www.bardelpuerto.com

### Bodega Cigaleña ★★★R

Andrés Conde, who is a passionate wine lover, offers a fabulous choice of more than 1,200 wines—with real treasures from Rioja, Burgundy, the Loire, the Mosel, and the Jura—in this endearing, 60-year-old family-run inn. There is also fine comfort food to accompany such wines—from a chunk of tuna with red peppers to a terrific steak and fries.

Calle de Daoiz y Velarde 19
Santander
Tel: +34 942 213 062

### Casa Cofiño ★★★R

In a hidden, picture-postcard-beautiful village, this former café has a breathtaking wine list and the best *cocido montañés* (thick beans-and-meat soup) you will find anywhere in the region. The meatball stew is justly revered by the faithful customers.

Plaza Mayor
Caviedes
Tel: +34 942 708 046

### Cenador de Amós ★★★★R

Jesús Sánchez is Cantabria's leading cook, inventive without ever losing touch with his roots, as his Cantabrian hake with an onion juice attests. The restaurant is off the beaten track but not far from Santander, and the trek will be amply rewarded.

Barrio del Sol s/n
Villaverde de Pontones
Tel: +34 942 508 243
www.cenadordeamos.com

## Asturias

### Casa Gerardo ★★★★R

The *fabada* (Asturian bean stew) remains a monument here, and traditional dishes are generally best in this well-established restaurant. But young Marcos Morán has brought some fresh ideas in such dishes as clams with Ibérico ham and a pea purée; and tangerine soup with roasted pineapple ice cream and dark chocolate with olive oil. The menu here is now much more varied and complete.

Carretera AS-19 Gijón a Avilés km 8
Prendes
Tel: +34 985 887 797
www.casa-gerardo.com

## Casa Marcial ★★★★R

Nacho Manzano is the leading force behind the revitalization of Asturian cuisine, while paying full respect to the region's products and traditions. Manzano's take on *pitu caleya* (free-range chicken, in the Asturian dialect) is legendary— one of the tastiest, most tender chicken dishes anywhere. His fried sardine with smoked potato, onion, egg, and corn shows more than a modicum of genius.

La Salgar s/n
Arriondas, Parres
Tel: +34 985 840 991
www.casamarcial.com

## El Retiro ★★★R

Young Ricardo González, a Nacho Manzano alumnus, is back in his family's restaurant, serving simple, regional, modern fare with great purity and lightness. Try his fresh albacore *escabeche*. Local customers wouldn't let González stop making old favorites—and he's happy to oblige.

Pancar, Llanes
Tel: +34 985 400 240

## Real Balneario ★★★R

This is northern Spain at its best—a golden beach on the Bay of Biscay, large bay windows, and a pleasant dining room where, for three generations, the Loya family has been serving great traditional food and, now, some new creations, too. Seafood is phenomenal, as is the tripe with fries.

Avenida Juan Sitges 3
Salinas
Tel: +34 985 518 613
www.restaurantebalneario.com

Galicia

## Casa Marcelo ★★★★

Marcelo Tejedor is the "godfather" of the Nove group of young Galician chefs, and his imaginative cuisine is also the best in the region. Only full-meal tasting menus are available, but they change constantly and offer great variety, with pleasant surprises assured behind such brief, cryptic descriptions as "potato-leek with egg yolk and bacon," "hake from Celeiro, lemon pil-pil sauce, and green bell-pepper broth," or "piña colada."

Rúa Hortas 1
Santiago de Compostela, La Coruña
Tel: +34 981 558 580
www.casamarcelo.net

## El Mosquito ★★★R

Shunned by modernists, this remains a haven of Galician traditions, serving some of the best (and biggest) fried Dover soles anywhere, as well as the not-to-be-missed *filloas* (sweet custard-filled crêpes).

Plaza da Pedra 4
Vigo, Pontevedra
Tel: +34 986 224 441
www.elmosquitovigo.com

## O Retiro da Costiña ★★★R

The García brother-and-sister team strikes a perfect balance between Galician classics and more daring twists. The dining ritual includes selecting your wines directly in the cellar while enjoying some Cantabrian anchovies. Then you move on to simple pleasures like a scallop on toast with raf tomato jam or the sea bass cooked two ways with slow-cooked leeks.

Avenida de Santiago 12
Santa Comba, La Coruña
Tel: +34 981 880 244
www.nove.biz/ga/o-retiro-da-costina

## Pepe Vieira ★ ★ ★ ★

Xosé Cannas, with his minimalist but tasty cuisine, and his brother Xoan, with his stupendous cellar including many of the wines produced by Spain's winemaking wunderkind Raúl Pérez, make a visit here very rewarding. Xosé's daring creation of scallops with a potato-and-lard cream has become an instant classic.

Camiño da Serpe s/n
Raxo-Poio, Pontevedra
Tel: +34 986 741 378
www.pepevieira.com

## Solla ★ ★ ★ ★ R

Pepe Solla, the founders' son, hasn't forgotten the huge steamed langoustines (not to mention Atlantic prawns, lobsters, spiny lobsters, spider crabs, and so on) that made this restaurant famous. But he has added his own cutting-edge creations, including oysters with apple and instant *escabeche* or the *maigre* (a cousin of the sea bass) with an eggplant purée and roast-vegetable jus.

Avenida Sineiro 7
San Salvador de Poio, Pontevedra
Tel: +34 986 872 884
www.restaurantesolla.com

## Yayo Daporta ★ ★ ★

Somewhat misunderstood by the conservative local customers, this daring young chef creates with a light touch and great ingredients. Slowly at first, then increasingly, the patrons are finding their way to this charming granite house in the old town and enjoying the hake in a "steam" of Albariño, cockles, and wakame. The desserts include a well-chosen accompanying glass of sweet wine—for instance, a white-chocolate soup with wild red-berry sorbet is served with the Casta Diva Cosecha Miel Muscat.

Rúa Hospital 7
Cambados, Pontevedra
Tel: +34 986 526 062
www.yayodaporta.com

# The Magic of Aged Rioja

Every now and then, Spain offers the opportunity to buy certain decades-old wines (especially Riojas) at not-altogether-unreasonable prices. These are usually wines from private cellars that come onto the market when their owner dies or reaches a very old age. But of course these occasions are too rare to be of much use for most readers of this book. More interesting will be details on where to buy truly old wines and where to find restaurants storing them that can also provide excellent gastronomy to match the magic of a well-aged Rioja.

It is advisable to keep expectations under control here, for Spain is not a country with a long tradition when it comes to cellaring wines in shops or restaurants. There are, therefore, few really special places. But some of the few that do exist will be revealed here, and betraying this secret will surely bring upon us the curse of those aficionados who frequent them. In any case, our readers deserve the best possible advice—especially if they have been patient enough to reach this page!

The absolute star in terms of old Riojas (and other wines, including impressive verticals of Mouton and Vega-Sicilia), even boasting a bottle of 1880 Marqués de Riscal, is Restaurante Rekondo in San Sebastián (Paseo de Igueldo 57; www.rekondo. com). If you are fond of scouring wine lists for hidden treasures, show up a few hours in advance... If you prefer purchasing wines to take home, there may still be old Riojas at Eceiza Vinos, also in San Sebastián (Prim 16; +34 943 466 814).

Without leaving Guipúzcoa, and right opposite the Cantabrian Sea, Restaurant Kaia, in Getaria (General Arnao 4; www.kaia-kaipe.com), has an impressive menu and an even more remarkable cellar. Make sure to share with Igor Arregi your genuine passion for old Riojas, and he will likely show his treasures and allow you to pick some very

special jewel. A third and more obscure reference in Guipúzcoa, also most deserving of attention, is Hotel Restaurante Etxeberri in Zumárraga (www. etxeberri.com). Please do not tell anybody...

Still in the north of Spain, in Santander, a real wine lover's pilgrimage destination is the cellar/restaurant La Cigaleña (Daoíz y Velarde 19; +34 942 213 062), where one can pick from the wine list or ask for the expert advice of Andrés Conde, a sage despite his youth. Some 160 miles (260km) east, Casa Consuelo, near Luarca in Asturias (Carretera Nacional 634, km 511; www.casaconsuelo.com) is another hidden gem, boasting an impressive list of old and very old Riojas, including all the historic vintages by López de Heredia.

In the opposite corner of Spain is another must-visit destination for the wine lover thirsty for aged Rioja (especially from the 1970s and 1980s, though there are some wines from the 1960s, too): Restaurante Bodega Bellavista, in El Alquián, near Almería (Urbanización Bella Vista; +34 950 297 156; www.restaurantebodegabellavista.com). Here, another passionate young connoisseur—Paco Freniche—is at the helm.

Rioja itself excels more in its shops than in its restaurants, though in Haro we have one of the greatest wine-loving (and wine-savvy) chefs in Spain: Juan Nales, in his Restaurante Las Duelas at Hotel Los Agustinos (www.lasduelas.com). It boasts an extensive and very sensible wine list, lacking only old vintages.

As for wine shops where old wines may still be available, in Haro there are several Juan González Muga shops (www.gonzalezmuga.com), as well as Vinoteca Rodríguez Alonso (Conde de Haro 5–7). El Rincón del Vino has a cellar with old vintages in Logroño and Ezcaray (www.rinconesdelvino. com). And of course there are also the producers themselves, some of whom still store (very) old vintages for sale, with the bonus of optimum cellar conditions.

**Left:** Historic bodegas such as La Rioja Alta may offer mature vintages for sale, as do some shops and restaurants in Spain

# The Finest 100

Producers or wines appear in alphabetical order within their category.
A star (★) indicates what is, in our opinion, the finest of the fine.

## Ten Best-Ever Riojas

Castillo Ygay Gran Reserva Especial Blanco 1946
CVNE Imperial 1947
Marqués de Cáceres 1970
Marqués de Riscal Cuvée Médoc 1945 ★
Monte Real 1964
Torre Muga 1994
Viña Bosconia 1954
Viña El Pison 2004
Viña Real Reserva Especial 1954
Viña Tondonia Gran Reserva Blanco 1964

## Ten Best Reds from Rioja

Aurus
Cirsión
Contador
Contino Viña del Olivo
La Nieta
Prado Enea
La Rioja Alta Gran Reserva 890
Remírez de Ganuza Reserva
Viña El Pisón ★
Viña Tondonia Gran Reserva Tinto

## Ten Best Whites from Rioja

Abel Mendoza Malvasia
Artadi Viñas de Gain Blanco
Capellanía
Contino Blanco
Mártires
Plácet
Pujanza Añadas Frías
Qué Bonito Cacareaba
Remelluri Blanco
Viña Tondonia Gran Reserva Blanco ★

## Ten Best Values in Rioja

Aldonia
Allende Tinto ★
Artadi Viñas de Gain Tinto
Luberri Maceración Carbónica
Muga Crianza
Sierra Cantabria Crianza
Valenciso
Viña Alberdi
Viña Real Reserva
Viña Tondonia Reserva Blanco

## Ten Best Wines from Navarra

3Pulso
Arínzano
Capricho de Goya ★
Chivite Colección 125 Blanco
Esencia Monjardín
Gran Feudo Viñas Viejas Reserva
Izar de Nekeas
Pago de Cirsus Selección Especial
Palacio de Otazu Altar
Santa Cruz de Artazu

## Ten Best Albariños from Rías Baixas

Contra a Parede
Davila
Do Ferreiro
Do Ferreiro Cepas Vellas ★
Fefiñanes
Fillaboa Selección Finca Monte Alto
Goliardo A Telleira
La Val Crianza Sobre Lías
Lusco Pazo Piñeiro
Pazo de Señorans Selección de Añada

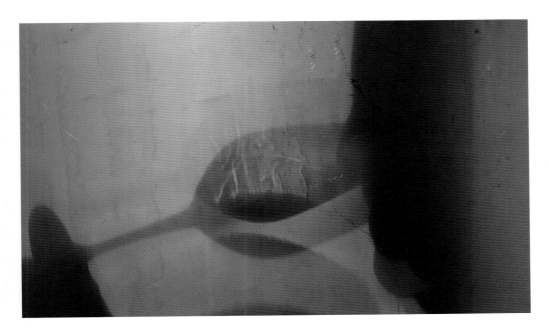

**Ten Best Whites from Galicia Outside Rías Baixas**
A Trabe Blanco
Algueira Blanco Barrica
As Sortes
Coto de Gomariz Colleita Seleccionada
Emilio Rojo
Guitián Godello
Guitián Godello Sobre Lías ★
Lapola
Sketch
Viña Meín

**Ten Best Reds from Galicia**
A Trabe Tinto
Abadía de Gomariz
Alcouce
Algueira Pizarra
D Ventura Viña Caneiro
El Pecado
Goliardo Espadeiro ★
Lalama
Quinta da Muradella Finca El Notario
Sameirás Tinto

**Ten Best Wines from Bierzo**
Altos de Losada La Bienquerida
Carracedo
Luna Beberide Reserva
Moncerbal Corullón
Paixar
Pittacum Aurea
Tares P3
Tilenus Pagos de Posada
Ucedo
Ultreia de Valtuille ★

**Ten Best Cantabrian Coast Wines**
Ameztoi
Corias Guilfa
Egia Enea
Gorrondona
Itsasmendi No.7 ★
Lusía
Picos de Cabariezo Roble
Ribera del Asón
Señorío de Otxaran
Txomin Etxaniz

# Glossary

**alta expresión** Literally "high expression," a term coined for concentrated, dark wines aged in new oak (mostly French) produced since the 1990s as a reaction to the degraded image and quality of most "traditional" Rioja. The wines were more international in style but soon fell out of favor with critics and consumers and lost market share, giving way to more balanced and elegant wines. It was finally dubbed *alta extorsión* by some, given the stratospheric prices of some of these wines.

**Barrio de la Estación** Railroad neighborhood; the district next to the train station in Haro, in Rioja, where many wineries were established in the 19th century

**blanco** white

**bodega** winery

**buena** good; one of the official vintage qualifications issued by the Consejos Reguladores of the *denominaciones de origen*, a third category behind *excelente* and *muy buena*. Its real meaning, however, is mediocre—no good vintage is defined as less than *muy buena*, "very good," in this age of PR-style paeans.

**calado** cellar

**Camino de Santiago** St. James's Way, the route(s) pilgrims walk to Santiago de Compostela

**cepas viejas** old vines; a term loosely used, since it is not regulated. (It is said that a grower answering his cell phone, when asked where he was and what he was doing, answered, "Planting old vines.")

**ciudad** city, a step up from *pueblo* (village); title granted to Haro in 1891

**cono** a synonym of *tina*, vat

**cosechero** artisanal wine producer in Rioja, making unoaked reds, most likely in the carbonic-maceration style,

following the old method; quite popular in the Basque Country; also applied to this style of wine

**crianza** literally "rearing" or "upbringing," but also used for a category of wines aged in oak barrels for a minimum of 6–12 months (depending on the region) and a further year in bottle before being sold

**cueva** cave, a word with a prehistoric connotation

**denominación de origen** (DO) appellation of origin, equivalent to the French AOC

**denominación de origen calificada** (DOC) the highest rank of appellation; only Rioja and Priorat are in this category

**dominio** domaine, estate. (Do not confuse with Dominico, which is a monk of Dominican order.)

**en vaso** head-pruned: pruning method equivalent to the French *gobelet* (*vaso* means goblet)

**Estación Enológica** Enological research station; the famous one in Rioja was located in Haro

**fermentado en barrica** barrel-fermented

**finca** estate (as in property)

**fudre** Spanish adaptation of the French *foudre*; a receptacle for wine, usually quite large and made of wood

**gran reserva** great reserve; a category of wines aged in oak barrels for a minimum of 24 months (in most regions) and a further two to three years in bottle before being released

**joven** young; used to designate unoaked wines

**minifundio** system of land ownership with very small plots; found in the north of Spain

**muy buena** very good; the second of the categories in the official vintage qualifications, behind only *excelente*

**pago** vineyard. (*Vino de pago* means single-vineyard wine.)

**País Vasco** Basque Country

**paraje** rural spot; used by some wineries to specify an area but not exactly a single plot of vines

**parcela** parcel, plot

**parra** literally "grapevine" but normally reserved for climbing vines grown pergola-style

**peludo** hairy; not a proper wine term or any characteristic of Rioja or its inhabitants, but rather a clone of Tempranillo called Tempranillo Peludo, whose leaves have a hairy underside

**pintxo** Basque spelling for *pincho* (meaning skewer), a variant of tapas normally inserted or held together by a toothpick or skewer

**quinta** country house; wine estate

**raro** rare, in the sense of unusual. (It is not used to indicate the degree to which meat is cooked.)

**reserva** reserve; used for a category of wines aged in oak barrels for a minimum of 12 months (in most regions) and a further two years in bottle before being released

**Riojano** name given to people from Rioja; literally meaning "from Rioja," it also applies to foods, costumes, traditions, etc.

**roble** oak. Also used as a semi-official or unofficial category for wines aged in oak but without reaching the minimum time required to achieve the crianza label, for a minimum of four to six months depending on the regions; sometimes also called semi-crianza

**rosado** rosé or pink wine

**seco** dry

**sobre lías** on the lees; *sur lie*

**solcacos** Galician (and Portuguese) word for terraces

**suelos amarillos** yellow soils; the name given to the clay-limestone soils in Rioja Alavesa and the western part of Rioja Alta

**suelos rojos** red soils; the name given to the terra rossa soils rich

# Bibliography

in iron and clay, from which they get their bright color

**temprano** early; the origin of Tempranillo's name

**tina** vat

**tinto** red

**trasiego/trasiega** racking; there is no agreement as to whether the action is a feminine or a masculine one, and therefore both forms of the word are often found

**variedades** grape varieties

**variedades mejorantes** literally, "improving varieties," a euphemism referring to French or international grapes but also to Tempranillo when used away from its northern Spanish homeland

**venajos** communal vegetable gardens belonging to Haro's city council, rented to the inhabitants for private cultivation

**viña** vineyard, but also vine

**viñedo** vineyard

**vino** wine

**vino de autor** author's wine, or designer's wine (loose translation); a wine in which the winemaker's signature is the most important thing—a concept that was often used as a synonym for *alta expresión*. A crazy idea if you have good terroir...

**vino de la tierra** literally "wine from the land," or "wine from the country"; a category of wine equivalent to the French *vin de pays*, with rules a little more flexible than the DO, usually in terms of permitted grape varieties. This category is being phased out under new European Union regulations.

**vino de mesa** table wine; the lowest official category. But some brilliant wines fall into this category because they don't follow the rules for DO or even *vino de la tierra*. This category is being phased out under new European Union regulations.

Michel Bettane and Thierry Desseauve,
    *The World's Greatest Wines* (Stewart, Tabori and Chang; 2006)

Oz Clarke and Margaret Rand,
    *Grapes & Wines* (Websters International, London; 2001)

Luis Díaz,
    "Ni la Mencía es Autóctona ni el Albariño Procede del Rin" (*La Voz de Galicia*; December 29, 2005)

Pierre Galet,
    *Dictionnaire Encyclopédique des Cépages* (Hachette Livre, Paris; 2000)

Iñigo González Inchaurraga,
    *El Marqués que Reflotó el Rioja* (LID Editorial Empresarial, Madrid; 2006)

Juan Goytisolo,
    *Señas de Identidad* (Seix Barral, Barcelona; 1966)

Jose Luis Hernáez Mañas,
    *As Castas Galegas de Videira: Estado da Investigación* (Estación de Viticultura y Enología de Galicia, 1999)

Alain Huetz de Lemps,
    *Vignobles et Vins du Nord-Ouest de l'Espagne* (Institut de Géographie, Bordeaux; 1967)

Julian Jeffs,
    *The Wines of Spain* (Faber and Faber, London; 1999)

Hugh Johnson and Jancis Robinson,
    *The World Atlas of Wine* (5th edition) (Mitchell Beazley, London; 2001)

Manuel Llano Gorostiza,
    *Los Vinos de Rioja* (Banco de Vizcaya, Bilbao; 1983)

—, *Un Vaso de Bon Vino* (CVNE, Bilbao; 1979)

Jesús Marino Pascual,
    *Museo de la Cultura del Vino Dinastía Vivanco: Arquitectura* (Dinastía Vivanco, Briones; 2005)

Agustín Muñoz Moreno,
    *Geología y Vinos de España* (ICOG, Madrid; 2009)

José Peñín,
    *12 Grandes Bodegas de España* (Pi & Erre Ediciones, Madrid; 1995)

—, *Cepas del Mundo* (Pi & Erre Ediciones, Madrid; 1997)

—, *Guía Peñín de los Vinos de España 2010* (Peñín Ediciones, Madrid; 2009)

John Radford,
    *The Wines of Rioja* (Mitchell Beazley, London; 2004)

*La Rioja: Sus Viñas y su Vino* (Gobierno de La Rioja, Logroño; 2009)

*Rioja Alavesa* (Asociación para la Promoción de la Rioja Alavesa, Vitoria; 1998)

Jancis Robinson,
    *Vines, Grapes and Wines* (Mitchell Beazley, London; 1986)

Manuel Ruiz Hernández,
    *Estudios Sobre el Vino de Rioja* (Gráf Sagredo, Haro; 1978)

*Las Rutas del Vino en España,* (Ciro Ediciones, Biblioteca Metrópoli, Madrid; 2006)

Julio Sáenz and James Bishop,
    *Tres Siglos de La Rioja Alta SA* (La Rioja Alta, Haro; 2009)

Ion Stegmeier,
    *Navarra: La Cultura del Vino* (Gobierno de Navarra, Pamplona; 2008)

George M Taber,
    *In Search of Bacchus* (Scribner, New York; 2009)

Luis Tolosa Planet and Mikel Larreina Díaz,
    *Bodegas y Vinos de la Rioja* (LT&A Ediciones, Barcelona; 2005)

*El Vino Entre dos Siglos* (López de Heredia, Haro; 2007)

*Viña Tondonia, un Pago, una Viña, un Vino* (López de Heredia, Logroño; 2007)

# Index

# Authors' Acknowledgments

Víctor de la Serna dedicates his work on this book to his wife Carmen, his son Juan, and his daughter Cristina—wine lovers, all—and to his youngest daughter Cecilia, who will soon be a wine lover, too— or so he hopes.

Luis Gutiérrez would like to dedicate this book to his parents, Luis and María Teresa, and to his wife and children, Claudia, Alex, Ana, and Blanca.

Jesús Barquín wishes to dedicate his work to his beloved wife Lola, true coauthor of everything in his life, not least their daughter Violeta and son Álvaro. He also addresses very special thanks to Professor Ernesto Suárez Toste for his generous and invaluable help with all kinds of linguistic issues.

The authors want to extend their gratitude to the following people for their friendship and generosity: Montse Alonso, Ramón Coalla, Alberto Fernández Bombín, Mario García, Mariano and Alberto García, Miguel Laredo, Florian Miquel, Dirk Niepoort, Estanis Núñez, Quim Vila and Ignacio Villalgordo.

# Photographic Credits

All photography by Jon Wyand, with the following exception:
Page 9: The Battle of Nájera, from an illuminated manuscript of Froissart's *Chronicles*; © Photos 12 /Alamy